The Innovative Woman

Creative Ways to Reach Your Potential

By

Norma Carr-Ruffino

CAREER
PRESS

THE CAREER PRESS, INC.
Franklin Lakes, NJ

THE INNOVATIVE WOMAN
Cover design by DesignConcept
Edited by Jodi L. Brandon
Typeset by John J. O'Sullivan
Printed in the U.S.A. by Book-mart Press

To order this title, please call toll-free 1-800-CAREER-1 (NJ and Canada: 201-848-0310) to order using VISA or MasterCard, or for further information on books from Career Press.

The Career Press, Inc.,
3 Tice Road, PO Box 687
Franklin Lakes, NJ 07417
www.careerpress.com

Library of Congress Cataloging-in-Publication Data

Carr-Ruffino, Norma.
 The innovative woman : creative ways to reach your potential / by Norma Carr-Ruffino.
  p. cm.
 Includes index.
 ISBN 1-56414-545-X (paper)
  1. Women—Psychology. 2. Businesswomen—Psychology. 3. Businesswomen—Life skills guides. 4. Self-realization. I. Title.

 HQ1206 . C269 2001
 305.4—dc21

                                             00-069668

Dedication

To Erica, Linda, Frances, Bobbie, Elisha, Andrea,
Vickie, Lauren, Natalie, and Meghan.
And to Fredo, who's always there.

Contents

How This Book Can Change Your Life

Y ou can change your life so dramatically if you really open up to the powerful ideas in this book. That means opening up to greater adventure, surprise, excitement, delight, achievement, and deep satisfaction. As a woman, you have many advantages in this arena of innovation—feminine attitudes and values you can build upon.

Your Career

If you're ready to work with the many facets of your Creative Self, and to develop your creative potential, you'll become more innovative in your business and professional life, as well as in your personal life. You'll do this not only by learning about recent research regarding your three brains and seven intelligences, but also by recognizing how you use them as you go about your daily life. You'll begin to sense the role that each intelligence plays in your ability to innovate. You'll learn how to boost the power of each intelligence and apply each one to the opportunities and problems you encounter at work and at home. You'll begin to sense how your brains integrate all of these intelligences in ways that enhance your ability to function in the world more innovatively—with Creative Intelligence.

Maybe you're already working on your innovative skills but find that the materials available, although helpful, are really scattered bits and pieces of the puzzle. The Creative Intelligence Model is the first comprehensive framework that enables you to pull all the ideas and techniques together. With this model, you'll have a framework for stashing all the ideas and information you'll ever encounter on the topic of creativity. And you'll see the role each plays in your personal Creativity Profile.

You'll take advantage of the tools I've designed to help you develop your creative potential. These tools include:

- *Sparklers*—The how-to's that help you recognize and apply the many types of intelligence that compose your Creative Intelligence.

- *Innovative Questions*—Those questions most likely to get at the heart of the situation so you can move through problems and go for those great opportunities.

- *Creative Processes*—Processes that stem from each of your intelligences and that you can apply to problem—opportunity situations in your life.

- *Self-Awareness Opportunities*—Exercises to help you get to know yourself and to see your environment in new ways.

- *Case Situations*—Real-life problems that give you a chance to apply your new innovative skills.

Your Team and Your Company

You're about to boost your innovative skills—to develop new techniques and processes for recognizing opportunities in the swirling marketplace of the New Economy, the highly networked, global marketplace. You'll learn how to diagnose and solve the problems you encounter there.

After you've worked on building and applying the creativity that stems from your seven intelligences, you'll explore ways to apply your new innovative skills on the job. For example, you'll learn how to spark team creativity through the power of synergy and creative collaboration. You'll explore how to thrive in the innovation age by being more open, adaptive, and wholistic—and how to help your team members and company to use these techniques to survive and thrive. You'll explore ways to ignite change within your corporate culture, changes that encourage everyone to be more creative. You'll learn to recognize ways that your corporate culture may block creativity and how to become a change agent, helping people shift to new mental models that spark creativity. And finally, you'll learn how to find the niche that's most innovative and satisfying for you.

Your World

A key innovative skill is the ability to step back and take a larger view of your immediate environment, to put it in a more global perspective. When you apply your Creative Intelligence in positive ways, grounded in the compassion of Emotional Intelligence, you influence your team, your company, the New Economy, and the planet. You spark that higher frequency of vibration we're longing to resonate with. Here's my vision of the role of Creative Intelligence.

Enchanted Millennium

Swirling chaos flows into fluid patterns
Creative genius divine in the making
Pulling from the cosmos a lightning bolt of success
Creative Intelligence in the New Millennium
Grounded in heart love
Soaring to a shining sparkling tomorrow
Laughing with joy
The Nature Goddess is birthing a new species of fireflies.
They emerge through mystic portals
Soar around the globe and throughout the cosmos to a brilliant future
Signaling to life's lovers
Explore, explore, explore!

Norma Carr-Ruffino
Professor of Management
San Francisco State University
April 2001

Part 1:

Recognizing Your Own Creativity

Chapter 1

You Were Born Creative:
Reclaiming Your Potential

Your creativity is waiting for you like a dancing partner.
Barbara Sher, author

What's the hottest, most in-demand skill you can bring to today's workplace?

Innovative skills are what business leaders want. They say:

We need people who know how to generate new ideas, who can get a sense of the next new thing. We'll fight to hire people who become inspired by a vision of a new product that delights customers, who find creative solutions to old problems—people with ideas that feed the bottom line.

Innovation: The Hot New Skill

Creative people are now the crown jewels of the workplace.

Every savvy executive says that the organization's biggest challenge today is finding true talent. If you have true talent, you not only have the right skills, but you also have passion and commitment. You're a dynamo. You get it done. If you've got this, you'll not only succeed in your career, but there are no limits. For companies that have enough of this human talent, there are no limits—and the best leaders know it.

As a woman, you finally have more advantages than barriers in this hot new arena—if you know how to leverage your innate intelligences into innovative skills. You're advantaged because the culture has given you more freedom and encouragement to express your emotions and to act on your intuition—to use the entire range of your intelligences.

You want to become more creative—to develop innovative skills—but how can you do that?

Most people believe they're not creative—that artists, inventors, and geniuses are creative because they were born with a special gift.

A few people believe that you can learn to be more creative. These people buy books, take classes, and do exercises designed to boost creativity. The results are pretty spotty. Why?

No comprehensive model for personal creativity has been available until now.

The books, articles, and courses on creativity and innovation each offer only a bit, a piece of the creativity puzzle (some large, some tiny, some effective, some not). We've been like the mouse trying to figure out what the elephant is like by checking out a toenail or a neck hair. We've needed a map of the whole elephant—and now we have it.

Solving the Creativity Puzzle

The Creative Intelligence Model, which you'll use to reclaim your creative potential, offers the holistic map we've all been needing and wanting.

Any creativity theory, idea, strategy, or technique that you know—or will ever learn—can be plugged into this model. Any creative experience you'll ever have, or hear about, will fit.

Bottom line: You'll build powerful innovative skills that are hot property in the workplace.

But I'm not a creative person, you say? Do you have a belief barrier to creativity? Western culture has long relegated creativity to a corner of our lives, instead of seeing life itself as creative. So if you're buying into this old piece of consensus reality, then creativity has little meaning in your life. But everything coming out of recent scientific research says:

You are creative. All of life is constantly creative.

The mere fact that you are here, alive in physical reality, is proof that your creative potential exists in every cell of your body, in the very strands of your DNA. All you must do to access your creativity is become aware of your potential, use some simple techniques to boost the seven intelligences that make up your Creative Intelligence, and practice applying them to actual opportunities and problems that exist all around you. Now, exactly what does it mean to be creative and innovative?

What Is Creativity? What Is Innovation?

Creativity is coming up with new ideas.

Innovation is putting new ideas into practice in ways that add value. In order to be innovative you must not only come up with a new idea, but you must experience that new idea in action. You must emotionally experience it as real and commit to making it real in the physical world. And the people who must work with your new idea also must have the sensory experiences and emotional commitment that are needed for the idea to become an innovation that makes a difference.

Team innovation is a discipline in which something completely new and precious is born out of the unrehearsed interplay of talented people. New technology comes from the innovative ideas of people. Savvy organizational leaders understand that if they put people first and provide the right environment, their people will create and adopt the technology the organization needs.

Why Innovative Skills? Why Now?

Our competitive global marketplace is far more complex and chaotic than anything we humans have ever experienced. And Internet connections have accelerated this complexity, creating a New Net Economy. Dotcom startup companies have played the major role in creating this New Economy, and this has created major challenges for traditional giant corporations. They've come to realize that they must become part of the New Economy or die. The infotech marketplace has changed the rules of doing business. It's changed the way we think about the most valuable assets of a business, and even how we view the business itself: as an idea factory. All this means that we've brought about the Innovation Age—a time when innovative skills are seen as a firm's most valuable asset.

Complexity, Chaos, and Innovation

Now is the perfect time to be a creative person, because this is the age of complexity thinking, which means thriving on chaos by relaxing and allowing new meaningful patterns to emerge in your mind. Key elements of the New Economy include continually evolving technological change, the lightning-fast global communication, and a constantly shifting global marketplace.

To become a complexity thinker, your first goal is to become comfortable with a certain level of chaos. Just allow it; let it be. Your next goal is to detect patterns emerging from this chaos. Ask yourself, Which of these patterns points to a new opportunity for me or my company? Ultimately, you're looking for clues to the Next New Thing—as well as the problems such change can bring. You need to know when and where to bring order to the emerging patterns and how to harness them for your own purposes. That means recognizing what paradigm you're in, when it is about to shift, and how this fits in with a typical high-tech life cycle. (For more about this, see Chapter 10.)

Dotcom Startups and Shape-Shifting Giants

The New Economy is emerging as a high-tech, startup world of constant innovation, fast-paced reinvention, shifting alliances, intense teamwork-based achievement, and high-stake risks that result in dazzling profits or devastating wipe-outs. This is the world of the dotcoms—the Amazons and eBays.

The high-tech startup world is having a huge impact on the traditional multinational corporations—the Walmarts and General Electrics. The giants cannot ignore the largest business gold rush in history. They are shifting the shapes of their customer channels, their organization charts, and their corporate culture so they can survive and thrive in the Net Economy.

Both the startups and the shape-shifting giants are outsourcing many of their functions so they can focus their resources on what they're really good at. When a corporation devises a breakthrough innovation, success depends on being the first to market it. This is so crucial that it makes good financial sense to pay other firms to help them get there first. This opens up many opportunities for specialists, consultants, and other startups to fill the niches. Such firms may do any of the functions—from handling all the corporation's accounts payable to training high-tech teams to hit the ground running when the corporation hires them as a team.

Infotech Networks

The New Economy is a networked economy that lets you make your career niche a more innovative one. This economy not only demands that you be more innovative, it richly rewards you when you come through. You can tap into the wealth of information available through the Internet (infotech) to help you clear your mind, to find the space for more communication, and to hurdle barriers to dreaming up new ideas. Infotech is allowing all businesses— even manufacturing firms—to become idea factories.

We've still got to have factories, but we must change their focus from mass production to continuous creativity. All companies must come to see themselves more or less as idea factories. They must apply the principle of interdependency:

Principle of Interdependency

Ideas are dependent on successful products.
Successful products are dependent on ideas.
Both ideas and products are dependent
on the effective management of creativity.

Our mindset is shifting from a mechanical, observer-observed separateness to a wholistic, interdependent connectedness. Competition is more about exploiting an aspect of interdependency, of being part of an ecological whole, than about beating out another company. Mastery is about moving from an abstract intellectual understanding of something to an understanding that's *cellular*, integrated into your worldview.

We have computer networks and related technology that let us play with ideas without the former limitations of time and space. We can preserve our creative energy while we vastly expand our creative choices.

New Creative Roles

In 1999 futurist Rolf Jensen predicted whole new job categories in the emerging marketplace, roles that feature the buying and selling of new dreams that fulfill people's heartfelt desires. Young companies, high-tech companies, and companies just wanting to lure innovative people into their workforce are already integrating such creative job titles into their companies. Some of these job titles are:

- Chief Energizing Officer (CEO).
- Envisioneer (Product Designer).
- Director of Fun (Administrative Director).
- Chief Evangelist; also Sultan of Spin (Public Relations Director).
- Alpha Geek (Chief Programmer).
- Minister of Dollars & Sense (Chief Finance Officer).
- Head People Officer (Director of Human Resources).

These are real titles that don't seem any more far-out or futurist than Jensen's future dream jobs:

- Director of Mind & Mood.
- Court Jester.
- Vice President of Cool.
- Chief Imagination Officer.
- Director of Intellectual Capital.
- Visualizer.
- Assistant Storyteller.
- Chief Enacter.

Let's face it, most of these jobs call on typical feminine traits and skills. Which ones might fit your talents and passions?

In this book, you will first explore all the intelligences that make up your creative potential. Then you'll explore ways to use your innovative skills in today's workplace. You'll find answers to some key questions, such as:

- What are the most important skills for job applicants, managers, professionals, and entrepreneurs in this New Economy?
- Where is the best place for you, as a woman, with your particular talents, interests, and lifestyle needs?
- What kinds of jobs, projects, and activities turn you on?

You'll delve into those things that fire your passion and drive in Chapter 4. And in Chapter 13, you'll get a better sense of the field of play that's emerging and just where you're likely to thrive. For example, you might want to explore some of the new Internet careers. You should certainly consider how your people skills and your innovative skills qualify you for New Economy roles. Or you might be ready to launch your own business startup, joining the millions of other women who are doing just that—by using their Creative Intelligence.

The global marketplace endlessly demands the imaginative, the new, the experimental, the faster, the better, and the cheaper. The high level of market competition in that world puts a premium on creative intelligence and innovative skills—the kind you'll learn to develop by working through this book.

Creative Intelligence for a New Economy: Using All Your Brain Power

You are almost certainly more intelligent than you think you are. That's because you have many types of intelligence—categorized here into seven types—and about 90 percent of your intelligence has little to do with typical cultural ideas about what intelligence is.

Intelligence experts are learning ways to boost overall intelligence—especially Creative Intelligence—by recognizing the various types of intelligence that humans actually have access to. One powerful approach is to work with seven intelligences that stem from your three brains. You can easily become aware of each type of intelligence when it's in action. You can use some simple techniques for boosting each type of intelligence—and increase your *smarts* throughout your life. Finally, you can practice using each intelligence as you recognize new opportunities and devise new ways to respond to them—and when you generate creative solutions to problems. You can gain skill at weaving together the intelligences you've expanded in ways that produce new ideas and innovations.

You learn how to move beyond the self-limiting patterns and boundaries of your Basic Intelligence and how to harness the energies of your Motivational and Emotional Intelligences. You can link these powerful lower-level intelligences to your higher-level intelligences, such as intuition. This is how you build your Creative Intelligence and innovative skills.

You can use strategies for recognizing the various types of thinking processes—from rational, logical linear thinking to associative, connective, relationship thinking to sensory thinking that uses your five senses to bring the outside in (visual seeing) and to bring the inside out (imagining, visualizing). You can and do link all these intelligences to your Intuitive Intelligence, which is your connection to the universal Web of Life. You can use your intuition in ways that provide feedback, so you begin to trust your intuitive hits. This weaving together of all the threads of your brainpower equals Creative Intelligence.

This Creative Intelligence model will help you use more of your brainpower—as you become more creative in the way you view reality and function within it, and as you develop the innovative skills you apply to opportunities and problems around you.

> People use only about 10 percent of their brainpower.

Intelligence experts have been saying this for decades. Have you ever wondered why we use so little of our brainpower? Most experts now believe it's because of Western culture's love affair with the straight line. In science, academia, and business, we have been so caught up in the rational, logical, step-by-step analytical approach, separating ourselves—the observers—from what we're observing, that we've ignored our other types of intelligence. Now we're beginning to see Rational Intelligence as only one of at least seven types of human intelligence. When you do this, you free yourself to use much more of that precious brainpower—and to become much more creative.

You're about to move beyond Rational Intelligence—to explore all your intelligences. In the future, when you need creative ideas, you'll have a whole array of creative resources to pull from. You'll understand how your seven innate intelligences feed into the creative process and how to continually expand those intelligences that make up Creative Intelligence. You'll have a set of skills for recognizing new opportunities and solving problems that crop up.

3 Brains = 7 Intelligences

You actually have three brains: the neocortex connected with your thinking processes, the limbic brain connected with your emotional processes, and the basic pattern-parameter brain connected with your instinctual and routine behavior, as symbolically depicted in Snapshot #1 on this page. These are related to your seven types of intelligence as follows:

- Basic Pattern-Parameter Intelligence—concentrated in the basic brain, or brain stem-spinal cord.
- Emotional and Motivational Intelligences—concentrated in the limbic brain.
- Rational Intelligence—concentrated in the left neocortex.
- Associative, Sensory, and Intuitive Intelligences—three powerful intelligences concentrated in the right neocortex.

The words *concentrated in* imply that the intelligences are not restricted to a certain part of the body. In fact, research indicates that every cell in your body is highly intelligent, and that *molecules of emotion* travel throughout your body and are an aspect of Emotional Intelligence.

Snapshot #1 Symbolic Picture of the Three Brains

(From back of head)

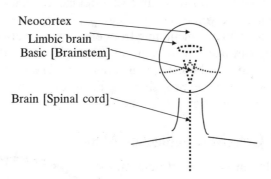

Snapshot #2 Seven Intelligences and What They're About

7 Intelligences	What They're About: Associated Words
Basic	reptile brain, brain stem, survival, attraction,
> Pattern	repulsion, perseverance, living in the present
> Parameter	moment, dream state programming, repetition, habits, imitation, deception territory, boundaries, limits
Emotional	mammalian brain , limbic brain, people skills, feelings, love, empathy, compassion, caring, joy, elation, anger, influencing, open to influence
Motivational	desire, wants, goal, drives, life purpose, limbic brain, mammalian brain

Snapshot #2 Seven Intelligences and What They're About (cont.)

7 Intelligences	What They're About: Associated Words
Associative	right brain, neocortex, similarities, comparisons, similes, relationship to, connection with, analogies, metaphors
Sensory (spatial)	right-brain, neocortex, image, imagination, fantasy, visual, musical, tones, chords, dancing, movement, motion, athletics, smelling, tasting
Rational	logical, sequential, intellectual step-by-step, mathematical, scientific, I.Q., SAT, GMAT, neocortex, left-brain
Intuitive	right-brain, neocortex, inner knowing, ESP, psi, between the lines, wholistic, global connection, spiritual, inner connections, beyond time-space

◆ ◆ ◆

You can start using your Associative Intelligence now by reviewing Snapshot #2. Study the words in the column opposite each type of intelligence. These words relate powerfully to what each intelligence is all about. If you can understand how these words relate to each intelligence, you'll begin to recognize which intelligence you're using at any particular time. By raising your awareness of when you're functioning from emotional intelligence or sensory intelligence, you can begin to beef up each intelligence and eventually put them all to work toward boosting your creativity. Then study the Creative Intelligence Model shown in Snapshot #3. Focus on the process you can use to expand each of your seven intelligences.

Snapshot #3 Creative Intelligence Model

Creative Intelligence = 7 Intelligences

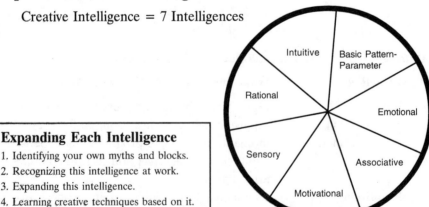

Expanding Each Intelligence
1. Identifying your own myths and blocks.
2. Recognizing this intelligence at work.
3. Expanding this intelligence.
4. Learning creative techniques based on it.
5. Applying creative techniques to situations.

Note: The pie and its segments are a theoretical model; the proportions are approximate and symbolic, as the exact proportion that each intelligence plays in creativity cannot be pinpointed.

Behavioral Pattern-Parameter Intelligences of the Basic Brain (Doing)

The basic brain consists of your brain stem and spinal cord. It's sometimes called the reptilian brain because it's been in the evolutionary chain the longest of the three brains, and reptiles have this type of brain. DeBeauport, whose research-based book *The Three Faces of Mind* won a Hoover Book Award, found that three major intelligences stem from this brain: Basic, Pattern, and Parameter Intelligences, which we will combine for discussion purposes. These intelligences are crucial for removing personal blocks to creativity, such as rigid habit patterns, limits, or boundaries you place on yourself, and denial of dreams. But in general, Basic Pattern-Parameter Intelligences are less directly connected to creativity than the other intelligences.

Basic Pattern-Parameter Intelligence focuses on what you instinctively move toward and move away from—those people, situations, and things you tend to seek out and embrace, and those that you avoid. These movements become your habits, routines, and little rituals, and developing this intelligence requires that you recognize your own habit patterns as well as those of others. Most of these patterns are deeply ingrained in your culture and family. They're based on what you were taught and what you decided about life. Some patterns are necessary and helpful in your current life. Other patterns form barriers to creativity and innovation and tend to sabotage your efforts to develop new skills and to change your life.

Parameter Intelligence refers to limits or boundaries. Your basic-brain movements, toward things and away from things, all take place within specific boundaries and limits—your own, those of others, and those of organizations. They're related to your territory and your comfort zone and to the concept of paradigms and paradigm shifts—rules and boundaries for succeeding in a particular situation or paradigm and moving beyond these limits to create new paradigms. You boost your Parameter Intelligence by recognizing unnecessary and limiting boundaries, rules, and paradigms—your own and others.

Emotional Intelligences of the Limbic Brain (Feeling)

All mammals have a limbic brain. It's sometimes called the middle brain because it lies under the neocortex and above the brain stem. One of its major functions is producing the emotions we need in order to conceive and nurture our young and to relate together in groups in order to raise them.

Emotional Intelligence is your awareness, expression, and management of your emotions, including your feelings and moods. It allows you to tune into the feelings and moods of other people and therefore is the key to developing your people skills, which are built upon empathy and compassion. Emotional Intelligence includes how you are affected by people, things, or situations, as well as how you affect or influence them.

Motivational Intelligence refers to what turns you on in life, what you want or desire, what you feel passionately about. It's built upon self-awareness—knowing what you like to do and are good at, seeing how this ties in with your purpose in life and why you're here, and finding your niche in the workplace where you can achieve this purpose or life mission. It's the drive to fully develop and express yourself creatively.

Right Brain-Left Brain Intelligences of the Neocortex (Thinking)

Your neocortex is made of up two distinct halves, often called the left brain and the right brain. Rational Intelligence is a function of your left brain, and your right brain is the seat of three intelligences: Associative, Sensory, and Intuitive.

Rational Intelligence is seated in the left neocortex. It's sometimes called left-brain thinking. You use it to study how the parts of things work and fit together into a whole, with a special focus on the parts. You use it when you focus on step-by-step reasoning, cause-and-effect logic, and how things occur over time. This is virtually the only intelligence that has traditionally been respected and nurtured in Western academia, science, and business. That part of the brain, perhaps 10 percent, that most educated adults use most often is the seat of left-brain Rational Intelligence.

The right neocortex, where you do *right-brain thinking*, provides you with three major types of intelligence. This type of thinking is simultaneous, spatial, associative, whole-to-parts, with more focus on the whole, and timeless.

Associative Intelligence is what you use when you focus on relationships between things: how things are alike or different.

Sensory Intelligence occurs when you use your senses—when you see, hear, smell, taste, and feel your body moving kinesthetically in space. It's related to visualizing things, drawing them, expressing them musically, dancing, doing sports, cooking creatively, and so forth.

Intuitive Intelligence is your higher-level inner knowing. It bypasses or aids the step-by-step, sequential-time, cause-effect ways of learning and goes directly to more wholistic, timeless experiences. In a sense, all life over all time may be felt as having a wholeness and a connection that are timeless. We're learning more about how we are all energetically connected and how we can naturally tune in to other persons, their feelings, and their life situations.

Now that creativity in the workplace is such a hot skill, moving beyond Rational Intelligence is becoming respectable. Although it will always be essential, Rational Intelligence is only a small slice of the intelligence pie.

Accessing Your Creative Intelligence

Your creative intelligence is the result of using all seven of your intelligences at the appropriate times and in the best combinations and interactions. The best way to access and integrate all of them is to spend more and more time totally present in the Now and to develop the art of complete acceptance of What-Is in each present moment.

This Total Presence empowers you to use your Creative Intelligence as a synergy that integrates all your intelligences. This results in a brilliance that's greater than the sum of the parts—and it's sometimes called the *flow* factor.

The Power of Now

Many people are beginning to break out of their inherited collective mind-patterns, which have kept virtually all of us imprisoned for ages. Some call this mass consciousness, while others call it consensus reality. In contrast with Rational Intelligence, the one true Source within—the Intuitive Intelligence—contains no theory or speculation. Your most powerful source of creativity is through this intelligence, for it accesses the original Source Energy. This creative source has many names, including All-That-Is, the Web of Life, God, and Spirit. Humans seem to have great agreement that it exists, generally, and little agreement about what it is, specifically.

You can only access Intuitive Intelligence when your rational mind is still and your attention is fully and intensely in the Now, the present moment—moment by moment by moment. Descartes threw us for a loop when he declared *I think; therefore I am*, and people actually lived their lives in accordance with his declaration. We now know that we're much closer to the truth when we say,

> I am. Therefore, I think (and feel and act and intuit)....

You are a center of consciousness, designed to be self-aware. You are. Period. That comes first, before all else.

How can you be fully present in the Now? How can you fully accept what is in that moment? How can you do that in more and more of the moments that make up your life? Let's begin to answer these questions with two powerful analogies used by author Eckhart Tolle in *Stuck in the Mud* and *Flashlight in the Fog*.

Stuck in the Mud

Suppose you're stuck in the mud. How much energy will you spend on such thinking patterns as, *Oh, no, this can't be happening to me. What a disaster! This can't be real—I'll wake up from this nightmare soon. Why did Joe tell me to go down this path? It's all his fault. If only....* You're filled with emotions that follow from your resistance to What-Is, your denial of What-Is, blame, your rationalizations, and your projections. You experience a whole array of stressful emotions, such as fear, doubt, irritation, anger, and resentment. In contrast, if you fully enter into the present moment, with full consciousness, and full acceptance of what is happening—all your energy can go toward solving the problem. You are free to access all your intelligences to come up with creative ideas for solving this life-situation problem. This is the highest level of Creative Intelligence.

Flashlight in the Fog

Imagine that you're surrounded by fog—a cloud of past resentment, guilt, drama, and a mist of future worry, fear, and possible nightmare scenarios. The light of your conscious focuses on the present moment—and your acceptance of What-Is in that moment is the flashlight that cuts a clear path through the fog. It shows you the way to go and guides your actions.

Acceptance of What-Is

You don't have to accept the overall situation, but just the tiny segment called the Now. Also, complete acceptance of What-Is doesn't necessarily mean that you just hang back and do nothing. You may make plans, set goals, and take action to initiate change and achieve goals. But when you do it from a place of acceptance, you're connected to the Web of Life through your Intuitive Intelligence, which flows through your actions. So you do it with an appreciation and a joy that takes you more deeply into the Now. You dramatically enhance the quality of everything you create, as well as the quality of your experience moment by moment. Bringing this quality into each moment as you plan and take action means that the future you will experience is more magical. It may be that the lessons you're allowed to learn are more potent, or that the moments you experience are more joyous, or both.

Non-acceptance, in contrast, hardens your egomind and strengthens your sense of being separate from the Web of Life. You're more likely to feel threatened by people and Nature. Your body tenses up, contracts, and becomes more rigid and hard. The only way to permanently release this tension is to practice acceptance in the Now on a regular basis.

Complete Presence in the Now

It's impossible to be totally present and accepting in the present moment and also be unhappy or negative. This silent, intense presence can dissolve your egomind patterns. They may recycle for a while, but they won't run your life, especially if you continue to stay present and accepting on a regular basis. As you go about your daily life, you can focus on what you're doing and still feel your inner energy bodies at the same time. You can learn to stay rooted within. Try this and see how it changes your state of consciousness and the quality of what you do. See how it boosts your creativity as you open up to the Now channel to Source.

See the Self-Awareness Opportunities at the end of Chapter 2 for suggestions on finding time to practice this awareness. Then, the moment a challenge presents itself, go within at once—before habitual reactions take hold—and focus as much as possible on your inner energy fields for a few seconds. Feel the inner energy bodies so you can immediately become still and present as you withdraw attention from the egomind. Your response will then come from this deeper level, infinitely more intelligent and creative than your egomind.

How All Your Intelligences Work Together

In your daily life, your three brains, with their various types of intelligence, work together to help you protect yourself and to learn, grow, and create. You rarely use, say, only your Basic Intelligence of moving toward and moving away from something or just your Pattern Intelligence of following old imprinted habits. Usually these basic experiences are accompanied by some type of emotion, ranging from very mild to intense. And these emotions fuel your motivation to take action. They also help you to remember and to learn because the more emotional the experience, the more vivid it is in your memory.

From Visioning to Intuiting. When you have a vision of something new that you want to create or achieve, it's probably based on some similar pattern or type of thing that you have already experienced. You associate this old experience with a new vision that goes beyond the old parameters and patterns. Often you tap your intuition for inspiration about what to create next in your life and for guidance on how to respond to life's challenges and opportunities.

Intuitive messages may come to you through your dreams via the basic brain, through your feelings via the emotional brain, and through your senses, associations, and thoughts via the neocortex.

Complex Learning. You learn, or gain intelligence, by using all three brains. For example, using your basic brain you learn primarily by trial-and-error experiences and by imitating role models. Using your emotional brain, you learn through your feeling responses to various experiences. They provide a charge that motivates you toward or away from such experiences. Using your neocortex, you learn by analyzing, planning, and evaluating in a rational way. You learn by associating one thing to another—comparing, contrasting, and studying relationships. You learn through your senses—seeing, hearing, smelling, tasting, and touching things in the physical world. You also learn by tuning into messages from your intuition, which puts together all the other learning. Your intuition also brings in information from the interconnected Web of Life at all three levels of consciousness: subconscious, conscious, and superconscious.

Innovative Skills. In today's job marketplace, you boost your value by boosting your ability to use all your intelligences to respond creatively to today's rapidly changing problems and opportunities. Many of these problems-opportunities are taken on by teams of people. Therefore, learning how to function creatively within a team, how to lead team innovation, and how to apply creative group techniques are crucial skills that you will learn in this book.

You need all your intelligences to recognize paradigm problems and opportunities and to take the lead in creating paradigm shifts and responding to them. You'll learn how to step back and see the big picture so you can ignite the changes your organization needs. You can take a lead role in recognizing which problem solutions can leverage a paradigm shift. You can identify opportunities that the most recent Next New Thing has opened up. And you can help develop innovative responses to the ever-emerging marketplace.

Using Creativity in
Problem-Opportunity Situations

You can use your Creative Intelligence in every area of your life where you encounter problems that need solving and opportunities to contribute something to the world and to your own growth.

We're shifting from the old mechanistic way of thinking of problems and opportunities as *out there*. We're playing with a new organic way of thinking. We view opportunities as the Next New Thing made possible by the current New Thing. We see problems as ongoing feedback about how our ideas are working in consensus reality.

The Problem-Opportunity Viewpoint

Do you think primarily in terms of problems you must solve? Or do you focus primarily on opportunities for getting ahead? How about both? Creative people tend to see problems as opportunities to create something new or better. They also realize that opportunities can contain inherent problems that must be addressed if a project is to be successful.

Opportunities signal a chance to initiate something new that leads to a better life or to a new source of business profits. Problems signal a need for you to make a current situation work more effectively by getting to the root of a problem, exploring many alternate solutions, and selecting the best solution for your purpose.

Both opportunities and problems may be hidden from your awareness, so learning to recognize them is a valuable skill. Although problems are often noticeable because they may be in your face and may bug you, making sure you don't settle for solving superficial problems is important. Learning to ask key *why* questions to get at deeper *root* problems is also a valuable skill.

You'll be using many creative techniques to resolve problem-opportunity situations. Realize that a particular creative technique may be highly effective for working on one stage of the problem-solving process and not particularly effective for another stage. Problem-opportunity stages are usually thought of as parts of a rational process, but creativity can occur at every step of the process. You can greatly boost your results by using Creative Intelligence to respond to the problem and opportunities around you.

Problem-Opportunity Stages

The problem-opportunity process can be seen as having six major stages. At most of these stages, you'll begin by exploring and generating ideas and follow by analyzing and evaluating the ideas and selecting the best ones.

As a woman, you're especially likely to relate to a new/ancient way of organic thinking that reflects Nature's creative process, according to Linda Leonard. For example, to create new plant life, we follow this process, which also applies to problem-solving:

1. We understand the environment, prepare fertile soil, and dig into it when the time is right.
2. We plant the seeds of new life.
3. We protect the seeds (and developing plants) from invading competitors and environmental disaster.
4. We wait for the seeds to germinate and grow.
5. We harvest the produce.
6. We appreciate the produce and the process, learning from it what we did effectively and ineffectively. We begin the process again, armed with new information from the experience.

This is Nature's Way, and you can use it along with the traditional problem-opportunity approach, which focuses on finding answers to Key Questions.

When you explore and generate ideas, you need an open, free, imaginative approach that uses your right-brain intelligences. These intelligences include your intuition, your ability to associate or connect things, and your five senses, especially your ability to imagine and visualize something new. You allow your emotional intelligences to come into play in the exploratory process. You break out of your basic brain's old patterns and limiting parameters to move toward new possibilities. When you're exploring, let your rational left brain rest, because evaluating in order to organize and plan tends to kill the idea-generating process. Evaluation just throws a wet blanket on your idea factory.

When you've generated enough ideas, then use your Rational Intelligence to review them, organize them, evaluate them, and decide on which ones to use to take you to the next stage of the process. Then test your final decision for its emotional and intuitive validity.

Stage 1. Analyze the environment.

Key Questions:

- What opportunities are now possible because of the latest New Thing?
- What Next New Thing is now possible?
- What are the ongoing opportunities, threats, comparisons with competitors, and other environmental issues?

You'll begin by exploring the environment and generating ideas about how the environment is affecting your situation and how the situation, in turn, is affecting the environment. In this exploration-generation phase, use all your intelligences except the rational, which can block the flow. When you've generated enough ideas about what's going on in the environment, then use the rational process of reviewing, organizing, evaluating, and selecting the ideas to take you to the next stage of the process.

Nature's Way. This is the time to honor Nature's seasons of time and preparation of fertile soil. It's a time to surrender old beliefs and methods, to leap into the unknown to discover new visions, ideals, and feelings, so you might bring them into being. It's a time to let go of the old boundaries and to let be the complexity and chaos of a situation. It's a time to be open to what comes up, giving up the need to control that process. It's a time to face the death of the old so rebirth of the new can occur.

Stage 2. Recognize problems and opportunities.

Key Questions:

- What possibilities have opened up?
- What Next New Thing is now possible?
- What problems need to be solved?

Now that you have explored the environment and generated a wealth of information, it's time to select from that bounty those opportunities that give you the most leverage and those problems whose solutions would be most crucial and profitable for you to reach.

The process involves sifting through information, making connections among bits and pieces of information, recognizing how certain information fits into your situation, identifying the most important opportunities and problems, and selecting the ones you will devote your attention and energy to.

Nature's Way. Plant the seeds of new life, new ideas. The first three phases are the time of toil. You apply self-discipline and work as you gather the information (energy), prepare the soil or environment, and plant the seeds of new ideas.

Stage 3. Identify root problems, opportunities, and assumptions.

Without a precise explanation of a problem, you can't solve it. At this stage, your goal is to develop a precise explanation, one that provides the necessary foundation for the phases that follow.

Key Questions:

- ❧ What is the underlying or root problem that we need to address?
- ❧ What hidden assumptions do we have that may be faulty?
- ❧ What opportunities are we overlooking?

Again, begin with exploring and generating ideas about which of the issues you explored in Stage 2 are actually problems or opportunities that need further exploration—as well as possible assumptions that are faulty. Follow with reviewing, organizing, evaluating, and deciding which ideas to take to the next stage.

Nature's Way. Protect the seeds (and developing plants) from invading competitors and environmental disaster. You continue the time of work, attention, and self-discipline.

Stage 4. Let new information incubate.

Now comes the easiest time, if you're naturally intuitive, or the hardest time, if you've become trapped in rational control games. It's a time of rest and relaxation, of diverting your attention to other projects and activities. Be willing to let the project *go underground*, consciously forgetting it but knowing that it's working in your subconscious mind. Be as open and receptive as you can to intuitive hunches, flashes of insight, little glimmers of ideas. It's great when your intuition brings you ideas with unmistakable fanfare and clarity. More often than not, the messages are subtle, symbolic, and puzzling.

Nature's Way: This is the time of waiting for the seeds to germinate and grow. Be willing to let all the information and ideas you've gathered incubate in the warm recesses of your mind (that is, let them hibernate in your subconscious for a while). The seeds will sprout in this darkness underground, in the fertile soil of a receptive mind, where you've planted them.

Remember the story of the overanxious farmer, who went out in the night to check on the sprouting seeds and to pull on them so they would grow faster. He ruined his crop. Be willing to let go of the need to control the process and trust that it will flow in Nature's creative way.

Stage 5. Generate alternatives.

Key Question:

- ❧ How many creative ideas, solutions, or plans can we come up with that address this problem or opportunity?

The process is first rational-creative, then purely creative. Organize all the information and ideas to get a handle on them. Then explore the information, make random associations, and remain open to emotional, sensory, and intuitive input in order to generate ideas.

Nature's Way: Protect the seeds and the new growth. Let them freely generate, develop, and grow. Don't thin out the new plants until you see which ones are most likely to thrive in this environment.

Stage 6. Choose from alternatives.

Key Question:

- ❧ Which plan has the best chance of bringing us the most success in this situation?

The process is rational. This stage is all about evaluating and deciding. It's primarily rational, but your final decision must *feel* right. Use your emotional and intuitive intelligence to evaluate it.

Nature's Way. Continue to protect the new plants, thinning them out so the best ones can thrive, weeding out superfluous plant growth, and nurturing and protecting the plants until it's time to harvest the produce. Now is the time to bring the new to fruition, to harvest the fruits of your work.

Stage 7. Sell, implement, evaluate results, and follow up.

Key questions:

- What can we do to get the people we need behind this plan?
- What do we need to do to make the plan work?
- How can we get the best results from this plan?
- What feedback mechanisms do we need to set up in order to evaluate how well the plan is doing? Do we have a good Plan B or C if Plan A doesn't work out as we expect?
- What can we do to minimize the risk factor and to boost the success factor of the plan?

The process has four steps, all of which require you to explore and generate ideas:

1. Sell the action plan. Explore ideas for selling the plan, generate ideas, and select the best ones.

2. Implement the plan. Explore ideas for carrying out the plan, generate ideas for how to do it, and select the best ones.

3. Evaluate the results of the plan. Explore ideas for the kinds of feedback you need to best evaluate how well the plan is working. Gather the evidence. Using this feedback, evaluate the overall plan and each of its aspects.

4. Follow up to improve the plan. Based on the evaluation of plan results, explore ideas for solving any newly discovered problems and taking advantage of newly discovered opportunities, generate new ideas for modifying the plan, and select the best ones.

Nature's Way. This is the time to appreciate. Feel gratitude and appreciation for the harvest, and for the creative process. Now is also a time of giving and sharing—getting others involved in the harvest of ideas. It's a time of reflection and review, of learning from the experience. Then the cycle will start again as you envision something new that can be created—and you pass along the creative gift, inspiring others to create.

Would you like to practice applying this process to a problem-opportunity situation? See the Case Situation that follows.

Case Situation: Kid Fun

Stevie Ruiz is 13 years old. His company, Kid Fun, is only two years old. Stevie is president of the company, which is owned in equal fourths by Stevie, his mom **Donna**, his dad **Alfredo**, and **Luis Martinez,** the CEO. The company makes toys, which are invented by Stevie and his mom Donna.

Kid Fun's initial product, Water Talkie, was Stevie's idea. He hopes to help other children realize that the goal of becoming a successful inventor-entrepreneur is as exciting as becoming a rock singer or a basketball star—and probably more attainable.

Ever since he was a baby, Stevie has demonstrated a persistent curiosity. He's always been fascinated by how things work, taking apart intricate items such as clocks and radios—with his parents' blessing! That same sense of wonder propels his budding business career. His parents have created an environment where he can freely express his ideas, and this has given him great confidence in his creative ability.

The idea for Water Talkie came to Stevie on a family vacation in the Bahamas when he was 10 years old. He went snorkeling for the first time with his dad. Stevie got very excited over the underwater sights and he wanted to chat with his dad about them, but how can you chat with your face in the water? Back at the beachside café, he started thinking about making a contraption that would allow underwater talk. He began drawing ideas on drink coasters. Stevie's dad says, "You want to encourage that kind of creativity." On the airplane going home his grandmother gave him a notepad and pencils. His drawings began to look like a megaphone. Stevie pinpointed the major problem: *How am I going to keep the water out?* At home, he began searching on the Internet for information. He decided to find two soccer cones, cut off the tips, and replace them with snorkel mouthpieces. He used a toilet-bowl screw to clamp the cone opening, changing it from a round shape to an oval.

The family enlisted Luis Martinez as a partner on the project because of his business expertise and connections. Stevie designed a mouthpiece for the toy, and Luis brought in a dental engineer, who combined it with a blow valve and a tube taken off a snorkel. The result was a product that allows users to talk with underwater partners who are less than 15 yards away. Stevie took $267 of his own savings and worked with his partners to develop packaging for the toy.

Stevie's mom Donna had some previous success in marketing inexpensive novelties. She had developed *The Formula* for making money, which she describes this way: You start with an inexpensive product idea, something that costs less than $2 to make and retails for around $10. You put dynamic packaging with that. You sell in very high volume. Finally—and this is the step that most people don't follow—you go out to get a large order that will cover your costs before you do anything about manufacturing the product. Also, it's critical not to depend on the retailers' ability to sell the product. You must make the right agreement when you take the order from the retailer: *You buy it, you own it; we don't buy back product that you can't sell.* It's very important that inventors do that, so the retailer is motivated to find ways to generate sales of the product—not just stick it on the shelf and see what happens.

According to The Formula, it was time to get a big Water Talkie order. Stevie wrote a letter to the head of Toys R Us and followed up with a phone call. The CEO asked Stevie to come to the headquarters office to show him the product. After a two-hour presentation, Stevie and his mom got an on-the-spot order for 50,000 units. They were off to a great start, but what next?

What potential problems and/or opportunities do you think Kid Fun faces now? Using the seven-step problem-opportunity approach, apply the process to Kid Fun's situation. Keep in mind the following two questions.

1. What kinds of products should Kid Fun develop next? In general? Can you think of some specific toys that Kid Fun should consider?

2. What specific recommendations would you make as a consultant to Kid Fun?

(After you try your hand at this, check the feedback that follows.)

Case Situation Feedback

Stage 1. Analyze the environment. No situation occurs in a vacuum. You must always ferret out those occurrences and trends going on around you that represent significant opportunities or threats. In Kid Fun's case, these include other toy manufacturers, especially pool toy manufacturers, trends in what kids are attracted to and what they're doing these days, as well as the entire retailing scene, including the Internet and e-commerce.

Stage 2. Recognize problems and opportunities. At this point Kid Fun seems to have many opportunities and no problems. The main job of the players in the company is to explore the numerous opportunities—now and in the foreseeable future—sift through them, and select the best bets for focusing their money and attention. Especially important are opportunities for new products and determining which products will appeal to kids. Here the main asset is Stevie. If he's really excited about a toy, chances are other kids will be also.

Stage 3. Identify root problems, opportunities, and assumptions. Kid Fun's players must be careful to uncover hidden assumptions about the marketplace and how future products will fare there. Can they assume that because Water Talkie is a pool/water toy, their future toys should also be pool toys? Is that their niche? They must explore all reasonable opportunities to add to their product line—the various types of products they could develop—and the array of channels to distribute and retail their products.

As a new company, Kid Fun does not have enough money to expand rapidly, which may limit the ability to take advantage of market opportunities. If Kid Fun's principals decide that generating adequate financial backing is a problem, they must explore the many sources of funding that could be made available.

Stage 4. Let new information incubate. Now is the time for the principals to focus on other activities and projects, relaxing and holding the intention to remain open to insights in intuitions about Kid Fun's next moves.

Stage 5. Generate alternatives. Kid Fun's principals must now organize all the information they've gathered, analyze it, sift through it, make associations and connections, and listen to their senses, their emotions, and their intuitive messages.

Stage 6. Choose from alternatives. Kid Fun's principals must select the best method for financing future operations. In fact, they decided to keep the firm private and swing a loan from the banker who had financed them from the beginning. They developed a business plan that described three new products Stevie had designed. All are water toys because Kid Fun's players decided that is their best niche for now.

- ❧ Pool Peepers is a water mask designed to let the wearer see out. People looking at the wearer will not see a water mask but a face mask that looks like a lobster, frog, or dragonfly.
- ❧ Pool Pogo is another product that kids will like but parents must be sure it won't damage the pool.
- ❧ Bin-Aqua-Lars are underwater binoculars. The major issue is how far apart to position the lenses.

Stage 7. Sell, implement, evaluate, and follow up. Kid Fun must sell this plan to their banker. They must sell their toys to retailers. They must get the toys perfected, manufactured, and delivered to retailers on time. They must continually evaluate how well the toys are doing, whether improvements are needed, how they can improve the toys, and how satisfied their customers are. They must do the same kind of follow-up with other key stakeholders in the business, such as their retailers, suppliers, shippers, and banker.

Kid Fun has in fact grown rapidly in the past two years. They secured more than $400,000 from their banker. Sales quadrupled last year, with accounts increasing from 18 to 125, including 250 Kmart stores and 600 Target stores, as well as stores in seven foreign countries. Foreign sales now make up about a third of total sales. Very helpful are sales in South America, Australia, and southern Africa, where the seasons are reversed. This means summer-season sales of pool toys are spread out over the entire year. As far as overhead, Kid Fun still has no full-time employees. The four principals do nearly all the work, and other duties are either contracted out or handled by part-time employees.

Chapter 2

Spark Your Creativity

Anything is possible. Put no barriers on your mind. Let it go.
If you nurture and feed the mind, it's amazing what you can
come up with.
Ron Johnson, Mosaic Events Management

Are you beginning to sense your creativity potential? A powerful way to see your creativity at play is to try out some new activities designed to ignite that spark that's there inside of you. Here are some "sparklers" that will help you get started. You'll find many more sparklers in the chapters that follow.

Sparkler #1: Turn on Your Creative Self and Turn Off Your Sabotaging Self

You have many selves, or many aspects of your one self. Some of your selves tend to sabotage your creativity while other selves glorify and enhance it. See if you recognize some of your sabotaging selves. But don't get discouraged, for each sabotaging self has an alter ego—one or more creative selves. You can always shift your consciousness to a creative self. They are all there within.

Your Sabotaging Selves

You can sabotage your creativity in many ways. Here are some of your sabotaging selves:

1. Rational Cynic. This self lacks faith, is frustrated with imperfection, doubts, doesn't care, and asks *why bother*? Alter egos: Lover, Witness.

2. Critic. Your rational Critic self may either function as a scary opponent who discourages your creativity, or she can help you make the important decisions you need to make in order to lead a healthy and creative life. If she teams up with your Tyrant and Cynic selves, she can destroy your creative impulses. Alter egos: Lover, Witness.

3. Tyrant. Your meanie self uses rational intelligence to gain absolute control over your other selves. She censors the creativity you want to express in your external life and tries to end your inner work by stifling your inspiration and spirit. She bullies you until you become her victim. Alter egos: Nature Spirit, Wise Fool.

4. Perfectionist. This picky self undermines your Sensory Intelligence by visualizing the impossible dream and setting up goals you cannot possibly reach. She can cause you to believe that you'll never do it right, that you'll never measure up, and that you can't expose your work to others' criticism. As a result, you may feel like a failure, fear that you're a fraud, give up, and abandon your creative projects. Alter egos: Nature Spirit, Lover.

5. Pampered Princess. Your *me-me* self begins thinking she's better than most everyone else and takes all the credit for creating. The rational egomind feeds the Pampered Princess with inflated fantasies of fame or lures her to rest on her laurels. She's motivated by egomind strivings instead of by doing the work. Alter egos: Witness, Adventuress Artisan.

6. Conformist. Your *same-o* self undermines your Basic Pattern-Parameter Intelligence by clinging to habits and limits, trying to avoid the risk of change, and thinking this will provide her the safety and security she needs. She discourages your Adventuress Artisan self, and if she teams up with your Tyrant self, she'll keep you inside your box. Alter ego: Gatekeeper.

7. Escape Artist. This slippery self evades the anxiety and tension of creative acts in a number of ways:

- She may escape into your *Sluggard* self, the passive, complacent, inert self who undermines your Basic Intelligence. Alter egos: Gatekeeper, Gardener.

- She may shape-shift into your *Compulsive Doer* self, the busy workaholic with no time for creativity, who undermines your Motivational Intelligence by doing the wrong things. Alter egos: Gardener, Adventuress Artisan.

- She may become your *Dilettante* self, who undermines your Emotional Intelligence by seeking pleasure in worldly distractions, dabbling in many projects and never bringing any to fruition. Alter ego: Adventuress Artisan.

Your Creative Selves

Your creative selves are lively and full of natural spirit and expansive emotions. They use your various intelligences in ways that boost and spark your creativity. Here are some of your creative selves:

1. Lover. This heartfelt self also connects with your heart center and Associative Intelligence, dealing with you and the world compassionately. She participates passionately in life's flow. She accepts imperfection, has tolerance for the learning curve, and takes an active role in the creative process by joining and sharing with others in the work of the creative life and in enjoying its achievements. She acts from her heart and asks others to collaborate.

2. Witness. This honest, assertive self is tied to your heart center and Associative Intelligence. She gives you the courage to stand your ground and the wisdom to know how to do it. She observes and remembers, recording the words and behavior of your Tyrant self, dealing with the fears and anxieties that your Tyrant self plays on.

3. Nature Spirit. This creative self feeds your Sensory Intelligence, your creative soul, with the imagination that brings inspiration. She invites you to co-create with nature. Invite her in by grooving on Nature—for at least a little while every day.

4. Wise Fool. This highly intuitive self is the most creative you. She's willing to step off into the unknown, not knowing the way or the outcome, but trusting that her Intuitive Intelligence will help her stumble upon the wisdom she needs to reach her destination. She sees the creative process as a quest, a search for the path of discovery.

5. Adventuress Artisan. This courageous, hard-working self actively opposes the Conformist, purposefully breaking out of old patterns and boundaries by taking a leap of faith, risking failure, and moving in a new direction. She's highly motivated to break out of old parameters because she sees creativity as a gift that she's grateful for. She knows she must work collaboratively and work throughout her life in order to hone the skills of her craft and to live out her life purpose.

6. Gatekeeper. This wise guardian self feeds your Basic Pattern-Parameter Intelligence. She stands guard at the border between the conscious mind and the unconscious minds—to keep you from retreating into unconsciousness, falling into *sleep*, to avoid the strain of creative work. Meditation takes you to your sentinel, and being alone allows you to get in touch with your superconscious and subconscious and bring them up to the conscious level. Relaxing in nature can help you make this connection.

7. Gardener. This energetic, nurturing self feeds your Motivational Intelligence, planting the seeds of hope, faith, and commitment to the creative process. She is the doer, the self who does the creative work.

Sabotaging Selves	Alter-Ego Creative Selves
Rational Cynic	Lover, Witness
Critic	Lover, Witness
Tyrant	Nature Spirit, Wise Fool
Perfectionist	Nature Spirit, Lover
Pampered Princess	Witness, Adventuress Artisan
Conformist	Gatekeeper
Escape Artist	
Sluggard	Gatekeeper, Gardener
Compulsive Doer	Gardener, Adventuress Artisan
Dilettante	Adventuress Artisan

As you take up the Self-Awareness Opportunities that follow, remember to take some of your creative-self time to focus, one self at a time, on the self-sabotaging selves that you sense are blocking your creativity. Practice shifting your focus to the alter-ego creative selves that can break through the blocks.

Sparkler #2: Leverage Your Energy

Moving beyond your limiting habit patterns and boundaries requires that you learn how to change. In fact, learning itself is nothing more than seeing and responding to changes and finding ways to leverage those things that make a difference. If you can make minor adjustments at the leverage points, the changes can produce major impacts on your environment. Go beyond the simple cause-and-effect elements of a situation and learn to identify the leverage points.

Leverage points are places where small inputs produce major results. Look at the results, both positive and negative, of energy applied at these leverage points. For example, a little mistake in the beginning of a new phase could have catastrophic effects as it expands. A small positive adjustment could have a major favorable impact that expands as things develop.

How do you find those leverage points? First, get unstuck from your old beliefs and ways of thinking. Imagine yourself as being very flexible, able to adapt, always innovating—not only in what you do, but also in how you do it. Practice being flexible and open in the way you think, learn, teach, and create new ideas and practices. Question your ideas and be willing to change them when they no longer support the actions you need to take in order to succeed. Innovative questions are constructive ways of always asking *why* instead of going along with the same old routine.

If a little energy creates great returns, what if you swarmed around a leverage point and ramped up the energy input? This is sometimes call flocking resources, or clustering them, in order to move quickly through a barrier or to speed up the completion of a project. So a good question to ask when time is of the essence is: *How can I swarm resources around this leverage point in order to meet the time target?*

Innovative Questions for Leveraging Energy

Ask yourself these questions any time you want to get more bang for your energy buck.

1. What activities do I (my firm) put *a lot* of energy into but get *small* results from? Why do I (we) continue doing these things?

2. What activities do I (my firm) put a *little* energy into but get *major* results from? How do I (we) account for this? What can I (we) learn from this?

3. How does this paradox—of small inputs producing large results—relate to the ratio of information to infrastructure in my career (firm)?

    ◆ Do *small* changes in infrastructure (physical, material stuff and old habits) produce *large* changes in productivity?

- Do *large* changes in infrastructure produce *small* changes in productivity?
- Do *small* changes in information (including new mental models, stories, symbols, theories) produce *large* changes in infrastructure?
- Do *large* changes in information produce *small* changes in infrastructure?
- How can I (my firm) find and create new leverage points?

Sparkler #3: Open Up to Your Creative Self

To spark your creativity you must open up to all your intelligences and allow that creative child that's still in there to come out and play. For the next week or so, focus on one of these "sparklets" each day. Maybe you'll want to photocopy this list and place it by your calendar to remind you to open up.

- Day 1: Today I'll be curious. I'll ask good questions and find good answers.
- Day 2: Today I'll give myself the freedom to play creatively.
- Day 3: Today I'll really listen, observe, and stay centered.
- Day 4: Today I'll venture into the unknown and stay there a while, just to see what happens—even if it's a little scary.
- Day 5: Today I'll open up my intuitive channels.
- Day 6: Today I'll keep my senses open to discovery—and intuitive messages.
- Day 7: Today I'll capture my unique inspirations.
- Day 8: Today I'll nurture the possibilities of innovation—by nurturing my Creative Self (and that of my team members) and rewarding innovation and creative risk-taking.

Self-Awareness Opportunities

SAO #1: What are your creativity-limiting beliefs?

Purpose: To begin to recognize how the beliefs you've picked up from culture and from your personal environment may be limiting your creative potential.

Step 1. Identify your beliefs. Check off the beliefs in #1 that you hold or think you may harbor. Complete the sentences in #2–7 and then reflect on the beliefs you have just expressed.

1. *Creative people are*:
   - Overemotional.
   - Impractical.
   - Unrealistic.
   - Children who refuse to grow up.
   - Egomaniacs.

- Difficult to live with.
- Poor wage earners.
- Martyrs who must suffer to achieve greatness.
- Likely to abuse alcohol and drugs.

2. *To be a creative person, I'd have to give up...*

3. All creative people are alike; they're . . .

4. I can't be a creative person until . . .

5. If I really expressed by soul's longing . . .

6. Creative people are never very good at . . .

7. I had a friend who was very creative and now she's (he's) . . .

Step 2. Rewrite. Rewrite each of the sabotaging beliefs that you identified in Step 1. Some examples of rewrites are provided to stimulate your thinking. Focus on fully accepting your rewritten beliefs. If you take some *quiet time* each day for yourself, spend a little of it focusing on these new beliefs for the next few weeks.

Creative people:

- Are often more in touch with their emotions.
- Sometimes don't agree with consensus reality.
- Are able to experience the world with childlike wonder.
- Have a strong and healthy sense of self.
- May value developing their talent and making a contribution above making money.
- Are likely to become rich and famous in the New Economy.
- Are likely to achieve inner power and self-control.

SAO #2: Make creative-self time.

Make a daily date—15 minutes with your Creative Self: 10 minutes for meditation and at least five minutes for creative expression.

Step 1. Creatively Visualize. Find a quiet, comfortable space where you can surround yourself with little meaningful symbols and treasures.

During your 10 minutes of meditation, breathe deeply, relax fully, and let go of mind chatter. When chatter comes in, don't get hooked into it; watch it pass on by. Let yourself go deep, sensing your inner energy bodies. Stay focused on your senses—on how you feel, sense, hear, smell, and taste. Move into a total acceptance of What-Is in the present moment.

Once you're deeply relaxed, focus on one or more of the following:

Sabotaging and Creative Selves. Ask your Intuitive Self, *Which self is sabotaging me at this time?* Listen for some sense of the answer. Go fully into that Sabotaging Self, fully accept it, and stay with it till you come out on the other side. Be open to a Creative Self that is ready to come in and take over your attention. Allow that Creative Self to fully expand and stay around.

What Next? Ask your Intuitive Self that's connected to the living universe, *What next?* Listen, sense, feel, and intuit.

New Creation. The answer to *what next* may give you a sense of what you want to create next in your life—for yourself and the world. Imagine that you have already created it. In your imagination, be there; be your creation. Experience it all in great detail for a few moments. Tune into the feelings—your own and others'. Then let it go; put it out into the universe, with the intention: *this or better, for the highest good of all*. Trust that it will come about in the best way possible.

Step 2. Creatively express. After you've done a brief meditation with visualization, take at least 5 minutes to express yourself creatively in some way—focusing on what came up during your meditative time. Find some methods for stimulating your creative expression. Write, speak into a tape recorder, draw, role-play alone or with a buddy, sing, or dance. Honor your expressions and save what you can—at least write some notes about each expression. You could also start a collage, an idea book, or a creative journal. Do what turns you on, what's fun, what wants to come next.

SAO #3: Be fully accepting of the Now.

Practice a full focus on the Now, along with total acceptance of what is—during meditation time and also at those odd times that are usually stressful. For example, any time you're forced to wait—such as in traffic, in grocery store lines, or at a doctor's office—use that time to feel your inner energy bodies. Go more deeply into the Now by going more deeply into your energy bodies. When thoughts come in, just watch them and let them go on by, each time coming back to what you feel, hear, see, and sense in the Now.

Fully accept What-Is in this moment. Rest in the *no-time, no-thing* of each present moment. Once you achieve this state, you may want to practice a What-Next phase of listening and a New-Creation phase of visualizing.

SAO #4: What's your Creativity Quotient?

Purpose: To get an idea of your current level of creativity and to receive feedback on how well you have developed each of your seven intelligences. Your Creativity Quotient will indicate which intelligences you have most strongly developed and least strongly developed, and therefore, which ones you may want to focus on most intensely.

Instructions: To the left of #1–49, write either a, b, or c (a=agree; b=in-between or don't know; c=disagree). For #50, follow the directions provided.

1. Whenever I solve a problem, I'm sure that I'm following the correct procedure.
2. It would be a waste of time to ask questions if I had no hope of getting answers.
3. I concentrate harder on what interests me than most people do.
4. I feel that a logical, step-by-step method is best for solving problems.
5. In groups I sometimes state opinions that seem to turn some people off.
6. I spend a great deal of time thinking about what other people think of me.
7. It's more important to do what I believe is right than to try to win others' approval.
8. People who seem uncertain about things lose my respect.

9. More than other people, I need to have things interesting and exciting.
10. I know how to keep my inner impulses in check.
11. I'm able to stick with difficult problems over extended periods of time.
12. On occasion I get overly enthusiastic.
13. I often get my best ideas when I'm doing nothing in particular.
14. I rely on intuitive hunches and the feeling of rightness or wrongness when I move toward the solution of a problem.
15. When problem solving, I work faster when analyzing the problem and slower when putting together the information I've gathered.
16. I sometimes get a kick out of breaking rules and doing things I'm not supposed to do.
17. I like hobbies that involve collecting things.
18. Daydreaming has provided the impetus for many of my more important projects.
19. I like people who are objective and rational.
20. If I had to choose, I would rather be a physician than an explorer.
21. I can get along more easily with people if they belong to about the same social and business or professional class as I do.
22. I have a high degree of artistic sensitivity.
23. I'm driven to achieve high status and power in life.
24. I like people who are most sure of their conclusions.
25. Inspiration has nothing to do with the successful solution of problems.
26. When I'm in an argument, my greatest pleasure would be for the person who disagrees with me to become a friend, even at the price of sacrificing my point of view.
27. I'm more interested in coming up with new ideas than trying to sell them to others.
28. I would enjoy spending an entire day alone, just thinking and hanging out.
29. I tend to avoid situations in which I might feel inferior.
30. In evaluating information, the source is more important to me than the content.
31. I resent things being uncertain and unpredictable.
32. I like people who follow the rule: "Business before pleasure."
33. Self-respect is much more important than the respect of others.
34. I feel that people who strive for perfection are unwise.
35. I prefer working with others in a team effort to "doing it by myself."
36. I like work in which I must influence others.
37. Many problems in life cannot be resolved in terms of right or wrong solutions.
38. It's important for me to have a place for everything and to have everything in its place.

39. Writers who use strange and unusual words merely want to show off.
40. I'm different, and I don't mind being different.
41. I don't necessarily play by the rules.
42. I have trouble being accurate, punctual, and proper.
43. I'm sensitive to the art and beauty in more than art and beauty.
44. I see things where others do not.
45. I think about new things but usually don't take action on them until others do.
46. I'm content with the average or normal.
47. I know when to let go and how to do it.
48. I have faith in my vision, my craft, and the creative process.
49. I'm able to concentrate and to focus energy on a single goal.
50. Circle the 10 words in the following list that best describe you.

absent-minded	acquisitive	alert	cautious
clear-thinking	courageous	curious	dedicated
determined	dynamic	efficient	egotistical
energetic	enthusiastic	factual	fashionable
flexible	formal	forward-looking	good-natured
habit-bound	helpful	impulsive	independent
informal	inhibited	innovative	involved
polished	practical	predictable	quick
realistic	resourceful	restless	modest
observant	open-minded	organized	original
perceptive	persevering	persuasive	poised
retiring	self-confident	self-demanding	sociable
stern	tactful	thorough	understanding
unemotional	well-liked		

Before you score your responses (see pages 43-45), examine the ways that your personal beliefs, traits, and habits are related to the seven types of intelligence that make up your Creative Intelligence. Your scores are related to these types of intelligence.

Typical Creative Traits—by Type of Intelligence

Your Creative Intelligence at work depends upon certain personal qualities. Research on what makes people creative indicates that certain learned beliefs and habits are usually present. The tendencies are categorized according to the type of intelligence each draws upon—and each item in the Creativity Quotient self-assessment is related to one or more of these types of intelligence.

Basic Pattern-Parameter Intelligence

- ❧ You've learned to overcome obstacles and keep going; you don't give up.
- ❧ You've learned to keep going through many rejections, learning from each one.

- ✎ You have a strong urge to go beyond established limits, to break rules, and make up new rules. This means you understand paradigms and paradigm shifts. You know that in order to take a creative lead in solving problems within a paradigm, you must see outside the current boundaries and rules and create new ones that work.
- ✎ You question conventional wisdom. You frequently ask why.

Emotional Intelligence

- ✎ You're passionately curious and inquisitive.
- ✎ You have a passion for the new. You've become fascinated with new combinations, new forms, new ways.
- ✎ You have enough confidence and love of adventure to risk looking foolish—for the work.
- ✎ You've learned to view life's successes and failures as learning experiences, rather than issues of ego and self-worth.
- ✎ You can see lessons where others might see failures.

Motivational Intelligence

- ✎ You've found a sense of your purpose in life and have found work that has meaning for you and ties into your life purpose. This enables you to feel a passion for the work and to get lost in it.
- ✎ You're able to get into the *flow*.
- ✎ You're motivated by goals and task-focused.
- ✎ You're energetic and productive.
- ✎ As you become more creative, you become more consumed by your work.
- ✎ You like some alone-time to pursue your passions.

Rational Intelligence

- ✎ You've learned to generate a large number of new ideas.
- ✎ You're comfortable with not knowing while you gather information and work through learning processes.

Associative Intelligence

- ✎ You've learned to see relationships in new ways.
- ✎ You use the power of metaphors, analogies, and other ways of learning through association.

Sensory Intelligence

- ✎ You've learned to think in images and visualizations.
- ✎ You often think in terms of tones, or chords, of musical harmony.

ᕭ   You often rely on taste, smell, or your kinesthetic sense to achieve
     what you want or to create something new.

ᕭ   You've learned to see things in new ways, so you can often see
     things others miss

Intuitive Intelligence

ᕭ   You're open to intuition, fantasy, imagination, feelings, new ideas,
     artistic expression.

ᕭ   You often get ideas that "just come to you."

ᕭ   You often trust your inner knowing when making decisions and
     choices.

Scoring

To compute your Creativity score, circle and add up the values assigned
to each item. The values are as follows:

	a agree	b between	c disagree	Type(s) of intelligence that this statement relates to
1.	0	1	2	Basic Parameter; Rational
2.	0	1	2	Basic Pattern
3.	3	1	0	Motivational
4.	-1	0	3	Emotional; Rational
5.	2	1	0	Basic Parameter
6.	-1	0	3	Basic Parameter; Motivational
7.	3	0	-1	Basic Parameter
8.	0	1	2	Emotional
9.	3	0	-1	Association; Emotional
10.	1	0	3	Emotional; Basic Parameter
11.	4	1	0	Basic
12.	3	0	-1	Motivational
13.	2	1	0	Intuitive
14.	4	0	-2	Intuitive
15.	-1	0	2	Intuitive; Associative
16.	2	1	0	Basic Parameter
17.	0	1	2	Associative
18.	3	0	-1	Sensory—Visual
19.	0	1	2	Associative
20.	0	1	2	Motivational
21.	0	1	2	Associative
22.	3	0	-1	Sensory
23.	0	1	2	Motivational
24.	-1	0	2	Associative
25.	0	1	3	Emotional

	a agree	b between	c disagree	Type(s) of intelligence that this statement relates to
26.	-1	0	2	Emotional; Basic Parameter
27.	2	1	0	Associative
28.	2	0	-1	Motivational
29.	0	1	2	Emotional
30.	-2	0	3	Associative
31.	0	1	2	Associative
32.	0	1	2	Sensory
33.	3	0	-1	Emotional
34.	-1	0	2	Emotional
35.	0	1	2	Motivational
36.	1	2	3	Motivational
37.	2	1	0	Basic Parameter
38.	0	1	2	Basic Parameter
39.	-1	0	2	Associative
40.	2	0	2	Basic Parameter; Emotional
41.	2	0	2	Basic Parameter
42.	2	0	2	Basic Parameter
43.	2	1	2	Sensory
44.	2	1	2	Sensory
45.	–1	0	2	Motivational
46.	–1	0	2	Associative; Motivational
47.	2	1	0	Intuitive
48.	2	0	2	Intuitive
49.	3	0	-1	Motivational

50. Follow these instructions to figure your score on the word association question:

   The following words have values of 2:

   * adventurous
   * bold
   * courageous
   * dedicated
   * dynamic
   * energetic
   * flexible
   * independent
   * innovative
   * involved
   * observant
   * passionate
   * perceptive
   * resourceful
   * self-demanding

   The following words have values of 1:
   * alert
   * determined
   * forward-looking
   * humorous

- informal
- open-minded
- patient
- playful

The rest of the words have values of 0.

Add up the total values of the words you selected to get a composite score for # 50.

To get your total score:

Add up the values you scored for all. Compare your scores to the following:

100 to 142 = exceptionally creative

70 to 99 = very creative

50 to 69 = above average

40 to 49 = average

20 to 39 = below average

below 20 = not creative—yet!

Follow-up: For each of the 50 items, review your response and score.

Note which intelligences your positive scores are related to. These are traits, beliefs, and practices you can build your creative intelligence upon. If you expand the time and effort you devote to these, you'll expand your Creative Intelligence.

Note which intelligences your negative scores are related to. Make a list of beliefs, attitudes, and habits you want to change in order to boost your creativity. Focus especially on the chapters devoted to these intelligences and the Self-Awareness Opportunities within those chapters.

No matter where you are now, you can develop these intelligences that make up your Creative Intelligence by engaging in the processes presented in this book. What you learn here is merely the beginning—the planting of the seeds of creativity. It's up to you to continue the developmental process throughout your career—and throughout your life.

Part 2:
Using All Your Creative Potential— 7 Intelligences

Chapter 3

Move Beyond
Habit Patterns
and Limitations:
Basic Intelligence

> You do not become enlightened by imagining figures of light,
> but by making the darkness conscious.
> *Carl Jung*

Your brainpower is amazing. You have three brains: the basic, the limbic, and the neocortex. Your basic brain has several major functions. It guides you toward what you need in order to survive and thrive and to move away from what you don't need or want. Your basic brain allows you to easily establish repetitive habit patterns. Habits in turn allow you to successfully cope with the overwhelming stimuli that you receive every second, by filtering out most of it. Your basic brain lets you establish and recognize boundaries or parameters. All this habitual moving toward and away from within your territorial boundaries can either block your creativity or enhance it. This brain is also associated with your dream state, each night creating a dream reality that can be a powerful source of your creative breakthroughs.

Terms to associate with this Basic Pattern-Parameter Intelligence include:

> survival, attraction, repulsion, repetition, imitation, deception, habit patterns, territory, boundaries, limits, perseverance, living in the present moment, dream state

Overcoming Limiting Patterns That Block Creative Intelligence

As a woman, many of your habit patterns may serve you well in the New Economy. For example, you probably have a head start in the people skills department—relating well to people, making people connections, understanding others' emotional responses, and knowing how to make people feel comfortable and cared for.

On the other hand, you may need some creative strategies for moving beyond cultural myths that limit you, strategies for setting your own boundaries and limits. You can learn how to recognize your own beliefs and fears that have grown out of these myths. You can then establish some new self-empowering beliefs. In this chapter you'll learn how to change old thinking-feeling-acting patterns that no longer serve you—overcoming your personal barriers to developing innovative skills.

Cultural Myths and Stereotypes

You can gain creative power by recognizing the cultural myths and stereotypes that can be barriers to fully developing your Creative Intelligence and innovative skills. You can overcome such barriers by identifying them, becoming aware of how they affect you personally, recognizing them in action, heading them off at the pass, and taking specific action steps that help you break out of their sway.

Myth #1: Women are not as creative as men.

You've heard this myth expressed in many different ways that cover virtually all the creative arts and professions. Most versions ignore the fact that almost all cultures for the past 5,000 years have been patriarchal cultures that relegated women to the kitchen and the bedroom and made them second-class citizens. As a result, women's creativity has been essentially ignored by cultural leaders and historians, swept under the rug with other stray bits of lint.

"All the great artists have been men," is one version of the myth. In response, many women artists have organized in recent years into women artist guilds and associations. They own their own galleries, sponsor art shows, and generally promote women artists and their work.

"All the great writers have been men," is the literary version of the myth, and women authors are responding in ways similar to women artists. Seminars and study groups designed for women writers have sprung up in recent years—as well as associations of women authors who review and promote each others' work.

"All the great chefs are men" is especially galling, given that food preparation through the centuries has traditionally been women's work. The implication is that even in those skills that women specialize in, they can't excel because they aren't creative; they just don't have it. Enjoying a gourmet meal at Post Trio in San Franciso recently, I endured a short lecture on this topic. A highly educated San Francisco business executive who dabbles in gourmet cooking as a hobby mentioned that great chefs have always been men. I had to point out that one of the most famous, highly creative chefs of the 20th century is Alice Waters, owner of Chez Panisse in Berkeley, California, just across the Bay

Bridge. I also noted that in a recent article in the *San Francisco Chronicle-Examiner,* the top 50 Bay Area chefs were named, and about one-third of them were women. The myth prevails, and it's up to us to tell the new stories.

"All the great business leaders are men." Basking in the sun, while we enjoyed lunch at the San Francisco Museum of Modern Art's sidewalk café, I was jolted by this comment from an international business executive. We were discussing the amazing high-tech ventures bursting on the Silicon Valley scene. "None of the leaders are women," he said. The implication was that women just don't have creative vision. I had to point out that in fact an association of women CEOs of high-tech Bay Area firms was meeting on a regular basis. I had been collecting articles about top-level women executives in high-tech companies—and there are hundreds of them.

Myth #2: Women's work is not as valuable as men's.

If women are not as creative and visionary as men, it would follow that their work is not as valuable. A large part of this myth is that women are not serious about their careers, they just work for *pin (extra) money*, and they are not the primary breadwinners in the family.

We all know that the result of this myth has been that women are paid less for comparable work in virtually every field and every type of job.

In 1998, women as a total group earned 75 percent of men's earnings. Minority women made even a smaller proportion: African American women 67 percent, Latino American women 58 percent. This is a major pay gap. Still, it's a distinct improvement over the gap of 33 years earlier—when women as a total group earned only 58 percent of men's earnings, according to the U.S. Census Bureau. Here are some pay gap figures for the past few decades:

1966	58%
1980	60%
1990	72%
1996	74%
1998	75%

Cultural Explanations

Many of the highest-paying jobs that don't require a degree involve danger or hard physical labor. These jobs are traditionally held by men, in some cases because few women want them. Some of the gap is because many jobs traditionally held by women don't pay as well as men's jobs. For example, social workers are typically female, but they have many of the same duties as typically male probation officers, who are paid much more. Many women are in low-wage jobs, such as secretary and cashier, or in low-wage industries, such as service and childcare. For this reason, as well as for childcare reasons, the poverty rate of women-headed families is 10 times that of male-headed families. They account for more than one-third of poverty in the United States.

Mothers are far more likely than fathers to leave the workforce for several years to raise the kids. When they do, their skills get rusty and their careers suffer. Because of the fear that female employees will have children and leave, some employers won't give women the same training or opportunities as they give their male colleagues.

Looking at executives who earn $150,000 to $500,000, some see men pushing harder for the extra pay than women do. They say some of the gap is because of family. They think age can be a factor, with younger women more likely to push for equal wages, but not always.

Men tend to place more value on their services. For example, some Yale undergraduates wrote an essay about computer shopping and put a price tag on the essay. A panel judged the essays of the female students as just as good as those by the male students. But the women set their price 18 percent lower than the men did.

Things are changing. More bachelor's degrees are now being awarded to women than men, and more women are developing good work experience to prepare for higher positions. Therefore, more women are getting into managerial and administrative jobs and into high-paying professional jobs, such as doctor, attorney, and professor.

Stereotyping and Discrimination

The reason the gap has narrowed at all may have little to do with increased equality for women. It may be due as much to the fact that men's wages have stagnated as women's wages have increased. For example, during the 1990s, inflation-adjusted median wages for women grew just 0.8 percent, while men's wages fell 6.7 percent.

The pay gap reflects a lot about stereotypical attitudes, which in some cases translates into overt discrimination, according to the AFL-CIO Web site for working women (*aflcio.org/women*). How can we explain that female attorneys earn nearly $300 a week less than male attorneys and that female professors earn $170 a week less than the males? In fact, an investigation in the late 1980s could not explain 12 percent of the wage gap, indicating that stereotyping and bias were probably the cause, according to the Economic Policy Institute.

Another indicator of discrimination is that women who belong to unions fare much better, because unions negotiate uniform rules concerning wages. For example, according to the U.S. Labor Department (1999), in 1995 women who were represented by unions had median weekly earnings of $523 compared with $386 for other women in the full-time wage-and-salaried workers category. This is a wage advantage of 36 percent.

The men who run the companies know about the pay gap but don't believe they are the cause. For example, in one survey, 52 percent of human resources executives said they believe women are being paid less than men for comparable work, but only 21 percent thought it was happening in their own companies, according to researcher Dave Murphy.

Myth #3: Dreams don't count.

Most people in our culture either say they don't dream, or they assume that dreams are meaningless. Yet research shows that we all dream every night. Further, without this dream time we couldn't function in our wake time. Those rare people who do see meaning in their dreams have been the more creative ones among us. They include the great geniuses and inventors throughout history who have used more of their brain capacity than ordinary persons use. Einstein used his Basic Intelligence to dream the theory of relativity and often spoke of the necessity of using Intuitive Intelligence to make new break-throughs. Elias Howe dreamed the process that led to the first sewing machine. And the list goes on.

Other Cultural-Belief Blocks

Cultural myths that devalue creativity are based on faulty beliefs. You've just reviewed some of them. Here are some more that are based on outmoded do's and don'ts, taboos, and stereotypes:

- ᠀ Fantasizing and reflecting are a waste of time.
- ᠀ Logic and reason are all that matter.
- ᠀ Intuition and personal judgments are too fuzzy and changeable to be worth much.
- ᠀ Any problem can be solved by scientific thinking and enough money.
- ᠀ It's not good to be too inquisitive (curiosity killed the cat).
- ᠀ Problem solving is serious business—so humor and having fun are to be avoided during the problem-solving process.

Perceptual Blocks

Although cultural beliefs affect perception, your perceptual blocks tend to also be personally unique to you. You don't see what you don't believe is there, which creates perceptual blocks, such as these:

- ᠀ Accepting as fact information that's really assumption.
- ᠀ Recognizing you have a problem but not identifying the root cause.
- ᠀ Ignoring information that gives clues to the underlying (root) problem.
- ᠀ Focusing on only a part of the problem, or focusing on solutions rather than defining the problem.
- ᠀ Assuming you can apply what works in one case to another.
- ᠀ Information overload.
- ᠀ Failing to use all your senses and intelligences.
- ᠀ Seeing situations as problems and ignoring the opportunities they can offer.

Emotional Blocks

Cultural beliefs influence your attitudes, which influence your thinking, which influence your feelings. Many of these beliefs play to your fear of change, fear of the unknown, and the resulting need to feel safe and avoid the new and risky. Some feelings trigger attitudes and actions that interfere with your free-dom to explore and manipulate ideas, your ability to fluently and flexibly conceptualize (create ideas and theories), and your ability to communicate ideas to others in persuasive ways. These emotional blocks include:

- Fear of failure.
- Fear of making a mistake.
- Fear of risk-taking.
- Impatience: the inability to tolerate ambiguity (uncertainty) and chaos.
- Snap judgments: being too quick to judge people and new ideas.
- Tenseness: the inability to relax, incubate ideas, sleep on it.
- Distrust, suspicion, lack of openness, closed-mindedness.

Rational-Logical Blocks

Rational-logical blocks stem from misuse or over-reliance on left-brain logic. Here are some common blocks:

- Not choosing the right mental approaches.
- Unwillingness to use new solution approaches, which limits the number of alternative ideas you can generate.
- Using only those techniques that have worked for you before.
- Reluctance to use intuitive techniques.
- Inability to abandon an unworkable approach and try something new.

Environmental Blocks

Does your environment contain creativity blocks? Even if you work independently or own your own business, you can create blocks to your own creativity through the cultural beliefs you've adopted. Here are some typical blocks:

- Few goals or rewards for creativity. Have you set some simple goals? Do you notice your little successes and reward yourself in some small but satisfying ways?
- A rigid, mechanistic, authoritarian way of operating—either your own way or that of the people around you, the people who have major influence in your life.
- Allowing an autocratic person, who values only his or her own ideas, to dominate you.
- No training for creativity. Are you taking some time and energy to develop innovative skills?
- Little or no support for creativity. Are you surrounding yourself with a support system of people who value creativity, are creative themselves, and encourage your creativity?
- Few if any creative successes to build upon. Are you developing your creative impulses, refining and honing them, and sticking with it until you have some small successes?
- Punishing mistakes and failures—and ignoring the willingness to risk and to learn from mistakes. Are you able to see a *failure* as

merely the first round of working toward a goal? Can you see *failure* as part of the process of learning what not to do next time? Do you reward yourself for having the courage to risk failure?

Sparking Your Creativity Through Basic Intelligence

You can spark your creativity through your Basic Pattern-Parameter Intelligence in so many ways. In doing so, you will learn how to access the energy of your basic brain, decide which patterns to keep and which to change, and tap into all three levels of consciousness to master meditation and dream states. You'll also learn to master pattern-change processes, use them for interrupting old patterns and making new pattern connections, understand what to expect and how your emotions tie you to old patterns, how to spark your energy level, and how to increase your options. Here are the sparklers that guide you in doing all that:

Sparkler #1: Learn How to Access Basic Brain Energy

To get in touch with your basic brain, try the following techniques.

1. Rhythms. Enter into the rhythms of what's happening. Slow down the speed of your breathing, thinking, and other body functions. Focus on rhythm, action, and movement. Notice them while doing ordinary physical routines, such as walking, dressing, or working out. Notice how you're moving easily and attending to the action within a defined space and time, without much distraction of thoughts or feelings. Sometimes the rhythm, action, or movement is more intense as when you're in sync while dancing, swimming, or playing ball.

2. Instinctual Movement. Notice how people seem to instinctively move toward or away from people, places, ideas, colors, feelings, things, and events. Notice how you do this.

3. Observation. Go deep into your inner body. Step outside your egomind and observe it in action as if it did not really belong to you. See it in the context of all that's around you—while keeping your emotions as neutral as possible and accepting What-Is. Look for patterns, limits, and boundaries. See how your behavior serves you—or does not.

4. Dreams. Pay attention to your dreams for information from your basic brain, and your subconscious and superconscious minds.

5. Addictive Patterns. Notice your addictions, your patterns or habits that you feel compelled to do. Which ones are constructive? Which are neutral? Which ones are a form of self-sabotage?

6. Withdrawal Patterns. Have you withdrawn or distanced yourself from beliefs, thoughts, feelings, decisions, and actions that are beneficial to you? That's how people develop antisocial, addictive, and even criminal habit patterns. When you withdraw again and again, until you are no longer aware of your avoidance, it becomes an automatic habit. Neither reward nor punishment seems to have much success in changing antisocial behavior unless it takes into consideration this basic brain patterning and conditioning and deals with changing the habit patterns at their root origins.

Sparkler #2: Decide Which Patterns to Keep and to Change

Observing your habit patterns and parameters sounds easier to do than it actually is. But this is some of the most important personal growth work you'll ever do, and it will pay off by removing some major blocks to higher-level creativity. The self-awareness opportunities at the end of this chapter will help you do this work.

Revisit the Scene of Key Life Decisions

Get in touch with problem patterns, one at a time. Meditate to find connections between the pattern and critical incidents from your past. Revisit the old scenario to see it in new ways and to make new decisions in order to change the old habit pattern. Get in touch with the needs, wants, and feelings you had at that time, whether it was last year or, more likely, when you were a child. As an adult, give your former self what you needed at that time: the nurturing, support, love, whatever the need. Now let the former you make a new conclusion and decision about the situation. Let these new beliefs, thoughts, feelings, and decisions serve as the basis for new habit patterns.

What is the ineffective habit pattern you want to break up? It's always based on a belief or cluster of beliefs. Get a sense of what this belief could be. What new beliefs will you adopt to replace the old? Repeat your affirmations of new beliefs. Develop some new patterns, new rituals, that focus your mind and re-establish new beliefs. Ritual is made up of belief, conscious thought, and perhaps some art or music to vividly symbolize the belief. Find ways to consciously act-out your new habit patterns. Remember, repetition creates new habit patterns.

Break Out of Limiting Boundaries

To begin with, learn to accept, without the need to explain or defend, the fact that you and others are territorial. Learn to respect rather than invade others' territories and to understand that you have territorial rights also. The inner-body emotions of humor, curiosity, openness, and flexibility can be very helpful here.

Set some reasonable limits and boundaries for expending your energy. This means that the signals you send out and the ones you let in make sense. It means you focus your energy and attention on those things that are most important for your growth and survival. Otherwise you'll scatter yourself all over the map and won't be able to achieve much of anything.

Two major problems you can create for yourself are:

- Believing parameters last forever.
- Ignoring the fact that life's rhythms keep changing.

You're most likely to try to hold onto old parameters—including home territory, relationships, friends, jobs, etc.—when you experience a sudden loss of parameters. Pay special attention to parameter behavior at the following times:

- The end of a relationship (or a major relationship shift, or fear of such a change).

∞   The end of a job.

∞   The change of home.

Do you try to defend your parameters by controlling people and situations? This is an old paradigm that is not successful or satisfying in the long run. All you can really control is yourself—your own beliefs, attitudes, decisions, and action choices. Try this new paradigm:

1. Understand life as a dynamic rather than static process—feel it, act it, as a dynamic process.

2. Evaluate your current parameters.

3. Stay flexible, loose, moving toward and away from.

4. Change parameters, or create new parameters, when energy drops. Shift to what you want, like, and love. Shift to what represents a new, high-energy experience.

5. Wear your reality lightly—don't let it weigh too heavily. Review your values, beliefs, habits, and roles. How do they need to shift? Remember, we're all here to learn! We don't have to do it right the first time.

6. Act out your Basic Intelligence by moving toward new growth and away from old limitations.

Sparkler #3: Tap into All Levels of Consciousness

You are constantly accessing three levels of consciousness: the conscious, subconscious, and superconscious. You're aware, of course, of those times when you're in the conscious mind state. You can easily bring information from your subconscious and superconscious minds into your awareness by learning some very simple meditation and dream-recall skills.

First, be aware that when your brain activity is measured, the resulting electro-encephalogram reveals that you access four major brain states. The following outlines these four states:

∞   **Beta** state occurs at 13 to 25 brainwave cycles per second. This is the rational, active state.

∞   **Alpha** state occurs at 8 to 12 cycles per second. This is the drifting, hypnogogic state you experience just before and after sleep. In this state your intuition is high, your connection to the subconscious and superconscious mind is strong. This is a good time to focus on goals, problems, and questions that you want answered. Closing your eyes encourages the formation of the alpha state.

∞   **Theta** state occurs at 5 to 7 cycles per second. This is the deep meditation state. Your intuition is very high. This is a good time to be open to information, messages, answers, and inspiration from your subconscious and superconscious mind.

∞   **Delta** state is 1 to 4 cycles per second. This is the state of deep or full sleep. Dreams occur during this state and your intuition is very high.

To take advantage of these brain states and to access information from your subconscious and superconscious minds, you need to develop some skills. To reach the meditative state, you need to deeply relax. To tap information and create new realities, you need to visualize situations and results. To bring them into your everyday life, you must let go of fearful needs and shift to relaxed desires. To gain information from the dream state, you must learn to program your dreams and to interpret them.

Use the Power of Now

As a woman you probably find it easier than your male counterparts to feel your emotions and to be in your body instead of in your egomind. The energy frequency of the rational mind and its tool, the egomind, appears to be essentially male. It's centered in your male side, and the men you know probably have a tougher time getting it under control and putting it in its proper place. Rational egomind resists letting go, fights for control, uses, manipulates, attaches, and tries to grasp and possess. The traditional God of many religions is a projection of the collective human mind in its journey of the past few thousand years. This God is a patriarchal, controlling authority figure that is often angry and sometimes vengeful. No wonder people often live in fear.

You can go beyond your rational egomind and reconnect with the deeper reality of Being. As a woman you'll probably find it easier than your male friends to do this because you tend to have the needed qualities: nonjudgmental acceptance of What-Is, an openness that allows life to be, and the ability to hold all things in the loving embrace of your knowing. The Being-energy is soft and yielding, yet infinitely more powerful than the egomind, which is hard and rigid.

Learning to focus on the present moment—and to totally be in the here and now—is a powerful way to aid the relaxation process and to turn off egomind chatter. This chatter is often associated with guilt, resentment, and worry. Remember: When you're feeling guilty or resentful, you're really living in the past. When you're worrying, you're living in the future. Action in the here and now is the only way to influence events. The key is to focus on the present moment and determine what, if anything, you need to do. If you need help with this, repeat the relaxation process in SAO #1: Be-Here-Now Consciousness (page 70) for *getting in the here and now*. It's designed to bring you into the present moment by helping you focus on the sensations your body is experiencing now. Practice it frequently when you're not under stress, and you'll soon be able to use it quickly, even in stressful situations.

Master Relaxation Processes

The goal of relaxation processes is to cut through tension and egomind chatter to reach a deeply relaxed state. As with all the techniques and processes for commanding your inner-body resources, these may take some time to master in the beginning. With practice, however, you'll be able to use your skills even in the midst of stressful situations, and you'll be able to go into deeper states of relaxation more quickly.

Achieve the Alpha State Advantage

The ultimate goal is to be able to move into a state of relaxation so deep that you're producing alpha brain waves. Although biofeedback mechanisms are available for helping you develop this ability quickly, you can learn well enough without them. Research indicates that closing your eyes helps to achieve this relaxed state that lets you communicate more effectively with your subconscious. You can give it new messages, even messages that override key decisions about life that you made long ago—viewpoints that no longer serve you. You can enlist the aid of your subconscious in reaching your goals and solving problems—so that your verbal and nonverbal actions are well-integrated and your entire being is moving toward achieving what you decide you want in life.

You get double payoffs, therefore, for learning to relax deeply. The relaxation alone is an immediate antidote to stress. It enhances your sense of well-being, your health, and potentially your longevity. In addition, when you combine it with visualization—that is, mental imagery—it helps you create the life you want. But more about that later.

Set the Stage

Four conditions are helpful for mastering these relaxation processes:

- ✎ A quiet, calm place as free from distraction as possible.
- ✎ A comfortable body position.
- ✎ A mental focusing device to help you shut off your egomind chatter and go deep within yourself.
- ✎ A passive attitude that lets you merely observe distracting thoughts, let them go, and bring your conscious mind back gently to your focusing device. Keep in mind that you can't *make* relaxation occur; you can only *let* it occur.

Once you've set the stage, experiment with the processes included in SAO #2: Deep Relaxation (page 71) to find the ones that work best for you.

Visualize the Results You Want

Once you're in a deeply relaxed state, you can talk to your subconscious and tell it what you want. Your subconscious is amazingly competent at moving you toward the results you request—if you'll only relax and let it do its work. It tunes in better to pictures and feelings, however, than to words. That's why visualizing results and getting in touch with the feelings you want to experience along with those results is so powerful.

How to Visualize

What if you have difficulty *making pictures* when you close your eyes? Don't worry. Everyone differs to some extent in the way they visualize. If you see no picture at all, you're still thinking of it in your *mind's eye*, and that's adequate. It may help to think of what it might be like if you *could* see the picture you're thinking about. Think in terms of *allowing* pictures rather than making them.

When to Visualize

When should you practice your visualization skills? Shortly before going to sleep each night is a time preferred by many people, because it's a quiet time when they're ready to relax fully. To make the most of your personal power, practice deep relaxation and visualization at some time every day so that it becomes a deeply ingrained habit—a way of life that you can put to use almost automatically. If you do this, you'll soon discover that you can use these skills quickly, with your eyes wide open, and with no one the wiser any time you're dealing with potentially stressful situations. You'll be able to stay centered or to regain your composure quickly even if you're taken by surprise.

The processes described in SAO #3: Visualization (page 72) are designed to enlist the aid of your subconscious in handling specific types of situations. You can adapt them to any kind of situation; just remember that important final step: letting go.

Learn to Let Go

Have you ever observed someone sabotaging herself because she was trying too hard? You probably thought, *Why doesn't she relax a little?* Can you think of a time when you probably sabotaged yourself by trying too hard or caring too much? Why do people do this? Usually it happens because they're too strongly attached to having the situation turn out just the way they want. They cling—perhaps desperately—to the idea or picture of certain end results. Therefore, they create a tension-producing need to achieve those results, often accompanied by fear that they won't.

Think Preferences, not Needs

Think of some situations in which you achieved the results you wanted—times when you moved relatively effortlessly toward your goal. Think of top athletes who have done that. Top achievement is usually a result of *relaxed concentration.* You fully intend to achieve certain results, and your mind and body are focused on the process of doing so. You *desire* and *prefer* those results, but you don't desperately *need* them, and you're not focused on fear connected with failure to achieve the results.

Prevent Self-Sabotage

You prevent the self-sabotage caused by tension-producing needs when you add a letting-go step to the visualization process you use for goal-setting. SAO #4: Letting Go of Needs (page 74) offers several techniques for this final step of the personal power process. Remember that when you let go of your goal, you retain a clear picture of having it, but you release the needs and fears related to not having it. This process frees you to work toward your goal in a relaxed, confident way, which in turn makes it easier to gain the cooperation and support of others. But you must truly become comfortable with the idea of *not* achieving your goal. If letting go is accompanied by sadness, regret, or unwillingness, you need to work on your fear of failure.

Allow Abundance

You can also adopt a viewpoint that there is abundance in the world. When you let go of your goal pictures, you *put them out into the universe.* The view that there is abundance in the universe implies that everything that happens eventually works toward your benefit. Therefore, if you give a goal situation your best shot, you're confident of achieving it. If it doesn't turn out the way you pictured, then your deep inner self had the wisdom to know that those results were not best for you at this time. That's the time to ask, *What lesson can I learn from this?*

Use Your Dream Time

Psychoanalyst Carl Jung was the first respected leader to give dreams an importance similar to that given by aboriginal tribes. Jung wrote of dreams as images that can convey important messages from the subconscious mind, messages the conscious mind may not recognize. The messages therefore often appear as symbols, metaphors, and archetypes that have universal meanings among human beings.

You can even use your sleep time to move you toward your creative goals. For years we've heard managers say, before making an important or difficult decision, "Let me sleep on it and get back to you tomorrow"—and for very good reason. Your subconscious mind is very powerful, and the superconscious mind is infinite. You can draw on these resources almost effortlessly by using the dream state to help you see opportunities and solve problems, resolve conflicts, and come up with new ideas.

Problem-Solve and Create

A powerful combination is visualizing results and then "sleeping on it" to help solve problems or create new results. Other techniques include writing down brief notes about your dreams upon waking, or during the day as you recall them, and interpreting your dreams. See the SAOs at the end of this chapter.

Expand Personal Awareness

Once you become accustomed to using your sleep and dream time, consider taking it a step further into pure research. Jungian analysts believe that your dreams can provide symbolic information about what's going on in your life at the subconscious level—and bring you helpful information through your superconscious mind from the interconnected Web of Life. You can expand your awareness and see relationships, events, and problems from a broader perspective by tapping into your dream world. You are the best interpreter of your own dreams and at a deep level, you already know the meaning of universal symbols. But to relearn their meanings, see Betty Bethards' *The Dream Book: Symbols for Self-Understanding*, a small, simple book that I have found to be the most helpful.

To sum up, follow these suggestions for using your dream time to spark your creativity:

1. Trust your own experience.
2. Open up to your dreams. Be willing to be gullible, vulnerable, a believer—at least for a while. Take a *what if...* approach.
3. Break up your patterns, your habits, in order to open up to new ideas and to create newness in your life.

4. Program your dreams—to solve problems, get new ideas, have new experiences.

5. Play with symbols to interpret your dreams. Your subconscious and superconscious minds love pictures and symbols, so your intuition often brings messages in symbolic form.

6. Connect dream time and wake time. Become aware of how your dreams may be responding or anticipating what's going on in your wake-time life.

Call on Your Superconscious

Your greatest resource of inner power is your superconscious mind. Keep that concept in mind as you work to spark your Basic Pattern-Parameter Intelligence through waking meditations and nighttime dream work.

Work with your Negative Ego

Your Negative Ego is the part of you that judges whether people are better-than or worse-than you (or some standard you devise). It's that part that's over-concerned with how people judge you as better-than or worse-than. When you give your Negative Ego control, it uses manipulation and games to try to control people and events. You're usually not conscious that you've given your power to your Negative Ego, because you established these patterns early in life and then forgot about them.

Work with Presence, empowerment

Become aware of old, now-ineffective habit patterns that live in your subconscious mind. Revisit your past, if necessary, to re-experience critical situations that led you to make key decisions about life. Perceive these experiences anew, make new decisions, and create new habit patterns. Retrieve your visions and dreams from the past, keeping the lessons you learned, the gifts and treasures. Risk moving forward to connect with the Web of Life, with an ever-changing Now that becomes the future. Let's anticipate expanding your Emotional Intelligence: See how often you can let go of emotions that focus your attention negatively on the past (resentment, revenge, guilt) or the future (worry) and spend more of your time fully present in each moment of Now.

Work on your inner-body environment

Focus on beliefs and thoughts that you can experience as true and beautiful—that trigger expansive, love-based emotions, especially trust, respect, enchantment, peace, wonder, compassion, inspiration, and intrigue for the unknown. Cherish your heartfelt desires and passions as creative generating energies. Begin with yourself—love for yourself, self-trust, self-respect—and then expand those emotions to the world in general and to the people in your life. If you feel threatened by people or situations in the world, do a reality check about the real dangers. Then ask yourself how you can protect yourself. Keep in mind this purpose in all your meditations and goals: *with harm to none and for the highest good for all*, an intention that can keep you on track. In these ways, you work through your Intuitive Intelligence connection with the superconscious mind, to connect with All-That-Is.

Sparkler #4: Use Pattern-Change Processes

You can pick and choose from many change processes to become aware of your basic pattern-parameter actions, identifying those that are helpful and those that block your creative potential.

Identify Types of Behavior Patterns

Think in terms of the types of patterns you follow. Certainly people follow their own relationship and work patterns. You can extend this awareness to your work organization, looking at profit or productivity patterns.

Relationship Patterns. Notice your relationship patterns. When you want to connect with new role models or deepen current connections to a person, consider these actions:

- Observe these people's patterns, mirroring them, learning from them, searching for deeper patterns of meaning, and appreciating their patterns.
- Observe these patterns to discover their key rhythms.
- Identify yourself with all the persons that you closely observe, focusing on one at a time.
- Begin to move in their rhythms, mirroring them.
- Accompany them as they go about their activities.
- Quiet your rational and emotional brains, letting your basic pattern-parameter brain lead the way.
- Keep their rhythms when you're with these people.

If it's a personal relationship, ask yourself, *Does this relationship expand my life or contract it?* If it's a work relationship, keep in mind that building authentic work relationships, inner person to inner person, is essential for team creativity.

Work Patterns. Notice your work patterns. Gently guide yourself, seduce yourself, into the rhythm of the work you need to do.

Productivity-Profit Patterns. Start noticing the patterns of work and relationships in your organization. How are they productive or non-productive? Research indicates that people who learn to recognize profit patterns are better able to anticipate new sources of profit before they develop. This means they're more likely to come up with creative ideas for capturing *tomorrow's profit zones*, according to Mercer Management Consulting.

Use Pattern Intervention Processes

You can find many processes for breaking old habit patterns that undermine your creativity and success, processes for establishing new patterns. For example, you can revisit old scenarios. What happened last year is still alive in your memory. So is what happened when you were three years old. That child is still a vital part of you, and you can nurture that child now as an adult. In your mind you can revisit childhood events and perceive them through new eyes. When you do, you'll find it easy to change the decisions and beliefs you established back then. You can do that in *now time*.

You've just explored the process of connecting with role models who can inspire and teach you. Another process is to notice how certain behaviors link together into a pattern. You can then change just one little behavior that's a key link in the chain. This can break up the behavior pattern, leaving space for creating a better one. See the SAOs at the end of this chapter (beginning on page 70).

Forming ingrained habit patterns does not happen in one cycle. Behavior chains linked together are repeated numerous times before they become automatic patterns that function near or at the subconscious level. It stands to reason that you may not change some of your most ingrained habits after one cycle of new behavior. Such change often involves one step forward and two steps back—and hopefully progresses to two steps forward, one step back. Remember, just being able to recognize that you've *done it again* is great progress! And the steps backward can offer you a new perspective if you choose. They can help you to remember the old behavior more vividly and to see how far you've really come—and where you're heading. The steps back can give you the momentum you need for the next step forward. Think of repatterning your habits as a spiraling process. Each time you recycle back through the habit pattern, you do it at a higher level of awareness.

Sparkler #5: Understand Emotional Ties to Your Habits

Some major emotional ties that keep people stuck in their ineffective habits include worry, guilt, resentment, and revenge.

Worry

Worry is negatively living in the future. On the other hand, suppose you're intelligently concerned about probable future threats and you follow up immediately with reasonable action to prevent threatening events from occurring or to minimize their impact. This is a positive way to create an optimal future. Worry is actually socially accepted addiction. People tend to nod approvingly when you express worry. You may conclude: *If I worry about you, that means I care about you.... If I worry about events, that means I care about them.*

Actually worry tends to create anxiety stress in the Now. Instead of getting stuck in worry, move into the present moment. Be totally conscious in the Now. Accept the What-Is of this moment. Then ask, *What can I do about it NOW? What can I not prevent?* or, *What is too far-fetched for me to spend energy trying to prevent?* Listen for clues, staying in the Now, and when you get a sense of what actions make sense, be ready to go out and do it!

Then let go of worry. Trust the universe to work toward the highest good. The only reason to go to a worst-case scenario is to face your fear dragons and realize that you can survive the worst that could reasonably happen. Then let it go. Have the intention to create best-case scenarios and realize that you have the strength to live through the worst.

Guilt, Resentment, and Revenge

These emotions involve negatively living in the past and creating stress in the Now. Instead of getting stuck in guilt, resentment, or revenge, ask, *What can I learn from these past events NOW?* Get it! Then ask, *How can I forgive myself* (guilt) *and others* (resentment) *for these past events?* Here are some constructive thoughts:

- *Remember: We're all growing*. Even though we do things that hurt, we're all doing the best we can, given our stage of growth.

- *Don't take it personally*. The hurtful things we do are connected with our life scripts, our stage of personal growth, and our habit patterns, parameters, fears, and other limitations. When someone hurts you, don't take it personally. That person would have reacted the same way toward anyone who represented to them what you did at that point in time.

- *Forgive—yourself and others*. Feel gratitude for the experience. Let go of guilt, resentment, or revenge. Forgive not necessarily because the other person deserves it—but because *you* do. When you feel forgiveness and gratitude, you give yourself a great gift—a lightness, a freedom that opens up your heart and mind to let in new ideas and experiences. You expand your creative potential!

Sparkler #6: Use Basic Intelligence to Spark Your Energy Level

When your body signals stress—when you experience pain, illness, boredom, fatigue, accidents—it's time to use your Basic Pattern-Parameter Intelligence. Ask yourself some questions, such as:

- *What are the major routines of my day and night?*
- *How are they creating this body signal?*
- *What patterns or beliefs are keeping me in my stressful routines?*
- *How can I move away from these routines, patterns, beliefs?*
- *What new ones could I try?*

You have two basic choices about how to break out of old patterns and become more creative:

1. *Growth by Crisis*—ignoring messages or signals from the subconscious and superconscious. When you do this, the message must get stronger and stronger, to the point of serious illness and even death.

2. *Growth by Design*—allowing information and messages from the subconscious and superconscious into your consciousness.

Sparkler #7: Keep Your Options Open

Are you limiting your creative options by thinking about decisions in either/or terms? Do you tend to think, *Either I have to put up with the boss's nasty comments or I have to quit?* This gives you only two possible options. Open up your options by thinking also in both/and terms: *I can both work with a boss who makes nasty comments and maintain my self-respect while limiting the boss's behavior by doing x, y, and z.*

Some decisions should be limited to two either/or options, but in most situations there are actually dozens, if not hundreds or even thousands, of small variations in the many responses you could make or initiatives you could take. In some cases the best decision may involve *either this, or that or that or that or that*, etc. In other cases it may involve *both this, and that, and that, and that, and that. . . or some combination of all these*. So don't think the world apart into this *or* that when it's actually this *and* that, an interconnected web.

Innovative Questions to Root Out Stuck Beliefs

Ask yourself these kinds of questions any time you suspect old stuck beliefs are blocking your creativity:

1. What are my (my firm's) beliefs and assumptions about how to succeed?
2. Are they still valid?
3. What are the new trends and the emerging environment?
4. What are the limits of those trends and that environment?
5. What would be different if they were followed out to their logical conclusion?
6. What does this mean for what I do (my firm does)?
7. Are the things I'm (the firm is) currently doing really making any sense?
8. Is the frontier we're currently exploring basically a closed frontier? Have the wars been won? Has the game been defined?

If the answer to the last question is yes, then your firm has no role to play in that game any longer, because you can't change its rules. This game is not where you can get high leverage.

Marketplace Change at the Level of Mental Model

You have some good information now on how to expand your Basic Intelligence at the personal level. How can you look with a fresh eye at the habit patterns and territorial limitations within your organization, your industry, and your field? How can you begin to see the need for change at the level of mental model?

Marketing to consumers is changing, for example. Successful marketers are always looking for adjacent possibilities—as well as evolving lifestyle changes—so they can come up with the Next New Thing that fits new lifestyles.

Trend projections are based on the environment of the immediate past. They are number-driven and somewhat linear. But lifestyles are what count now, and they're more complex in nature. Many complex factors interact to produce a lifestyle. They reflect many unpredictable interactions within the culture. They're not always obvious on the surface. Look at a few basically related lifestyles of people around you and ask some innovative questions:

1. What are people doing differently?
2. How have their lives changed? How are their lifestyles different? What are the changing lifestyles in an emerging new environment?

3. What needs and wants does this create—that aren't being met?

Lifestyle situations change fast, and the younger Net Generation usually adapts more easily to these changes.

Beyond Customer Demand to Adjacent Possibilities

In the New Economy, focus groups and market surveys no longer play the key role in new product development. This statistical approach to what customers want doesn't work as it used to. Everything that's rooted in that way of thinking is tied to the status quo. For example, it makes no sense to ask people who don't use computers what they think of broadband computer access. Customers didn't ask for personal computers or personal radio/tape players. These products emerged when the available technology and evolving lifestyles made them the Next New Thing. In today's environment, the hottest ideas develop because of adjacent possibilities, not because of customer demand.

Co-Evolution of Mental Models

New mental models, all functioning at the same time, enable things to become more complex—to develop higher levels of organization that didn't exist before. The new models incorporate innovations that didn't exist before but that were always a possibility, waiting for the process to unfold.

Here's the paradox: As you move toward more complex levels of organization, you find a simplicity that wasn't available or even possible on a lower level of complexity. *High-level simplicity "emerges" from low-level complexity,* according to Deutsch. For example, it's much simpler to write a paper or a book using a computer, which is itself extremely complex.

Recognizing complexity can help you to use mental models more effectively in order to find patterns and possibilities that did not previously exist in the current complexity of the business world.

Wide-Open Opportunities

A major reason why businesses have wide-open opportunities for innovation is that new technologies have freed so many employees from the drudgery of doing routine work. Computers and robots take care of that now, so people are free to use their imaginations, to daydream and brainstorm, and to follow up on their ideas. They can use all of the intelligences instead of being trapped in the rational. They have more time and freedom to step back and see a bigger picture with many diverse realities. Understanding that there is no *one right way* helps them move beyond old biases and stereotypes. They're more likely to see the bright side of change and the risk it entails—and so a willingness to try out new mental models and new practices emerges.

However, many in the Net Generation have a short attention span and little patience for long-term investigations. Even though much of the drudgework is done by computers and other equipment, lifestyles and ambitions may mean they have few blocks of time to really daydream, meditate, visualize, and tap into all their Creative Intelligence. And many have little sense of ongoing history, little sense of place and community, and no strong vision of a personal future, or collective future. Mastering these concepts gives you a creative advantage.

Creative Processes Using Basic Intelligence

Here are some creative processes that call upon your Basic Pattern-Parameter Intelligence. They help you to organize your thoughts so you can recognize the patterns and parameters of a situation. Apply each of them to the case situation that follows on page 69.

Look for Patterns

Go over all the available information in your case situation. Look for patterns, boundaries, relationships. Draw a diagram that shows these patterns or relationships. Seeing the data visually helps trigger your Basic Pattern-Parameter Intelligence, leading to a deeper understanding and creative ideas.

Fishbone Pattern Diagram

The main purpose of the fishbone pattern diagram is to generate a list of possible causes of a problem-opportunity situation. You organize causes into a fishbone pattern diagram in order to see patterns and relationships.

At the center left edge of a sheet of paper, write a brief phrase that describes the problem-opportunity situation and circle it. This is the head of the fish. Draw a straight line, representing the fish backbone, from the head to the right edge of the paper. This line is the backbone of the fish. Next, draw straight lines that are angled off from either side of the backbone. These are the vertebrae or fishbones that you'll use to organize problem causes.

Put the simplest, most obvious causes first, near the head of the fish by writing them beside a fishbone, circling them, and attaching them to the fishbone with a straight line. Try to put causes that are similar or closely related along the same fishbone. Consider putting causes that pull against each other on opposite sides of the backbone. Continue to brainstorm causes, putting the most subtle and complex ones near the tail.

When you feel you've listed all possible causes, study the diagram for relationships—patterns, limitations, and hidden opportunities. You may want to re-do the diagram to show a different pattern of relationships. Use your imagination to find unique ways to arrange the list of causes. Ask such questions as:

- ✤ Have all parts of the problem-opportunity situation been explored and all possible causes listed?
- ✤ What are the relationships between causes?
- ✤ What is the relative importance of these causes?
- ✤ Which ones are surface causes and which are root causes?
- ✤ Will solving simple causes and issues first help us to handle the more complex ones?
- ✤ What sequence will be most effective to handle the problems?
- ✤ What opportunities might be hidden within this situation?

Why-Why Pattern Diagram

Why-why is similar to the fishbone pattern, but it's a more powerful diagram for getting at the root causes of a problem. Write the problem-opportunity statement on the center left side of a sheet of paper and circle it. Ask why this problem is occurring and list the causes under the problem statement, beginning at the top of the page, circling each one, and moving down the page in column form. For each cause ask, *Why is this occurring?* and list each reason to the right of the cause, circling it and connecting by a straight line to the cause. If you need to delve further into any of the reasons why, again ask, *Why is this occurring?* and write the answers to the right of the reason, circling and connecting.

Examine the diagram for patterns, limitations, root causes, and hidden opportunities.

Mind Mapping

Write the problem-opportunity statement in the center of a sheet of paper and circle it. Brainstorm ideas about how to solve the problem or explore the opportunity. Write your major ideas on lines drawn outward from the main statement, as highways from a city would be drawn on a map.

As you think of new aspects that relate to a major idea, write them on (minor) road lines drawn outward from the (major) highway line. You can go into further detail by brainstorming ideas for each new aspect and writing it on street lines connected to a road line.

Use your imagination to highlight relationships by using colored pens, highlighting, circling certain ideas, starring them, and so forth.

Study your mind map, looking for patterns, limits, associations, relationships, and new ideas.

A Final Word

The first step in building your Creative Intelligence is to become aware of the old patterns and limitations that are blocking your access to creativity. Now you have some tools for doing that, as well as some ways to boost your Basic Intelligence and apply it to your workplace opportunities and challenges. The next step is to work with what drives you toward a more creative life: your Motivational Intelligence. But first, try your hand at the case situation and the SAOs that follow.

Case Situation: Fast Print, Inc.

Instructions: Practice using the creative processes by applying them to this case situation. Compare your answers to the case questions with those in the Case Situation Feedback at the end of this chapter.

Fast Print, Inc. performs two major functions—printing and copying—with 12 shops in a large metropolitan area. **Renee Carter**, CEO, inherited the company from her father nearly five years ago.

About 90 percent of the company's revenues comes from printing jobs. These are done primarily for privately owned corporations, such as banks, retail stores, and sports teams, but also for some nonprofit organizations. Fast Print produces presentation folders, business cards, pamphlets, brochures, posters, newsletters, coupons, tickets, and similar printed matter that these organizations need. Most of the large printing jobs come from repeat customers.

The other 10 percent of Fast Print's revenues comes from its copy service. About half of the copying jobs are for law firms, and the other half are jobs are for commercial or retail businesses.

Fast Print relies on getting its new customers through referrals and word of mouth. It has only two salespersons. One salesperson, **Jeff**, has been with the company for 30 years and has a very large client base. He keeps track of clients with help from a digital assistant in a computer database. He normally does not acquire new clients, but keeps track of current ones. **Jennifer**, the other salesperson, has been with the company about five years. She doesn't have a large client base. She networks her current clients to obtain new clients and referrals. She keeps track of her customers in a Rolodex.

Both salespersons regularly call their clients to see if they are satisfied with their orders and if they need anything else printed or copied. The individual store managers call the customers when their orders are ready. The customers usually have their orders delivered.

One of Fast Print's biggest problems right now is competition for printing and copying jobs. In many instances, owners of office buildings are installing in-house printing and copying stores for use by all the businesses in their building. These businesses find that such in-house print shops are closer, more convenient, and often less costly. Similarly, many schools and universities have installed their own in-house print and copy centers. They do many print and copy jobs, large and small, so they represent a significant market segment as well.

Copy competitors are a problem for Fast Print, also. Kinko's is its greatest competitor for copying jobs, because Kinko's has more locations and most of their stores are open 24 hours a day. Many of them are located near universities. Kinko's and other, smaller copy shops have taken away about 20 percent of Fast Print's copying jobs in the past year.

Another competing factor is that more small businesses and home office owners are buying their own copiers. New technology allows for cheaper, more reliable copy machines.

Today sales reps Jennifer and Jeff are meeting with CEO Renee Carter and her executive team to discuss all these problems and to generate some creative solutions. They will address these types of questions:

- What are the surface problems and the root problems that Fast Print is facing?
- What opportunities is Fast Print overlooking?
- How can Fast Print expand its market share and revenues?

Self-Awareness Opportunities

SAO #1: Be-Here-Now Consciousness

Purpose: To bring yourself fully into the present moment as an aid to letting go of concerns about the past and the future, to prepare yourself for deep relaxation.

Variation 1: Focusing on the Five Senses

Step 1: Breathing. Take a few deep breaths.

Step 2: Seeing. Become internally aware of what you see around you. Look at it in detail as if you've never seen it before. Pretend you just arrived from another planet. Notice colors, patterns, and textures.

Step 3: Hearing. If the situation permits, close your eyes. What do you hear? Notice every little sound, identify it, and describe it mentally.

Step 4: Touching. Focus on your sense of touch—the feel of your clothes against your skin, the air on your skin, the floor under your feet, the chair under your seat if you're sitting. Describe the sensations to yourself.

Step 5: Smelling and tasting. If there are noticeable odors around you or tastes in your mouth, become aware of them; identify and describe them.

Did you notice that your focus moved away from your mind and its internal chatter about the past or future and into your body and what it was sensing in the present moment? Here's an alternate technique that may work for you.

Variation 2: Progressive Muscle Relaxation

In this process, you bring your attention into the present moment by focusing on your body, and you also begin the relaxation process. You will alternately tense and then relax all the muscle groups in your body, beginning with the toes and moving upward.

Tense up the toes of your right foot, hold it, then quickly release them all at once. Notice the resulting feeling of relaxation in those muscles. Continue up your right leg, tensing and relaxing the calf muscles and the thigh muscles. Then do the left leg; next, progress up through the various muscle groups in the trunk of your body, then the right and left arms, and finally the neck and head. Pay special attention to the muscles of the jaw line and between the eyes; both are places where we tend to retain tension. Then let any tensions that's left rise up through an imaginary opening in the crown of your head.

SAO #2: Deep Relaxation

Purpose: To experiment with various methods of deep relaxation.

Deep relaxation begins with deep breathing. The goal is to slow down your breathing pattern, which automatically slows down your other bodily processes.

Start with one of the breathing processes. Then move into one of the focusing devices. If you have trouble moving out of a focus on egomind chatter and into an accepting attitude, do a process for getting in the here and now.

Deep breathing variation 1: Breathe in through your nostrils, counting slowly as you do so; hold the breath, starting your counting over again; breathe out through your mouth, with your lips slightly parted, again counting. The actual process: Breathe in 1-2-3-4-5; hold it 1-2-3-4-5; breathe out 1-2-3-4-5. Each time you repeat the process, extend the time you take to breathe in, hold it, and breathe out, counting to 6, then to 7, etc. See how long you can extend it.

Deep breathing variation 2: Visualize yourself stepping onto the top of an escalator. As you breathe slowly in and out, watch yourself descending down the escalator into a deeper and deeper state of relaxation and count: 10-9-8-7-6-5-4-3-2-1.

Deep breathing variation 3: Close your eyes, take a deep breath, and enjoy the pleasure of feeling yourself breathe. As you breathe in, say quietly to yourself, *I am*. As you breathe out, say to yourself *relaxed*. Or say, *I am...calm and serene* or *I am...one*.

Deep breathing variation 4: Focus all your attention at the tip of your nostrils. Quietly *watch* in your mind's eye the breath flowing in and out past the tip of the nostril. Count from 1 through 10 each time you breathe in and each time you breathe out. Continue counting from 1 through 10 each time you breathe in and out until you're completely relaxed.

Focusing device 1: Candle flame. Place a lighted candle about a foot in front of you and focus all your attention on the flame. As thoughts float by, notice them, let them go, and gently bring your attention back to the flame. This form of relaxed concentration can help you notice how your thoughts and senses keep grabbing at your awareness. The goal is to free your awareness from its identification with thoughts. We cling to our senses and thoughts because we're so attached to them. While focusing on the candle flame, you start becoming aware of that clinging and attachment and the process of letting go.

Focusing device 2: Centering. Focus all your consciousness into the center of your head. Visualize a point of light about a foot in front of your eyes. Now focus all of your attention on the point of light.

Focusing device 3: Grounding. Visualize the center of the Earth as a very dense place of rock or metal. Focus all of your attention on the center of the earth, and picture a huge iron bar there. Next bring your attention to your spinal cord. Visualize a large cable or cord running from the base of your spine all the way to the center of the Earth. Picture a big hook on the other end of the cord, and hook it into the bar at the center of the Earth. Feel a slight pull toward the center of the Earth and a slight heaviness of the body.

Focusing device 4: Your peaceful place. Think of a place where you usually feel especially serene, relaxed, and happy, such as the beach, the forest, a meadow, or the lake. Picture yourself there. Re-experience in your mind's eye all the sights, sounds, smells, and tastes you experience there. Focus on your sense of touch, too—the sun, the water, the air on your skin, and the sand, earth, or grass under your feet. Bring in as much vivid detail as you can. Get in touch with the positive feelings you experience there—your sense of well-being, confidence, serenity.

SAO #3: Visualization

Purpose: To practice envisioning what you want to create in your life.

Step 1: Focus on the here and now and move into a deeply relaxed state by using any combination of processes from SAO #1.

Step 2: Select the visualization that applies to your situation from the ones listed here (or adapt one of them to fit your situation).

Step 3: Use one of the letting-go processes from SAO #4.

Basic Visualization

1. Create a clear, concise, consistent picture. In your inner mind's eye, develop a clear, concise picture of the desired outcome you want, the end result, the state of being, especially the feeling tone within you and flowing between you and others, in this state of having what you want. Don't get into *how* the result will come about, but stay focused on the end result you want.

2. Charge it with passion. Allow your passion, your strong desire, to charge that picture with energy.

3. Become the essence of that picture. What one word best describes the picture for you? Is it success, abundance, joy, love, peace, elegance, competence, connectedness, or something else? *Become* that quality as you focus on your mind's-eye picture.

4. Replay the experience. When you come out of your meditative visualization, sit still for a few moments while you replay the experience a time or two. This helps you to remember it fully. Jot down a few words about key aspects of the visualization.

5. Persist until it materializes. Bring up the picture as often as possible, each time seeing the same clear picture—not fuzzy, vague, or changing—each time charging it with passion and desire, and each time freely letting it go. The more attention and focus you give it, the greater the likelihood of success.

Visualization variation 1: Accessing Creative Self

Relax deeply. Imagine yourself in a very safe, comfortable space—sensing it in vivid detail, using all your senses. Move to the edge of that space and imagine a portal into another realm—a beautiful realm with golden light pouring through the open portal. You are about to reunite with your Creative Self. Step through the portal into the light. Look around for your twin, your Creative Self. Greet this Self. Look for ways you are alike and ways you are different. Listen to what your Creative Self has to tell you. Look around and see what type of space this Self hangs out in. Ask this Self how you might bring her or him back with you into the everyday physical world. Listen for the answer.

When you're ready, thank your Creative Self and ask if you can meet again. Embrace this Self and feel the creative power surge flow into your own body. Step back through the portal. Gradually expand your consciousness out and up, filling the space of your body with your own awareness. As you return, feel the creative energy—alive but peaceful—that is within you. Bring that feeling back into your physical body. Slowly, gently open your eyes, recall the experience, and jot down some notes about it.

Visualization variation 2: Problem resolution

Relax deeply. Get in touch with your problem situation. If thinking of it or picturing it causes you to feel anxious, focus again on a relaxation technique. Repeat this process until you're able to picture your problem situation without feeling anxious.

What do you want the end results of this situation to be? How do you want it to be resolved? Picture that happening—in vivid detail, bringing all your senses into play: colors, patterns, textures you see; sounds you hear; and things you touch, smell, and taste. Picture your interactions with the other person(s) involved, focusing on your specific feelings and feelings flowing between you and others; for example, understanding, acceptance, warmth, and goodwill. Focus on the pictures and feelings until you feel quite comfortable and secure with them. Now use a letting-go technique to release them.

Visualization variation 3: Goal achievement

Follow the process described in Variation 1, but instead of focusing on a problem situation, focus on a goal you want to achieve. Picture yourself actually achieving the goal. Include all the people involved in helping you reach the goal; focus on the positive feelings flowing between you and them. Now let go.

Visualization variation 4: Evaluating goals

You can carry the process used in Variation 2 a step further to help you evaluate possible goals. (For example, if you're not sure whether getting a master's degree should be merely one alternate activity for achieving a career goal or a goal in itself, picture yourself having achieved the career goal without the master's degree.) Picture all the consequences of having achieved the goal. How do you feel about each? Is anything missing? What? Would a different goal have led to better results?

Visualization variation 5: Handling stage fright

Use this process to overcome the *jitters* that accompany any type of presentation you plan to make before a group. For best results, practice the visualization several times before your presentation. Just before going to sleep the night before the presentation is an especially good time to visualize positive results. Follow the process described in Variation 1, but instead of picturing a problem situation, picture yourself making a successful presentation. See yourself focusing on the major thrust of your message and getting it across in a clear, dynamic, persuasive way. See your audience understanding and accepting it. Feel your expansive inner-body emotions and theirs. Now let go.

SAO #4: Letting Go of Needs

Purpose: To experiment with processes for letting go of the need to cling to the results you want, to put your purpose out into the universe, trusting that all will work to your benefit.

Step 1: Move into a state of deep relaxation (SAO #2).

Step 2: Visualize the end results you want (SAO #3).

Step 3: Let go of your pictures of end results by one of the following methods (or devise your own method for putting your goals out into the universe):

Variation 1: Hot air balloon

Picture a beautifully colored hot air balloon with a lovely passenger basket. It's tied to the ground with velvet ropes. Put the picture of your end results into the basket—and the feelings related to the picture. Untie the ropes and watch the balloon float away, up into the sky and away toward the horizon. As it floats out of sight, repeat to yourself, *Let go, let go*.

Variation 2: Space capsule

Follow the process described in Variation 1, substituting a sleek space capsule for the hot air balloon. Picture all the latest technology and equipment for controlling the capsule. Put your end results inside the capsule; lock it; and watch it blast off and disappear into space.

Variation 3: Bottle at sea

Follow the process described in Variation 1, substituting a large glass bottle for the hot air balloon. Put your end results inside; place the cork in the bottle top; and throw the bottle into the ocean. Watch the tide carry it out to sea; see it disappear toward the horizon.

SAO #5: Programming Your Dreams

Purpose: To set up your dream time so it will provide you with valuable information for creative projects, new ideas, and problem-solving.

Step 1: Preliminaries. It's best not to set an alarm but merely to tell yourself what time you intend to awaken. Try this on weekends first, when you don't feel pressure to be somewhere at a specific time. Learn to instruct your subconscious and to trust this ability.

Keep a pen and paper beside your bed so you can jot down a few notes about the night's dreams before arising. Dream time is wispy, and dreams disappear all too easily in the hard light of day.

Step 2: Programming. Before you go to sleep, think about a problem you want to resolve, an opportunity you want to tap into, or a question you want to find an answer to. Formulate your desire into a brief question, such as *Should I go to work for ABC Co. or XYZ Co.?* or *What opportunities am I overlooking?* or *What should I do next?* Hold the question in your mind as you drift off to sleep.

Step 3: Recalling. When you awaken, lie still, drift, and allow dream memories to come in. Don't reach for your notepad too soon. When a wispy memory comes in, follow it. Allow your consciousness to drift back into the dream, to relive the details and patterns of it. Then jot down the key elements of your dream. Pay special attention to the overall feeling tone of the dream. If you had to define the tone, what would you say? Scary? Romantic? Nurturing? After you've completed your notes, give the dream a title and date it.

SAO #6: Interpreting Your Dreams

This process is adapted from one developed by Elaine DeBeauport. You can use your Rational and Intuitive Intelligences to interpret dream messages from your basic brain.

The Energy Within Me

The first technique focuses on your inner-energy body and its messages.

Write your dream on lined paper, skipping every other line. Go back and underline key words and images that stand out as important, that have emotional punch. For example, *I was speeding along in my car and I was fighting with my best friend.*

Above these underlined words or images, write the characteristics, qualities, or traits that each one represents to you. For the image my car, the key trait might be *rugged, speedy,* or *beat-up*. For the image best friend, it might be *gentle, weird, honest,* or *serious.*

Write the symbolic story of the dream above the original story, using the phrase *the energy of* (key word or image) *within me* when you come to key words or images. From this example, a sentence might be, *I was speeding along in the energy of ruggedness within me, and I was fighting with the energy of weirdness within me.*

The Poet Within Me

Another powerful dream interpretation technique is to write your dream as a poem. Dreams have much in common with poetry: They originate in your basic brain, and your left-brain rational mind doesn't know how to interpret them. But your wholistic right-brain mind does. This is the mind of associations, the senses, and intuition, so it tunes into dream messages, just as it tunes into poetry with its metaphors and analogies.

SAO #7: Breaking a Link: Pattern Intervention

Purpose: To break up old habit patterns by working with one link in the behavior chain.

The breaking-a-link process includes these steps:

1. What are your major behavior patterns—for better or worse? Identify and list as many as you can.

2. Which habit patterns are self-empowering—especially in keeping you open to new ideas? Mark them as ones you want to keep.

3. Which habit patterns are self-sabotaging? Mark them as ones you want to change. Avoid making them wrong. Fully accept the fact that they have served their purpose in the past.

4. Take the first habit pattern that you want to change. Notice how it causes you to react to a particular type of situation. List the links in your chain of reaction. (*I see a stranger. I mentally clam up. I try to avoid contact or to get away as soon as possible*, etc.)

5. Decide where you want to intervene—at which step, breaking which link?

6. Imagine two or three possible substitute actions, and then choose one.

7. Mentally see your old reaction in exaggeration or write about it; then see or write the word STOP when you reach the *breaking link.*

8. Remember to practice this new reaction every time you encounter a situation that triggers the old habit pattern. In this way you replace the old link with a new *breaking link.*

9. Reward yourself in some small way in order to support the new link.

10. When you're ready, work on the next habit you want to break.

Case Situation Feedback: Fast Print

Surface problems:

- Losing business to in-house print shops.
- Kinkos' 24-hour operation, especially copy service targeted to students.
- Increased use of home copiers.

Root problems:

- Net loss of revenues.
- Inadequate increase in new customer accounts to offset lost revenues.

Overlooked opportunities:

- Greater demand by certain companies for high-end print work that includes:
  - Providing high-level computer graphics and other artwork.
  - High-end design work for an entire project.
- Demand by new startup firms for logo, trade name, and similar work. An entire package could include everything: company signs, stationery, business cards, brochures, flyers, product labels, etc.
- Signage. Most companies, especially startups, need many signs. Fast Print could include coordinated packages of signs that include a company logo.

Ways to expand market share and revenues:

- Focus on the overlooked opportunities.
- Change company image. Fast Print may be an outdated name now that the copy end of the business has decreased. Image Design & Print might be an alternate company name.
- Recruit new customers. Jeff and Jennifer need to pool resources and brainstorm ways to make the best use of total customer/contact database. Get all this info into a computer database that can gather and report the information needed to identify customer opportunities, needs, and problems.

Chapter 4

Live Your Passion:
Motivational Drive

You make the road by walking it.
Anonymous

Still wondering what you want to be when you grow up? Many talented, high-powered adults say they're still not sure about that. Finding the answer is fun because it involves answering some very personal questions, such as:

- What do you feel excited about? Passionate about?
- What types of books or magazines do you like to read?
- What kinds of people do you like to talk with?
- When you have free time, what kinds of interests or projects do you spend time doing?
- What are you dying to learn about?
- How would you define success (your own)?

Hopefully, your definition of success includes doing meaningful, enjoyable work and making a contribution to the planet. You now have a chance to learn how to find the path of your unique life purpose—and to bring more passion into your career and your life. This is a key factor of Motivational Intelligence, which you'll incorporate into building your Creative Intelligence. You've thought about the type of niche that interests you, one that will make use of the innovative skills you're developing. You're about to learn more about that—and how to harness the Motivational Intelligence you need to move into your niche.

From there it becomes easy to develop your own set of clearly stated goals, to set priorities that help you balance career and personal life, and to plan projects, activities, time targets, to-do lists, and schedules that work best for you.

Imagine moving up from your brain-stem-spinal-cord area, the seat of your Basic Pattern-Parameter Intelligence, to the midbrain, or limbic brain, centered below and under the large neocortex. This emotional brain is central to two of your intelligences: Motivational Intelligence and Emotional Intelligence. Motivational Intelligence is all about the passion to achieve, to find your purpose, and to stay *on purpose*.

Terms to associate with Motivational Intelligence include

> desires, wants, passions, goals, drives, life purpose, emotional-limbic-mammalian brain

How Motivational Intelligence Works

Motivational Intelligence goes beyond your deepest conditioning about what you *should* want to do. It thrives on what you came in physical life to do—your life purpose. Motivational Intelligence based on life purpose gives you great strength to break out of your self-sabotaging patterns, and to form new self-empowering patterns. Unless you feel the desire to experience and achieve things in life, and you feel strongly enough to learn very specifically what it is you really want, you're likely to sabotage your own efforts and finally destroy your Life-Passion, gradually losing interest in everything.

Motivational Intelligence is the capacity to recognize what you want and what moves you to action. It's about listening to your inner self and observing what excites you, interests you, gets you going. It's making up your life in your own way, based on your own desires and passions, setting and achieving your own goals, not someone else's. It's using your sense of your own life purpose to guide yourself through a *process* of desiring and creating—over and over throughout your life.

You gain access to your passion through identifying your life purpose and following it. When you're standing in your life's purpose, when you're *on purpose*, the passion is always there, and possibilities live everywhere. You feel powerful and capable of achieving your goals. So getting in touch with your passion will always get you out of your rut and onto a higher road. In this way, passion gives you access to your inner power.

The Wanting-Satisfying Process

To want is forever; satisfactions are temporary, according to intelligence expert Elaine DeBeauport. Wanting is an emotional process of expansion that goes on continually in the emotional brain. Satisfaction is the resting point in the process of desire.

Satisfaction is to wanting as conclusion is to thinking—a form of temporary closure. You can feel, and even express, many desires without satisfying them, and you don't have to criticize yourself for wanting. You don't need to act on every desire or rush to satisfy them all. Wanting and desiring are emotional indicators of what you've allowed yourself to be affected by. They tell you what you love. If you decide your wanting is not pleasant or life-giving, or that it's too expensive, you can shift your focus to more life-enhancing desires. Use your Rational and Intuitive Intelligences to give yourself reasons for shifting your interest. Use your basic brain of action to withdraw from this desire. Use your Rational Intelligence to notice that you don't feel good doing it and to quit.

What should you do when you feel dissatisfied?

So what should you do when you do not feel satisfied, when you're not getting what you want? Here are some ideas:

- Realize that every time you satisfy a desire, you can rest and celebrate instead of criticizing yourself for wanting more.
- Use your Rational and Intuitive Intelligences to select the desires that are aligned with your life purpose and that make sense for you now.
- Use your Rational and Intuitive Intelligences to establish your priorities, referring back to your emotional brain to see if that's what you really want.
- Use your Basic Pattern-Parameter Intelligence to decide when it's time to rest or to act on something else.

The wanting-satisfying process will last forever and indicates that your emotional being is alive and well.

Coming from Deep, True Desire

You need to encourage that passion that comes from deep, true desire in order to strengthen yourself to live, to identify old patterns that either don't work or actually sabotage you, and to create new patterns that enable you to bring your goals into reality.

Which of your desires are superficial? Are you *conditioned* to want something or do you really want it, regardless of your conditioning? See the vital connection between conditioned patterns and wanting. Realize that you can want independent of your deepest conditioning.

Are some of your desires actually Negative-Ego desires to be better-than, to merely impress others, or to feel less worse-than and therefore a special case? Negative Ego will always eventually bring what you do *not* want. The key question to ask yourself: Do I want this for my own deep satisfaction? Would I want it even if others ignored or despised it?

Learn to identify your true, deep passions. Use this deep wanting to guide yourself away from old conditioned patterns that no longer serve you. Then enlist all your brain systems to building your Motivational Intelligence: vivid, wonderful visions and goals of your neocortex, supportive habits and patterns of your basic brain, and expansive emotions of your emotional brain.

Remember: When you are into your passion, you are totally here in the present moment. You are completely charged and focused. You are oblivious to distractions. You forget yourself, your troubles, and your day-to-day life. You hitch yourself to something bigger. Sounds like the definition of creative flow, doesn't it?

The "Flow" Factor

Have you ever been so carried away with an activity that time flew by because you were so wrapped up in what you were doing that you forgot all about time? Afterward, did you ever assess your performance? Did you notice whether what you did was innovative, new in some way? The experience of Creative Intelligence in action is called the *flow factor* by University of Chicago professor Mihaly Csikszentmihadlyi. His research indicates that when you're in the creative state of flow, these things are going on:

1. *You have clear goals.* This means you must know how to see clearly what needs to be done and know how to set clear, on-target goals.

2. *Your activity becomes the goal.* The work becomes an end in itself because it has deep meaning for you. This means you have learned what truly motivates you, have some sense of your deeper purpose in life, and are able to find work that helps you achieve that purpose.

3. *You forget time.* Time flies by as you become caught up in the work. Time is just an extended present in which you're making meaning.

4. *You're totally focused.* You've learned how to focus your consciousness so that the level of awareness you need to do the job merges with your actions. You screen out distractions. This means you can sustain a single-minded focus on what you're doing, so you're aware only of what's relevant here and now. It's a matter of intense concentration. It also means you don't worry about failure. You're too involved to be concerned with failure; it's not an issue.

5. *Your skills match the challenge.* This means you know how to seek out appropriate challenges, have gained some problem-solving skills, and have developed the confidence you need to take on new problems.

6. *You move beyond ego concerns.* You're not concerned with protecting your ego. Strangely enough, research indicates that your intuition expands when you're in the flow state. You're able to tap into information from all three levels of consciousness: conscious, subconscious, and superconscious.

7. *You get immediate feedback.* You know how to get information about how your work is judged, and you're able to accept constructive criticism.

We know flow involves Emotional Intelligence and Motivational Intelligence because it produces positive emotional experiences. Flow involves meaningful activity, what people classify as *work* when they love their work. In fact, people are three times more likely to report that such positive experiences occur at work than at leisure according to Csikszentmihadlyi.

One way to increase the percentage of time you experience flow in your work, therefore, is to boost your Motivational Intelligence. That's because this intelligence is all about discovering what really lights your fire—and basing your goals and activities on that. Your work then holds meaning and value for you. You can see also that the practice of being fully present in the Now will help you achieve the flow state.

Motivational Profiles: 6 Types of Workers

A survey of thousands of Shell employees by the Herman Group suggests six types of workers, ranging from those who focus primarily on the clock to those who focus on getting personal fulfillment from their jobs. How well do you think these people understand their own wants, desires, motivations, life purpose, and goals? How effectively do you think they go about satisfying these wants? Do any of these profiles describe your patterns?

Clock Punchers

- Ended up in current job by chance, not design.
- Satisfaction level is lowest of all groups.
- 75 percent would make a different career choice.
- Typical demographics: female, no college education, earns less than $30,000.
- Typical occupations: cashier, waitress, hospital orderly.

Paycheck Cashers

- Priorities include good income and good benefits.
- Not focused on stretching abilities or changing the world.
- Happy in their cubicles.
- Typical demographics: young, male, ethnic minority, no college degree.
- Typical occupations: blue-collar or non-professional white-collar jobs (factory worker, entry-level word processor, etc.).

Ladder Climbers

- Priorities include job security and company loyalty.
- Working their way up to a better job.
- Typical demographics: female, modest education, good income; 48 percent earn more than $50,000.
- Typical occupations: skilled blue-collar supervisor, middle manager.

Risk Takers

- Want to get rich quick.
- Always seek opportunities to make bucks.
- Job hop, looking for better jobs.
- Typical demographics: young, male, educated, successful; 40 percent earn incomes of more than $50,000.
- Typical occupations: software entrepreneur, commission salesperson.

High Achievers

- ꙮ Leaders who take initiative.
- ꙮ Planned their career path early on.
- ꙮ Highest income group: 25 percent earn more than $75,000.
- ꙮ Typical demographics: male, highly educated.
- ꙮ Typical occupations: professional (lawyer, surgeon, CPA, upper management).

Fulfillment Seekers

- ꙮ Want to make the world a better place.
- ꙮ Seek jobs where they can contribute.
- ꙮ Team players rather than leaders.
- ꙮ High satisfaction with their work.
- ꙮ Typical demographics: white, married.
- ꙮ Typical occupations: teacher, nurse, social worker, public defender.

Sparking Your Motivational Intelligence

You can easily spark your Motivational Intelligence—the level of motivation you feel and the skill with which you use it to create the fulfilling life you want. You can begin by identifying your deep desires, what you're good at, your life purpose, the goals and activities to achieve that purpose, and ways to stay *on purpose*.

Sparkler #1: Give Your Motivation a Quick-Charge

You can boost your level of motivation by falling in love with life and by identifying what turns you on and moving toward those situations.

Any Love Affair Will Do

You need a high level of motivation in order to guide yourself and sustain your life within the all-pervasive Web of Life. You need it in order to fully participate in life itself. The secret is to know that you are one with the Web of Life, one with the energy of all life. You *are* energy. You *are* life. Identify yourself with the Web of Life so you can take your rightful place within it.

If you identify with all energy, with the Web of Life, you'll feel that you belong, that you're a member of it, and you can continually accept and receive energy. Become aware of how this Web of Life affects you and how you affect it. If the flutter of a butterfly wing in Japan affects the weather in California, what impact do your thoughts and actions have?

Your love of life is precious because it's your deepest connection with all creation. Use your love of this Web of Life to boost your motivation level. You know that what you love is what moves you most deeply, so find something to love. *Any love affair will do.* Love a sunset, a tree, an animal, a person, an idea, a cause, a career. It's your way of saying *yes* to life—honoring what's here, approaching it, penetrating it, surrounding and integrating yourself with it.

You get a sense of that oneness and that emotion when you focus fully on the Present, accepting What-Is in each moment. Live your emotions. Use your turn-ons to know yourself, to stay passionate, excited, truly and vibrantly alive.

When you doubt or question life, you drain off some of your energy. Your rational mind can doubt and question any aspect of life. Your basic brain can wrap life into a package of duties and bury your energy under a pile of *shoulds*. Your emotional brain can get worn out from dealing with all this. Free your emotional brain by encouraging yourself to *be* what you feel like being, to *do* what you feel like doing, to *have* what you most want. Free yourself to experience whatever feelings come up—happiness or anger or love or sadness. Allow yourself to go fully into all these emotions; on the other side, you're likely to discover what you really want.

Find Turn-Ons That Light Your Fire

What excites you? What kinds of situations, people, food, drinks, ideas, music, sexuality, challenges, work, art, sports, hobbies, weather do you really groove on? What kinds of recognition, flirting, compliments, rewards turn you on? Exactly what is it that gets you excited? Observe your reactions to life so you can know consciously what excites you. Keep asking yourself these kinds of questions:

- What makes me feel excited and expanded?
- What starts me trembling with excitement?
- What stirs me into motion?

Only this fuel can keep you motivated and really in love with life.

Desire is a deep, passionate, and unclear feeling. It takes skill to observe it in all its subtleties. Feeling and observing are two different skills. Watch and observe your body to see what gets it to act. What moves you to pick up the phone, plan a trip, write a letter, or go to see someone? What causes you to repeat that action over and over? Notice what stimulates you to move; is it good company, someone in need, money, a compliment, God, status, making love, childhood dreams, what?

This information provides clues to identifying your life purpose, what you want to learn in and contribute to life. This information also can help you decide on the best approaches to take, the kinds of interim goals and rewards that will work for you, and the kinds of activities to plan for achieving those goals.

Use these turn-ons as the fuel to throw again and again on the fire of your motivation. The secret to conscious motivation is being willing and able to notice which turn-ons work for you and to find ways to create those turn-ons to continually fuel your fire. Feed that fire so it won't go out in the difficult times, so you can stay in the wanting, the longing, the desiring.

Sparkler #2: Find a Life Purpose

Your life purpose, and your motivators, are tied to what you like and what you're good at. Do you really know what they are? Can you list them quickly? If not, don't worry. Many people aren't clear about the kinds of things they're good at and really enjoy. They feel there may be many things they could do or would like if they only knew more about them or had a chance to try them—especially in the career area.

What Do You Like? What Are You Good At?

The only way to identify your skills and interests is to start with what you know now. Then, as you learn more about various jobs and careers, you have a basis for evaluating how well they fit your skills/interest set. At the end of this chapter you'll find SAO #1: What Do You Like to Do? What Do You Do Well? (page 93). It will help you identify your skills and interests.

Your most valuable resource can be people who are working in the field, industry, company, or position you are considering. Use your networking skills to locate these people and to arrange some informational interviews. Ask them such questions as:

- ☙ Where do you see the industry going in the next few years?
- ☙ Tell me about your career path.
- ☙ How did you get your job?
- ☙ What do you like best and least about your job?
- ☙ Could you describe a typical day on the job?
- ☙ What is the average salary for this type of position?
- ☙ What is the single type of thing I could tell you about myself that would help me get a job?
- ☙ Is there anyone else I could speak to? In a particular job or department? In another company?

Why Are You Here?

Underlying and surrounding what you like and what you're good at is your life purpose. Ask yourself:

- ☙ Why am I here?
- ☙ Why did I come into this world?

We all came here to learn certain lessons to make some kind of contribution to the world—your life purpose is composed of these two aspects. SAO #2: What's Your Life Purpose (page 97) is designed to help you get in touch with this. Once you get some sense of your life purpose, you'll begin to understand your primary motivators. Then you can assess all your goals and activities in the light of how well they align with your life purpose. It's a great way to keep yourself *on purpose*.

> Your life purpose, or mission statement, is a long-range overview of what you believe you want to do with your life—why you're here and how you fit in the overall scheme of things.

You may never have some specific experience that tells you, *This is your life purpose*. George Bernard Shaw said, "Your life purpose is simply to help the purpose of the universe." This is a good starting point, but you'll want to get more specific than that.

How can you realize what your life purpose is? If you had no life purpose, you wouldn't be here on Earth, so you *can* learn to recognize that purpose.

In the meantime, author David Spangler says, "I don't know what tomorrow brings. I don't know which task I should undertake. I don't have a sense of my life purpose at this moment. But right now, here in front of me, there's someone or something to interact with. I can honor that person or situation, that place or object, and I can give my whole heart to it." This is a choice. You can choose to give yourself and your passion in that way to call forth the good in someone or something else. In this way you create your own calling, moment by moment.

Over your lifetime, your life purpose will undoubtedly grow and shift, but there will be a consistent core or thread. That core is what makes your life purpose different from your goals, even long-term goals. When you become consciously aware of your life purpose, you can consciously set goals that are aligned and integrated with that purpose. Your day-to-day activities can lead you in the direction that seems right to you. People who have managed to *get it all together* in this way say their achievements became more meaningful to them. The work itself—and the resulting achievements—began to bring deeper satisfaction and joy.

When you're on purpose, you have a deeper, more sustainable source of motivation that keeps you working toward your goals. The line between work and play becomes fuzzy, because those activities that you see as part of your life's work, you also see as important, satisfying, and the source of fun and joy in your life. In addition, work that you love to do, you learn to do well, and the work that you do well is the most likely to bring in the money you want. Isn't it elegant that the work that brings you joy is most likely to bring you abundance? All it takes is getting in touch with your deep desires and how they reveal your life purpose.

Sparkler #3: Develop Clearly Stated Goals

Once you have some sense of life purpose, you're ready to move into the goal-setting process. This includes the precondition of allowing for abundance, then brainstorming the particular things you want to achieve that align with your life purpose. After that you refine and rank a short list of goals that are clear and specific.

Allow Abundance in Your Goals

Do you approach goals from a viewpoint of scarcity? Do you think, *Because there are not enough resources for everyone to have all they need, then the more I get, the less there will be for someone else?* Women are more likely than men to think in these terms, and as a result they hold themselves back. To break that cycle, think of all the things that are perceived as scarce. Jot them down.

Now, step back, try a new worldview. If you analyze the world's resources—such as food, fresh water, housing, education, health care, money, time, energy, love—you may realize that we have adequate resources, and even abundance, if a critical mass of people were to decide to manage these resources properly.

The World Game Institute determined in 1992 that within 10 years we, as a global society of humankind, could solve all major global problems and create a vital, sustainable economy for all people. We could have adequate resources for all. We have the technology to do this, and we could raise the money if we managed our resources differently. The cost? About $ 250 billion a year for 10 years. The amount spent on *defense* globally? About $750 billion a year. This estimate is based on 1991 statistics provided to the World Game Institute by UNICEF, Worldwatch Institute, Rocky Mountain Institute, and World Resources Institute.

Surely we could collectively choose to have not only adequacy but sustainable abundance. Abundance thinking reflects individual beliefs or collective beliefs about the key resources in life. Here are some powerful beliefs:

- Take money—our creative energy becomes money; we can think of it as green energy.

- Or time—there are always 24 hours in a day; we have abundant time to achieve our top-priority goals once we clarify them and weed out the nonessentials.

- Or energy—all that exists in the universe is energy; the only problem is finding and using the best form of energy for each of our purposes.

- And love, which exists in our minds and hearts—the more love we give to ourselves and others, the more we tend to receive, and the more we have to give back again. The only limits are our fears that shield us from giving and receiving love.

When you come from an attitude of abundance, you can move more freely toward your goals. Because there's plenty for everyone, your successes don't need to be built on someone else's failures. Your having more doesn't mean that someone else has less. It's a win-win attitude: Everyone can win. On the other hand, our culture also has a tendency to make heroes of greedy multimillionaires and billionaires. The type of abundance discussed here is aligned with the concept of *right livelihood*, earning a living in ways that contribute to humanity. It means going beyond the need for greed and sharing the wealth with those who help you to create it.

For the past 20 years, U.S. women have filled two-thirds of new jobs and will continue to do so well into the next century. Women dominate the New Economy as workers, professionals, and entrepreneurs. If you're older than 35, you probably set your career goals in the days when women were a minority. You probably set them too low and may be holding yourself back. Try this process:

- Visualize yourself in a leadership role. Are you uncomfortable with that picture?

- Do you hold self-limiting beliefs about your workplace role?

Discomfort with wielding power and self-limiting beliefs about workplace roles are women's two primary internal barriers to achieving career success. Both barriers are related to what you've learned about how women should be in our culture.

As you complete SAO #3: What Are Your Goals? (page 98), focus first on setting goals that tie in to your life purpose and the contribution you want to make. Secondarily, but with clarity, focus on the type of abundance you want for yourself—whether it be abundant relationships, abundant health, abundant joy, abundant material resources, and so on. When you're *on pur-pose*, doing what you're here for, the abundance will materialize in the best form for you.

Be Clear About What a Goal Is

The term *goal* as used here is synonymous with *objective* and is quite different from an activity in the following ways:

- A goal is a specific end result you want by some stated point in time. Activities are things you *do* in order to achieve your goal.
- You may *enjoy* an activity, but that doesn't make it a goal.
- There may be a variety of feasible and acceptable activities that can help you reach your goal.

The activities are a means to an end. The end is your goal. That's why it's so important to separate goals from activities—so you'll be clear about what you're really after and feel free to consider alternatives for getting there.

It's also important to have a clear picture of your goals. Write them down. You're much more likely to achieve written goals than mental ones. They're more specific—and they're easier to remember, to update, to revise, and to mark off once they're achieved. And the marking-off increases your sense of satisfaction and your motivation to keep achieving.

Distinguish Between Specific and Vague Goals

Look at the differences between the vague and specific goals shown in Snapshot #1. Most of us tend to carry around a mixed bag of *wants*. Many of them are vague; some we picture as activities instead of what we hope to gain *from* those activities. We usually wish we had these wants now, and we dreamily hope to have them someday. We must transform such dreamy wants into clear, specific goals in order to achieve them. How specific? Preferably specific enough so that on the target date you've set for attainment of the goal, you *know* for sure whether you've achieved it or how close you've come to it, and anyone knowledgeable on the subject could also tell.

Snapshot #1: Vague Vs. Specific Goals

Vague Goals	Specific Goals
To make more money.	To earn $50,000 next year.
To move up in the company.	To be a department manager by....
To get ahead in life.	To have an MBA degree by....
To have more free time.	To have at least one month of free time per year by....
To travel more.	To travel to Africa for 3 weeks in....

Distinguish Between Goals and Activities

In many cases, only you can decide whether a *want* is a goal or just an activity. Ask yourself, *Why do I want to do this?* If the act or process of doing something is what you desire, then it's probably a goal for you. If the activity is mainly a *means* to having something you desire, then it's not a goal for you.

For example: *Why* do you want more free time? Is it to have more time to pursue a hobby, develop a skill, or travel? If so, then those activities are your goals and having more free time is a *means* to that end. On the other hand, you may want freedom to do things on the spur of the moment, to pursue whatever tickles your fancy from time to time. If so, then having more free time is indeed your goal.

Here is another example: Why do you want to have a master's degree? Is it to get a better job, make more money, or feel the personal satisfaction of having the degree, regardless of its other advantages? Suppose you find that the major reason you want a degree is to increase your earnings. You might find a number of alternate career paths or ways of becoming qualified for a particular career path that would take less money, time, and energy than getting a degree.

When you find it difficult to decide whether a want is a goal or merely an activity you enjoy that is a means to another end, try this:

- Get comfortable; relax as fully as possible.
- Close your eyes and try to visualize yourself once you have achieved your goal.
- Think about how you feel. Are you satisfied with that particular end result? Are you satisfied with the *way* you got it? Is anything missing? What would you have done differently if you could?

Sometimes visualizing end results and how you feel about them can help you decide what you really want. For example, if you visualize yourself holding a particularly desirable job *without* having gotten the degree, you may determine whether having a degree is your true goal.

Brainstorm, Refine, and Rank Your Goals

After you spontaneously generate a random list of things you want in your life, the next step is to evaluate the list, sorting out activities from goals, adding goals you may have overlooked, rewriting them so that they are specific and contain time targets, and ranking them in order of their importance to you. Most people find it helpful to categorize them by life area, such as career area, personal development, and private life. SAO #4: Refine Your Goals (page 98) guides you through this step.

Sparkler #4: Plan Your Activities and Set Priorities

Consider which activities will provide the best avenues for reaching these goals. Write down any and all activities you can think of that might help you achieve your goals, taking one goal at a time. At this point, do not rank the activities. Again, fantasize, brainstorm, and let the creative-child part of you take over. Send your judgmental counterpart out of the room. Be daring. Be outrageous. When you've listed activities for all life areas, summon your critical, practical, reasonable side to help you select the activity that is most feasible and the most likely to contribute to your first goal. Rank that activity 1.

Rank the second most likely activity 2, and so forth down to the least likely activity. Repeat for each goal.

Does your list of activities boggle your mind? If so, start picking out the activities *you are willing to spend at least five minutes on during the next week.* Now remove from your list all activities you are *not* willing to spend five minutes on. Such activities may be important, but obviously they're not important enough to occupy your time right now, so you'll probably never get to them. Do some of your goals now have no activities listed for them? Go back and list other activities; rank them and delete the impractical ones. Keep going until you have for each goal a list of activities that are important to you and are things you are willing to begin acting on right away. Once you've completed all the SAOs to this point, you should be close to knowing:

- What you want.
- What you can do to get it.
- What you will do about it in the next week.

Develop Short-Term and Long-Term Action Plans

You'll probably want a one-month action plan, a one-year plan, and perhaps a five-year plan. Think broadly as you complete the longer-range plans, focusing on goals rather than on activities.

To accomplish the most, make a one-month plan *every* month. Use it as the basis for your weekly and daily to-do lists. Compare months to see how you're progressing toward long-term goals. Finally, remember to reevaluate your decisions regularly to be sure that your goals reflect what you really want in life and that your activities are the best ones for getting you there.

Here's the total, ongoing process you'll be following to get what you want in life:

- Setting goals and priorities.
- Developing specific action plans with prioritized activities to help you reach those goals.
- Periodically reevaluating your goals, action plans, and priorities.

Make Your Plan a Reality

Now it's time to work your plan. Here are some general suggestions for bringing your mental plan into physical reality.

Envision and focus. Use relaxed concentration and visualization as a technique to command your inner resources so that all your actions tend to move you toward your goals, which gives you a powerful focus.

Act. Begin this week, even if you undertake only a five-minute activity for each goal.

Communicate. Let the important people in your life *know* about the goals they may be able to help you with. For example, let your boss or mentor know about appropriate career goals.

Get support. Make a list of the people who can help you and give you support as you work toward your goals. Decide the best way to enlist their aid. Include support systems in your plan.

Enjoy. Make the *process* of achieving your goals as enjoyable as possible. It's important to keep your eye on the end result you want, but it's also important to relax and enjoy yourself along the way. In fact, your enjoyment of an activity should be one of the criteria for selecting it.

Negotiate. Use your goals to help you achieve specific results on the job that will serve as the basis for negotiating promotions and raises later.

Focus. Don't get so carried away with the *activities* that you lose sight of the *goal.* Use your action plan to chart activities; mark them off as they are completed and as the goal is achieved. As mentioned earlier, it helps if you keep a list of your top three or four goals handy and refer to it regularly. Some successful women keep their lists (and/or symbolic pictures of their goals) posted where they'll see them daily in their homes or offices.

Overcome barriers. Become a problem solver who can figure out how to overcome barriers to reaching goals. Don't let procrastination, interruptions, and distractions keep you from achieving your goals. Manage your activities.

Reevaluate. If you're having unusual difficulty in achieving a goal, ask yourself whether the goal is right for you. If it is, then reevaluate the activities you have selected and look for new ones.

Keep goals flexible. Your goals are not set in concrete. They're just part of a plan that can be changed as *situations* change.

Congratulate yourself. When you achieve a goal, remember to give yourself credit and reward yourself.

Keep setting goals. Once you have achieved a major goal, set another one to take its place. You say you've earned a rest? You don't want another major project for a while? Then your new goal might be to have a specific number of additional unstructured hours each week, month, or year to do as you please.

The object is to be clear about what you want and what you're doing with your time and your life—so that you're making clear choices rather than drifting.

Sparkler #5: Keep Checking Your Motivation Level

To keep yourself on track, keep asking yourself, *What's my motivation level now, on a scale of 1 to 10?* If it's 5 or below, you need to take a new look at your goals and priorities. In the middle of a project, ask yourself:

- What am I feeling?
- What feedback am I receiving?
- How does it make me feel?
- What am I wanting now?

Use your feelings as a signal to readjust your plans, rather than ignoring them, which can lead to sabotage. Know what you really want—to save time, money, and heartache. Invite your rational brain into more accurate, more efficient, and realistic planning. Feel the blocks so you can move around or over them. Within these blocks may be the necessary energy and information you need to complete your project successfully. Consider these suggestions:

- Feel what it is that you truly want.
- Experience the desire; love your longing.

If your feelings are unpleasant or painful, keep the following in mind:

- Don't shift to *thinking about* the wanting or the doing.
- Don't move away from *experiencing* your wanting at a gut level.
- Don't intellectualize or postpone it.

The only way to know how to want is to experience the wanting and let it motivate you.

Sparkler #6: Cross the Gap from Wanting to Having

Say you haven't been aware of your life purpose and you haven't been achieving your goals. Try this attitude: *Where I am now is simply where I am now. The universe attaches no value judgment to it. The gap between where I am and where I want to be creates a healthy tension that can move me forward.*

You won't move forward unless you stay clear and honest about where you are now. When you start to deny failure or pretend success or start to settle, you drain your *moving-forward* energy and momentum.

Try this: Focus on where you've been (that you don't want to be) and where you are now (that you don't want to be). Notice how that energy feels. Now focus on where you want to be, what you intend to have, what you're committed to moving toward and achieving. Notice how that energy feels.

Think about the quality of energy you feel when you're moving away from what you *don't* want. Doesn't it have a negative quality? This focus is not a powerful way of creating what you want in your life. Say, for example, you have a problem with owing money and you focus on solving that problem, which is getting rid of what you don't want, what you are *against*. Your focus on that problem can lead you to pay off your debt, but if that's as far as it goes, you're likely to repeat the pattern, accumulate debt again, and face a similar problem. That's because you're not generating a positive attractor energy that draws a positive outcome into your life. Shift your focus to what you are *for*, what you intend to achieve, and this automatically generates the electromagnetic energy that attracts it to you.

Creative Processes That Use Motivational Intelligence

Every innovative technique you can imagine is related to your Motivational Intelligence. That's because you must be motivated to actually use a creative technique before it can do you any good. The most important creative activities involving your Motivational Intelligence are those that help you get in touch with your life purpose, the big fire that runs your engine. Having a sense of life purpose also helps you to recognize and use all those little things that turn you on, that light your fire and keep your Motivational Intelligence growing. The Creative Techniques that follow will help you do that. The cases will help you apply your Motivational Intelligence to real-life situations.

List Your Passions

Note: Work on this technique after you have completed the SAOs concerning life purpose and goals.

Successful people who passionately love life and love their work are likely to have lists of things they want to explore, do, see, launch, write, or achieve before they die. For some it's a mental list, but written is best. For example, the best travel agents have a list of places around the world they want to see. Successful writers keep a list of topics they want to explore and possibly write about. Business entrepreneurs have a list of new types of businesses they would like to research and perhaps launch before they retire. Professionals keep a list of career areas they would like to explore and experience. Here are suggestions for making your own list:

- Make lists of topics you want to explore, goals to achieve, people to meet, places to see, and so on.
- Put your #1 desire first and rank order each list.
- Draw or paste small pictures or symbols, in color, on your list—to spark a multisensory, emotional charge.
- Put the list where you'll see it regularly, renewing your awareness of it, but not where you'll see it so frequently that it becomes invisible to you.
- Revise the list as your interests change and as you complete items.

A Final Word

Using your Motivational Intelligence is so important because no matter how creative you are, unless you have the passion and drive to actually do something with your creative ideas, they'll wither and die. You're on the road to living out your life purpose, the ultimate motivational engine. From now on, whenever you wonder *what next?* your answer will be *whatever fits best with my life purpose as it's unfolding at this time.* Motivational Intelligence is all about your passion for life, and it's seated in your emotional brain. Next, it's time to explore the whole range of emotions—and your Emotional Intelligence. But first, work with the SAOs that follow.

Self-Awareness Opportunities

SAO #1: What Do You Like to Do? What Do You Do Well?

Purpose: To get to know more about yourself by identifying your key interests and skills and to organize these into career building blocks.

Instructions: Follow the instructions given in Parts A through D. Then examine the Showcase Examples and set up a similar sheet with seven columns for analyzing your own favorite activities—what you enjoy doing.

Part A. Interests

Step 1: What excites you? List three times in your life when you felt passionate and excited. Think of three special times when you could say *I did that and it feels good.* Get started by writing the first one that comes to mind, and the other two will probably come back to you.

Step 2: What do you gravitate toward? Ask yourself some probing questions, suggested by career specialist Richard Bolles:

1. What kinds of problems do you like to solve?

   a. Problems in which the main focus is on the people (or animals)—their thoughts, feelings, desires, conflicts, learning, healing, etc.?

   b. Problems where the main focus is on knowledge, information, or data?

   c. Problems where the main focus is on things, such as cars, houses, pictures, etc.?

2. What kinds of questions do you like people to ask you?

   a. What they should do next?

   b. What a situation really means?

   c. How to make things work?

3. What kinds of knowledge do you like to bring into a conversation or situation?

   a. Knowledge about what makes people tick?

   b. The history of something? How culture comes into play?

   c. How something works? How to do something?

4. What are your favorite words? What kinds of words do you find yourself using over and over? Ask people close to you to notice the words you frequently use, especially words that they don't hear others using as often. Your vocabulary often reveals areas that are close to your heart.

5. What are your favorite activities, hobbies, avocations, etc.? (Note: most of these are also industries.)

6. What's your definition of *fascinating strangers*? What do they like and what are they're good at? What kind of work do they do? What kind of activities are they involved in?

7. What kinds of magazines and books do you browse through or buy at newsstands or bookstores? Within those venues, what types of article attract your attention so that you're likely to read them?

8. What Internet sites do you frequent? Look at your bookmarks to detect patterns.

9. If you watch game shows on TV, which categories do you like for contestants to pick because you stand a good chance of getting the right answers and you enjoy the information in those categories? What types of TV shows do you watch? Pay special attention to educational channels or other programs that are educational and informative. Which shows are you likely to watch?

10. If you were to write a book, what subject would you write about?

Step 3: Interpret your answers. Questions 1, 2, and 3 have three categories of answers: a, b, and c. Count the number of "a" answers you gave. This score reflects your people orientation. Count the number of "b" answers you gave. This score reflects your information orientation. Repeat for your "c" answers. This score reflects your technical orientation.

Question 4: Count the number of words that you think fall into the "a" category of people orientation. Repeat for the "b" category, information orientation, and for the "c" category, technical orientation.

Questions 5-10: How do your answers fit into the people-information-technical categories? Do other categories or patterns emerge? What do your patterns suggest about your key skills and interests?

Which category—a, b, or c—has the highest score? What do your patterns suggest about your key skills and interests?

Step 4: What do you like to do? Now that you've played with your likes for a while, summarize them in column 1 of your seven-column table. (See the Showcase Example on page 96.) Just randomly list, as they come to mind, 20 things you most enjoy doing. Don't attempt to respond to the other columns until you have completed the first column.

Step 5: Why do you like those activities? Now find out what your *liked* activities have in common. Analyze each activity listed in the first column by responding to the other columns.

In column 2, opposite the first activity, place a minus sign (–) if you most enjoy doing this alone; a plus sign (+) if you enjoy this activity with another; or a slash (/) if you have no preference.

In column 3, place an *I* for activities in which you experience intimacy, perhaps *I* + for deeper levels of intimacy. If you don't experience intimacy, place a minus sign.

In column 4, note activities that carry a risk factor with an *R*. Use a plus or minus sign to show risk level.

In column 5, write the approximate date you last engaged in the activity.

In column 6, identify the primary need filled by engaging in this activity; that is, what motivates you to get involved: a need to achieve (*A*), to exercise power (*P*), or to interact socially (*S*)?

In column 7, identify the types of skills or knowledge that you use when you engage in the activity. Write one word that symbolizes each skill or knowledge area used in this activity. Looking at all your activities, how do they fit with your *people, information,* and *technical* scores?

Step 6: Rank your *liked* activities. Rank the activities in order of the degree of enjoyment you derive from each. (See page 96 for a sample chart.)

Ashley realizes that her chief skills used in party-going and hanging-out are communication skills with a healthy dose of empathy and intuition. Her skills in writing and making presentations are also primarily communication skills, in these cases allied with the ability to visualize past and future events and to organize her thoughts and feelings about them. She sees the chief skills she uses in photography and travel as being able to visualize what she wants to do and achieve and to follow through. In shopping for collectibles, her chief skill is applying the information she has gained through study and shopping experiences. She can see a strong skill pattern of visualizing, communicating, and organizing—allied with a strong need for social interaction and intimacy, followed by achievement need, in low-risk activities.

Showcase: Ashley's Favorite Activities

1	*2*	*3*	*4*	*5*	*6*	*7*
Favorite activities:	alone – other+	intimacy level	risk factor	last did	need met	skills-knowledge used
Entertain	+	I+		6/2	S	visualize
go to parties	+	I		5/13	S-P	communicate-intuit
hang out with close friends	+	I+		6/18	S	communicate-intuit
take photographs	–	–		6/2	A	visualize-act
travel	+	I	R	1/5-15	S-A-P	visualize-act
write letters, reports, diary	–	–		6/18	A-P	communicate-organize
make presentations	+	–	R+	5/20	A-P	communicate-organize
shop for collectibles	+	I	R	6/15	A-S	apply information

*Needs: A=achievement need P=power need S=social/belonging need

She repeats this process in a separate list for what she does well. She finds that most things she does well are also on the favorite list. She identifies those activities that appear on both lists as her core skills—the ones to build a career around.

Part B. Skills and Knowledge

Step 1: What do you do well? If possible, complete this part a day or so after you complete Part A. Complete column 1 by listing, in random order, 10 things you honestly do well; take no more than 20 minutes.

Step 2: What do your skills have in common? Complete columns 2 through 7 as instructed in Part A.

Step 3: Rank your skills. Rank the things you do well in order of their importance to you; also consider your level of expertise in each activity.

Part C. Patterns and Insights

Step 1: What patterns can you find? What interrelationships do you see among the different factors, such as alone/with another, intimacy, risk, need fulfillment/motivation, and types of skills and knowledge? What patterns seem to emerge concerning what you enjoy (interests) and what you do well (skills/ knowledge)? Notice the date column (column 5). Are you developing your most likely talents or neglecting them? Are these truly the interests and skills you most enjoy and that seem most important to you? Or do you wish they were, or believe they should be? If so, where do these wishes and beliefs originate? From family? Friends? Teachers? Describe the interrelationships and patterns in writing. From this deep inner source comes your passion for your work and for life.

Step 2: What insights pop up? What insights emerged from this exercise? State in writing how these insights affect your image of yourself, what you want in life, and what talents and contributions you have to offer.

Part D. Career Building Blocks

Look over your interests, skills, patterns, and insights. Identify some common building blocks of skills and interests that could form the foundation for a career. Take several sheets of paper; consider each page a block. Give each block a label, and within each list the types of interests, skills, and knowledge that apply. Play with your blocks, moving them around in different combinations and configurations to fit various types of jobs and careers. Remember: Each of your skills is transferable—these skills go everywhere with you. It's up to you to recognize them and use them. Ask yourself, *Where would I be happiest using these basic skills?* Remember, you'll be most effective where you are the happiest. Each of your skills is potentially a marketable skill. It's up to you to find the company and situation that needs this skill. So once you identify your package of transferable, marketable skills, it's a matter of doing some research and informational interviewing to determine how your skills would fit in with some company's needs or a set of customer needs.

SAO #2: What's Your Life Purpose?

Purpose: To help you determine your life purpose.

This approach to identifying your life purpose asks you to look at your role models, those people who have influenced you the most. Your relationships with all the important men and women in your life always hold hidden meanings.

Step 1: Explore your feminine side.

- Who are the important women in your life—past and present? List five or six women.
- What are some strengths of these women? List them and then notice types of strengths that most of them have in common.
- What are some weaknesses of these women? List them and then notice types of weakness that most of them had in common.

These are the feminine strengths and weaknesses you came in to work with—to build on the strengths and to work on the weaknesses.

Step 2: Explore your masculine side.

- Who are the important men in your life—past and present? List five or six men.
- What are some strengths of these men? List them and then notice types of strengths that most of them had in common.
- What are some weaknesses of these men? List them and then notice types of weakness that most of them have in common.

These are the masculine strengths and weaknesses you came in to work with—to build on the strengths and to work on the weaknesses.

Now combine your feminine and masculine strengths. How do these suggest your life purpose—what you came to contribute? Then combine your feminine and masculine weaknesses. How do these suggest your life lesson—what you came to learn?

Step 3: On a card write your life purpose and life lesson.

Make it easy to remember your life purpose and to speak about it when appropriate. Write a brief one-liner, *My life's purpose is . . . .* Do you feel empowered when you say this? Is it easy to recall this line? If not, rewrite it until it's easy to remember and you feel empowered when you say it. Then print it on a card, with colorful embellishment and symbols if you like.

Keep this card on hand in a place where you'll notice it from time to time—as a reminder that keeps you on track when you need to remember goals and priorities.

SAO #3: What Are Your Goals?

Purpose: To begin the process of identifying those goals that are most important to you.

Step 1: Your mission. Write your personal mission statement (life purpose) in one sentence.

Step 2: Your goals. Keeping in mind that a goal is a specific end result, list your five most important goals. Include goals related to family, career, and personal development.

SAO #4: Refine Your Goals

Purpose: To help you weed out activities from goals, to make your goals as specific as needed, to identify all the goals that are important to you, and to prioritize them so you become clear about which are the most important to achieve.

Step 1: Distinguish between goals and activities. Look at the list of goals you made in SAO #3. How many are actually activities? Eliminate them.

Step 2: Redefine your goals to make them more specific. Select the following items that reflect your goals and fill in the blanks to make your goals specific. At this point, don't rank or evaluate their practicality or relative importance.

- To have $_____ in assets by _____.
  (date)

- To be_____ by _____.
  (job position)   (date)

- To have a relationship with_____ in which we
  (description of person)

  _____ by _____.
  (feel, believe, do...)   (date)

- To weigh _____ by_____.
  (pounds)   (date)

෨ To have a _____ by _____ .
    (degree or certificate)   (date)

෨ To retire with $_____ a month income (or equivalent) by _____.
                                                        (date)

෨ To have_____ days of free time per year by _____.
                                                    (date)

෨ To learn_____ by _____.
    (specific skills or knowledge)   (date)

෨ To travel to_____ in_____ for _____.
                         (date)   (length of time)

෨ To spend_____ hours a _____ in mutually satisfying
                    (days, week, month, year)

    activities with_____.
                (description of person[s])

෨ Other goals:

Step 3: Brainstorm. List other goals that don't fit into the preceding categories. Be as outrageous as you like. Use the enthusiastic, creative-child part of your personality to brainstorm. Send that critical, practical part of you *down the hall* till later. Make your goals as fantastic or as simple as you like. Anything goes!

Step 4: Evaluate and rank. After you've freely and wildly listed any goals you can think of, start asking which one of all your goals is the most important (include all goals in Steps 2 and 3). Put the number "1" in the space to the left of that goal. Continue the process for the second most important goal, the third, and so forth until all are ranked. Do you want to delete any goals? Can any outlandish ones be modified or combined to make them more realistic? Are they all specific?

Step 5: Categorize by Life Areas. What are the major life areas that are important to you? For most people they're career, personal development, and private life. Sometimes goals overlap, and that's great, but pick the category that's most relevant to the goal at this time. Having goals in all areas helps you to focus on your need to create a balanced life.

SAO #5: Add Power to Your Goals

Purpose: To help you increase the power and effectiveness of your goals.

Step 1: Visualize a Passion Pyramid

Imagine a Passion Pyramid that looks like the one shown here.

Step 2: Identify your passion factor.

Think about your life purpose and visualize being on that path. How passionate do you feel about being on this path? Would you describe your passion factor as "Hot-Hot,"

"No interest," or somewhere in between? From the list provided here, pick the number that best represents the passion you feel about your life purpose and your current path.

0 = Hot-Hot
9 = Hot
8 = Turned-On
7 = Excited
6 = Enthusiastic
5 = Interested
4 = Possibly Interested
3 = Lukewarm
2 = Little Interest
1 = Almost No Interest
0 = No Interest

Repeat the process for your top long-term goals and your top three short-term goals.

Find your passion factor for each of your major planned activities. Repeat the process for key activities on your current to-do list.

Do you need to make some changes in your life purpose, your path, your goals, or your activities? What changes can you make that will ramp up your passion factor?

Step 3: Visualize end results.

During a quiet time, relax deeply and imagine being *on purpose*, actually achieving your top-priority goal and living the end result of having that goal. Focus on what you are doing, having, and most of all *being;* that is, how you feel, how others feel, how relationships are affected. Note any conflicting feelings or thoughts that come up—thoughts about barriers to achieving the goal or about payoffs for not achieving it. Repeat for each goal.

Example: Need help making your vision more powerful? Try this technique: Imagine you are looking through a glass door. On the other side is a beautiful life, just the life you want. See the scenery, the people, your home, your life there. Become aware of where you're standing now, your life now with its events and with your beliefs. Grab the handle and open the door, but don't go in yet.

Notice how welcome you feel, the sounds and sights and breeze and scents. Look around and see everything you want—all the parts of your dream vision: family, career, friends, personal development. Now, look back at where you've been and around at where you are now. Then look in front of you, all around, at where you want to be. Know that all you need to do to get to this other side is to feel strongly the intention to do that.

Ask yourself, *Do I want this? Is this my intention?* If the answer is yes, then step forward and step in. Now you're in the land of possibilities, where goal visions come true. Trust that now you're standing in your life purpose, your intention, your commitment. How does it feel?

Step 4: Check the source of each goal.

Are you sure this is *your* goal? It is very important to establish this. If you are trying to achieve a goal because someone else thinks you should, you can never give it the full level of commitment, passion, and enthusiasm you give to goals that come from deep within you. The achievement of others' goals can never bring you the joy and fulfillment you deserve, and you will never reach the same level or quality of success as you will with your own goals. So analyze each important goal in this light. Have you chosen this goal because it's what you think someone else would admire (for example, a parent figure, spouse, influential friend, teacher)? Or is it truly what *you* want in your life?

Step 5: Apply the energy/emotional level test.

If you have difficulty ranking a goal—or if at any point in the goal-setting or goal-implementing process, you are pulled between two alternatives—try the following analysis. First, be sure you have developed an adequate foundation for making the decision, through self-analysis of your life purpose and deepest desires and through gathering the information you need. Then ask yourself the following questions:

- ✤ Do I feel energized when I think of a particular choice?
- ✤ Do I sense a drop in my energy level when I think of the choice?
- ✤ Which option has a special glow around it when I picture it? An emotional attraction?

Then ask yourself, *If the decision were based solely on emotion, which alternative would I choose?* You will probably experience the greatest success when you go for the alternative that energizes you and brings up positive feelings, such as a sense of freedom, well-being, growth/expansion, or enthusiasm.

Step 6. Ask, What else is possible?

Keep asking that question each time you set up a goal vision. Get at least three or four other possibilities beyond the goal vision before you stop. This process will help you to include all the elements you really want in your vision.

Think ahead to the point when you will have your goal vision—say a year from now. As your Future Self, look back over the past year in terms of the following questions:

- ✤ How was it for you?
- ✤ What did you achieve?
- ✤ How were people involved and what happened in relationships?
- ✤ What would you change?

Look at all the goals you achieved. Ask, *What would make my life easier? What would make it more magical and exciting? How can I link together all my goals in a more creative, magical way?* If you want to live every day with passion, take a look at your life purpose. Then design a project or set some goals that seem bigger than your life—a project or goals that you're not sure how to achieve.

Step 7: Turn old blocks into new cornerstones.

For each major goal, examine your current and past beliefs and attitudes, thoughts and feelings, decisions and choices. Are any of them likely to block your success in achieving the goal? What new beliefs and attitudes could you adopt that would support this goal? How can you change your thoughts so that you let go of nonproductive thoughts and focus on positive thoughts that enhance your chances of success? What old decisions—about yourself and others or your place and your roles—might be inappropriate now for what you want to achieve? What actions (based on your beliefs, attitudes, thoughts, feelings, and decisions about you and life) have you made in the past regarding goal achievement? What new action choices might be better? Now do this:

- List goal #1.
- List current beliefs, attitudes, and so on that conflict with achieving your goal.
- Identify new ones that would support it and list them.
- Repeat the process for each major goal.

SAO #6: What Activities Will Achieve Your Goals?

Purpose: To generate activities leading to achievement of your top goals in each life area.

Step 1: List Career Goal #1. Then list at least four activities that would lead to the achievement of Goal #1.

Step 2: List Career Goals #2 and #3 and their activities, as you did for Goal #1.

Step 3: Repeat the process for personal development and private life goals. After you have listed activities for *all* goals, rank the importance of the activities listed for each goal.

SAO #7: What Are Your Most Productive Career Activities?

Purpose: To help you identify your most productive career activities.

Part A. Ask Career Questions

By now you should have a specific type of job in mind as your key career goal. You should also be able to describe your ultimate career goal—the top position you're aiming for. To help you identify the activities most likely to help you reach that goal, look at the following questions. (Note: See John Wright's *The American Almanac of Jobs and Salaries* for some of your answers.)

- What type of company do you have in mind? Can you pinpoint a specific company?
- What type of degree, courses, or other training will you need?
- What specific skills and knowledge will be required? At what level of ability?
- What kinds of people could tell you more about the job, help teach you what you need to know, help you get your foot in the

door, help you gain favorable visibility within the company, and introduce you to people who can help?

- What jobs will you need to hold in order to prepare yourself for your *ultimate* career goal?

- What functions do you need to have experience with?

- How do these functions link up with each other? (For example, what are the links between production and sales, sales and marketing, etc.?)

- Can you get some actual job descriptions your target company has prepared for these jobs?

- Which staff positions would give you the best chance of moving into a line job?

- Which line jobs provide the basic experience you'll need?

- Once you have a career plan, who can give you the most helpful evaluation of its effectiveness?

- Is the plan workable in view of the other top priorities in your life?

Follow-up: Use your answers to help complete the remaining SAOs regarding goals.

Part B. Brainstorm with a Friend

Brainstorm with a partner about ways to achieve a particular goal. What types of activities might work? If your goal is to go to Paris, what do you need to get there? How can you get the time, the money, and any other resources you'll need? Next, work on your partner's goal.

Part C. Create Mutual Support with a Friend

Discuss a key goal with a friend. Tell her the specifics of the goal and the actions you plan to take. Verbalizing your commitment, as well as writing it down, tends to strengthen it. Your friend should also share one of her goals with you. Set regular dates to discuss what actions you actually took and how they worked out. Dream expert Gayle Delaney and I made this process work for us when we were each writing our first books. We agreed to phone each other every Friday to discuss our progress. I certainly wanted to be able to tell Gayle that I had moved along in my project. If Thursday arrived and I hadn't written all week, I was motivated to write something rather than admit on Friday that my project had been neglected. Gayle felt the same way about her progress.

Part D. Make Your Goals Visible

Find methods of keeping your goals up front, of staying focused, or making them real to you.

Pick three top goals. Write them on a business card, along with the target dates. Put the card where you will see it many times a day: tucked in your dresser or bathroom mirror, in the clear-plastic window of your wallet, on your desk calendar, or in another visible place.

Draw vivid symbols of your top goals, using colored pens or pencils if possible. Put them on a card and display them as discussed previously.

Showcase: Ashley's Life Purpose

Purpose: To give you an example of how the life purpose exercise is applied and to help illustrate the relationship among life purpose, goals, and activities.

After Ashley completed the self-awareness opportunities for identifying life purpose and setting goals and activities, her results looked like this. The elements of Ashley's life purpose look like goals and in a sense they are, but they are actually a long-term mission statement—or even a lifetime goal. Notice the ways in which her life purpose overlaps into all three life areas and leads to an integration of the three areas. You may not see this degree of integration in your life purpose at this point in time, but it's not unusual for the areas to become more integrated over time.

Ashley's Life Purpose: Leader/Manager/Teacher

Career area: To develop leadership and managerial expertise in the business world. To continually learn about the ways of this world and grow from these experiences.

Family/friends: To build loving relationships of many kinds—family, personal, professional.

Personal development: To continually learn about the philosophical and spiritual aspects of life—what life is all about.

Integration: To help others learn the types of things I've learned and am learning. To bring together my learning in the business, personal, and philosophical/spiritual areas of my life to enrich all areas.

Ashley's Top Three Goals in March, current year:

1. To complete my MBA degree by December.
2. To negotiate a promotion to sales manager, based on my MBA, by December.
3. To find and join or establish a women's personal growth group by June.

Ashley's Top Three Activities to complete this week:

1. To complete a report on workforce diversity for management class.
2. To contact 12 customers in order to meet sales goal for this quarter.
3. To attend an evening seminar on women's roles in creating community.

SAO #8: Draft an Action Plan.

Purpose: To prepare an action plan to help you focus on top-priority goals and activities for the coming month.

One-Month Action Plan

Step 1: From goal to-do list. List your top-priority career goal. Under it, in order of importance, list the major activities, with their target dates, that you plan to complete this month. Put the most important activity on your To-Do list for *today* and keep it on the list until you have accomplished it. If you haven't acted on this activity within seven days, go back and reevaluate your goal and activities.

Step 2. Repeat the process for career goals 2 and 3.

Step 3. Repeat the process for any top-priority personal development goals and private life goals that you want to include.

Longer-Term Action Plans

Step 1: List the top three career goals, with target dates, you plan to accomplish in one year.

Step 2: Repeat the process for your personal development and private life goals.

Step 3: Make longer-term plans, such as three-year, five-year, or 10-year plans—using the time frames that make the most sense for your life.

SAO #9: Do a Life-Purpose Follow-up.

Purpose: To revisit your life purpose from a different angle and apply it to an important goal.

Remember, Motivational Intelligence is about knowing and following your wants and desires. Ultimately, it's about achieving your purpose in life

Step 1: Look for additional clues to your purpose. Ask yourself these kinds of questions:

- What fulfills me?
- What thrills me?
- What is a passion for me?
- What lights me up?
- What am I willing to commit to?
- What would I love to be doing? To achieve?
- What would make me thrilled to get up in morning?

Listen to your inner self. Meditate for at least a few minutes every day (when you awaken or as you fall asleep, for example) with your life purpose or goals question in mind and listen for your future. Discover who you can become.

Step 2: Verbalize your answers. First to yourself, then to others. Put them in writing.

Step 3: Visualize a plan. Once you get in touch with what your life purpose seems to be (it's okay if you're not absolutely sure), ask, *How can I go about making my contribution? Achieving what will fulfill me?* Decide on a major project or achievement. In the following example, opening a new business is the end goal. What is your end goal? Close your eyes and visualize, using this process:

- Picture your Passion Pyramid.
- Picture your achievement at the top.
- See your goal: exactly how it looks, who's there. Sense how it feels.

- ↪ Visualize yourself in that place. It's done. Declare it. Know it.
- ↪ Give that a date.
- ↪ Now ask, *What did I do right before that?* In the example, *finding a location* is the activity. Name your activity and give it a date.
- ↪ Before that? In the example *getting financing* comes just before the end goal. Name yours and date it.

5. Open the business—date
4. Location—date
3. Financing—date
2. Business plan—date
 1. Research—date
NOW

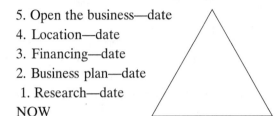

Work your way back down the pyramid to Now. In the example, the steps backward are *developing a business plan* and *researching the field*.

Now create a second pathway down the other side of the pyramid—as your Plan B, an alternate plan that provides options for you.

Step 4: Do it in writing. Now that you've visualized the achievement process, put it in writing. Draw the pyramid on a sheet of paper. Make each step a brief statement, a one-liner, or a picture—anything that's a powerful symbol and reminder for you. Hang the picture where you can see it every day. Consider making a separate picture of the step you're currently working on and placing it where you see it often. Focus primarily on the current step, with the overall plan in the background.

Step 5: Bring it to work. Bring your life purpose to work. If you're not passionate at work, ask yourself what traits or characteristics you can bring to your job that will allow you to express more passion there. Is there a part of your life purpose that you can bring into a work project or task?

Step 6: Make a Vision Board. Look for pictures in magazines and brochures that turn you on because they symbolize some aspect of your goal vision or life purpose. Cut them out, collect them for a while, and then create a collage on a poster board. Now you have a powerful visual image of the life you want to create. Keep it where you see it regularly. This helps to bring your ideas from the higher, finer energy levels into the denser physical energy level—to make them physically *real* to you.

Chapter 5

Direct Your Emotional Power

Think of crying as singing. You wouldn't want to keep a song
inside when you had an urge to sing.
Crying reminds us that we're moved by life's sorrows and
beauties and we're participating in them all fully.
Alexandra Stoddard, writer

Do you really feel your own feelings? Do you cry when you're sad, yell when you're mad, laugh when you're glad, hug when you feel affection? How about picking up on others' feelings? If you're a typical woman, you have a strong advantage in this area of intelligence. As you grew up, you were probably allowed to express most of your feelings. Lucky you.

Emotional Intelligence is your ability to understand and manage your own feelings—and to understand the feelings of people around you. It's emotional awareness, the ability to know which emotions you're feeling and why. It's realizing the links between what you feel and what you think, do, and say. Managing your emotions doesn't mean denying or suppressing *negative* feelings. That doesn't work anyway, because accepting What-Is in the Present is the key to accessing all your intelligences.

What does work is to assess your beliefs, which affect your attitudes, which affect your thoughts. You can begin to notice how one thought triggers another and how certain types of thinking invariably lead to certain kinds of feelings. You can learn to break up self-sabotaging thought trains by focusing on different, equally true thoughts. Thoughts trigger feelings. Change your thinking and you change the feelings you experience.

Terms to associate with Emotional Intelligence include:

influencing, being open, feelings, empathy, compassion, people skills, elation, anger, frustration, limbic-mammalian brain

The Mind-Body Nature of Emotions

Thinking, feeling, and knowing all take place throughout your body, in every organ and cell. Scientists now know that your heart has many brain cells that are in turn connected to your head brain. Candace Pert, an award-winning scientist, says, "White blood cells are bits of the brain floating around in the body. This means that knowing is a phenomenon that expands throughout the body. So is feeling."

Molecules of Emotion

Cellular knowing and feeling operate through an intricate chemical network of *peptides,* a network that integrates your mental, emotional, and biological activities. Peptides are the biochemical (physical) form of emotions. Most peptides, if not all, alter emotional states and behavior. Each peptide may evoke a unique emotional "tone" or vibration. The group of about 60 peptides may constitute a universal biochemical language of emotions. Throughout your body are cells with receptors in their membranes that allow these peptides to enter the cell.

The limbic system of your brain is highly enriched with peptides, but it's not the only part of the body where peptide receptors are concentrated. The entire intestine is lined with peptide receptors and may explain "gut feelings" (when you experience your emotions in your gut). All sensory perceptions, all thoughts, and all bodily functions involve peptides. The nodal points of the central nervous system, which connect the sensory organs with the brain, are rich in peptide receptors that filter and prioritize sensory perceptions. All your perceptions and thoughts are therefore colored by emotions.

Endorphins and other chemicals are found in the brain, immune system, endocrine system, and throughout the body. These molecules are released from one place, diffuse all over the body, and tickle the receptors on the surface of every cell in your body. These neuro-peptides, brain chemicals, and their receptors on your cell surfaces are the molecules of emotion. These brain chemicals can be described by locating their effect on a scale between quietness and excitement. It is a two-way communication system between various body systems.

If you're depressed and you refuse to shift to "I-can" thinking and other active, self-empowering thought patterns, you're depriving your brain and body of natural excitants. If you're continually frustrated and refuse to focus on thought patterns that calm you, you're depriving your body of the quiescent state that natural chemicals such as endorphins provide.

You don't need artificial mood-altering drugs when you know how to enter into emotional states, how to make use of them without harming yourself or others, and then how to shift out of them. You can become skilled in releasing the natural chemicals you need and want. Emotional Intelligence allows you to reclaim your power by experiencing all of your emotions in order to access your natural brain chemicals; to govern, protect, and exercise the organs of your body; and to receive emotional information for creating the life you want.

Creative Intelligence of the Heart Brain

Scientists are finding that when people use certain exercises for imagining their feelings within their hearts, they're able to break out of old emotional patterns faster and more directly than when they use traditional mind or brain imagery. The heart is a storehouse of emotional memories and energy patterns that make us who we are as individuals. In fact, the five small waves that make up your electrical heart signal create a unique energy pattern as personal as your fingerprint.

Research conducted by the Institute of HeartMath and reported in the *American Journal of Cardiology* indicates that your heart plays a large, independent role in drafting your emotional blueprints. Your heart's electrical signals shape the way your brain thinks about certain kinds of events, and your heart itself may be able to "remember" emotional experiences.

That's because your heart has its own brain: a network of neurons identical to many of the kinds of neurons and neural networks that your brain has. Your heart brain and head brain are connected by the "vagus nerve," which is made up of thousands of nerve fibers that continually flash messages between your heart and head brains. You don't think and remember only in your head. Memories are now seen as patterns of energy that groups of neurons can store in various parts of your body.

Creative Intelligence of the Heart

Your heart has a unique way of making its memories and ideas felt: It's your body's largest rhythmic generator, sending electromagnetic signals up to 5,000 times stronger than those from your head. That strong signal, combined with the surges of blood your heart sends throughout your circulatory system, can either harmonize or overpower and disrupt the weaker rhythms and currents sent by your brain and other organs. Your changing heart rhythms affect your brain's ability to process information, including:

- ❧ Problem-solving.
- ❧ Decision-making.
- ❧ Creativity.
- ❧ Feelings.

Your heart rhythm is the product of two types of hormones produced by your nervous system: adrenaline that revs you up and tranquilizers that relax you. Your heart also makes its own unique "balance hormone" that makes you feel serene and peaceful.

When your body and mind are relaxed, your heart beats in an easy, consistent (coherent) rhythm. Over time, those relaxed heart pulses entrain (that is, pull along after themselves) the weaker brain and body signals so they throb in sync with the heartbeat. *This is the flow state of creative intelligence.*

Stress (even positive stress excitement) disrupts the flow state. It causes the heart to beat in erratic rhythms, which in turn causes bioelectric incoherence. The heart beats fitfully, making synchronization among the body's organs and systems impossible. Prolonged incoherence leads to:

- ∾ Decreased brain functioning, including decreased creativity, empathy, and rational thought.
- ∾ Heart disease, impaired immunity, rapid aging, cancer, destruction of brain cells, and early death.

Unmanaged tension underlies up to 90 percent of all visits to doctor's offices. We adapt to unmanaged stress all too easily. It becomes a subconscious process, but we pay a price.

Stress-Damage Reversal

A powerful way to prevent or reverse this stress-damage process is to use Emotional Intelligence. Adopt beliefs, attitudes, decisions, and thought patterns that trigger the expansive inner-body emotions—especially the feelings of *forgiveness, appreciation, gratitude,* and *love.*

Prolonged and frequent experience of these love-based emotions reverses the stress-damage process and establishes bioelectrical coherence. The brain's electrical activity is brought into entrainment with heart rhythms. As you experience expansive feelings, the changed information flow from the heart to the brain can modify brain function.

A peaceful heart helps you think more clearly and creatively. When you focus on the images of love and appreciation in your heart center, you increase the likelihood that all kinds of body cells become synchronized around your heart's electrical signal. You gain power—creative, emotional, physical, and spiritual power. Heart-centered techniques can help you find within yourself new feelings of peace, empathy, and intuition that in turn result in greater personal creativity and productivity. See SAO #8: Heartfelt Stress Reduction (page 136).

Heart signals impact how you affect others and how they affect you. That's because your heart signal can entrain other persons' electrical brain patterns and alter their moods, making them more tranquil or tense. And their heart signals can have the same effect on you.

When you meet another person, who will have the most impact? That depends on which of you is the most aware and focused. If you're feeling *higher* than your friend, and you're also more focused than he is, he'll become more expansive during the meeting. On the other hand, if he's feeling *lower* than you, and he's also more focused than you are, then you'll begin to feel lower during the meeting. The impact may be fairly equal—where you're feeling a little more expansive than he, and the two of you have about the same degree of focus. When this happens, you leave the meeting feeling a little less *up,* and he leaves feeling a little less *down.*

Heart signals probably impact your Basic Intelligence as well. For example, when you take an instant dislike to someone, it's probably due at least in part to clashing heart rhythms. And love may be literally a matter of two hearts beating in harmony.

How to Spark Your Emotional Intelligence

The steps to Emotional Intelligence are simple but often difficult in practice. And practice is exactly what you need to boost this intelligence, which is so important for breaking through creative blocks and for opening up to intuitive messages about creative projects. Here's an overview of key aspects of building your Emotional Intelligence:

1. Recognize that emotions have a physiological basis within your brain and every cell of your body.

2. Give emotions equal status with rational thoughts, visual images, and intuition.

3. Move beyond gender stereotypes about women being "too emotional" and "real" men not being emotional.

4. Stop, slow down, feel your feelings. Do feeling meditations. Your feelings are states of consciousness. Learn to stay in your inner world without interference. Learning to feel is learning to travel in your inner world.

5. Process your emotions, especially those that you tend to avoid or suppress.

6. Feel and express your emotions when you want to, how you want to—realizing your many options for viewing events, thinking about them, and expressing your feelings about them.

Sparkler #1: Overcome Gender Stereotypes

Gender stereotypes can block both women and men from fully developing their Emotional Intelligence. The stereotypes center on beliefs that men are not, or should not, be very emotional and that women are more emotional and that that's okay as long as they don't try to become leaders of organizations.

Beliefs about raising boys and girls lead to some emotional problems for men. For example, girls typically get payoffs of sympathy or approval when they cry, show fear, express sadness or other tender feelings, show sympathy for others, and nurture others. Boys usually get disapproval or even punishment for such behavior. In our culture, little boys are trained to be "real" men from an early age through such messages as:

- Big boys don't cry.
- Big boys are brave and strong.
- Keep a stiff upper lip.
- Don't be a chicken.

Little boys are usually reprimanded or belittled when they cry, show sadness, or express fear. The result is that when little boys become men, they often repress and deny most of their emotions and eventually become numb to them. But most boys usually receive approval, admiration, or at least acceptance when they express dominance and anger in actions ranging from assertion to aggression. Such *masculine* expressions of emotion by girls, however, usually meet with disapproval or rejection.

Recognize Male-Female Emotional Patterns

These different socialization patterns set the stage for adult behavior. As they've grown up, most women have stayed in touch with their feelings and have developed the ability to express their emotions. However, they tend to be significantly less assertive than men. In contrast, most men have a healthy dose of assertiveness; some have an unhealthy dose of aggressiveness. But most men, in general, are significantly less aware of their feelings. They're therefore less able to verbalize them and act on them.

In the male-dominated business world, therefore, it is generally acceptable to express anger or aggression within certain limits. However, a display of tears or fear signals you can't handle the game; that is, you can't handle real responsibility on the line where key decisions are made and where the real power is wielded. It's especially important to manage fear because some political game players can sniff out the nonverbal signs of fear like bloodhounds, and they'll quickly move in for the kill if it suits their purposes. Others will simply assume that you're too weak to handle a leadership role. Obviously, women are at a real disadvantage here. They can be blocked professionally by these types of stereotypes:

- ᔕ Women are too emotional to be leaders; they go to pieces in a crisis. (This stereotype overlooks the fact that nearly all mothers get their children through the numerous crises growing up entails without "going to pieces.")
- ᔕ You can't afford to put someone in top management who might burst into tears in the crunch.
- ᔕ Women are just too flighty to handle a high-level leadership role.
- ᔕ Women don't roll with the punches like men do.
- ᔕ A man can keep problems in perspective better than a woman.

Manage the Differences

As a matter of fact, women *do* report being in positive moods and in negative moods about twice as often as men, according to author Ed Diener's 1991 research, which would indicate that women experience feelings more intensely. However, it does not follow that women are helpless victims of their feelings or must somehow act out all their feelings. Nor does it follow that men cannot begin to get in touch with the full range of their feelings and experience them more intensely. Remember: Infant boys actually exhibit more emotion than infant girls do.

Openness to feelings is essential to openness to intuitive information. Therefore, women are known to be more emotional and more intuitive than men, on average. Both of these states are normally governed by the right-brain, while rational thought and action are governed by the left-brain. Language, or verbal ability, is a rational, left-brain activity in which women excel, however. Women are obviously not lacking in left-brain abilities, but because their traditional roles centered on nurturing others, they focused almost exclusively on the language area, neglecting the strategic, tactical, mechanical, and mathematical areas.

In recent decades, careers using both right-brain and left-brain abilities have opened up to women. Many women have acquired the business and professional skills to move into these fields—and many have excelled in them.

Integrate Emotional and Rational Intelligences

Emotionally intelligent people on average appear to experience deeper, richer, and more expressive emotional lives, according to author Daniel Goleman's research. The traits of playfulness, sensuality, and spontaneity correlate with higher intuitive ability. In addition, it's significantly easier to develop rational abilities and intellectual intelligence than to develop Emotional Intelligence and intuition. To live up to your potential, honor and respect all your abilities—especially your Emotional Intelligence. Learn to express it appropriately in business and professional settings. Help others to understand and respect this type of intelligence.

Sparkler #2: Recognize Egomind Vs. Energy-Body Emotions

A powerful concept that can help you manage your emotions is the classification of emotions into two basic types:

1. Egomind emotions have an undercurrent of fear. They drain energy from your creative power, contracting it.
2. Inner-body emotions come from deeper and higher levels. They have an undercurrent of compassionate love. They're expansive and charge up your creative power.

We all intuitively understand the terms "contracting" and "expanding," because we experience them daily in our emotional life. Our language reinforces this concept with such contracting terms as *uptight, little black cloud, don't be so heavy, play the heavy,* and *got the blues,* and such expansive terms as *sunny, walking on air, being on Cloud 9,* and *lighten up.*

Your feelings continually expand or contract your heart. Are you able to feel your emotions, allow the expansive ones, and guide them in a continuous process through the inevitable contractions on to the expansions? You cannot stay in any one state all the time. What goes up must come down—and vice versa. But you can learn to ride the waves and avoid being stuck or drowned. Live the contracting emotional energies as well as the expansive ones, and learn that they can inform and enrich your life. Many typical feelings are categorized in Snapshot #1: Map of Emotions. This map is designed to help you identify your own feelings and to get a sense of how they range from mildly unpleasant to deeply painful, as well as from mildly pleasant to wildly euphoric.

Identify Your Egomind Feelings

Think about the feelings you associate with the stress in your life. Which emotions come to mind? Many people mention anger, embarrassment, resentment, frustration—feelings listed as contracting emotions in Snapshot #1. When you experience these stressful emotions, how do you respond? Do you focus within on stressful thoughts (the type that preceded the stressful emotion?). Do you clam up, close up, or even withdraw? These feelings are low-energy states that act as energy drains and cause people to avoid you—or to be attracted to you for the wrong reasons.

The Map of Emotions on page 114 shows the milder forms of egomind emotions at the top of each column, moving toward generally more intense feelings at the bottom. Key bottom-line egomind emotions are highlighted at the bottom of each column. The underlying, bottom-line emotion is fear, the realm of your negative ego. But how can fear be related to anger or rage? You'll work with such questions later as you bring root fears out of the shadows. For now, consider the research finding that anger, and in fact all the

Snapshot #1 Map of Emotions

	compassion	passion	wonder	LOVE
Inner-Body Emotions ↑	forgiveness	enthusiasm	awe	joy
	empathy	excitement	bliss	ecstasy
	commitment	eagerness	beauty	happiness
	devotion	desire	gratitude	enjoyment
	affection	optimism	imagination	peace
	caring	mindfulness	curiosity	serenity
	appreciation	openness	mirth, fun	certainty
	respect	honesty	playfulness	hope
	acceptance	sincerity	interest	calmness
	admiration	determination	amusement	satisfaction
	infatuation	perseverance	innocence	solitude
	tolerance	yearning	surprise	comfort
	connection	nostalgia	thoughtfulness	relief
	self-acceptance	self-confidence	self-awareness	self-love
Ego-Mind Emotions ↓	annoyance	ego-pride	somberness	distraction
	impatience	judgment	envy	mischievousness
	blame	dislike	jealousy	confusion
	resentment	pity (other)	hatred	caution
	frustration	disgust	hurt	vulnerability
	hostility	contempt	withdrawal	embarrassment
	stubbornness	revulsion	shock	shyness
	anger	condemnation	loss	self-pity
	rage	arrogance	despair	suffering
	hatred	defensiveness	humiliation	remorse
	powerlessness	doubt	paranoia	victim
	bitterness	worry	hopelessness	dread
	regret	anxiety	apathy	desperation
	sadness	resignation	victim, martyr	hysteria
	guilt	exhaustion	rejection	terror
	shame	**depression**	**loneliness**	**FEAR**

egomind emotions, involves some type of fear—fear of losing something you value or fear of not getting something you want.

Your tendency will probably be to judge the egomind emotions as bad or negative and the expansive ones as good or positive. Avoid that tendency, simply because it leads to denying your egomind emotions. Clearly, you normally enjoy the expansive emotions the most—and they are the typical creativity triggers—but you get valuable information from the entire range of emotions. That's how you learn and become more intelligent. And obviously, you sometimes need to experience fear, anger, and similar emotions in order to avoid disaster. Likewise, when you've suffered a significant loss, you need to feel the pain and sadness that goes with that. You need to go through a normal grief process. The more open you are to experiencing the egomind emotions that want to come up, the more quickly you'll be able to move fully into them, through them, and out the other side.

Once you become aware of egomind feelings, you're in a position to process them, so you can use that emotional energy to achieve what you want to create in your life. You may get some ideas for identifying or labeling your feelings by studying the Map of Emotions. Your goals are:

- ☙ To process egomind, low-energy, stressful feelings before they settle in and build into a mood.
- ☙ To process the feelings a mood contains if it does gain hold.
- ☙ To allow yourself to spend as much time as possible in the self-empowering, high-energy *expansive* feelings.

Some people say they fear evil, which is difficult to deal with because it's such a vague, nebulous force. Evil is a lack of respect for others and the acting-out of that disrespect. The more blatant the lack of respect, the greater the evil. It's always connected to a lack of self-respect. Let's make it personal: Wherever you harbor a pocket of self-hate, you'll express it as hatred for others. Self-hate is basically a lack of self-respect and is often expressed as lack of respect for others, who serve as a sort of scapegoat for you. Despising them makes you feel better, superior. This is Negative Ego in action. The cure is to root out your pockets of self-hate so you can build respect for yourself as a human being. The process helps you to feel empathy and compassion for others in the place of dislike or disgust or hatred. The process can lead to feelings of acceptance and ultimately unconditional love.

When you don't process egomind emotions, they don't go away. Instead, they build up within your mind and body. If you hide them away securely enough, they'll stay hidden until they express themselves as illness. If you're lucky, they'll first express themselves as an outburst or a mood. As you know, moods can last hours, days, or even years. You walk around with your little dark cloud hovering over you and all around you. Your cloud may take the form of self-pity, guilt, blame, resentment, anxiety, or some other dominant egomind emotion. How can this be lucky? If you become aware of your mood, you have the choice of getting at the root emotions and processing them before illness sets in.

Pain does teach. The energies of fear and separation and powerlessness do teach, for your intelligences use everything in the service of learning. But joy and abundance also teach. You have free will to choose how to grow.

Identify Your Inner-Body Feelings

In the Map of Emotions, the expansive emotions at the bottom of each column represent the beginning stages of personal expansion and usually begin with some type of self-love. They move upward toward the more intensely expansive feelings, with the key expansive emotions highlighted at the top of each column. The root emotion here is love, the realm of your intuitive connection to the Web of Life.

What happens when you process and release those egomind emotions and moods you experience? You free yourself to move into one or more of the *expansive feelings*. Think about what happens when you feel curiosity, excitement, admiration, empathy, love, happiness, or joy—any of the expansive emotions identified in the Map of Emotions. For all of us these emotions are an *up*, a *high*, and lead to reaching out to others, sharing and interacting with others in an upbeat way. They're high-energy states that act as energy boosts and therefore attract people to you—for the right reasons.

Expansive emotions feel light and airy, causing you to reach up and out toward life and toward other people. You experience a lot of space within the expansive emotions and therefore more possibilities. You're more willing to take chances, to do something new and challenging because you're focusing on the bright side of people and situations.

Consider "I Can-I Can't" Viewpoints: Power Vs. Blockage

When you don't get what you want, do you focus on the "I can't?" Do you react *passively*, from a sense of powerlessness, leading to sadness or boredom? Or do you respond *aggressively*, leading to feelings of frustration, resentment, and anger? In general, women in our culture feel more permission to feel sad—or most any other emotion except anger.

On the other hand, men have permission to feel anger—and not much else. Many men give themselves permission to feel only anger. They've therefore learned to channel *all* their feelings into the feeling of anger. Frustration, resentment, and anger can easily go into the extreme of hatred, which is a combined mental-emotional state, or into violence, which is a physical-emotional state.

When you can focus on the "I can" aspect of a situation, even when you don't get what you want, you tend to move through the sadness or anger more quickly. You can move on to thoughts that allow you to feel good or excited about life. When that happens, peptides fill your cell receptors, allowing little chance for viruses to enter the cells. When you focus on "I can," you take back your power. Here's a self-empowering goal: to live most of the time in the expansive, love-of-life side of the emotional map *and* to learn what to do when you fall into the egomind emotions.

Sparkler #3: Feel Your Feelings

Many people, especially men, have learned to control their feelings by suppressing them and pretending they don't exist. This practice creates a number of negative side-effects. Here's an overview of how you can process your feelings in a healthy way.

All feelings have a purpose.

Be willing to feel the whole range of feelings. That's what makes you a complete human being. Take emotions out of the either-or framework of negative and positive. Frame them as notes on a scale—with tonality, depth, volume, intensity, counterpoint, atonality, dissonance, and resonance. Which emotions feel thicker, slower, lower? Which are thinner, faster, higher? You can begin to recognize when you need to calm yourself and when you need to increase your excitement level.

Suppressed feelings don't go away.

They tend to build up inside until they reach the *explosive stage*. You tend to forget the incident that triggered the feeling and the fact that you suppressed the feeling. Therefore, your outbursts of anger, self-pity, fear, and so forth come as a surprise to you, and they're out of your control.

Suppressed feelings can cause illness.

Feelings that simmer and fester within you continue to create stress long after the stressful situation has passed. You then become vulnerable to stress-related illnesses, especially ulcers, high blood pressure, heart disease, cancer, migraine headaches, allergies, and asthma.

Suppressed feelings block personal growth.

If you deny your feelings as a way of coping with life, you'll become more and more out of touch with yourself—how you really feel about things, the way you really are, the true effects of people and events on your life, all the facets of the ways you really respond to those people and events.

Such denial will inhibit your personal growth and development as a creative, autonomous person. It will numb you so you can't feel your heart's desire. As a result, you'll find it more and more difficult to be clear about your values (and therefore your goals) and to evaluate situations and opportunities in light of those goals. This leads to such problems as tunnel vision, workaholism, and burnout. Therefore, you want to be able to feel your feelings.

When you're in touch with your emotions—when you're able to feel your fear, anger, and sadness as well as your excitement, compassion, and joy—you have a major advantage. For one thing, in order to process an emotion, you must be aware of it and able to feel it. For another, in order to empathize with another person's emotional state, you must be able to feel what they're feeling. People who repress and deny their feelings over the years become numb and have difficulty feeling anything, including what others are feeling.

Feelings can be a career plus.

Emotional Intelligence boosts your creativity and gives you a leading edge in the workplace. Business cultures traditionally haven't allowed much space to acknowledge emotions. Most business cultures don't embrace the belief that experiencing and expressing emotions can be beneficial. Nor do they have the tools or methods to access and acknowledge emotional expression. Yet emotions are always with us, always in play. So the business leader who knows how to help individuals and teams channel their emotional power has an obvious edge. The first step in gaining Emotional Intelligence is to become aware of the key stressors in your life and the feelings those stressors trigger within you. SAO #1: What Feelings Do Your Stressors Trigger? (page 132) will get you started.

Sparkler #4: Process Egomind Feelings

Dealing with stressful, painful emotions takes courage. But the investment pays off in mental health and powerful personal growth. Author Greg Braden said it well: "You always have the ability to see beyond the pain, into what the pain is saying to you. Your life is a gift through which you may come to see yourself from many viewpoints, and know yourself as all possibilities." Here's a basic overview of how to process emotions so that you can fully experience them and release them. In the sections that follow, you'll see how to work with emotions that are especially problematic, such as surface emotions that cover up deeper feelings, emotions that cluster and hang around as moods, and persistent anger.

Step 1: Identify the specific feeling.

Become aware of the emotion you're experiencing. Label the feeling as specifically as possible. Be sure you use a word that indicates something you *feel* and not merely a rational thought or character trait. For example, use *self-confident* or *certain* rather than *ready to make a move* or *decisive*.

Step 2: Locate the emotion in your body.

If it's an emotion, locate it in your body by identifying where you feel some tension, some tightness, some pain, some upset, something different, or something that doesn't feel normal.

Step 3: Get at root emotions.

Ask, *Why do I feel (anger, sadness, etc.). So what? What difference does that make? Why do I care about that? So what will happen if* . . . . Keep asking these kinds of questions until you feel a shift, a sense that you've reached the bottom line, the root emotion that's stressful for you. (More about this step later. If you're processing an emotion now, you may want to skip to the section on root emotions, then return to Step 4.)

Step 4: Fully experience all emotions that come up.

Allow the feeling to be there in your body; fully experience it being there. Be willing to feel the emotion with intensity. Be in the present moment with it, paying attention, with intent to fully feel it, fully believing that you can move on out of the emotion when it's processed. The crucial attitude is your willingness to feel the feeling, to let it get more intense if it needs to, to move deeper into another emotion, into a root emotion—or to get less intense. Be willing for it to change locations in your body—or to move anywhere on the emotional map that it wants to go. In order to get at root emotions and then to release them, you may need to use some SAOs, such as SAO #4: Worst-Case Scenario (page 133) and SAO #5: Put It in Perspective (page 134).

Step 5: Heal the emotion and the negative belief.

By using some simple acupressure techniques, along with some ways of thinking about your situation, you can actually heal the pain and damage of egomind emotions. And you do it at an energy-body level, which is much more powerful and lasting than working only at the physical-body level. For a very simple and powerful technique, see the Tapas Acupressure Technique (TAT), as described in SAO #7: Heal Painful Emotions and Beliefs (page 135).

Step 6: Release the emotion.

If you're willing to feel the emotion, and any related emotions that want to surface, you will eventually be able to release the feeling or allow it to be lifted. Let it go.

You may have trouble letting go of certain emotions. Some people say that in those sticky cases, it helps if they picture themselves surrendering to the flow of the universe and ask the universe to lift the emotion. Others say they call on their Higher Self to lift the emotion. Look to your belief system and find the greater power that can help you. The important aspect is to realize that you don't have to lift the emotion all by yourself. All you have to do is be *willing* for it to be lifted. Are you willing for it to be lifted? Can you believe you can get back to neutral?

Step 7: Review your options.

You have many options about how to view a situation or to think about it. You also have many options about what actions to take when you experience an emotional response to a situation. Here are some examples of various ways to view situations, followed by some options for expressing the emotions that come up in a situation.

Anger

Your boss is angry. If you can see the threatened little boy thrashing around behind his angry outburst, you feel more empathy than anxiety. Your empathic response is more likely to meet the needs of the *little boy's* anxiety underneath his anger. You're more likely to see a number of options for responding to the event.

Judgment

A friend betrays a confidence. What options do you have for perceiving this event, what ways of thinking about it? What will you say to yourself? Here are a few options you can try—to see what effect they have:

- She's not a true friend, she doesn't really care about me, and I'm devastated.
- Just wait. I won't get mad—I'll get even.
- She was feeling needy when she did that.
- She probably meant well
- It's about her problems. It's not about me personally.
- I can handle this.
- This won't really matter to me in the long run.

Envy

You feel a stab of envy upon learning that a coworker got a promotion to a job you'd love to have. Your knee-jerk reaction is to put her down and accuse the boss of being unfair. Ask yourself, *Are these envious thoughts working as a barrier to my creativity and achievement? Are they draining my energy away, giving it to this situation? Are they setting up an "I-Can't" dynamic? Do they reflect a fear that I'm not good enough? That I couldn't really get that kind of job—ever?* You can choose from a wide array of options for viewing the situation, for example:

- What's it like to be in her place? How does she feel?
- What did she do to qualify for that promotion? What are the steps?

- ✎ I admire her ability to get that promotion.
- ✎ That promotion is worth putting time and energy into.
- ✎ What can I do to get that type of job?

These types of thoughts can serve as a remedy for envious thoughts because they lead to an "I-Can" dynamic. Notice that these thoughts trigger empathy and admiration. Here you are mentally identifying with success instead of rejecting it.

Thinking triggers emotions. Think about a recent situation that triggered an upsetting emotion for you. What other ways could you have chosen to perceive the situation? What emotions might have come up in each of these ways? As you practice different ways of thinking about an event, you'll notice that very different types of thinking patterns lead to very different emotions. By choosing a specific thinking pattern, you can choose a different emotional response.

Options for Expressing Emotions

You also have many options about what to do in response to a situation and in response to your emotions. In the situation just mentioned, what are some actions you could have taken? What would be the likely outcome of each type of action? (More about options later in this chapter, including acting-out options.)

A major advantage of processing your egomind emotions as they occur is that you can avoid denying the emotion and getting stuck in "bad moods." Another power is that you can process your emotions internally. You don't *need* to share the process, though it usually helps to share your feelings with a trusted confidante. Processing is very active, but you can do it within. Doing so will allow you to build and maintain a professional image and make better business decisions. Keep in mind these two tips:

- ✎ Process egomind emotions *before* you make a business decision or take action.
- ✎ Try to make decisions and take action when you're experiencing expansive emotions.

Sparkler #5: Bring Root Fears Out of the Shadows

Some emotions play around near the surface of your consciousness, while others are rooted much deeper in your being and even at levels below consciousness. Processing an emotion, such as anger, can help you to become aware of deeper-level emotions. When you get in touch with root fears, bring them out of the shadowy subconscious into the light of conscious awareness, examine them, and fully experience them, then you are more likely to be able to release them. When you move into and through all the emotions brought up by an event and then release them, you move into a lighter space, a space rooted in love-goodwill. Root fears typically express themselves in all-too-common life problems, as shown in Snapshot #2.

You can begin the process of bringing root fears out of the closet by asking yourself such questions as:

- ✎ *Why am I angry?*
- ✎ *What am I afraid of?*
- ✎ *What do I fear will happen?*

Snapshot #2 Typical Root Fears

Root Fears: ⟶	How these fears express:
Not being good enough ⟶	**Self-worth issues**
Not lovable enough	Can't reach expectations for relationships
Not capable enough	Can't fully receive
Not deserving	
Abandonment ⟶	**Driving away relationships**
Rejection	"I'll leave before I get hurt."
Separation	"I'm always being left in relationships."
Loneliness	
Fear of living fully ⟶	**Inability to love or to express love**
Fear of surrendering to the flow of life	Need to control people and situations
Not trusting the process of life—based on fear of rejection and abandonment	

When you get some answers, you then may need to ask:

- *What difference will that make?*
- *Why do I care about that?*
- *So, what would happen then?*

The answers may be similar to these:

- *I won't get enough attention.*
- *I won't have any power.*
- *People will think....*

Underneath your anger or sadness or anxiety, you'll probably find you're concerned about not getting something you want or losing something you have. As Snapshot #2 indicates, you'll probably uncover a root fear that says one or more of the following:

- I don't really deserve....
- They'll think I'm not good enough.
- They'll find out I'm not really good enough.
- I'm not lovable or likable enough.
- I'm not capable enough.

As you continue the process of asking why, you may come to the next root fear:

> *I'll be rejected, abandoned, separated, and alone.*

This is the fear that you'll be without those human connections so crucial to your well-being. It's the bottom-line fear. You may then say to yourself, *Okay, so I don't want to feel rejected and lonely. Then why don't I reach out to others and connect?* This question may bring you to another root fear: the fear of living fully, of surrendering to the flow of life, of trusting yourself and the universe. It's rooted in the bottom-line fear that if you trust, reach out, live fully, you'll be rejected—either now or later when you become deeply attached—and you'll be abandoned.

The way these root fears express themselves in your life is truly ironic, for when you're holding them, they seem to attract to you the very results you most fear. When you harbor the fear that you're not good enough, people often can't see who you really are, so it's hard to create authentic relationships. And it's very difficult for you to fully receive from others when you harbor the feeling that you don't deserve, which in turn blocks productive or loving relationships.

When you're caught in the root fear of rejection and abandonment, you tend to drive away those who could have mutually supportive relationships with you, so you create being bypassed or left in relationships. You may drive people away by being needy and controlling because you fear losing the relationship—choking the relationship by holding on too tight. You may drive people away because you express your fear as defensiveness, often interpreting people's actions as slighting you. You may drive people away because you're afraid of giving more than you might get. This often results in the decision, *I'll drop him before he drops me.*

When you're caught up in such fears, and when people reach out to you in loving ways, you can't fully receive because you feel you don't deserve or you doubt their sincerity. When you fear giving yourself to the process of living life fully, you can't trust life, so you need to control people and situations. It's very difficult to fully feel and express love and goodwill when you're caught up in control issues.

The reason we call these emotions the contracting emotions is that when we experience them, we also experience a withdrawal from others—back into ourselves. This intensifies the feeling of isolation and separation—the most stressful of feelings. In contrast, when we process and let go of these feelings, we're able to reach out, to move outside our shell, to trust, and to expand. We rise up into the more expansive emotional realms.

Let Egomind Feelings Be a Learning Tool

You'll no doubt continue to create situations that bring up stressful emotions from time to time. We do this to learn more about ourselves and others—to test relationships, to test our own limits and capacities, and to continue our personal growth and development in general.

Most of us don't go around consciously creating stressful situations for ourselves, but stress still happens. It happens even to those who have made great strides toward becoming self-aware, taking responsibility, developing satisfying relationships, and creating their own success. The point: Don't become discouraged if you're not always able to create "the perfect life" or to always feel high. That higher part of you knows the lessons you need to learn and the path of growth you need to follow.

The key to creating the life you want is to understand your emotional life and to take conscious control of it by dealing constructively with all your feelings as they come up—and remembering that often your growth path is unclear and you must feel your way through to learn those lessons you need to master.

Follow the Anger Trail

Anger can alert you to problem situations and relationships that need attention and to what's really going on within you. This awareness can empower you to deal with the conflict underlying the anger, to build better relationships, and to learn more about yourself.

Dealing with Conflict

Anger's specific value in dealing with conflict includes:

- Helping you to identify hidden problems that can then be dealt with and resolved to strengthen a relationship.
- Getting the other person's attention and motivating him or her to deal with the conflict.
- Transforming internal anxiety or frustration into external conflict, moving you to action, and increasing your sense of power to influence situations.
- Building your confidence in speaking out and challenging others.
- Releasing frustration.

Building Relationships

Anger's specific value in building cooperative relationships includes:

- Signaling the value you place on another person—and perhaps your dependence or interdependence.
- Deepening your awareness and knowledge of others in your life and, as a result, learning more about their values and commitments.
- Allowing you to signal that you want to work out problems and improve the relationship, including how you work together to get things done.

Learning About Yourself

Anger's specific value in helping you to learn more about yourself includes:

- Motivating you to analyze the source of your anger and, as a result, learning more about yourself, your values, and your commitments.
- Motivating you to take vigorous action to deal with problems, achieve your goals, and build your skills.

When you don't express anger, others are often not clear if the problems are important to you and therefore whether they merit attention. They may not understand the depth of your concern.

Sparkler #6: Decide How to Express Feelings: Choices, Choices

You've figured out by now that you can't directly control your emotions and that trying to do so leads to denying and repressing them. What you *can* control are the choices you make for how to think about people and situations and how to act in response to them. You can control your choice to process those egomind emotions that do occur. When you process your emotions, you take conscious control of your emotional state. Sometimes emotions feel like a wild horse with you as their rider. You're tossed around, jerked about, powerless and helpless, at the mercy of the horse. Learning to process emotions is like learning to ride the horse, going with its movements but being in charge of the situation.

Other emotions feel like a whirlpool sucking you in, pulling you down. When you begin processing the emotions, you can quit fighting, take charge, go down to the depths where the whirlpool ends, and then move to one side with a powerful, releasing kick so that you can rise up to calmer waters. After you process an emotion, you feel more freedom to review all the options and choices you have for viewing situations and acting on them.

Intelligences Option

If feelings overpower you on the job, remember that you always have the choice of temporarily shifting out of that emotion by using your other intelligences. You can shift to other realities that involve thinking, imagining, sensing, or doing, which will move you out of emotional trauma for a time. For example, the sensory appeal of beautiful art or music is powerful. Shifting your attention to something beautiful to look at or listen to may be the fastest way to change your mood. You can always come back to the emotional experience and process it. You can access each of the three brain systems in a way that's fairly independent of the others, although the three usually work in tandem. To feel is a choice, a freedom, a decision to enter the range of feelings, as clearly as when you choose to watch a film or take a walk.

At times we all revert to old victim thought patterns—I-Can't thoughts that blame others or fate and drain our power. Even when you backslide into I-Can't thinking and egomind emotions flood in, you still have options for expressing and processing the feelings. You can choose what you say to yourself, what you learn from the experience, whether you interpret the event as a personal attack, how you interpret someone's criticism of you, and how you express egomind emotions.

Thought Options: There Are Many Ways I Can Think About This

Feelings become toxic only when you step out of your power and allow yourself to become victimized by them. You can take your power back by recognizing the many options you have for choosing a belief, attitude, worldview, or thought that starts a positive thought train. Learn which thoughts start a chain of thoughts that takes you into an inner-body emotion (from neutral to joy) rather than an egomind emotion (from irritation to terror). You have the power to choose how you want to perceive a crisis, an insult, or any other event and therefore what emotions may come up as a result of your perception.

Your perceptions are formed by your thoughts, or more specifically a thought that logically leads to another thought that in turn logically leads to another—and on and on. We can call this a *thought train*. For example:

- Your roommate growls at you as you enter the kitchen.
- You think, *Oh, no, she's in a bad mood this morning and she's going to take it out on me.*

❧ Then you think, *She's done this several times lately.*

❧ Next you think, *I'm getting sick and tired of her moods and being dumped on.*

What kind of feelings does this thought train arouse? What type of action does it lead to?

On the other hand, you can choose to think:

❧ *She's having a difficult morning.*

❧ Then you can think, *It has nothing to do with me.*

❧ Next, you're likely to think, *I'm having a good morning.*

❧ This may lead to the thought, *Maybe I'll have a positive effect on her, but she's free to feel any way she wants to feel.*

Compare the feelings that this thought train arouses—and the likely actions—with the previous thought train.

When you take charge of the situation, you have available to you the emotional energy you're holding within your body. You can let this *stuck energy* start flowing. You can use it to fuel expansive thought trains. Pay attention to your thought trains. Notice that when you hop onto a thought about what you are *for*, the bright side of the picture, the good that's there, and what you want to create in the situation, you board a thought train that can take you up through the expansive emotions. You can even go to the *top of the world,* emotionally speaking, to the heights of awe, wonder, passion, goodwill, love.

In contrast, when you hop onto a thought about what you are against, what's wrong, how awful someone is, or what you fear will happen, the thought train takes you down into the egomind emotions, even *down to the dumps.* Instead of focusing on what you're against or don't like, you can shift to the reverse: what you're *for,* what you do like and want.

If a stressful emotion keeps coming up, by all means process it. After that, remember that you can become aware of fear-based thoughts moment by moment and break your old egomind thought train patterns. Try this: As you inhale, pretend you're breathing in love/goodwill through your heart. As you exhale, breathe out blame, judgment, anger, and all the egomind emotions. Picture yourself emptying out the old and filling up with love/goodwill. Next, allow an appreciative or loving thought. Feel your energy expand as you hop onto an expansive thought train. If you make this process a habit, you'll find more and more upbeat people attracted to you. Positive energy attracts creative, supportive people like magic! Negative energy repels or, at best, attracts manipulators.

Of course, even when you get on a thought train that takes you to an egomind, stressful emotion, you still have many options about what actions to take. For example, even if you feel irritated or impatient with your roommate's mood, you can choose to fully experience those feelings without saying or doing things that are likely to antagonize her.

Crisis Options: Stay Poised in a Crisis

How do you deal with a crisis? Are you afraid you might fall apart? Be aware that you have many options for responding. Here's an effective process for mastering yourself in a crisis:

    ☞   Take a few very deep breaths.

    ☞   Experience the automatic slowing down of your physical processes and your egomind chatter.

    ☞   Have the intention of becoming grounded and centered.

    ☞   Go into slow motion, as if you were in a slow-motion movie.

    ☞   See yourself in charge of the situation.

    ☞   Move very deliberately.

    ☞   Take action to handle the crisis, one step at a time.

    ☞   If frantic or harried egomind thoughts come in, repeat the deep breathing.

You can use one or more of the relaxation techniques discussed earlier in this book. The simplest technique is simply to pause and take a few deep breaths. Don't say, *I must relax.* Instead, start breathing deeply. In fact, avoid telling yourself that you *should, must,* or *need* to do anything. Simply have the intention to follow these strategies.

Become very aware of the present moment. Have the intention of feeling centered and grounded in your body and very present mentally. All this helps you to rise above any chaotic egomind chatter. Feel your breathing slow down and your entire body slow down, including your chaotic thinking process. You must slow down enough to end the paralysis or the frantic rush to action—so you can take the necessary steps, one step at a time, to deal with the crisis.

Power Options: Use Self-Talk That Empowers

He made me so mad.... It made me so sad. When you talk this way, you tell yourself that you have no choices about how to view an event. You step out of your power and so give away your power to the person or situation who *made you mad.* This leaves a power vacuum that others who want power over people can sense from a mile away. You first become a victim in your own mind (*He made me mad*). Then you become a victim in someone else's mind, someone who thinks, *I can get this person to do what I want.*

Does a little self-talk really have that kind of power-draining impact? Yes. Everything you say to yourself programs the subconscious part of your mind about how the world is and how you should respond. If you've said *he made me mad* hundreds or thousands of times during your lifetime, you've programmed your subconscious to respond as if you're a victim. To change the program, stop yourself in mid-sentence or mid-thought and correct yourself: *I chose to see him as a threat and became angry* or *I thought he was belittling me, which triggered my anger.* Choose your own words, but be sure they reflect your power to choose.

Sometimes thoughts seem obsessive. When certain thoughts just won't go away, let them run their course, much as you process your emotions by letting them run their course. Don't beat yourself up because you've hopped onto a thought train to the dumps. It takes time to change old thought patterns, and growth is always two steps forward and one step back. The step back usually provides the momentum to take the next two steps forward.

Review Options: Look for Lessons and Growth Opportunities

As you grow in your ability to choose thinking or self-talk that results in expansive emotions, you'll sometimes slip into old thought patterns and take yourself straight into an egomind emotion. All is not lost. You not only have options for acting on the feeling, but you can also choose to learn from the experience. You have the option of seeing how difficult people and emotional upsets actually help you learn about yourself and how they can accelerate your personal growth.

Pay special attention to persons and behaviors that you don't like. Those traits and actions can show you the active parts of your personality that you think are too obnoxious to admit to and so you deny them. If you can begin to recognize them in yourself and admit to them, these traits and actions of obnoxious people can serve the invaluable purpose of showing you what you need to work on next in your personal development.

When someone betrays you, for example, you'll probably experience a range of egomind emotions. At some point, ask yourself why you attracted such a person into your life. Is it because *you've* betrayed someone recently? Or wanted to? If so, you probably need to deal with betrayal issues within yourself. Or is it that you simply hold harsh judgments toward people who betray?

Not one of us has completely conquered the tendency to make negative judgments of others, so we all need to work on empathy, compassion, and acceptance of others as they are. Maybe betrayal is coming up in your life at this time because you're ready to develop greater empathy and compassion for betrayers. The bottom line: Instead of hanging onto the egomind emotions of an event (such as betrayal), you can focus on the lessons for growth and self-understanding, which in turn trigger expansive emotions.

Action Options: Experience Feelings Without Acting-Out

As you master the techniques we've been discussing, egomind emotions will become less and less a problem. Here's a strategy for constructively handling those egomind emotions that do occur.

Accept your feelings.

Be glad that you're able to experience the whole range of human emotions and that you're aware of being able to do so. Believe that a feeling isn't right or wrong, good or bad; it just *is*.

Let yourself fully experience your feelings.

Be aware of feelings in the present moment. Don't begin focusing on guilt (about past experiences associated with a similar feeling) or worry (about what will happen in the future). Stay in the here and now by focusing on your senses—what you're seeing, hearing, touching, and so forth.

Choose not to act-out.

Tell yourself that you're choosing not to act-out your feelings because to do so would be inappropriate and self-defeating.

Decide whether and when to give feedback.

You may decide it's appropriate to *tell* the person who triggered the feeling what you're feeling. If you do this effectively, it's not acting-out, and the feedback can be constructive to that person. (See the earlier discussion of managing anger.)

If you can't give feedback calmly, postpone it.

As a general rule, you don't have to respond immediately to anything. When your feelings are too overpowering for you to *experience them out* quickly, it's more professional to delay responding. You can act-out your feelings in privacy, if necessary. Later, when you're ready to deal with the problem situation, you can do so without having to deal with explosive feelings at the same time. To postpone gracefully, it helps to have some exit lines in mind. Your exit line is what you say before you change the subject or excuse yourself from the scene. Here are a few examples:

- *I'd like to check on a few things before I give you my answer (respond to that, discuss that).*
- *May I get back to you at/on...?*
- *Let me think about that for a while. I'll get back to you at/on....*
- *I'm glad you brought that up. I must leave for a meeting (or appointment) now, but I want to talk with you about this as soon as I return.*

Use substitute acting-out.

Tell yourself that you'll enjoy acting-out your feelings in an appropriate way later. Sometimes just telling yourself this can defuse the situation enough for you to deal with it effectively at the time it occurs.

You can visualize throwing darts at a picture of the person on a dartboard. (Some people even have dartboards in their office for this purpose.) Here are other substitutes:

- Any game that requires hitting a ball: Pretend the ball is the person or thing you resent and really smash it.
- Jogging or walking: Pretend you're stepping on the person you resent *if you need to!*
- Karate: Pretend your opponent is the person you resent (but don't get carried away!).
- Any physical exercise: You can work off the bottled-up energy of unexpressed feelings by reminding yourself while you're exercising that you're working out those feelings. Be aware of the situation and the resulting feeling you're now working out. You'll probably be free to rest peacefully once the tension and energy drain of unresolved feelings is eliminated.
- Hitting a large stuffed doll: Try to knock the stuffing out of a large doll, animal, or dummy.
- A quick mental acting-out: Instead of visualizing the dart-throwing incident, you can picture yourself telling off the other person, kicking him or her in the seat of the pants, and so on. You may be able to work out the feeling in a few seconds and go on to deal with the situation calmly.

Expression Options: Express Feelings to a Trusted Friend

Another way of handling your emotions is to talk them out with someone. The more stressful your job, the more essential it is to have at least one trusted friend that you can *let your hair down* with. It's best if such friends are not connected with your job. Although business friends may understand the problems better than someone outside the company, it's risky to be completely open with them. True friends are rare. Most people are lucky if they have five or six at any one time in their lives. For the relationship to be truly mutually supportive, it should include these aspects:

- You can be yourselves with each other.
- You are interested in each other's well-being.
- You really listen to each other.
- You don't make judgments about each other's character, feelings, or behavior. (To avoid making judgments, think in terms of behavior that works or doesn't work, that appears to be constructive or destructive, rather than what is right or wrong, good or bad. Deal more with what is rather than with what *should* be.)
- You confide in each other about the joyous events in your life as well as the problem situations.
- You both feel more lovable and capable as a result of the friendship.
- You can trust each other's judgment about revealing shared confidences.

Frequently you can gain insights into problem situations and learn more about yourself by discussing things with a friend. Such discussions can also be very helpful in *experiencing out* any leftover, bottled-up feelings you may have. This type of friendship can help both parties keep a balanced perspective on life.

Research indicates that women have a knack for reaching out to close friends when the emotional going gets tough. Women's ability to rally round with a hot cup of tea, a little shopping spree, a heart-to-heart talk, a good cry, or a big hug seems to work wonders in healing those wounds from the slings and arrows of outrageous office politics. Men are often in awe of this power, and they would do well to try similar techniques, adapting them to men's ways of bonding and hanging out.

Emotional Intelligence in Your Workplace: Gratifying Customers' Emotional Needs

Future success in the business world lies not so much in selling products as in selling dreams that appeal to people's emotional needs. People are captivated by stories that appeal to their emotions. Companies are finding they must create stories about the firm and its products if they want to make them emotionally memorable and appealing. All kinds of companies are challenged to do this—whether they produce consumables, necessities, luxuries, or services.

Everyone in the firm must nurture these stories, because good ones amount to the company's greatest asset. Because stories about the company and its products are so crucial, companies are learning to value the storytellers who create them. Storytellers are not limited to the creative advertising department. They need to exist throughout the company, especially at the executive level. At the top, if you want to win the enthusiasm of employees and the respect of the general public, you must create an appealing myth that weaves together the company's history and traditions.

Futurist Rolf Jensen defines six emotional markets where companies sell dreams and experiences that meet customers' emotional needs—along with the product or service that goes with it. How could your organization profit from one or more of these markets?

The Self-Identity Market offers products that proclaim the owner's identity, such as distinctive fashions, accessories, automobiles. Distinctive luggage may say, "I'm a stylish, savvy world traveler." An SUV may say, "I'm a down-to-earth but adventurous guy," while a hybrid electric car may say, "I'm an environmentalist." This market meets needs for self-awareness, self-love, and self-acceptance (as well as ego-pride and arrogance).

The Love-Friendship Market offers gifts, such as perfume, flowers, candy, and knick-knacks, as well as opportunities to enhance togetherness, such as restaurants, entertainment, and home photography. Unique experiences are featured, such as the *genuine* Irish pub or the bookstore-cafe offering "issues" discussions. This market meets needs for togetherness, belonging, and showing gratitude.

The Peace of Mind Market offers the comfort of the familiar, perhaps a feeling of small-town friendliness in a bank or boutique or retro nostalgia in a restaurant or bar. It meets needs for comfort, relief, certainty, calmness, and appreciation.

The Care Market offers pets and pet experiences, such as hotels that provide guests with *housedogs* they can take for walks, kennels that offer custom environments and experiences for your pet, and electronic pets. This market meets needs for caring, nurturing, empathy, compassion, and devotion.

The Social Convictions Market offers green products and services, those that honor or protect the environment, animals, workers' welfare, and human rights. Where the Care Market meets needs for caring, nurturing, empathy, compassion, and devotion at the one-on-one level, this market meets it on the global level, with a special focus on commitment, conviction, and optimism.

The Adventures Market offers safaris, theme parks, sports, and action/adventure films and programs. It meets customer needs for excitement, playfulness, fun, newness, surprise, curiosity.

Creative Processes Using Emotional Intelligence

Here are some creative processes that call upon your Emotional Intelligence, especially the emotion of empathy—one of your most powerful people-skill emotions. Apply these processes to the problem-opportunity situations you encounter.

Your Current Case Situation: These creative processes will work best in situations that you are personally involved with. Close your eyes and ask yourself, *What problem-opportunity situation is most important for me to address at this time?* Listen for an answer. Jot down a brief outline that tells the story of your situation. Then apply the following techniques to it.

Role Playing

Who are the key players in your problem-opportunity situation? Pick the most important player and pretend you are that person. Get inside her head or his skin. Walk around mentally in her shoes or in his body. See the situation from that person's viewpoint. Describe it as she sees it or as he feels it. How does this person want the situation to be handled or resolved? This requires the emotion of empathy. Complete the role-playing process as follows:

- What insights does this suggest for you?
- Repeat the process for other key players.

Be-Its

Carrying the idea of role playing a step further, you cannot only pretend to be another person, such as a key player, you can pretend to be the problem, be the opportunity, be the company mission, be the current goal, be the future, be any aspect that may be important.

What elements, besides key people, are crucial to your problem-opportunity situation? In your imagination, be that element (be the product, be the customer, be the billing-shipping process, etc.). If you're being a product, imagine yourself as the source of the product, going through every step of becoming the finished product.

If you're being an object that your company processes in some way, ask yourself such questions as *What can happen to me? Where should I go next?* and *What if I went to the Accounting Department next?*

Let your imagination play and run wild. What insights come to you? Write them down.

Be or Ask a Famous Person

Through your superconscious mind, you can have access to all the geniuses and important people who have ever lived and who will ever live. You can learn to tap into this information through empathy and intuition. Even if you don't believe in your ability to do this, try it. It's fun.

Regarding the case situation you're working with, if you could pick the brain of anyone who has ever lived, who would it be? Think of a famous person—or any person you admire—a person you believe could understand and provide sound advice in this situation. Relax and turn all your attention to this process. Get in touch with all the qualities that you associate with this person. Use the emotion of empathy to tune into this person, to become this person.

Now, as this person, review the problem-opportunity situation. How do you see it? What actions could you take? Which approach would be most effective? Write down any insights, ideas, suggestions.

Be or Ask an Outsider

Look for an entirely new take on the situation. Try these methods:

- Talk it over with a child and ask for ideas. Listen carefully. A child may still have the advantage of being open, spontaneous, curious, and flexible.
- Ask anyone who is outside the situation. An outsider's fresh take on the problem may bring new insight.
- Pretend you are a child, an outsider, even an alien from another planet. Imagine how this being would view the situation, ideas they might have.

Self-Awareness Opportunities

SAO #1: What Feelings Do Your Stressors Trigger?

Purpose: To raise your awareness of the connection between certain stressors and related feelings so you can process them effectively.

Note: You don't need to have artistic ability to do this exercise. The power of the exercise lies in your ability to imagine, to visualize. Your drawing can be very simple, crude, childlike, or symbolic. In fact, the power lies in the symbolism.

Step 1: Identify and draw your stressors. What stressors impact you now, in your current life? Make a drawing that symbolizes the stress in your life as follows:

- Draw a picture of yourself—it can be a stick figure, a symbol, or as realistic as you like.
- Symbolize in some way all the pressures and demands that you're aware of—using drawings, words, or other symbols.
- Show the intensity of each pressure, demand, or anxiety by drawing arrows, bridges, or other connections between the pressure and you. Indicate intensity by the size, thickness, darkness (or similar means) of the connections. Remember, even positive change can be stressful if you perceive it has a disruptive effect.

Step 2: Identify your feelings. For the first major stressor, get in touch with the feeling(s) you experience when you focus on that stressor. What feeling(s) have you felt when the stressor was especially active?

Step 3: Process your feelings. Process that feeling, using the process described in this chapter. Repeat for feelings related to other major stressors

SAO #2: Draw and Redirect Your Stressful Emotions.

Purpose: To gain mastery of your stressful emotions so you can channel them into useful forms of self-expression.

Step 1: Identify a stressful emotion. Think of a stressful emotion that recurs in your life. It may be an emotion you have difficulty mastering, one that sweeps you up in its force, one that you act out in destructive ways. It may be an emotion that recurs in your dreams and is troubling to you.

Step 2: Draw the emotion. If you have difficulty seeing it as a symbolic or physical entity, do SAO #6: Observe Your Stressful Emotions (page 134). The emotion might look like a dark cloud, a tornado, a lightening bolt, a solid bunker, a shield, a smoking gun, a raging fire, an icicle, a vise or hand that squeezes—you get the idea. See the emotion as raw energy.

Step 3. Draw the channeling of the emotional energy. Draw a protective container around this raw energy-emotion. Now draw a mini-power plant: From the container of raw energy draw power lines and transformers coming out of the container and going to your house, to your brain or other body area, to your job, to a relationship—to anything you see as needing this energy. Every time you become aware of feeling this emotion, visualize it being transformed into positive energy that you can use to help achieve your goals.

SAO #3: Tap Your Emotional Power.

Purpose: To relax before a meditative visualization, before programming dreams and going to sleep, or any other time. This exercise is very simple. Follow these steps:

- ❧ Think of a time when you felt unconditional love, when you received it or gave it. What feelings come up now when you recall this incident? How do you feel now? Identify your feelings, such as confident, optimistic, friendly, outgoing, calm, happy, and joyful.

- ❧ Allow the feeling(s) to prevail throughout your body-mind as you go into meditation, go to sleep, or engage in some other activity.

Note. These expansive feelings have been studied and found to be connected with higher immune levels, healing, and wellness. On the other hand, certain contracting emotions have been studied and found to be connected to low immune levels and illness. They include anger (hostility, rage), depression (sadness, self-pity, guilt, hopelessness), tension (agitation, nervousness, anxiety), and repression (denial of anxiety). When you feel stuck in one of these emotions, try this power exercise for a quick shift.

SAO #4: Create Your Worst-Case Scenario.

Purpose: To regain a sense of peace and self-confidence during emotional upset.

Step 1: Do the process for getting at root fears discussed in this chapter (in Sparkler #5: Bring Root Fears Out of the Shadows, page 120).

Step 2: As you work through that process, imagine the worst thing that could possibly happen in your current problem situation. For example, if it's a career situation, the worst thing may be losing your job. Imagine that you've lost your job.

Step 3: When you get to a *disastrous* bottom line, ask yourself:

- ❧ Is this the end of the world?

- ❧ Will life go on?

- ❧ Can I survive?

See yourself in that scenario (in this case, without a job). Fully experience the feelings that arise in connection with that picture. Get comfortable with your ability to deal with that scenario.

Step 4: Ask yourself, *What could be worse than this?* For example, you can't find another job that's comparable to the one you now have. Repeat Step 3 for dealing with this new scenario.

Step 5: Keep going until you get to the worst thing that could reasonably happen.

For example, what type of job could you undoubtedly get? Could you deal with that low-level job—at least for a while, until something more appropriate comes along? Become comfortable with this worst-case scenario.

You'll find that imagining the worst-case scenario will bring your fearful shadows and ghosts out of the closet into the realistic light of day. This process will bring you to a sense of competence for coping with whatever comes up.

This in turn will bring a sense of peace and self-confidence that will serve you well in dealing with the current issue.

SAO #5: Put It in Perspective.

Purpose: To help you put an emotional upset into perspective.

How Bad Is It?

Think about the current situation that has triggered some contracting emotions for you. Refer to the trauma scale showing various levels of damage that could occur to your body, ranked from top to bottom in order of perceived impact, pain, loss, and so forth. Which item on the trauma scale best corresponds with your current *traumatic* situation?

Trauma Scale:

1. Stubbed your toe.	5. Lost your toe.
2. Cut your toe and needed a bandage.	6. Lost your foot.
3. Needed stitches in your toe.	7. Lost your leg.
4. Broke your toe.	8. Became paralyzed from the neck down.

Ten Years from Now

Picture yourself 10 years from today. Picture any other persons involved in this situation. From that perspective, looking back to this time in your life, ask yourself:

- ✎ Ten years from now, how important will this problem be?
- ✎ Ten years from now, what response will I wish I had made?

SAO #6: Observe Your Stressful Emotions.

Purpose: To help you become master of your emotions, to put them in perspective, to allow one part of you to move outside an emotion and observe it while another part of you fully experiences it, and to contain raw emotional energy and then transform it into useful forms of self-expression.

Step 1: Create an internal observation room. When you sense the onset of one or more strong, stressful emotions, picture yourself in a mental room inside your head. Imagine yourself stepping back from the emotion and sitting down in an observation chair. From here you'll observe your feelings as separate entities.

Step 2: Stack feelings in the middle of the room. As the first feeling comes up, imagine yourself placing it very carefully on the floor in the middle of the room. If other feelings want to come in, allow them to do so and carefully stack them one on top of the other.

Step 3: Carefully observe the feelings. Now take one feeling at a time—or the whole stack if that's what seems to be needed. Sit back and watch the feeling—its color, its shape, and the nuances of its emotional tones. Watch the feeling. Don't judge it or put it down but observe it. Some typical thoughts that might come up are:

- ❧ *Oh, there you are again!*
- ❧ *So, that's what you look like!*
- ❧ *My, you're very dark today.*

Step 4: Experience and let go. Allow yourself to fully feel the feeling in your body while the observer part of you watches it in your mental room. When the force of the feeling has passed, let it go. If you have difficulty letting it go, ask that it be lifted. What you're left with is the energy that was being wrapped around the feeling.

SAO #7: Heal Painful Emotions and Beliefs.

Adapted from the work of Tapas Fleming (1998).

All the meridian lines in your energy body end at your third-eye acupressure point. All your chakra energy centers come together at the back of your head. Work with these key body points to shift your emotional energy. When you heal at the energy body level, you automatically heal the physical body. The Tapas Acupressure Technique (TAT) is a very quick, simple process that is also very powerful. Mental focus is the key here.

Step 1: Practice the TAT hand position.

- ❧ Your index finger and ring finger (1st and 3rd) find the indentations that "feel right" at the inner eye areas on either side of the bridge of your nose.
- ❧ Your middle finger (2nd) finds the indentation that represents the "third eye" between your eyebrows, just above your nose.
- ❧ Your other hand is cupped across the back of your head, just above the nape of your neck.
- ❧ Lightly touch and hold these acupressure points as you do the following steps.

Think of a problem situation you want to resolve—a situation, emotion, belief, trauma, allergy.

You are going to make several statements in relation to this problem. For each statement, your task is to just "be with" that statement. That's all. Simply focus your attention, be aware of clear intention, and notice what comes up. Then move to the next statement.

Ask yourself, *On a scale of 1 to 10, how strong is this belief (trauma, condition)?*

Step 2: State the problem.

Formulate a statement that expresses the problem in a way that feels right to you. For example, "I need for people to like me in order to feel good about myself." You may want to stress the belief by saying, "It's true that...." Holding the TAT hand positions, make the statement several times. Then rest and be with it.

Step 3: State the opposite.

Think of the opposite condition. Formulate a statement that expresses that for you. Focus on What-Is, using these ideas: "what happened has happened...I experience this condition...I hold this belief...and that's all right." Examples of an opposite statement are, "It's not true that I need people to like me in order to feel good about myself," or "I can feel good about myself even if people don't like me."

Holding the TAT hand positions, make the opposite statement several times. Then rest and be with it. These two steps may be all that's needed, but if the issue is deep-seated, you'll need more.

Step 4: Heal all the origins.

The next statement reflects your intention to heal all the origins of the belief, trauma, allergy, or other problem condition. You don't need to identify the origins; just intend to heal them. The statement might be, "All the origins of this belief (trauma, condition) are healing now." Holding the TAT hand positions, make the statement several times. Then rest and be with it.

Step 5: Heal all the energy storage places.

This statement reflects your intention to heal all the places where this belief, trauma, or condition are stored—in your body, your mind, your life, and all the parts of you. The statement might be, "All the places where I've stored this belief are healing now—my body, mind, life, and all parts of me." Holding the TAT hand positions, make the statement several times. Then rest and be with it.

Step 6: Forgive yourself and others.

This statement reflects your intention to heal everyone you have ever blamed for this belief, trauma, or condition—including yourself. You may want to include your vision of the Creator in this statement, using your own words. A statement might be, "I forgive everyone that I've blamed for this belief (trauma, condition), including myself and the Creator." Holding the TAT hand positions, make the statement several times. Then rest and be with it.

Ask yourself, *On a scale of 1 to 10, how strong is this belief (trauma, condition) now?* If there is still some charge, work through the statements again. Repeat until the charge is gone.

SAO #8: Heartfelt Stress Reduction.

Purpose: To shift out of stress-related emotions.

When you experience feelings such as worry, frustration, agitation, recognize the feelings and process them. If you have difficulty releasing them, try this process:

- Concentrate the feelings in your heart.
- Concentrate all your attention on your heart.
- Pretend you're breathing with your heart. Breathe in through the heart.
- Think of something that triggers feelings of love or sincere appreciation.

- Channel that thought-feeling into the warm, loving emotional energy of your heart.
- Soak your contracting emotion in this warm energy.
- Hold that image in your heart for at least 10 seconds. This will calm your heart, and then your mind and body.
- Ask your heart the best way you can take care of yourself and still be able to do the things you need to do.

SAO #9: Clear Out Egomind Energy.

Purpose: To boost the power of your inner work.

Step 1: Focused Breathing. As you do your deep breathing to relax, say to yourself:

Breathe in...love.

Breathe out...fears.

Breathe in...love.

Breath out...negative ego, negative judgment.

Breathe in...love.

Breathe out...pain from the past.

Step 2: Visualization. To deepen the relaxation, use this visualization:

- Focus into your heart area.
- Bring in love/white light through the crown of your head.
- Bring it down into your heart area and let it fill your heart
- Let love and caring radiate out from your heart.
- Feel love, caring, connection, compassion, and gratitude.
- Open the eyes of your heart.
- See beyond the trivial to the big picture.
- See the pathway of your life.
- See what needs to be next for you.

Chapter 6

Make Connections:
Associative Intelligence

If at first the new idea is not absurd, there's no hope for it.
Albert Einstein

Are you good at putting together things that don't normally *belong* together—and coming up with something new that works? Sometimes you improvise because you don't have what you need. Other times you just play with new combinations because it's fun. Either way, you're using your Associative Intelligence. Sometimes it really pays off. Here's an example:

> A man was experimenting with various glues, looking for one that would permanently attach one piece of paper to another without damaging the paper. He absentmindedly placed a piece of paper coated with one version of the glue onto a stack of papers. Later he noticed that even though the glue-backed paper had stuck, it came loose easily—and it left no mark. Instead of seeing the glue as a failure to permanently bond two pieces of paper, he associated the temporary bonding ability with the need for place markers, removable messages, and other paperwork problems. The Post-it notes phenomenon was born—thanks to one man's use of Associative Intelligence.

Your ability to see relationships between things—how one thing associates with another—is one of your most powerful intelligences. It's mainly about putting together What-Is, in a new and different way. It's a key to your Creative Intelligence.

You use your Associative Intelligence to directly perceive something, to freely associate one thing with another, or to link two ideas together in your mind. Thinking in this way is often the first step in moving from rational left-brain thinking to right-brain thinking, which also includes your Sensory and Intuitive Intelligences.

Through Associative Intelligence, you relate the specifics, the details you focus on through your basic and emotional brains—your attractions, re-pulsions, emotions, desires—with the general, the big picture—planetary and universal concepts, principles, and ideals. This is the linking, connecting intel-ligence. Terms that will help you understand what your Associative Intelli-gence is all about include:

> similarities, comparisons, relationship to, connection with, analogies, similes, metaphors, neocortex, right brain

How Associative Intelligence Works

Associative Intelligence works to increase your Creative Intelligence by relating the wide variety of things you encounter to the big picture, the Web of Life. It relates all kinds of strange things, making new connections and linkages.

Relating to the Big Picture

You've learned about your basic-brain intelligences, as well as your emo-tional-brain intelligences. Now you're ready to explore the intelligences of your highest-level brain, the neocortex, which has two distinct halves, often called right-brain and left-brain, as symbolized in Snapshot #1. They are con-nected by a bridge of nerve fibers called the corpus collosum. Your left brain is associated with the right side of the body (left-brain, right-handed) and is the seat of your Rational Intelligence, which we'll discuss in detail in Chapter 7. Your right brain is therefore associated with the left side of your body and is the seat of three important intelligences: Associative, Sensory, and Intuitive. All these right-brain intelligences have a capacity for catching glimpses of a larger whole, a greater truth, a bigger perspective. All have a sense of timeless-ness, of being able to access all time in the Now. All include getting a sense of the whole before focusing on the parts.

Taking Charge

Have you allowed your rational mind to be the master of your life? Now you can make it your slave, your tool. You can step into your rightful place. Your whole self, your creative self, your higher self can be the master. You do this by using your right-brain intelligences as new-idea generators and your rational brain as evaluator and implementer.

Integrating Right and Left

Creative Intelligence is *not* a matter of using either the wholistic right brain or the sequential, rational left brain, but of using both as partners in the creativity process. Instead of *either-or*, it's a case of *both-and*. In most situations, you'll want to let the right brain processes run free without interference from your rational left brain. After your wholistic right brain has sensed, intuited, connected, and associated with all kinds of things and generated a batch of ideas, your rational left brain can come in to ground your ideas in physical reality. You'll use it to organize the new ideas, to evaluate them, and to put them to work in the world of consensus reality.

Snapshot #1 Neocortex Intelligences

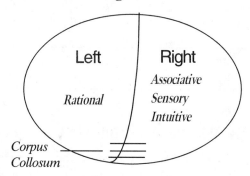

Discovering New Connections

When you use your rational left-brain thinking, you focus on questions that get at specific facts: who, what, where, when, why, and how. You connect fact, ideas, or actions in a step-by-step linear sequence, selecting on an either-or basis, using verbal symbols and math symbols. This is linear or straight-line thinking.

In contrast, when you use your right-brain Associative Intelligence, you freely make connections without regard to sequence. In the process of connecting one known idea with another, you may come up with just the brilliant new idea you need. Here, instead of a straight line is a free-form associative process:

- ❧ Direct perception of the person or object.
- ❧ Discovery.
- ❧ Multiple connections.
- ❧ Dynamics among and between persons and objects.
- ❧ Both-and.
- ❧ No limits.
- ❧ Abundant ideas and discoveries.

Associative thinking is associating, linking, relating, connecting with whatever and whomever you want. Its main quality is total freedom. It can free you to make an immensely larger number of connections, bringing to life other unused areas of your brain. These new connections will increase your intelligence and can provide the first step toward accessing the *unused* 90 percent of your brainpower.

Three functions of Associative Intelligence, which make it an especially powerful factor in generating creative responses to problem-opportunity situations according to Elaine DeBeauport, are:

1. *Direct Perception*. When you directly perceive something, you relate to the person, object, or situation as-is, without applying labels, symbols, concepts, conclusions, or evaluations.

2. *Free Association*. When you freely process a situation, you make connections without being distracted by sequence or cause and effect. Instead you search among images and thoughts in a state of mental freedom.

3. *New Arrangements*. You link and rearrange associations, make new connections, and relate things in different ways and by different methods in order to make new compositions.

Direct Perception

Every word in our language is a symbol that stands for something that has its own reality, its own existence. When you experience a symbol for something, that is a substitute for directly experiencing the actual thing.

You use your rational brain to think mainly with verbal and mathematical symbols. Associative Intelligence gives you a choice: You can either relate to symbols of people (employees), things (espresso coffees), or situations (lunch meetings in the cafeteria) and link them in various ways, or you can associate directly with the person, object, or situation.

Direct perception serves as an entry into all the intelligences of the right brain. When you perceive directly, you can free yourself of the left-brain rational labels, assumptions, conclusions, and concepts and relate to an entity from many different angles or viewpoints. You're free to see the complexity of what you're experiencing before you have to relate to the accepted symbol for it. You can decide where to focus your attention.

When you think of associating things, you probably think of linking them together. This linking is much more powerful if you're first able to *de-link* the words, symbols, labels, stereotypes, and assumptions from that person, object, or situation. When you do this, you're better able to *just be with* that entity in its being-ness. You free yourself of preconceptions and assumptions about it. You bypass the cultural and gender labels, stereotypes, concepts, assumptions, and symbols. You take in your direct experience of persons, things, and ideas as if they are brand new.

Now you're free to be with that entity's reality—to notice and associate with any aspect of it—not just those aspects triggered by labels or symbols of it. Now you're free to associate continually with the reality of that entity according to your own perceptions, desires, and creativity in the moment.

Snapshot #2: Perceiving Things Directly

Look at the image in Snapshot #2 on page 142. Try de-linking—forgetting about—all the words, labels, stereotypes, and beliefs you normally connect with this type of image. What you see here is a symbol for a living being, of course.

Imagine that you're looking at the original living cat. Focus fully on being here now in this present moment—no past and no future, just the now.

Imagine just *being with* this being as if you had never seen anything like it before. Be totally open to letting it be exactly what it is. This is direct perception. It requires *being here now*—totally conscious and present in the present moment. In the next few days, as you encounter various people and animals, try perceiving them directly. Start building a habit pattern of direct perception.

Associating Things Freely

Innovation comes from a new way of seeing, making a new guess about what will work. Although most of the *scientific method* is rational, what makes it powerful is the associative process of looking into the unknown, catching glimpses of new ideas, associating them with known ideas, and arranging and rearranging ideas into new patterns.

The artistic process is similar. For example, a painter focuses on a subject, looks for new ways to express what she sees there, and arranges and rearranges these new perceptions until she finds the *right* design. Associative thinking is essential for scientists, artists, businesspeople, and everyone involved in creative thinking.

When you change your patterns, your routines, or your habits, you usually trigger a new way of seeing. Ideas come pouring in and collide, making new connections. When you take any kind of trip—even a day trip—to a new place, you get out of your rut. You come back a different person. It may be a tiny difference, but those differences can add up to innovation.

Making New Arrangements

When you link together in new ways the people, places, ideas, concepts, things, colors, foods, or smells that you perceive, you're using Associative Intelligence. Your mind freely wanders and roams all over your known experience and unknown imaginings, free from the limits of cause and effect. You're free from the rational need to assess, measure, judge, or reach a conclusion, free to begin a voyage of discovery.

You make meaning by linking together your glimpses of ideas and flashes of insight, your mental maps of things. You play with these ideas, moving them around, linking them together, and seeing how they connect with a problem-opportunity situation you're working on. You explore their nuances, their subtleties, and their mysteries to discover something new about them. You try them out in various patterns or arrangements—until you find new meaning.

Building Relationships: Gender Differences

Associative Intelligence is all about relationships—and that includes human relationships. Here we find distinct gender differences. Research indicates that males typically see the world as a hierarchy where they must gain or maintain status. Females typically see it as a web of connections where they must make and maintain relationships.

Status Vs. Connection

Even as young boys, the male groups focus first on hierarchy. They all jockey for position because the high-status boys get many privileges and make life miserable for the low-status boys. They become sensitive to the way anything that anyone says may affect their place in the hierarchy. Early in life, an important aspect of boys' culture is the language of insults, some playful, some not—and this continues into adulthood.

Women see this kind of behavior as aggressive. It seems as if men are frequently putting down others. Men see it as defensive, making such comments as: *Because people will always try to put you down, you have to protect yourself. The best defense is usually an offense: I'll put you down before you put me down.*

Girls' groups focus more on connection. Instead of measuring how high people are in a pyramid (hierarchy), they measure how close or distant each girl is to other girls in a web of personal connections. Girls are likely to have a best friend and perhaps a small group of close friends. If they don't like a girl, they just avoid her rather than associate with her and then mistreat her.

Girls become very sensitive to being left out, while boys become very sensitive to being put down. The same words in a conversation may therefore be interpreted by a woman to mean *you're pushing me away* and by a man to mean *you're trying to control me* according to researcher Deborah Tannen.

Polarity Vs. Unity

The male focus on hierarchy and put-downs extends to a tendency to argue. Ritual opposition is used to stage a fight as a way of accomplishing something that isn't really so much about fighting as gaining or maintaining status.

Also, boys are more likely to set up an argument as a form of fun, a ritual way of determining who's going to come out on top. Girls will fight if there's conflict, but not as a form of entertainment.

The love of argument is intensifying throughout all the media. The press, for example, changed after Watergate and the coups of *Washington Post* reporters Woodward and Bernstein. Many journalists began to believe that any journalism worth doing brings down the mighty. In politics, opening up primary systems to public vote has led to candidates fighting in such a public way that they destroy each other before the election.

Many people in our culture, especially the men, have become obsessed with reducing every issue to a two-sided argument. That type of conflict has been ritualized into a kind of game, where entertainment is perceived as dull unless a fight breaks out. Often it's fighting just to be fighting—generating lots of heat and throwing very little light on the issues. Anthropologist Deborah Tannen says that we need to move beyond polarity thinking. We need to argue about the real stuff and explore real issues rather than let a lot of phony, ritualized arguments take over. As a woman, you can use your influence to encourage people to explore issues—in order to learn more, to get a variety of viewpoints and ideas, and perhaps to come up with creative solutions. We need creativity in all areas of life—the political, economic, and social, as well as in business and personal life. Everyone can benefit by moving beyond polarity thinking, which is a major block to creativity.

Innovation Showcase
Barbara Corcoran on Associative Intelligence

Barbara Corcoran is chairman and founder of The Corcoran Group Real Estate in New York. She credits her success to a lively imagination that loves to put things together in new and different ways.

"I've always been able to think of an idea a minute," she says, "so this has always kept me feeling fresh and cutting edge. I'm also very competitive, so not only do I want to have a brilliant idea, but I want to think of it first."

Barbara is constantly trying new things and reconfiguring ideas, as well as people. In 1989, in the midst of a recession, Barbara borrowed an idea from a farmer's wife who lived near her country home. The farmer's wife needed to get rid of some puppies, so she displayed them with a sign that read, "first come, first served." The puppies went—fast. Back in New York, Barbara applied the technique to a real estate problem—how to sell apartments in a building where no one was buying. She told her brokers that all the apartments would have the same price, and they would be sold *first come, first served*. The building sold out in record time and her company made $1 million in profits that day.

Risk-taking has also played a large part in Barbara's success. When she was young and made her first sale, she took that money and hired a new salesperson. So even then she was taking chances on people and on building the company. She adds, "But more than that, I think, I had a lot of determination—so I was bound to make this thing work."

Sparking Your Associative Intelligence

You can spark your Associative Intelligence by applying it to the way you gain new information and expertise and to the way you create new relationships and revive old ones.

Sparkler #1: Play with Links

Word play is powerful. Putting together bizarre and ridiculous combinations of things makes you laugh. Both absurdity and wit give you a quick way to overthrow the tyranny of the right way, the status quo, the given, the known. For example:

- Look at the wall and rename it zebra.
- Stare at a rug and call it satellite.

This can break the connection you've established between the thing and your words for it. It can push you into thinking in the picture language of the sensory-visual intelligence.

Even more powerful than word play is *picture play*—moving various images around in your mind and making new connections among them—because it's closer to direct perception. Your most creative inspirations may come to you not in words but in visual images.

Activity play is also powerful, especially when you combine it with *picture play*. For example, Einstein often asked questions that linked together two or more unrelated activities. As he mentally answered the questions, he formed mental pictures of the activities, such as:

- What would it be like to ride a beam of light and at the same time look back at a clock?
- What would happen if I dropped a coin while standing in an elevator that was dropping?

This play at combining activities is a key feature of creative thought. Such associative thinking occurs at a stage before you connect your pictures with words or numbers—where you directly relate to the pictures, moving pure images around in your mind's eye. It can lead to new insights that you can later find the words or symbols for—to communicate them to others.

Try using this type of associative play to understand relationships in a new way.

Sparkler #2: Learn on the Right Side

Because our schools have traditionally viewed learning almost completely as a rational, left-brain activity, most people continue to limit their learning activities to the rational mind. Stop to think about your learning process. By far, the most prolific learning period of your life was from birth to age 5 or 6. Did you really learn primarily by rational thinking? Kids learn by associating Mom's touch with her voice, with comfort, and with survival. Kids pick up nonverbal information before they learn the language, using their wholistic right-brain intelligences to determine who's okay and who's not.

To spark and speed up your learning capacity, and therefore your Creative Intelligence, use your right brain as well as your left brain. For example, a book is a very rational learning tool, but you can also use right brain methods for grasping a book's information. Try these actions:

- Read the pictures and graphics before you read the words.
- Before reading the main text, scan the non-text materials, such as headings, subheads, tables, graphs, sidebars, and opening quotes—to get a sense of the overall organization plan, the key ideas, and the information that merits special treatment by being highlighted in tables, graphs, or boxes. This gives you a sense of the priorities and relative importance of various topics.
- As you read the main text, pay attention to how it relates to the pictures, graphics, and other non-text materials and make the connections between them.
- If there's a summary at the end, review it *before* you read the main text to get a sense of the bottom line.
- As you read, bring the materials alive by relating them to your own experiences.
- If the material is abstract, ask yourself these kinds of questions: *What does this statement really mean? How does it apply to real-life*

experience? How would this concept or idea work in my life? How would it look, sound, and feel in this real-life situation? You should be able to visualize concrete examples of each concept.

- Consider skipping around in the text if that would help you get a better grasp of the materials.
- As you read (or hear someone speak, if it's a lecture), visualize how the information applies to life in general and to your life in particular.
- Discover ways to link new information to things you already know.

These right-brain techniques will boost your understanding and your learning capacity.

Sparkler #3: Relate Creatively to People

Much of your creativity relies on building collaborative, synergistic human relationships. You often must work with a team of people to create innovative responses to problem-opportunities. Also, in business the goal of your creative efforts nearly always involves customers or users of a product, process, or service. And you virtually always must sell your innovation to the right people in order to make it a success.

Finding creative ways of dealing with people is a brilliant skill that enriches your career as well as your personal life. You know that rational thinking focuses on making evaluations and coming to conclusions. It requires skepticism, continuous doubting, and questioning. Although this approach can work quite well for evaluating your own ideas, it's hardly the best approach for building relationships with people. How to win friends and influence people has always centered around paying attention to them, showing more interest in their concerns than in your own, and relating to their concerns by showing that you've had similar experiences that enable you to empathize with theirs.

Relate Beyond Rational Limits

When you use your Rational Intelligence to form and maintain relationships, you severely limit your possibilities for building a wide range of exciting, interesting friends and associates. Your rational mind relates by:

- Trying to understand people by adding up what they've achieved, what they own, how many friends or contacts they have, and other external measurements of human worth.
- Dealing with people based on their *place* in a social group, an organization, or the society in general—the status trap.
- Dealing with people based on cultural myths, stereotypes, or labels.
- Identifying parts of human beings, summarizing these parts, then proceeding to criticize them and doubt them based on this incomplete information and resulting conclusions.
- Assuming that having met someone or spent time with them means you completely know that person.

ᗺ   Criticizing, doubting, and concluding, which results in judgments
that are actually mental traps. These traps severely limit your
voyages of discovery of other people.

In contrast, when you use Associative Intelligence to relate to people,
you perceive them directly instead of by their name, label, or other symbol.
How do you want to be perceived? Don't you hope that people will get to
know the real you, hopefully your best self? Do you want to be judged on some
isolated mood or action you took? You know that a mood and resulting action is not *you*. It's just a temporary energy flowing through you—unless you
keep repeating it until it becomes a rigid pattern that your friends can accurately predict.

Give people a fair chance. Try taking the first steps toward friendship
and love, using the Associative Intelligence techniques of directly perceiving,
linking, associating freely, and making new arrangements.

Relate by Direct Perception

The associative technique of directly perceiving people as unique beings
is a rare and well-appreciated quality that can help you relate to who a person
really is. It opens you up to really finding out about a person, like turning a
fresh page, a blank unknown that's ready to be filled in. When you start with a
blank slate, you're inspired to find out how to fill it. If you start with labels,
stereotypes, and assumptions, you think you already know most of it. This is
really a type of arrogance on your part.

Direct perception is a great approach to meeting someone new. It can
also be very powerful for shifting a stuck relationship with someone you've
known a long time. Try tossing out all of your past conclusions and judgments
about an old friend and be with that person as if for the first time.

Relate by Free Association

Relating by free association is a de-linking process. You de-link your
labels from the person. When you want to make a fresh start, try thinking
about the person's body as billions of cells in constant motion and change, an
endless possibility of discovery. Use this process:

1.   See that some of the person's energy is obvious and much of it is
     hidden, aspects that you can only glimpse.
2.   Ask yourself, *What can I intuit here? What can I relate to? What
     affects me, moves me, interests me, intrigues me?*
3.   Realize you can't really *know* others. You can't measure them or
     completely understand them, but you can catch glimpses of them.
4.   Ask yourself, *What's going on? What's happening with this person?*
5.   Begin by finding something, any little thing, that pleases you,
     that you can relate to.

When you focus on what *kind* of person someone is, you judge, label, and
conclude. This closes your mind to what's really happening with this person
and in the relationship the two of you are having. When you focus on what
your relationship together will *be*, how you *are* together, you're able to freely

associate with the person and to notice how the relationship is moving along. You can focus on the energy or communication that develops between the two of you, whether it:

- Feels more like rapport or like reporting information.
- Is open and agreeable or blocked and tense.
- Is abundant or minimal.
- Has a clear, high quality or is full of static and interference.

Begin the contact with a process of free association. Then move on to finding links and continue by looking for other associations, ways to relate to one another.

Relate by Linking

Associate what you find out about a person with your own interests and experiences. Express appreciation of what you find in the other person and share something of your related experience. This gives you a link to connect and bond with the person. Finding those connections also motivates you to continue exploring, to learn more about the person. These connections are the conversational links for making that exploration fun and charming. They allow you to participate in the give-and-take of meaningful conversation and to show that you understand and can relate to the person's interests and experiences.

When you use associative thinking, you can use a process to explore, discover, find some aspect you can appreciate in every person you meet—and you use that aspect to forge a new relationship. You can feel comfortable in meeting anyone or going anywhere. With this tool you can creatively reinvent old, stuck relationships and inspire them with new life.

Your rational mind may come in to judge what's *missing* in the other person. When this happens, you don't have to conclude, separate from, or destroy the budding relationship. Instead, you can shift out of your rational thinking and into an associative process. See the person as a fresh page free of labels or judgments. See the person as a new combination of energy that has never before been this exact configuration. (It's true!) Search for something, anything, that's interesting, pleasant, or admirable. Just get a glimpse. Focus on that, give it detail, express your interest, and make the connection. Remember: *You don't have to buy the whole package* (the whole person). *You can love the glimpses that you really like and leave the rest*, according to Elaine DeBeauport.

Creative Processes Using Associative Intelligence

Here are some creative processes that call upon your Associative Intelligence. Apply these processes to the problem-opportunity situations you encounter.

Word Associations

Write down a word or two that may (or may not) represent your problem, your situation, or some aspect of it. Then write down another word that comes to mind, that you associate with the first word. Now write a third word that you associate with the first word. Keep going, listing related words till you have a nice list. Review your list, looking for insights to hidden problems, opportunities, solutions, and options.

Dictionary Springboard

This is a variation of word associations. It's designed to strengthen your ability to make associations and think in metaphors. This in turn will help you build skill at using signs and symbols as springboards to intuitive knowing.

Open a dictionary at random. Leave your mind blank as you let your finger spontaneously land on a word. If you get a highly technical word, move on to another.

Say the word; read the definition out loud. Then keep on speaking, saying anything that pops into your mind, whatever is triggered by the random word. Jot down the words as you say them. Once you have a list of freely associated words, review the list to explore connections and images that range outside your personal experience.

Free Associations

Free associate in this way:

- Write a one-word summary of your problem or situation.
- Looking at that word, write down the first word that comes to mind.
- Look at the second word and write down the first word that comes to mind.

Keep going till you have a nice list. Look at these words. See how each of them gives you some insight into the situation. Can you use any of these words to draw analogies that could lead to a solution or new idea? Notice words that stand out for you and use them to brainstorm new associations, ideas, or solutions. You're looking for thoughts that might in turn lead to solutions or unrecognized opportunities.

Here is a variation of the free association process, using a business issue:

- Pick a product, service, process, or other item that you might want to change.
- List the qualities or attributes of this item.
- For each quality, do a free association, listing all related items that come up.
- How does each free association apply to changing the item, solving a problem, or recognizing an opportunity?
- What ideas do the free associations, in combination, suggest?

Qualities and Attributes

After you have defined the problem, draw a large circle, like a clock's face, and write the numbers 1 through 12 around the clock's face. In the center write the problem-opportunity definition as a brief statement or question. Identify 12 qualities or attributes of the situation. Write a one-word symbol of each of these 12 attributes beside the 12 numbers on the clock's face.

Begin with the first quality. Free associate, brainstorm, and/or mind map any thoughts that come up about this attribute. Move on to the second quality, work on it, and continue until you have generated ideas for all 12 qualities.

What qualities can you combine? Perhaps you can see some likely combinations. If not, choose to combine some attributes at random. Play with the combining process. For each combination, free associate, brainstorm, and/or mind map. Continue until you feel you have enough ideas.

Associate with Poems, Songs, Etc.

Make up little poems, songs, and so forth that throw a new light or humorous slant onto the situation. Some people use such well-known songs as the Beverly Hillbillies' theme song, "Trouble in River City" (from *The Music Man*), and "Dixie" to parody current problems. Ask yourself what insights the song or poem suggests. This is especially good for recognizing problems and opportunities.

Associate through Metaphors, Similes, and Analogies

A seawave of change. Cooking the books. Metaphors usually treat one thing as if it were something else so that people can see a resemblance they would not ordinarily perceive. A metaphor is a figure of speech that links together two different universes of thought—oceans and economies, cuisine and accounting, for example.

Metaphors stimulate the imagination, appeal to the emotions, give vivid life to a challenge, and transform the intangible into an image that you and others can more easily grasp. Metaphors allow you to compare and link the literal reality around you with the figurative reality of your imagination, your emotions, your intuitive possibilities, your dreams, and your ability to dare to dream them. Metaphors are great for helping a team to share a particular vision.

Create some metaphors for your situation or problem. Ask yourself what insights the metaphors suggest for finding opportunities, hidden problems, or solutions. This process is especially good for generating options.

Similes are also associative in nature. *As cute as a ladybug. Sparkling, like a sun-struck pond.* Similes show how things are similar, usually by using such terms as "like" or "as." Create some similes for your situation or problem. Ask yourself what insights the similes suggest for finding opportunities, hidden problems, or solutions. Similes are especially good for generating options.

You can work with analogies, too. Here are two examples of analogies: Blades are to a fan as a propeller is to an airplane. A spider is to its web as a weaver is to the fabric. To associate through analogies, try this process:

- ✎ Consider two things that are essentially dissimilar and, by a direct analogy, show how they have some similarity. You can use anything: animals and how they function, equipment or toys and how they function, weather and how it functions.

- ✎ How can you apply certain facts, knowledge, or technology from another field to your current problem situation? For example, can you use facts from biology—such as how animals or plants function—to get new ideas?

- Create some analogies for your situation or problem. Ask yourself what insights the analogies suggest for finding opportunities, hidden problems, or solutions. This is a good technique for generating options.

A Final Word

Now you've entered the wonderful wholistic world of your right brain. The first intelligence you've encountered in this world, your Associative Intelligence, is such a powerful creative engine. Now that you've explored some creative processes that use Associative Intelligence, apply them to the case situation that follows—to start the skill-building process. Then cross over to the linear, sequential left-brain world, where you'll find an old friend: your Rational Intelligence.

Case Situation: 3D Adventures Vs. Megastar

Instructions: Practice using the creative processes by applying them to this case situation.

3D Adventure is a 13-year-old company that creates video games. One of its biggest competitors, **Megastar**, has a popular game called Jungle that features Grizmo, a large bear that engages in various battles in the jungle.

3D Adventure's latest hot game is called Tanks. Because 3D specializes in providing video material, it decided to create its own TV commercial for the Tanks product launch. As the team sat around, dreaming up ideas for the commercial, Otto Grant, a team member, started laughing. "Hey, wouldn't it be a hoot if we showed our tanks attacking Grizmo the bear?" he asked. The other guys started laughing. They all liked the idea.

The team created the TV commercial as a vignette that takes place in a laundry room. It begins with the famous talking bear, Grizmo, talking to the audience. Suddenly a group of tanks shows up and begins chasing Grizmo around the room, trying to blow him up. By the end of the commercial, Grizmo has lost a paw and he is on fire. The Tanks are victorious.

The public relations department scheduled the TV commercial to be shown primarily on Saturday mornings during popular kids' shows. The Tanks commercial definitely caused a commotion. Megastar has sued 3D Adventure for $3 million in damages. Its lawyers claim that 3D's team violated copyright laws by copying Grizmo and using him in a commercial. They also claim slander of Megastar's product, saying that the Tanks commercial implies the product is no good. As a result, sales of the Jungle game have fallen off.

- What are the root problems facing 3D?
- What opportunities is the staff overlooking?
- How could Emotional Intelligence help the 3D staff avoid these problems and capitalize on missed opportunities? What do you recommend?

Case Situation Feedback:
3D Adventure Vs. Megastar

Root problems:

- Not grounding free-ranging creative exploration in everyday marketplace reality. Not checking with a legal expert.

- Not following up team brainstorming sessions—where all ideas are welcome—with a rational evaluative process that predicts the dynamics that will likely be set in motion by a particular plan of action.

- Not using the associative process fully. Once they hit on the Grizmo idea, they could have started asking, *What else?* Because Grizmo appealed to them so much, they could have continued playing with that idea: What makes it so appealing? What else might be even more appealing?

Overlooked opportunities:

- Creating an ad that uses a vignette from the actual Tanks game. This would give potential buyers a foretaste of what to expect. The actual game should be more fun than the Grizmo scenario. If not, the team needs to improve the game.

Recommendations:

- The team needs to look at how their competitive approach gets them in trouble. What egomind emotions created the charge that made it so compelling to *steal* the Grizmo character? What alternate expansive emotions could they focus on instead?

- Only a good legal team is likely to get 3D out of the current situation, especially if Megastar can convince the judge that they've suffered a significant financial loss due to 3D Adventure's commercial.

- The team should agree on creative processes that are open and free-ranging, but that also include rational follow-up, grounding in marketplace reality, and checking with a legal expert.

Chapter 7

Balance Left-Brain Rational Intelligence

To have ideas is to gather flowers; to think, is to weave them into garlands.
Anne-Sophie Swetchine, writer (1781–1857)

Rational Intelligence is the one that men in our culture love best—as a general rule. As a woman, you may think you have not-so-hot aptitudes toward math, physics, high-tech innards, and technical mind's-eye manipulations. However, courses in these subjects are readily available in all our educational institutions, so skill building here is certainly doable. In fact, more and more women are majoring in such areas as engineering, math, science, and computers.

You already know that Western culture glorifies Rational Intelligence and either ignores or discounts most of the other intelligences. That doesn't make Rational Intelligence a bad thing. It's a glorious human gift—the seat of thinking and also of communicating and expressing your thoughts. So your Rational Intelligence is to be respected, but you'll want to use it to boost your Creative Intelligence, not undermine it.

When you're involved in rational activities, you:

- Engage in critical thinking and make predictions about what's true in reality.
- Gather information, then categorize and organize it.
- Criticize, doubt, and question information, processes, ideas, and results.

- ✎ Set strategies to achieve goals.
- ✎ Devise standards to measure achievement, controlling for irrelevant or disruptive factors.
- ✎ Select instruments to measure validity or achievement.
- ✎ Review information—comparing, judging, assessing, and evaluating.
- ✎ Reach conclusions and make recommendations.
- ✎ Decide on an action plan.

In carrying out these activities, your rational mind likes tightness and order.

This all sounds familiar, doesn't it? It's the venerated scientific method. These are activities you rely upon when you study, take exams, tackle problems, do research, and develop and complete projects. However, you can easily go astray if you misuse your powerful Rational Intelligence in two typical ways:

1. Relying almost exclusively on rational-mind thinking.
2. Getting trapped in judging, comparing, doubting, and controlling.

Terms to associate with Rational Intelligence include:

> logical, sequential, intellectual, step-by-step, mathematical, scientific, I.Q., SAT, GMAT, left-brain, neocortex

How Rational Intelligence Works

Your rational mind is an extremely important part of the creative process. When you use your Rational Intelligence, you ask questions and find answers that get at the specifics of a problem-opportunity situation: who, what, where, when, why, and how. You connect ideas or actions in a step-by-step linear sequence, selecting in an either-or way and using verbal symbols and math symbols. Western culture fell in love with this straight-line way of thinking, making it the source of many of our problems. What you'll want to remember is that Rational Intelligence is only a part of your Creative Intelligence—perhaps 10 percent. When you're working on a creative project, you use Rational Intelligence in certain ways for certain stages.

Typical Rational-Mind Activities

Both as part of the creative process—especially the problem-solving and decision-making phases—and as part of other rational-mind activities, you use Rational Intelligence when you judge, assess, evaluate, compare, doubt, criticize, ask why, investigate, research, analyze, control, organize, reorganize, create, innovate, review, follow up, and sell.

Judge, Assess, Evaluate, Compare

Throughout the rational phases of the creative process, you must judge, assess, evaluate, and compare all aspects of the situation, including the facts,

statements, explanations, ideas, conclusions, and proposed solutions you encounter. At some point you must judge their applicability, relevance, and effectiveness for your creative project.

Doubt, Criticize, Ask Why

Before you begin investigating any situation, you will typically have some
doubts or criticisms about the current situation. You'll ask why things are as they
are. Here are some rational-mind activities for this phase:

- Look at the whole situation.
- Find reasons why this problem-opportunity situation exists.
- Raise doubts and questions about it.
- At each stage of the process, ask why and find reasons why.
- Evaluate ideas about problems, opportunities, and
  assumptions.
- Continuously question until you discover critical differences
  between things.
- Make predictions about causes and effects.

Investigate, Research, Analyze, Control

Once you decide a situation is worth looking into, you'll begin the investigation, the research phase, engaging in the following rational-mind activities:

- Gather evidence.
- Observe the situation, breaking it down into all its relevant parts.
- Observe all the data in detail.
- Control the environment in which you test for certain cause-
  effect relationships.
- Observe the effects of a situation, analyze the causes, and each
  time search more deeply and more specifically for cause-effect
  relationships.
- Analyze the causes for good and poor results.
- Search more deeply and more specifically for cause-effect rela-
  tionships.
- Explain the causes step-by-step until you arrive at a conclusion.

Organize, Reorganize

One of the greatest challenges to many people is organizing the wealth
of information they find available today over the Internet and in other media.
Here are typical rational-mind activities for this phase:

- Organize ideas in a logical way.
- Make sequential, precise, and logical connections. (This contrasts
  with the Associative Intelligence you use to make more general,
  relational, and random connections.)
- Make detailed connections and order them in a sequential manner.
- Make logical links between cause and effect.

Create, Innovate

Your rational mind can either block creativity or enhance it. Once you get your information organized, you're ready to come up with new ideas, using these rational-mind activities:

- ❧ Select the best information and ideas for generating new solutions or responses to the problem-opportunity situation (bringing other intelligences into the selection process).
- ❧ When you find the critical difference, what is missing, go on to create alternatives.
- ❧ Search out and test the alternatives.
- ❧ Create a new whole, a new solution, program, or invention.

Review, Follow Up, Sell

The most creative ideas are worthless if you don't implement them properly. Reviewing, following up, and selling your ideas call for these critical rational-mind activities:

- ❧ Be exact.
- ❧ Give reasons to substantiate everything you say.
- ❧ Evaluate the overall plan and each of its aspects.
- ❧ Observe the effects of the plan.
- ❧ Review ideas about problems, opportunities, and assumptions.

Many of these rational activities involve doubting, criticizing, asking questions, and being objective rather than personal. These are valuable rational activities that can lead to trouble when done in the wrong place and time or when carried too far.

Creative Use of Rational Intelligence

Your Rational Intelligence is a double-edged sword. When you use it appropriately, it's incredibly powerful for sparking your Creative Intelligence. But just as the habit patterns and territorial limits of Basic Intelligence can block creativity, the activities typical of Rational Intelligence can lead you into self-sabotaging traps that undermine creativity.

About Judging, Comparing, Controlling

Although assessing the facts and conclusions is essential to the problem-solving process, limit your use of these activities. Your egomind thrives on judging, comparing, and controlling in ways that have a negative impact on you and on others. The very definition of Negative Ego is the mind that focuses on better-than and worse-than. To maintain your creativity, you can continually monitor your motivation: *Is this to show that I'm better-than or to complain that I'm worse-than?* Egomind thinking leads to contracting egomind emotions that are fear-based. One way your egomind fends off fear is to try to control people and situations. Although controlling experimental research situations can be productive, trying to control others is not.

About Doubting, Criticizing

When you're being rational, any fact, statement, or conclusion must be subject to doubt. You search for the critical difference that will provide the next logical step in order to continue the investigation. By questioning and doubting, you use your rational thinking to create a dynamic, open process that leads you on to continuous discovery. The trick is to doubt and criticize facts, processes, and activities—not people. You build relationships by fully accepting people as they are while still confronting problematic ideas and actions.

About Asking Questions

When you need to know something, your rational mind begins asking the reporter's questions: who, what, when, where, why, and how. The answers to these questions give you an analysis of the situation and help you to understand what you're facing. In this way you come to understand the different aspects of the problem, which enables you to start resolving the situation from various points of view.

About Being Objective

Abstract thinking allows you to set up theories about cause and effect—hypotheses or predictions about what would happen if you changed one or another aspect of the process or the situation. Objective thinking allows you to separate yourself from immediate action on a problem or an emotional reaction to it. Asking analytical questions helps you to distance yourself from the problem, to become more *objective* about it. With analysis you look at all parts of the problem and get data about it. Then you put together all the relevant data and make order in such a way that you reach a new understanding of the problem. You assume that for every existing situation, there is one, several, or many causes.

Problem-Opportunity Applications

You've already explored the creative problem-opportunity process and its six stages. Look at it again in light of the role your rational mind plays in this creative process—using the Kid Fun case as an example as you move through the problem-opportunity stages. See Rational Intelligence in action as it helps you to work with the problems-opportunities inherent in an actual case situation.

Summary of Kid Fun Case

Stevie Ruiz, age 13, is president of Kid Fun, a company owned in equal fourths by Stevie, his mom, his dad, and Luis Martinez, the CEO. The company makes toys, which are invented by Stevie and his mom Donna. Kid Fun's initial product, Water Talkie, was Stevie's idea. Water Talkie can be used while snorkeling and allows users to talk with underwater partners.

Donna had some previous success in marketing inexpensive novelties. She had developed *The Formula* for making money, which she describes this way: You start with an inexpensive product idea, something that costs less than $2 to make and retails for around $10. You put dynamic packaging with that.

You sell in very high volume. Finally—and this is the step that most people don't follow—you go out to get a large order before you start to manufacture your product. And it's critical not to depend on the retailers' ability to sell the product. You must make the right agreement when you take the order from the retailer: *You buy it, you own it; we don't buy back product that you can't sell.* It's very important that inventors do that, so the retailer is motivated to find ways to generate sales of the product—not just stick it on the shelf and see what happens.

Once a prototype and packaging for Water Talkie had been dreamed up, Stevie and his mom sold 50,000 units to Toys R Us.

Case questions:

- What potential problems and/or opportunities does Kid Fun face now?
- What kinds of products should Kid Fun develop next?
- What specific recommendations would you make to Kid Fun?

Stage 1. Analyze the environment.

No situation occurs in a vacuum. You must always ferret out those occur-rences and trends going on around you that represent significant opportuni-ties or threats. In Kid Fun's case, these include other toy manufacturers, especially pool toy manufacturers, trends in what kids are attracted to and what they're doing these days, as well as the entire retailing scene, including the Internet and e-commerce.

Key Question:

What are the ongoing opportunities, threats, comparisons with com-petitors, and other environmental issues?

Process:

First purely creative, then rational-creative. You'll begin by exploring the environment and generating ideas about how the environment is affecting your situation and how the situation in turn is affecting the environment, using all your intelligences except the rational critic. When you've generated enough ideas about what's going on in the environment, then use the rational process of reviewing, organizing, evaluating, and selecting the ideas to take to the next stage of the process.

Rational Activities:

- Look at the whole situation.
- Raise doubts and questions about it.
- Ask why.

Stage 2. Recognize problems and opportunities.

At this point Kid Fun seems to have many opportunities and no prob-lems. The main job of the players in the company is to explore the numerous opportunities—now and in the foreseeable future—sift through them, and select the best bets for focusing their money and attention. Especially impor-tant are opportunities for new products and determining which products will appeal to kids. Here the main asset is Stevie. If he's really excited about a toy, chances are other kids will be also.

Key Questions:

What problems need to be solved? What opportunities need attention? Again, begin by exploring and generating ideas about where the problems and opportunities lie, followed by the rational process.

Rational activities:

- Look at the whole situation.
- Raise doubts and questions about it.
- Ask why.
- Make logical links between cause and effect.

Stage 3. Identify root problems, opportunities, and assumptions.

Kid Fun players must be careful to uncover hidden assumptions about the marketplace and how future products will fare there. Can they assume that because Water Talkie is a pool/water toy, their future toys should also be pool toys? Is that their niche? They must explore all reasonable opportunities to add to their product line: the various types of products they could develop—and the array of channels to distribute and retail their products.

As a new company, Kid Fun does not have enough money to expand rapidly, which may limit the ability to take advantage of market opportunities. If Kid Fun's principals decide that generating adequate financial backing is a problem, they must explore the many sources of funding that could be made available.

Key Questions:

What is the underlying or root problem or need that we must address? What hidden assumptions do we have that may be faulty? What opportunities are we overlooking?

Process:

First purely creative, then rational-creative. Again, begin with exploring and generating ideas about which of the issues you explored in Stage 2 are actually problems or opportunities that need further exploration—as well as possible assumptions that are faulty. Then review, organize, evaluate, and decide which ideas to take to the next stage.

Rational activities:

- Ask why.
- Review ideas about problems, opportunities, and assumptions.
- Make sequential, precise, and logical connections. (This contrasts with the Associative Intelligence you use to make more general, relational, and random connections.)
- Organize ideas in a logical way.
- Evaluate ideas about problems, opportunities, and assumptions.
- Select the best information and ideas for generating new solutions or responses to the problem-opportunity situation.

Stage 4. Let new information incubate.

This is Intuitive Intelligence time, so Kid Fun's principals let their Rational Intelligence take a break from this particular project. They step back and shift their focus to another project or other absorbing activities. They're open to new insights and ideas that may pop up, adding them to their pool of information.

Stage 5. Generate alternatives.

Kid Fun's principals must now organize all the information they've gathered, analyze it, sift through it, make associations and connections, and listen to their senses, their emotions, and their intuitive messages.

Key Question:

How many creative ideas, solutions, or plans can we come up with that address this problem or opportunity?

Process:

First rational-creative, then purely creative. Organize all the information and ideas to get a handle on them. Then explore the information, make random associations, and remain open to emotional, sensory, and intuitive input in order to generate ideas.

Rational activities:

- Observe the situation, breaking it down into all its relevant parts.
- Observe all the data in detail.
- Find reasons why this problem-opportunity situation exists.
- When you find the critical difference—what is missing—go on to generate alternatives.

Stage 6. Choose from alternatives.

Kid Fun's principals must select the best method for financing future operations. In fact, they decided to keep the firm private and swing a loan from the banker who had financed them from the beginning. They developed a business plan that described three new products Stevie had designed (all are water toys because Kid Fun players decided that is their best niche for now:)

- Pool Peepers is a water mask designed to let the wearer see out. People looking at the wearer will not see a water mask but a face mask that looks like a lobster, frog, or dragonfly.
- Pool Pogo is another product that kids will like but parents must be sure it won't damage the pool.
- Bin-Aqua-Lars are underwater binoculars. The major issue is how far apart to position the lenses.

Key Question:

Which plan has the best chance of bringing us the most success in this situation?

Process:

Rational, followed by intuitive. This stage is all about evaluating and deciding. It's primarily rational, but before deciding on the new whole, allow some time for intuitive insights to emerge, remembering that these insights may come through the other intelligences (that is, through dreams, emotions, inner vision and hearing, etc.).

Rational activities:

- ✎ Search out and test the alternatives.
- ✎ Make logical links between cause and effect.
- ✎ Make detailed connections and order them in a sequential manner.
- ✎ Give reasons to substantiate everything you say.
- ✎ Be exact.
- ✎ Explain step-by-step until you arrive at a conclusion.
- ✎ Decide on a new whole—a new solution, invention, or program.

Stage 7. Sell, implement, evaluate, and follow up.

Kid Fun must sell this plan to their banker. They must sell their toys to retailers. They must get the toys perfected, manufactured, and delivered to retailers on time. They must continually evaluate how well the toys are doing, whether improvements are needed, how to improve their products, and how satisfied their customers are. They must do the same kind of follow-up with other key stakeholders in the business, such as their customers, retailers, suppliers, shippers, and banker.

Key Questions:

- ✎ What can we do to get the people we need behind this plan?
- ✎ What do we need to do to make the plan work?
- ✎ How can we get the best results from this plan?
- ✎ What feedback mechanisms do we need to set up in order to evaluate how well the plan is doing? Do we have a good Plan B or C if Plan A doesn't work out as we expect?
- ✎ What can we do to minimize the risk factor and to boost the success factor of the plan?

Process:

All four steps in Stage 7 require exploring and generating ideas, a process that is first purely creative, then rational-creative.

Step 1: Sell the action plan. Explore ideas for selling the plan, generate ideas, and select the best ones.

Step 2: Implement the plan. Explore ideas for carrying out the plan, generate ideas for how to do it, and select the best ones.

Step 3: Evaluate the results of the plan. Explore ideas for the kinds of feedback you need to best evaluate how well the plan is working. Gather evidence, observe the effects of the plan, analyze the causes for good and poor results, search more deeply and more specifically for cause-effect relationships. In this way evaluate the overall plan and each of its aspects.

Step 4: Follow up to improve the plan. Based on the evaluation of plan results, explore ideas for solving any newly discovered problems and taking advantage of newly discovered opportunities, generate new ideas for modifying the plan, and select the best ones.

Rational activities:

- ᕱ   Ask why and find reasons why.
- ᕱ   Gather evidence.
- ᕱ   Observe the effects of the plan.
- ᕱ   Analyze the causes for good and poor results.
- ᕱ   Search more deeply and more specifically for cause-effect relationships.
- ᕱ   Evaluate the overall plan and each of its aspects.

Kid Fun has in fact grown rapidly in the past two years. They secured more than $400,000 from their banker. Sales quadrupled last year, with accounts increasing from 18 to 125, including 250 Kmart stores and 600 Target stores, as well as stores in seven foreign countries. Foreign sales now make up about a third of total sales. Very helpful are sales in South America, Australia, and Southern Africa, where the seasons are reversed. This means summer-season sales of pool toys are spread out over the entire year. As far as overhead, Kid Fun still has no full-time employees. The four principals do nearly all the work, and other duties are either contracted out or handled by part-time employees.

Sparking Your Rational Intelligence

> Oh, you must fail! If you don't fail, you won't know the degrees of success.
> You have to fall down to learn how to improve.
> *Carol Bartz, high-tech executive*

Your rational mind is essential to creative problem-solving and to responding to opportunities in a creative way. The question you must continually ask is *how can I use my Rational Intelligence most effectively*? The answer always involves balancing the rational left brain with the wholistic right brain so that you don't get trapped in rational-only thinking. In fact, all the rational-mind traps hold the key to a related strength on the other side of the trait's coin. The reverse side of *doubting* and questioning is *curiosity*. The inverse of *judging* is *discerning*. SAO #4: Find Power in Your Personal Paradox (page 171) gives you a chance to explore your own traits.

Sparkler #1: Balance Judging-Doubting with People Skills

Judging, controlling, criticizing, and doubting are important rational activities for certain steps in the creative process. They can enable you to sift through a myriad of options and arrive at the best plan of action for your particular problem-opportunity situation. On the other hand, you must beware of making the "doubting judge" a personality that you use in all your interactions with the Web of Life, especially in building personal relationships.

Problems

You know that the creative process involves building creative relationships—with clients, customers, your work team, and people within the company who must approve your innovations, use them, or sell them. Ask yourself whether you're relying too heavily on Rational Intelligence in your personal relationships.

Your many years of rational training in academia, and perhaps in a business or professional life, have formed a mind lens that you look through. Do you see the world primarily from a rational mindset? This can be devastating for building human relationships. Your negative ego finds your rational mind very cooperative in running its better-than / worse-than program. Here's one way it works:

- ❧ You encounter a person.
- ❧ Your immediate mental question is some variation of *Is he better-than I am or is he worse-than?* (variations include better-than Tom, Dick, Harry, my ideal man, etc.).
- ❧ You take the other person apart as coldly and specifically as you would take apart a piece of equipment or a business problem.
- ❧ You probe for important traits or qualities that help to answer your question.
- ❧ You reach a conclusion about the person.
- ❧ If it's a favorable conclusion, you still have an automatic tendency to judge, compare, criticize, and doubt—to look for better-thans and worse-thans.

Are you likely to form a warm, nurturing, supportive relationship with this mindset? And if this is your primary approach to people, don't you, in turn, assume that other people pick you apart in the same manner? You use your own *better-thans* to feel better about yourself—and it may work, temporarily—but deep down you know there's always a *worse-than* around the corner, waiting to pounce. Ever wonder why so many people in our modern culture are isolated and alone, off in their own little cocoons, perhaps with immediate family and two or three close friends—if that?

This kind of rational criticism and doubt can wear away your self-esteem until you give up and prefer numbness or an impersonal world. You may decide it's better to ignore others and to control your life through focusing on acquiring things or solving problems instead of trying to forge a broad array of personal relationships. Let's face it: The rational mind is not skilled at living joyfully with people.

Remedies

To balance your Negative Ego's "doubting judge," bring in the people skills you've built, using your Associative and Emotional Intelligences. Remember the Associative Intelligence skill of direct perception that you practice: the ability to just *be with* a person, without needing to add anything or take anything away from that person or the experience. This is actually a form of *unconditional love*, worth its weight in relationship gold.

Remember also your skills at identifying those egomind emotions that seem to feed your doubting judge. Could they include one of these: annoyance, blame, resentment, hostility, anger, powerlessness, regret, guilt, ego-pride, judgment, dislike, pity, disgust, contempt, revulsion, condemnation, arrogance, defensiveness, doubt, worry, anxiety, resignation, rejection, mischievousness, confusion, caution, vulnerability, embarrassment, shyness, self-pity, suffering, dread, desperation, shame, loneliness, or fear?

Identify the primary emotion, go into it and feel it fully. Be willing to let it go into other emotions anywhere on the emotional map, including going into deeper, more-contracting feelings. Be willing to let it go, once you've fully processed it.

Remember what happens when you process and release egomind emotions? You free yourself to move into one or more of the inner-body emotions, such as curiosity, excitement, admiration, empathy, love, happiness, and joy. For all of us, these emotions are an *up*, a *high*, and they motivate us to reach out to others, to share and interact. You become more open to new possibilities in relationships. You're more willing to take chances, to do something new and challenging, because you're focusing on the bright side of people and situations.

Sparkler #2: Balance Being Objective by Connecting

Rational thinking traditionally calls for being objective so that you don't confuse your personal opinions, emotions, and biases with what happens in consensus reality. You'll find it helpful to use objectivity when the situation calls for rational thinking. However, if you get in the habit of always *thinking at a distance,* you'll create blocks to your creativity. Always go back to a balance between the sequential, logical left brain and the holistic, connected right brain. Keep in mind that true knowledge must come from relationship—from knowing the wholeness of life and the wonder of life. Remember that all things are interconnected in the Web of Life.

Deal with Paradox

Remember too that *reality* is often a paradox. Nobel physicist Neils Bohr said, "The opposite of a profound truth can be another profound truth." For example, both of these statements are paradoxically true:

- People are deeply caring and compassionate with other humans.
- Among animals, only humans deliberately torture and kill others from their own species.

Also true are these paradoxical statements from quantum physics:

- Energy vibrations materialize as waves.
- Energy vibrations materialize as particles. It depends on who's watching and what they want to see or expect to see.

Reconnect the Parts

When you analyze, you *think things apart* in order to study the parts. Remember to *think them together* again—to synthesize all the information you've studied into a whole picture. You may need to connect both ends of paradoxes to get that picture.

Abstract thought involves theoretical, hypothetical concepts and ideas that are not necessarily grounded in applied experiences. Such thinking may be idealistic and transcendent. Abstract thinking, therefore, is very important for certain stages of the creative process, tying in with your imagination and the visions that you create. By itself, abstract thinking is only a small part of human intelligence. It's usually not the sole basis for your everyday decisions and actions, which are never completely rational but are always colored by emotions. Your thoughts are always embedded in your bodily sensations and in those processes that contribute to the entire range of human intelligence.

Ground Yourself

After you've spent a great deal of time using Rational Intelligence, always come back into your body, your senses, and your intuitive messages. Ground theory and abstract relationships in your own experience by asking yourself such questions as, *How does this play out in reality and in people's actual experiences?* Think of examples from your own experience, or imagine how a theory would work in the physical world.

Sparkler #3: Balance Automatic Routines with New Ways

We've discussed some of the advantages and disadvantages of categorizing data and objects in order to organize them and effectively handle them in your mind. Related to this is routinizing those similar, recurring situations that call for problem-solving, decision-making, and action. You save huge amounts of energy when you go *on automatic* in repetitive situations, but you can also block out new ideas.

Problem: Over-Routinizing

When you're on automatic, you take in and use only limited signals from the world around you without letting other signals penetrate. This is good unless you fail to notice new elements that could change the situation. Then automatic behavior could limit your self-image, your decision-making success, your creativity, and your success.

Limited Self-Image. If you decide you know all about yourself, your boundaries, and your patterns—that they're fixed and done with for life—you'll be stuck with a limited, narrow self-image that can't grow.

Limited Decision-Making. Have you fallen into a routine decision-making process rather than selecting the best process and making your own decisions anew each time the situation changes? If so, you may get mindlessly seduced into activities that you wouldn't otherwise engage in. For example, the famous study on obedience to authority, which was done by Stanley Milgram at Stanford, showed that normally kind people could be extremely cruel. Participants administered painful electric shocks to people because they thought it was what other participants were doing. They believed it was what they were "supposed" to do.

Limited Creativity. Do you ever let automatic routines take over instead of being mindful and taking personal responsibility for results? This can prevent you from making creative choices. Routines can lead you to attribute all your troubles to a single cause, which in turn narrowly limits the range of solutions you might seek.

For example, do you blame your relationship failures on your parents, school failures on your teachers, or work failures on your boss? If so, you're more likely to repeat such failures than people who take some personal responsibility for results. They're likely to see many possible explanations for their situation and to try some new, creative solutions. Similarly, if you have an addiction and see the cause of your problem as purely genetic, you're likely to give up on the self-control—and the resulting creative ideas—that could lead to recovery. A single-minded explanation blocks you from paying attention to valid information that doesn't fit in with your *reason why*.

Limited Success. Carrying this automatic syndrome a step further, repeated failure in one area of life may cause you to give up in all areas. Research indicates that such *learned helplessness* then generalizes to situations in which you could in fact exercise control. For example, if you keep failing at relationships, you may assume you'll fail at that new people-oriented job you're interested in. You feel a sense of futility that prevents you from reconsidering the causes of the relationship failures. You remain passive toward the new job opportunity, even though you could handle the job with little difficulty.

Remedy: Keeping an Open Mind

In reality you'll be most creative and successful if you develop effective rational-mind habits and techniques while keeping an open mind to new information and a willingness to try new ways. If you're mindfully engaged, you'll actively attend to changed signals. Your behavior is likely to be more effective.

When you're open to different viewpoints, you begin to realize there are many viewpoints other than our own. There are as many fine gradations of viewpoint as there are observers. For example, has a friend ever accused you of having incorrect information, and you disagreed? He may have thought he was being frank. Suppose you opened up to an awareness of the many perspectives of the situation that you were giving information about. Could you accept that you both may be right? If so, you might be able to concentrate on whether your information conveyed the story you wanted to tell—or had the impact you wanted it to have (rather than concentrating on defending it as *right*). As a result, you'll gain more choices in how to respond, more options. And change becomes more possible for you.

Sparkler #4: Watch Out for Rationalizations and Projections

Your rational mind excels at rationalizing and projecting. You'll want to use it to help you be more creative, not to undermine your efforts.

Rationalizing

When you rationalize, you give rational reasons for something. You intellectualize the causes for certain effects. Rationalizing, used correctly, is a powerful engine of the reasoning process. But if you give this power to your Negative Ego, it will use it to make all kinds of excuses for you. You'll be able to convince yourself that no matter now irresponsible you've been, no matter what a mess you've created or cocreated, things are not *as they seem*. You can convince yourself of absolutely anything if you really want to and if you allow your Negative Ego to take charge. This is such a common occurrence that psychologists use the term *rationalization* to mean denying, avoiding reality, and making excuses.

The first step in avoiding rationalization is simply being aware and alert to the tendency. When you think you may be rationalizing, ask yourself, *Am I taking responsibility for creating this situation?* or *Am I denying, avoiding, or distorting what's really going on here?*

Projecting

Your Negative Ego loves to project its own *stuff* upon other persons in your life, attributing to them what you are thinking, feeling, or wanting while in that negative-ego mode. You can then point to another person as having certain problems that in actuality you are experiencing. This temporarily takes the spotlight off your own need to face your problem and *clean up your act*. This is another one of those human tendencies that's so common that psychologists have labeled it *projection*. When you find yourself criticizing and judging another person, ask yourself, *How does her problem reflect my own tendencies? Does his problem bug me because I haven't faced a similar issue in my own life?*

You'll want to watch out for rationalizations and projections, so you can minimize self-sabotage and keep opening yourself up to the expansive inner-body emotions that attract creative possibilities. On the other hand, remember that these are normal human tendencies. Don't make them wrong. Instead, see them as creative blocks. If you face your human frailties and smile at them, you free yourself to choose to move beyond them into more productive ways of using your Rational Intelligence.

Creative Processes Using Rational Intelligence

Here are some creative processes that call upon your Rational Intelligence. Apply these processes to the problem-opportunity situations you encounter.

Play Devil's Advocate

This process is especially effective at these problem-opportunity stages: "Identify root problems" and "Choose from alternatives." It calls on the doubting judge to assess ideas and processes. Work with one or more partners. Here's how it works:

- ❧ Take a position on what you think the problem or opportunity is—or what you think the response to it should be.
- ❧ The other person(s) plays devil's advocate by pointing out what might be wrong with your position and suggesting other positions.
- ❧ Each person in turn takes a position while the other(s) plays devil's advocate.

The process can help you to arrive at a better definition of the situation and ways to respond to it. It's important to criticize only ideas and information, not the person who volunteers them—and to express criticisms in ways that enhance this stance.

Process Ideas

This technique can be especially helpful at the "Choose from alternatives" stage if you have many ideas to choose from. This may occur when you are

working with a team. Put each idea on an index card or other media for display-
ing the idea and working with it. Process ideas in this way:

- *Combine* similar ideas.
- *Exclude* anything not related to the goal (put these in a separate pile for possible future consideration).
- *Modify*, where appropriate, by rewriting.
- *Defer* ideas that have merit but are not timely by putting into a separate pile to consider when the time is right.
- *Review* the ideas you've been processing, looking for new insights, ideas, and suggestions.
- *Organize* similar ideas into batches of seven or eight, if you have a surplus of ideas.
- *Label* each batch by topic or type of idea.
- *Rank* each idea within batches based on its usefulness or impor-tance to achieving the goal.
- *Reorganize* the ideas, placing the highest-ranked ones in one batch, the second-highest ranked ones in another batch, and so forth.
- *Evaluate* the results. What has this process suggested for choos-ing the best action plan?

Use SCAMMPERR Idea Processing

SCAMMPERR is an acronym for the following kinds of idea processing. It's used primarily in the "Generate alternatives" phase of the problem-
opportunity process, but it can also be used in other phases. SCAMMPERR
stands for:

- Substitute
- Combine
- Adapt
- Magnify
- Modify
- Put to other uses
- Eliminate
- Rearrange
- Reverse

Let's look at each of these steps in more detail.

Substitute

- What can be substituted?
- Who else could fulfill this need?
- What other procedure might work better? Other material? Color? Approach? Format?

Combine

- Combine ideas? Purposes? Talents?
- What could be merged with this?
- How about an assortment?

Adapt

- ✎ What other ideas can we incorporate?
- ✎ Can other processes be adapted?
- ✎ Whom could we emulate?
- ✎ Can we put the product or service into a different context?
- ✎ What ideas outside the field can we adapt?
- ✎ What else can be adapted?

Magnify

- ✎ What can be made larger? What if we made it really enormous?
- ✎ What can be added? Extended? Made longer? Higher? Overstated?
- ✎ What extra features could we add? What can add more value?

Modify

- ✎ How can this be altered for the better?
- ✎ How can we change the nature or meaning of any aspect of the situation?
- ✎ What other shape? New twist?
- ✎ How can we modify standard procedures? Attitudes?

Put to other uses

- ✎ What else can we do with this?
- ✎ What else can be done with the waste? Other uses as is? Other uses if modified? Other extensions? Other markets? Other fields?

Eliminate

- ✎ What can be streamlined? Omitted? Made smaller? Divided? Split up? Understated?
- ✎ What's not necessary?

Rearrange

- ✎ Other corporate arrangement? Payment plan? Pattern?
- ✎ Can we change pace? Interchange components? Change layout?
- ✎ What are the negatives?

Reverse

- ✎ Reverse it? Consider it backwards? Down instead of up? Do the opposite? Reverse roles? Turn it around?
- ✎ Do the unexpected?

A Final Word

Now you may be viewing this old friend, your Rational Intelligence, with fresh eyes. This is the intelligence that can trap you or empower you, depending on how you use it. So raise your awareness by completing the Self-Awareness Opportunities that follow. Then cross over again to your wholistic, timeless right-brain world. Dive in and revel in your Sensory Intelligence.

Self-Awareness Opportunities

SAO #1: Overcome Fear-of-Risk Blocks.

Purpose: To break through fear-of-risk barriers.

Fear of taking a risk is perhaps the most common block to creativity. When you want to pursue a new idea but are afraid, write a worst-case scenario. Detail precisely what could happen if everything goes wrong. This brings the fears out of the closet into the light of conscious awareness. When you deal with the precise information, you're able to logically analyze the possibilities and probabilities of success and failure. In other words, you can swap your fear of failure for analytical capability.

SAO #2: Play Devil's Advocate.

Purpose: To challenge your current rational-mind thinking patterns.

In working with your own personal growth, let your rational mind play devil's advocate.

Look at any relationship that's problematic. Ask yourself:

- *Where am I coming from Negative Ego?*
- *What am I denying?*
- *Am I rationalizing here?*
- *Am I projecting my own egomind workings onto someone else?*
- *Am I engaging in some type of self-sabotaging behavior?*

Use your doubting critic to pinpoint your creative blocks so you can choose to move beyond them.

SAO #3: Play with Rational-Mind Workouts.

Purpose: To boost the creative aspects of your Rational Intelligence.

Our culture is overflowing with rational-mind workout opportunities. Here are a few examples:

- Language has its own rational logic, so doing crossword puzzles and learning a new language are Rational Intelligence workouts.
- Math is obviously a rational-mind activity, so doing math problems is a good workout.
- A challenging puzzle or game can provide good practice.
- Browse a bookstore or the Web—using such search words as *brain builders, mind benders,* and *puzzles*—to find books of rational-

mind skill builders. The Mensa organization publishes dozens of books designed to stimulate rational thinking and improve your Rational Intelligence.

SAO #4: Find Power in Your Personal Paradox.

Purpose: To understand how your rational mind traps, and other egomind traits, hold the key to a related strength on the other side of the traits coin.

Note: This process is adapted from a process developed by Jerry Fletcher [1997].

Step 1: Find your core paradox pair of traits.

Randomly list your major personal traits, both those you view as strengths and those you see as weaknesses. Try to list 20 or 30 traits, focusing especially on the rationa-mind traps.

- Review the list, placing a plus or minus sign by each to denote strength or weakness.
- Find pairs of traits that are opposites, self-canceling, paradoxical, or strength-weakness.
- Work with these pairs for a while until you identify one pair that represents a central conflict that you repeatedly struggle with.

Examples: *do-nothing achiever, ambitious slowpoke, hesitant risk-taker, ruthless helper, spontaneous planner, careless planner, passionate robot, iron butterfly, gentle warrior, velvet jackhammer, cutthroat pussycat, creative imitator, vague analyst, meticulous tolerator, silken sergeant, compulsive free spirit*

Important: Instead of denying, avoiding, and rationalizing a weak trait, admit it, embrace it, and be willing to work with it in order to discover its constructive aspects.

Step 2: Explore the facets of your core paradox pair.

- Place your core pair of traits in the middle of a blank sheet of paper.
- Focusing on the *strength*, list above it other, related traits that are positive expressions of that core strength, becoming more positive as you move upward.
- List below that *strength* other, related traits that are negative expressions of that core trait, becoming more negative as you move downward.
- Focusing on the *weakness*, list above it other, related traits that are positive expressions of that core trait, becoming more positive as you move upward.
- List below that *weakness* other, related traits that are negative expressions of that core trait, becoming more negative as you move downward.

Important: Stick with expressions of the core trait, so that you have a vertical range of expressions of that same trait, from its most positive to its most negative expression.

Examples: Facets of Three Core Paradox Pairs

charismatic	enabler	real	visionary	trustworthy	peacemaker
doer	strong	natural	pilot	credible	gentle
lively	take charge	pristine	initiative	genuine	careful
intense	fearless	untouched	instigator	honorable	moderate
passionate	powerful	pragmatic	influencer	principled	nonthreat
enthusiastic	do-er	candid	guide	respectable	careful
enterprising	active	direct	committed	sincere	neutral
Energetic	**Steamroller**	**Crude**	**Leader**	**Honest**	**Wimp**
overwhelming	self-absorbed	thoughtless	self-important	tells all	passive
tiring	domineering	insensitive	weighty	righteous	ineffectual
insensitive	oblivious	uncaring	superior	better-than	fearful
steamroller	detached	rough	dominating	inflexible	weak
frantic	threatening	gross	frightening	obsessive	coward

Step 3: Discover your self-empowering and self-sabotage pairs.

- ✎ Discover your *self-empowering strength-weakness pair*, the most positive pair of traits that your core pair could lead to.
- ✎ Discover your *self-sabotage strength-weakness pair*, the most negative pair of traits that your core pair could lead to.

Examples of Self-Empowering and Self-Sabotage Pairs

Core Strength-Weakness	**Self-Empowering Pair**	**Self-Sabotage Pair**
Energetic Steamroller	Charismatic Enabler	Frantic Threatener
Crude Leader	Real Visionary	Gross Frightener
Honest Wimp	Trustworthy Peacemaker	Obsessive Coward
Other Examples:		
Do-nothing Achiever	Breakthrough Mapmaker	Carping Workaholic
Self-doubting Overachiever	Prepared Genius	Hopeless Drudge
Conventional Extrovert	Reliable Communicator	Shortsighted Windbag
Driven Indifferent	Focused Pressure-Resister	Obsessive Slob

Step 4: Define a problem situation, apply your strength-weakness pair.

- ✎ Describe a problem situation by writing a brief outline of its key facets.
- ✎ Think of all your options or choices for responding to this situation.
- ✎ Describe how this situation affects you—emotionally, psychologically, and practically.
- ✎ Evaluate your past responses and efforts to deal with this situation. How do these responses reflect your core strength-weakness pair? Have they been primarily from the negative, bottom self-sabotage pairs of traits or from the self-empowering pairs?
- ✎ How could you make better use of your positive, self-empowering pairs of traits (from the top half of your chart) in responding to this problem?

- Write a goal statement with a time target: *I'm going to find a way to...* and list the objective outcomes you would like, in terms of what the solution must include but leaving room for various ways the solution might be reached.

- Add a *from...to...* statement to indicate how the situation will change. For example: *"I'm going to find a way to move **from** being ignored by my contact **to** our developing a productive relationship,"* or *"**from** my getting no attention or action from my contact **to** our working together for our mutual success and profit."*

  Does this goal statement incorporate your self-empowering strength-weakness pair of traits? List action steps you can take, what you can do to act out this positive combination of your strength-weakness traits. How can these two conflicting traits work together to empower you to achieve your goal?

- Think of other situations that are creating tension and conflict in your life. Repeat Step 4, adding these suggestions where they apply:

  - Brainstorm with another person.
  - First work on the *weakness* trait of your core strength-weakness pair, choosing actions to raise it into balance with the strength.
  - Look at both core traits, even the weakness in its more positive expressions, moving up toward the self-empowering strength-weakness pair.
  - Work on embracing both traits, keeping in mind that both traits in your self-empowering strength-weakness pair work together to produce more power than the strength can produce by itself.

Notice how you tend to express self-empowering pairs of traits in tandem, but you swing erratically from side to side when you express the self-sabotage pairs of traits.

Chapter 8

Just Imagine:
Sensory Intelligence

Imagination is the highest kite we can fly.
Lauren Bacall, actress

You use your Sensory Intelligence when you relate to the world through your senses and when you learn through your senses. You're most familiar with the five senses you use to interact with your outer world: seeing, hearing, moving-touching, smelling, and tasting. Even more directly linked to your creativity are the senses for interacting with your inner world—inner vision including visualizing and imagining, inner hearing of verbal ideas or chords or tones, inner smelling and tasting sometimes based on vivid memories, and inner movement.

Most vital to your Creative Intelligence is your internal visioning ability. Vision, imagination, and insight are powerful links to Intuitive Intelligence and through that to the Web of Life. But as your grew up, you probably heard many belittling comments such as these:

- ❧ It's just your imagination.
- ❧ Stop daydreaming!
- ❧ That's total fantasy.

You may therefore have some self-limiting beliefs about your Sensory Intelligence. Not to worry. You can become aware of them and replace them with new self-empowering beliefs.

Here's a brief overview of the senses as they relate to Creative Intelligence:

- ✎ *Kinesthetic* intelligence includes movement in space, finding your way around, athletics, sports, and artistic expression through movement, such as dance, ballet, acting, and similar activities.

- ✎ *Aural* intelligence includes relating and learning through listening—through the sounds that resonate through your body, through soaring with beautiful music and expressing yourself through music.

- ✎ *Olfactory* intelligence includes relating and learning through your senses of smell and taste and includes artistic expression through preparing and appreciating foods.

- ✎ *Visual* intelligence includes relating and learning through what you see externally and internally—through your powers of visualization and imagination. It includes artistic expression through the visual arts and the appreciation of visual arts.

- ✎ *Crossover sensory* intelligence refers to combining or switching senses. Creative people often perceive or think in crossover terms. Does the smell of fresh-mowed grass bring up the color green in your mind? If so, you're crossing the olfactory and visual senses. An artist may see a musical rendition of Bach as a colorful tapestry. A musician may hear the brilliant purples and pinks of a sunset as vibrant musical chords. Such crossover is called synesthesia.

People vary in their patterns of taking in information. Most of us actually receive a mixture from all the senses but rely most heavily on one sense above all others. For most the dominant sense is vision, the images we take in. For some, it's the sounds, verbal and musical, that they hear. Some rely mainly on touch and body movement, while others focus on odors or fragrances. And of course creative chefs depend primarily on the combination of taste and smell.

Terms to associate with Sensory Intelligence include:

> image, imagination, fantasy, visual, musical, tones, chords, dancing, movement, motion, athletics, smelling, tasting, neocortex, right-brain

Innovation Showcase:
Melba Duncan on Sensory Intelligence

In 1985 Melba Duncan had a vision for a personnel placement firm. Somewhere between the bottom rungs of temp clerk placement and the top rungs of executive placement, she visualized a niche: She would specialize in pairing up top-level executive assistants with the executives who needed their services. Maybe she programmed her dreams because she awoke one morning with the vision vividly in mind.

For 15 years Duncan had worked as executive assistant to a high-powered Wall Street CEO. Many times, an executive who had visited her boss would call to ask if she knew of someone open to a job change—someone sharp, with nerves of steel and unshakable poise—someone just like Duncan herself. Frequently she had served as matchmaker, sensing when the chemistry would be right between the executive and an assistant she had in mind.

Duncan's innovative vision created a whole new genre of search practice. She blended her extensive knowledge of assistantship with her observation that this was an overlooked arena of the business scene, one that hovered beneath the notice of big executive-search firms. Want to know a trade secret? Duncan selects executive assistants who fit her visual model of success, so she can tell her executive clients. She told interviewer Nancy Austin:

The successful executive assistant is not a subordinate, but a business ally of the first order: You get executive attitude in a support role.

Today the Duncan Group is still the only retained search firm in the country that deals exclusively in the special world of administrative-support professionals. It's generating more than $1 million a year in revenues, and Melba is having the time of her life.

Sparking Your Sensory Intelligence

You may receive intuitive messages through your senses. Most people do, but people vary as to which sense connects most often with Intuitive Intelligence. And some people receive most or all of their intuitive messages as a wholistic *sense of knowing*, which doesn't seem to involve any of the senses. If you are like most people, however, you can spark your Intuitive Intelligence by boosting your awareness of sensory messages, especially those that seem to come from within—in other words, messages that are *not* clearly from your external environment, such as the ringing of a doorbell, the sight of a person at the door, the touch of her hand in a handshake, or the smell of her cologne. Your inner senses include:

- Seeing visual imagery, as a thinking process.
- Hearing sounds, music, tones, themes from within.
- Hearing messages, information, from an inner voice.
- Smelling and tasting by imagination.
- Thinking about certain body movements and feeling them in your mind; playing them out or practicing them (psycho-cybernetics).

Sparkler #1: Become More Sensual

Pay attention to your senses. Enjoy sensual experiences: the breeze on your skin, the fruit on your tongue, the lover's touch on your lips. Let them entice you and work their full magic. The experiences in Snapshot #1 on page 177 can give you some ideas. Let even the unpleasant sensory experiences interest you—the weird smells, little pains, messy sights. Raise your awareness of the whole range of your sensuality.

Sparkler #2: Make Sense Connections

You can make more sensory connections by connecting outer and inner senses, by connecting experiences to their expression, and by connecting one sense to another.

Connect Outer and Inner

Allow more input from your outer world. Try these techniques:

Snapshot #1: Sensory Highs

Falling in love	Friends
Laughing so hard your face hurts	Watching a spectacular sunset
A hot shower	Sleepovers
A special glance	Your first kiss
Getting mail	Being part of a team
Taking a drive on an intriguing road	Playing with a new puppy
Hearing your favorite song on the radio	Having someone play with your hair
Lying in bed listening to the rain outside	Sweet dreams
Hot towels out of the dryer	Hot chocolate
Walking out of your last final	Road trips with friends
A chocolate milkshake	Swinging on a swing
A long-distance phone call	Going to a really good concert
Getting invited to a party	Hanging out with close friends
Butterflies, fireflies, humming birds	Riding a bike downhill
Laughing till you cry	Hugging a person you love
A good conversation	Running through sprinklers
A care package	Laughing for absolutely no reason at all
The beach	Laughing at an inside joke
Laughing at yourself	Balmy summer nights
Midnight phone calls that last for hours	Getting out of bed in the morning and
Greeting the sunrise	rejoicing because you're alive!

- ✌ When you listen or read, visualize what the words are saying. See the experience, events, processes, people, relationships, and so forth.

- ✌ Draw quick sketches of how things look, where this would help you make it real, concrete, and memorable.

- ✌ Work with sensory input in your inner world. Meditation is a way of listening beyond your Negative Ego, rational-mind yada-yada. With practice you can learn to differentiate between ego-chatter and deeper-level information.

- ✌ Deeper-level information can help you put your current life and concerns into a bigger framework, the larger picture. You see clearly what's trivia and what's important. Your priorities fall into place. You engage in a higher-level thinking process that can lead to visions of what you and others can create in the future.

- ✌ Use this inner learning to boost your level of expectancy, your active belief in "I can."

- ✌ While in meditation, work with visualizations to express this inner learning in the outer world. For example, set related goals and visualize the goals as already achieved.

Connect to Experience and Expression

Remember: Everything you create or do happens first in your mind. So when you develop your inner senses, you give a powerful boost to your Creative Intelligence. For example, you expand your skills in:

- ✌ Observing and exploring the world.

- Learning about the world—by making connections between what you see, hear, touch, smell/taste, both externally and internally, and what you think and feel.

- Expressing yourself—through artistic creations based on what you see, hear, smell/taste or felt body movement, by producing a drawing, a painting, a song, a dance, a great dinner, a new business project, etc.

- Opening up to receive intuitive information.

Connect Sense to Sense

Be willing to fine-tune these senses. One way to do that is to practice synesthesia, the crossover of sensory input. Ask yourself these kinds of questions:

- What color is that sound? That word? That image or picture? That fragrance?

- What color is that touch, that physical movement (for example, a leap, a twirl)?

- What sound-tone is that color? That word? That image? That odor?

- What sound-tone is that touch or physical movement?

- What feeling does that sound have?

- What word triggers that image?

A feeling may elicit also a color, sound-tone, fragrance, touch, or physical movement. A word may elicit a picture, a color, a sound-tone, an odor, or a taste. Every one of the senses can cross over with any and all of the others.

Sparkler #3: Try Creative Culture Shock

As a creative person—whether your niche is in business, science, academia, or the arts—you need to continually cultivate new awarenesses. You need to clear your mind of old habits and search for input that's fresh, input that triggers creative insights—and you must refresh again and again through the years. Your biggest block to regaining that beginner's mind, the one that welcomes new ideas, is your belief that you already know it—the *been there, done that* reaction. You need to continually regain the curiosity and wonder you had as a little child: the *wow, that's amazing* reaction.

There's no better way to unblock your mind—to get back to that blank-slate beginner's mind—than to travel to strange parts of the world. If you don't have the time and money to go in person, try the next best thing. Travel in your imagination by immersing yourself in the strange worlds you can find in books and films and on the Internet. You'll find a cost-effective glimpse into the values, mindsets, and imaginations of people from other cultures. Buy yourself a ticket to a refreshing, shocking alien environment that assaults all your senses. Start with the one that seems most exotic and alluring to you at this moment.

You must keep looking outside for fresh input—whether it's in wildly varying fields of inquiry, talking to kids or old folks, taking up new hobbies or sports, whatever works to keep you moving mentally. You need to *know* what you don't know. You need to contact what is really new for you and recognize it as such through your beginner's mind. You can't leave to chance this fresh input and the powerful awarenesses that result from it. You need to plan for freshness in an intentional, systematic, and ongoing way. And then keep making new associations and connections between things—seeing new, weird, and wonderful analogies and relationships.

Sparkler #4: Allow the Magic

You've learned that such emotions as gratitude, forgiveness, curiosity, and wonder empower the creative process. They're magic. Let's look at wonder for a moment. This emotion arises from a sense of enchantment. And here's where your senses play a definite role. The garden has long been a metaphor for paradise, and lovely gardens enchant us all. We're transported to a wondrous sensory state by the rose's curled coral petals, the maple's quivering burgundy canopy, the lush emerald grass carpet, the iridescent flash of a hummingbird, and the tinkly splash of falling water. We're rapt in their fragrance, their beauty, their sounds.

Enchantment comes from opening up to nature—how it speaks to you, what it teaches you. It comes from allowing the wonder of the innocent child to return and to stay always within you. So open up to the enchantment your senses can bring to your life—not only from nature but from all your experiences. Here are some examples:

Kinesthetic touch

Rapture over the sensuous feel of handmade things; of fabrics, sculpture, and furniture; of moving your body in sport, dance, or any activity; of moving through life; of enchanted travel. Think of a time when your bodily sensations were vivid and divine, such as floating, soaring, or gliding.

Sound and silence

Groove on the music of enchantment. Think of a time when you heard sounds, other than words, that had a vivid impact on you. Allow the chimes, chants, bells, drums, strings, horns, and singing bowls to reverberate through your body.

Images

Glory in the beauty of nature and art. Think of a time when the beauty of the scene before you took your breath away.

Smells and tastes

Relish food and its preparation, presentation, and enjoyment. Think of a fragrance or odor from your past that was enticing and vivid. Allow into your awareness all the related memories connected to this sensory memory. Think of a taste, something delicious that you ate, or tasted through the atmosphere (such as salt air), that had a vivid impact on you.

Jump-start your Sensory Intelligence by hanging out in nature whenever you can—and really be with it in the present moment. The Muse of Nature's realm includes timing and movement. If you flow with time, that freedom and openness connect you to your Nature Spirit self. When you relax into tenderness, gentleness, and vulnerability, you open up to her magic.

When you listen to Nature's sounds and appreciate the beauty all around you, she flows in and enlivens your imagination. When you then allow your imagination to wander and wonder, you honor your Nature Spirit self. She'll gift you with beauty and playfulness, encouraging your child within to be free.

Your Nature Spirit self understands the seasons of nature and sees creativity as an organic, cyclic process of creation and destruction, life and death. She participates and co-creates within this cyclical process instead of trying to control it or fight it. Allow the old to pass away when the time is ripe, to make way for the new creations that want to spring out.

Sparkler #5: See Your Visualization Power

Imagination is internal visualization. Imagination may function most powerfully during meditation, when external distractions are minimized. So use your imagination!

Your right hemisphere will develop along with your left. You will energize both hemispheres and constantly expand the network of connections in your neocortex. You'll improve your memory and possibly your enjoyment of all your experiences.

Imaging or inner visual thinking is its own form of thinking. When you're exploring a topic or communicating about it to someone, use *I see* as well as *I think* to express the information. Both processes register in your memory and you may remember the image more vividly than the word. You have many ways of accessing your memory. When planning a new project or event, asking *What will it look like?* can be just as important as asking *What is the cause?* or *What is the effect?*

Every time you hear yourself saying *I think*, imagine yourself also saying *I see* or *It looks like* and create a mental picture related to that thought.

If you hear yourself saying *I think* when you're really imaging, rephrase your statement to reflect reality. Conversely, if you finding yourself saying *I see* when what's going on internally is actually a thought, rephrase the statement to *I think*. Then convert this thought into a picture and express what you see.

Periodically, as you read something, take a moment to visualize it. Even better, draw some images, either to help you grasp the material more deeply or to include in your writing to help readers grasp the information. Sketch relationships and images that help you understand the material, make it real, connect it to related information, show various types of relationships, and so on.

Before you begin to write something, visualize it: how it looks, relates, connects, and flows. After you have written, go back and review. Imagine that you're the reader or audience for this bit of writing. Visualize the story or information as that reader would probably be able to do. Notice important gaps and opportunities for enlivening the visual experience.

Sketch and doodle any time you feel like it. When you're learning about a new topic, seek out pictures, films, videotapes, and other visuals that can help to crystallize the concepts in your mind.

Any time you're listening to others, especially when they're conveying information or instructions, visualize how that information would look in physical form. See people using it or carrying out the instructions. Imagine the results.

Meditate for Deeper Messages

To practice internal visualization, close your eyes to prevent visual distraction and you may create more powerful images. The more relaxed your body becomes, the deeper you can go into your inner self. Actively imagine a person or a place until you feel as if it is in your presence. Stay still and quiet until images come that are not activated by your will. Let images present themselves on the screen of your mind. Let them pass by without becoming attached to them. Remain quiet and still, focusing on the screen of your mind without losing your concentration, and more images and colors will present themselves. Smells may also come. You tend to get more profound and comprehensive glimpses within your inner being when your eyes are closed than when they're open.

Every time you meditate, focus more deeply into this inner space of thin and rapid wavelengths, and other dimensions of life will occur. Focusing on an inspirational person that represents to you love, forgiveness, appreciation, and wonder can help you deepen into the thinner wavelengths.

Create the Life You Want

You can use visual intelligence to program your day or any future event or project. You can create images of the possible before it happens. Research on psycho-cybernetics has documented the power of mental rehearsal—over and over again since the 1950s. That's why virtually all the world's top athletes and artists use such techniques.

See yourself giving an important presentation, for example, presenting the information, answering questions, warmly relating to the people who will be there. This practice can help you to feel secure with the people and the event before experiencing it in your external reality. Visualizing the future allows you to realize what may be missing from your presentation or project. You can imagine how to change your presentation or fill in the missing parts of the project. You get to see and play the game ahead of time, rehearse it, adjust your action plan, refocus your attention, or change the plan.

You may want to visualize an ordinary day as peaceful, loving, connecting with others. You can enter the day more consciously, alert to what you need to do, seeing how to make it the kind of day you want, aware of what needs adjusting or how you might be more flexible, and so forth. This practice can lead to a day that is less stressful, and more fulfilling, creative, and joyful. Here are some suggestions:

- Focus on the event or project as if you are watching a film.
- Visualize each step of the event or project as it unfolds.
- If you're not satisfied with a particular part, go back and imagine how it could be most effective and fulfilling. Try some creativity techniques to come up with new ideas about how to handle this aspect. Now visualize it again.

- ◌ Allow yourself to be affected by this picture, and have the intention to create it most effectively.

- ◌ Focus especially on the end result you want and the feelings you have about that. Experience the feeling tone between you and others who are involved.

- ◌ On the other hand, be open to the idea that it could unfold even more effectively than you have imagined, and allow yourself to be flexible when the event actually occurs. Be willing to let go of the exact results you've visualized, to put it out in the world mentally and trust that *this or better—for the highest good of all* will emerge.

Use Past Experience to Boost Future Success

You can use this powerful visualization process to relive the past in order to boost your future success. You can use your imagination to build on past successes and current strengths. In the past you have experienced moments of great strength, great health, great flexibility, and so on. You can bring these moments and situations back to your consciousness and allow yourself to be affected by them in the present moment. You can also learn lessons from past *failures*, which are really just learning experiences, and you can go back and heal old wounds that still block you. Try these techniques while you're in a relaxed meditative state:

- ◌ Recall past successes that give you the confidence and the informational reminders for succeeding in your current projects and relationships. Pull up all the sensory information about how that past success felt emotionally as well as what you heard, saw, touched, smelled, and tasted.

- ◌ Learn from past experience what not to do. The only reason to go back to old hurts and *failures* is to ask, *What lesson did I learn? What if I could do it over?* Take the lesson and let go of the idea of *failure*.

- ◌ Re-experience past hurts that are still creating problems in your life. Rewrite history in ways that free up your creativity. In meditation, go back to that time and as a wiser adult now, give your former self what she needs to heal that situation.

Use Expectancy to Boost Your Creative Power

Expectancy is vision, the capacity to imagine and see a better tomorrow. Positive expectancy can help you visualize a better future—and to actually bring it about. Expectancy is a new vision of the future, different from what you're living in the present. You can convert these images of the future into a way of guiding your life. You can train your mind to focus actively and consciously on positive future images. You can actively construct the vision that you want to bring into reality. You may want to change some of your images as you go along, but your current vision can serve as your guiding star.

Remember, your brain is energy—and when you consciously guide this energy, you can create great things. When you don't do it consciously, your subconscious egomind does it without your awareness. Here is the paradox you must work with: You can create more of the kinds of things you want in life if you consciously guide your own energy. On the other hand, you're usually interacting with many people and events in the Web of Life and cocreating with them. You must also work with their energies and be flexible in allowing events to unfold in all their wondrous complexity.

The future can be a state that you first envision in your mind, which then happens or not, depending on many factors. We can all participate in helping to create a better future. To visualize the future is a capacity of your mind. Use it consciously.

Creative Processes Using Sensory Intelligence

Here are some creative processes that call upon your Sensory Intelligence. Apply these processes to the problem-opportunity situations you encounter.

Sensory Exploration

Focus on your problem-opportunity situation. Begin to sense it, using each of your physical senses in order to explore all aspects of the situation.

How does it look? Imagine—literally, figuratively, symbolically. Allow new insights. Write them down. Repeat this process for the other senses:

- What do you, or others, hear? What sounds do you connect with the situation?
- How does it smell?
- What does it taste like?
- How does it feel, by touch or movement, kinesthetically?

How can you more fully experience all aspects of the problem-opportunity situation? For example, if you are working on improving a service or product— or creating a new service or product—how can you live with current services or products that might be competitive? Test them yourself. Use them in your own life. Broaden and deepen your experience with this type of situation. What insights does this experience suggest?

Listening

To structure your listening, ask for input about your problem-opportunity situation. This includes:

- Who are the stakeholders in your problem-opportunity situation?
- How can you best elicit ideas, suggestions, information, or input from them?
- What process can you use that will inspire or motivate them to contribute?
- How can you be sure they feel rewarded for contributing, even if their ideas cannot be implemented at this time?

When someone discusses a problem-opportunity with you, be aware of opening up your mind to new possibilities. Listen to all ideas, including *far-fetched* ones, for the possibilities they may open up for you. As you listen, envision the possibilities that could be related to the idea the person is discussing.

For one week, pay special attention to open listening. Keep a record of your experiences.

Visual Stimulation

Visual stimulation is great for triggering new ideas. It's also powerful for holding in your mind your intention to create something new.

Collect magazines, brochures, and catalogs that have colorful pictures, including ads, that delight your imagination. Likely choices include travel and fashion magazines, travel brochures with inspiring destinations, and colorful catalogs of jewelry, clothing, and home furnishings.

Clip pictures that appeal to you and that seem in some way connected to what you want to create in this situation. Don't limit yourself—when in doubt, clip it. Range free and wide rather than tight and small. You may also find key words, sentences, and even brief articles to add to your creative collection.

Decide how you will put together and use these clippings, both to trigger new ideas and to symbolize your intention to create something new. Possibilities include:

- **Make a collage** on any size paper or poster board using paper glue. Or use a corkboard and push pins. Play with arranging the clippings in various patterns before you actually glue. Do you want to add your own lettering or drawings? When you've finished your collage, place it where you'll see it frequently. Each time you see it, be conscious of its symbolism, meaning, and impact for you.

- **Make file folders**, using some cataloging system to identify the type of clippings in each folder. Place your clippings in the folders. Set specific times, and put them on your calendar, to go through the folders, to remind yourself of your vision, and to inspire yourself. Add to the folders on a regular basis until you bring your vision into physical reality.

- **Other methods** might be posting one picture at a time on your desk, on your bathroom mirror, on the cover of your notebook, or on the dashboard of your car. What other methods might fit your lifestyle?

Mind Mapping

Mind mapping builds on the fact that your brain works primarily with key concepts in an interrelated and integrated manner. Here are suggestions for arriving at a visual display of these relationships:

- Write a brief definition of the problem, opportunity, or item in the center of a piece of paper and draw a circle around it.

- Ask *What are the major aspects of this problem-opportunity?* Write each one on a main line drawn outward from the central circle, similar to main thoroughfares running out from the city center.

- Ask *What are sub-aspects or key qualities of each of the major aspects?* Write these on branches (similar to streets) running off the main thoroughfares.

    ~ Use your ingenuity to add other visual signals, such as different colored pens for major lines of thought, circles around thoughts that appear more than once, connecting dotted or colored lines between similar thoughts, etc.

    ~ Study your mind map. What new relationships do you see? What insights, ideas, or solutions do they suggest?

Variation: Team Mind Maps

Ask your team to mind map a problem-opportunity situation. Then make transparencies of each mind map, or scan them into the computer, or use any way that works to give team members easy access to each others' mind maps. As members examine a mind map, have its creator explain her thinking. Visual mind maps showing creative connections can inspire further connections and spark new ideas.

Variation: Idea Collection

As insights, flashes, and ideas come to you (or your team), jot them down on sticky notes or index cards and keep them in a box where you can easily refer to them. Periodically take them out and arrange them on a bulletin board, desktop, or tabletop. Rearrange them and play with them, looking for relationships, patterns, combinations, and new ideas.

Team Visualizing: Idea Display

Here is a method teams can use to generate idea synergy:

1. The team identifies the problem-opportunity situation and defines it in a brief statement along with the goal of this team activity.

2. Members individually write rapidly as many ideas as they can on post-it notes or index cards, taking about 10 minutes to generate 15 to 20 ideas per member.

3. The facilitator collects the cards and redistributes them so that no member has her or his own cards. Encourage the use of humor in sorting the cards and discussing the ideas.

4. One member reads a card aloud. All members look for cards in their stacks that contain related ideas and read these aloud. The group gives this set of cards a name that captures the essence of the thoughts represented. This becomes an *idea set*.

5. The next member reads a card aloud, and the process is repeated until all cards are categorized into idea sets.

6. The idea sets may be combined into all-inclusive groups.

7. The team plays with the idea sets—connecting, arranging, and rearranging—to stimulate ways of responding to the problem-opportunity situation.

A Final Word

What's more fun than your Sensory Intelligence? Your vivid, visual imagination is so incredibly powerful in producing the new ideas you need—and showing you how to bring them into your physical reality. Become more and more aware of ways to use your senses more creatively. Play with the Self-Awareness Opportunities that follow. Then it's on to your final crown jewel intelligence—that shadowy, glittery, dreamy, symbolic, All-That-Is intelligence: your intuition.

Self-Awareness Opportunities

Here are some activities that will help you raise your personal awareness of Sensory Intelligence and take some action to build your innovative skills in this realm.

SAO #1: Express Your Thoughts and Feelings Visually.

Note: Adapted from the work of Barbara Ganim and Susan Fox, *Visual Journaling,* Quest Books; 1999.

Purpose: To become more aware of your visioning and imaginative power and to practice expressing your thoughts and feelings in a visual way.

Step 1: Set a focused intention.

When you set a focused intention, you send all the cells in your body the message that you have a clear goal behind the actions you are about to take. This helps your body to overcome resistance to change. Some examples of intentions are:

- ✎ I intend to understand the root of this problem.
- ✎ I intend to generate at least three creative solutions to this problem.
- ✎ I intend to select the best solution for this problem.

Step 2: Relax and visualize.

Use your deep breathing and other relaxation techniques. Then visualize the situation or person you want to learn more about. If appropriate, re-experience an event or emotion that you want to learn more about or to express more fully. Focus on the strongest physical sensation you're experiencing now, within your body. Imagine what this sensation might look like if it were a color, shape, or form—or all three. What would best express it visually?

Step 3: Draw your inner images.

Draw freely and quickly—to express, not impress. Above all, don't judge what you draw. When you finish, respond intuitively to the following questions, allowing your first response to be valid:

- ✎ How do you feel when you view the drawing?
- ✎ What does the drawing reveal about the problem? About the solution? About how you feel? About your emotional tone? What do the light or dark, bright or somber colors reveal? The shapes or images?
- ✎ How do you feel about the colors? What impact do they have on you?

- ☙ Does anything about the drawing bother you? If so, write about it.
- ☙ What do you like best about your drawing? Write about it.
- ☙ What have you learned about the problem or about your feelings from this drawing?
- ☙ Are these feelings connected to a specific issue, person, or concern? Write about it.
- ☙ Does understanding your feelings help you deal with the issue? If so, how? Write about it.

Take the attitude that you don't have to solve any problems now, though you may. Just enjoy understanding more about the problem and your feelings or being able to express yourself more fully.

Step 4: Get information from your drawing.

Get information by asking your drawing some questions. Look at the drawing as a whole and ask, *What are your trying to tell me about myself or my life?*

Pick one aspect of the drawing, such as one image or one color, and ask *What are you doing in this drawing? What are you trying to tell me about myself or my life?*

Pick another aspect and repeat the questions, until you have worked with every major part of your drawing. If an answer seems especially important, focus on it and ask it for more insight.

Step 5: Explore connections.

If you sense a relationship between the messages you receive from your drawing and other events in your life, past or present, ask yourself these questions:

- ☙ Are the feelings I expressed in this drawing similar to feelings I've had in other situations?
- ☙ Which life trends or personal patterns are the messages I get from my drawing connected to?
- ☙ Which messages might apply to some of my current life situations?
- ☙ How does this drawing help me understand who I am or who I could be?

SAO #2: Sense Information: Feed Intuition.

Purpose: To practice using your senses to receive intuitive insights.

Instructions: You can practice and develop the ability to receive intuitive insights from your higher consciousness—so that you can use them at will. The major barriers are believing you don't have imagination or intuitive ability and trying to *make* the messages come. Relaxed focus is the key; *allow* the messages to come. Let go of the need to make them come and be open to letting them in.

Step 1: Breathe.

Slow down your breathing process, taking more and more time to breathe in, to hold it, and to breathe out. Feel your body and mind slow down.

Step 2: Relax.

Continue with one or more additional relaxation techniques that work for you, such as those suggested in the Basic Intelligence chapter (Chapter 3). Aim to reach the alpha state of deep relaxation.

Step 3: Go into Higher Consciousness.

Focus all your attention in your feet. Hold it there. Then, step by step, focus your attention in your ankles, calves, thighs, and on up through your body to the crown of your head. Imagine that above your head is a magnificent Higher Self, Soul Self, Intuitive Self, Creative Self, Higher Consciousness, or some aspect of yourself that is much larger than your physical self. Allow your consciousness to move up into that Self. Become comfortable hanging out there for a few moments.

Step 4: Ask a question.

Ask this Self a question that's concerning you, such as *What should I do about...? What's going on with...?* or *How can I...?*

Step 5: Receive a message.

Be open to the various ways intuitive messages typically appear—how your various inner senses may be the vehicle.

Hearing words in your head

You'll have to practice and then note the results, because this intuitive channel can be confused with egomind thinking. Sometimes the verbal messages are soft and brief; other times they're loud and repetitive. It may help to focus inside your head in the area just above your ear level.

Seeing pictures, colors, or symbols in your mind's eye

Focusing inside your head in the area just above your eye level may help. You may sense visions indirectly, or you may see them like a movie. You may see colors or geometric shapes or other symbols instead of picture. Visual messages are certainly noticeable, but you may not know how to interpret them. Dreams are intuitive visual messages, so a good dream interpretation book may help you with these waking visualizations. Ultimately, it's your image and you must decide what it means, but try Betty Bethards' *The Dream Book* for guidance.

Feeling, sensing in your body

Intuitive messages sometimes come as feelings, most often in the stomach-abdomen area. It may help to focus on that area when you want to pick up an intuitive message about a person you're with. Feeling messages can be confused with Negative Ego-related, fear-based feelings. Hindsight can help you learn to distinguish among feelings. For example, looking back some time later, what did your strong feelings about that person really mean?

A sense of knowing

Sometimes intuitive insights come as a sense of knowing what's going on or what will happen. You may feel it throughout your being, especially in your mind, but it's not purely verbal. If the message is loud and clear, you'll know what to do. But it may come as a subtle flash or a glimmer. You must learn to notice these and to trust this type of knowing.

Try asking your Higher Self some questions, such as: *Does that little flash of insight mean I will get the job?* and *Does this mental image mean I should partner up with Jim in order to win the new account?* Be open to the answer—get a sense of a *yes* or *no* inner response. Then check it out. See what actually happens when you follow the advice. That way, you can learn to recognize and trust this intuitive knowing.

SAO #3: Create Your Personal Vision Collage.

Purpose: To create a visual link between your visualization of your Creative Self and the physical manifestation of that vision. You can also use this process for linking to physical reality your vision of the Next Big Thing you want to create in your life, or your next creative project.

Materials needed:

- ✎ Large pieces of paper—at least 18" x 24". It can be art paper, sheets of paper from an artist's sketch pad, blank newspaper, butcher paper, or similar paper that can be rolled up for carrying or storing.
- ✎ Magazines and brochures that can be cut up.
- ✎ Paper glue.
- ✎ Embellishment materials (optional).

Step 1: Prep—Creative Self Image. Imagine your Creative Self. Get a sense of what he or she looks like, either as a physical being or as a symbol. Draw that on a card. (Alternatively, draw the symbol or essence of your next creative project, or other vision.)

Step 2: Prep—Focus Phrase. Get in touch with your Heart's Desire, your What Next? in life. Develop that into a one-liner, a Focus Phrase. Put it on an index card.

Step 3: Gather pictures and words. Put your Creative Self Image and Focus Phrase cards in front of you—physical expressions of your Heart's Desire coming from your Creative Self to keep in mind what you're looking for.

Go through the magazines and brochures, cutting or tearing out pictures and words, placing pictures in one pile, and words in another. If you find an image that represents your Creative Self more vividly than your drawing, set it aside to use.

Step 4: Select pictures and words. Select the pictures that you want to use in your collage and put them in a "selected pictures" pile. Then select words that express your Heart's Desire and put them in a "selected words" pile.

Step 5: Arrange and glue. Put your Creative Self Image at the center of the collage—symbolically making this self the center of your dream vision. Play with arranging pictures around this center image—trying out different configurations until your heart center is happy with one. If you need more pictures, go back to the gathering step.

Play with placing words within your composition, between or on top of pictures, until you arrive at the configuration you like best.

Use paper glue to attach the pictures and words to the art paper.

Optional embellishment: You can embellish the collage with paints, colored pens, bits of fabric, trim, natural elements, glitter, feathers, leaves, anything that fits.

Step 6: Image write. First write a simple listing of the pictures and elements within your collage. Then, coming from your heart, from your Creative Self, use these elements in a simple story or poem about your Vision Collage. How does this image writing express the underlying meaning of your collage? How does it verbally plumb the depths?

Chapter 9

Weave Your Crowning Glory:
Intuitive Intelligence

> Out beyond ideas of wrong-doing and right-doing, there is
> a field. I'll meet you there.
> *Rumi, Sufi philosopher*

As a woman, your time has come to regain a cultural role that is your birthright, using your Intuitive Intelligence to serve as a link between the physical world and the spirit world of All-That-Is. Long before the patriarchy, there was the age of goddess worship, a time when women held leadership roles in the tribes and clans. Women's leadership roles included connecting with the spirit world, teaching people how to bring spirit connections into everyday life, and practicing the healing arts.

Of the seven intelligences, Intuitive Intelligence is the one that's most essential for creativity. Because it pulls together and uses all your other intelligences, it is your "crowning intelligence." It's also related to spirituality. It can give you clues to your inner destiny, your future. The greatest use of your intuition and your creativity is creating the life you want, the life that will be most fulfilling for you, the life that makes a contribution to the Web of Life.

The inner knowing of Intuitive Intelligence comes with apparent ease and elegance. We often refer to an intuitive message as a *hunch*, a *gut feeling*, or an *inspiration*. You're born with intuition, but it's like a muscle: You either use it or lose it—and if the world around you tells you that it's not real or doesn't count, and you believe that, then you'll lose it. But like a weak muscle, you can exercise it and make it strong again. And that's an effort well worth making.

In dealing with the world rationally, you hold it constant by means of categories you formed in the past. Through intuition, you grasp the world as a whole, in flux. You encompass your whole intelligence, also—for this inner knowing comes from your senses, from the association of your many connections, from your rational thinking, from the deeper limbic system of feelings, and from the basic brain of action. Information from these sources is woven into words, numbers, images, sounds, colors, shapes, insights, feelings, and actions. Your Intuitive Intelligence somehow puts together all the information and experiences you've ever come in contact with and are willing to access.

Intuition is a knowing from within, knowing without referring to logic or reason. It's *the direct knowing or learning of something without the conscious use of reasoning; immediate apprehension or understanding*, according to Webster's Dictionary. Intuitive knowing speeds up the creative process, as it's your direct connection to the Web of Life. Terms to associate with Intuitive Intelligence include:

> inner knowing, between the lines, wholistic, beyond time-space, universal access, global-inner connections, ESP, psi, superconscious, right brain, neocortex

Myths That Block Intuition

The many cultural myths about intuition tend to discount its value. Relegating its power to an amusing trait typical of women, similar to old wives' tales, discounts its relevance in rational Western cultures. Making it a weird trait further undermines its validity. Typical myths center around the belief that intuition is neither rational nor reliable.

Myth #1: It's only women's intuition.

Just as emotions are known as *women's territory* in our culture, so is intuition. And because anything in women's territory has been traditionally considered second-class, inferior, and therefore discounted, this means that intuition has been devalued in our culture.

Research indicates that businesswomen rely more on intuition than men do. Those who succeed are likely to realize that many men also rely on intuition but they express it in business terms. You may hear successful businesswomen say, *My feel for the marketplace..., My gut reaction...,* or *My best estimate....* Such women find that their intuitive insights are more likely to be accepted when they express them in ways the men are comfortable with.

Myth #2: Intuitives are weird people.

Because Western culture has traditionally not accepted intuition as a valid way of thinking, intuitives and psychics are usually viewed as *outsiders*. It's too bad. Society is so insistent that we conform to its norms. Yet Creative Intelligence (intuition, genius, etc.) is a measure of how far we're willing to deviate from the norm.

Myth #3: Intuition is irrational and unreliable.

Western society has not traditionally encouraged the use of intuition in everyday life, nor has it tried to teach intuition. The myth is that intuition does not conform to any logical process that can be replicated and depended upon to be reliable. The reality is that you cannot measure with rational techniques and standards a process that is wholistic, timeless, and dependent upon the inner life of the practitioner.

When you use your intuition to solve problems and make decisions, you're in good company. Recent research indicates that the higher your position in an organization, the more you must rely on soft data and intuition to make decisions. Most top-level decisions involve broad policy matters rather than operational details, depend on future events, and have such general implications that you cannot depend on hard facts and figures alone in reaching them.

A nationwide survey of 2,000 business, government, and academic leaders was conducted in 1982 by Professor Weston Agor, University of Texas at El Paso, and reported by author Gerard Nierenberger. He concluded that top-level leaders rely more on intuition than do lower-level managers. Moreover, women consistently score higher than men in intuitive ability. And Asian managers score higher than Westerners, presumably because of less focus on Rational vs. Intuitive Intelligence. The women were more reluctant to admit using intuition, however, fearing that it would be viewed as a sign of weakness. Agor did a follow-up study of the executives who scored in the top 10 percent in intuitive ability. Virtually all said they use intuition in making the most important decisions, though many said they do not reveal this fact to their colleagues. Researchers at Harvard, the University of Pennsylvania, and other prestigious institutions have reached similar conclusions.

As innovation becomes more and more the measure of survival and success in business, intuition plays an ever-larger role. Although effective executives certainly won't ignore relevant facts and figures, they must also take into consideration the feelings and opinions of other people, information gleaned from the company grapevine, and their own intuition about future probabilities.

How Intuitive Intelligence Works

It is by intuition that we discover... and by logic that we prove.
Henri Poincare, mathematician

You are an intuitive person—at least you were as a child. You may now be conditioned to ignore intuitive messages, but you can regain the ability. You can learn again how to connect to the Web of Life, how to recognize the many types of intuitive messages you receive, and how to use intuition to access information and enrich your life.

Connecting to the Web of Life

Nature is relentlessly irregular and nonlinear, and the inanimate world is much more nonlinear than we thought. In fact, most of the real world is nonlinear. We must go beyond rational, linear thinking in order to deal with reality.

Perception is what you make of what's *out there*. There is no absolute *out there* environment. There is only what you make of it—and that changes as your internal patterns of relationships change—as your believing-thinking-feeling-acting process changes.

How do you perceive reality? If you're like most people, you create abstractions of separate objects, including a separate self. Then you believe you belong to an objective, independently existing reality full of lots of selves or lots of fragmented objects. You probably extend this fragmented view to the whole human species, dividing it into different nations, races, religions, and political teams. You may believe that all these fragments—in yourself, in your environment, and in society—are really separate. This alienates you from nature and from other people.

But when you shift your conceptual focus from objects to relationships, you're able to realize that identity, individuality, and autonomy do *not* mean that separateness and independence are all there is. That's just a piece of the reality pie. If you were to regain your experience of connectedness with the entire Web of Life, your Intuitive Intelligence would return. Your creativity would blossom. If you're part of the Web, you can tune in to all parts of it. If you can see time as an abstraction—after all, there was no *time* when you were a baby—you can tune into all that happens in all times, according to author Fritjof Capra.

Receiving Intuitive Messages

You have many doors to your intuitive self, which is able to access information from the entire universe, past, present, and future, because it has a direct connection to the Web of Life. You access this information through all of your other intelligences: the dreams and instincts of your Basic Intelligence, the passion of your Motivational Intelligence, the feelings of your Emotional Intelligence, the direct knowing and connections of your Associative Intelligence, the deductions of your Rational Intelligence, and through all the senses of your Sensory Intelligence. You can access this information through your dreams, meditations, music, art, spontaneous encounters with the natural world—such as a bird, tree, or flower—and through many other channels. Your pattern of receiving intuitive messages is unique.

Through Basic-Brain Dreams and Body Messages

Dreams can be prophetic and play a role in your intuitive development. Dreams are part of Basic Intelligence, which you incorporate into your Intuitive Intelligence. Some dreams are Big Dreams that carry important information for you. You know now how to program your dreams to get answers to questions and to keep a record of them. You've had some experience at interpreting your dream messages. Hopefully, you're learning to trust your dream messages. You're ready to move on to some new ways of interpreting and using your dreams, as discussed in the Creative Processes segment of this chapter.

Your intuition takes in other information from your Basic Intelligence. You ask, *Should I move toward this person or away from him? Should I establish my personal boundary at this point or not? Is this the right action pattern to settle into?* Your Basic Intelligence feeds into your intuition to provide you with inner knowledge about whether to say yes or no to such questions. You can access this higher Intuitive Intelligence to identify which patterns and boundaries are no longer productive for you and which new energies you should move toward.

Notice messages from your basic brain, body messages such as an energy increase or decrease, a sudden attraction to or recoiling from something, or sudden nausea. Ask yourself, *What is my body trying to tell me? What message is it feeding into my intuition?*

Through Emotional Intelligence

When you use Emotional Intelligence to develop the feelings of empathy and compassion, your intuition can integrate these feelings with other information, such as higher-level desires from your Motivational Intelligence, and create an exquisite form of empathy, expanded boundaries, and attunement with the world.

Notice sudden changes in your feelings about a situation. Intuitive messages sometimes come as feelings, most often in the stomach-abdomen area. It may help to focus on that area when you want to pick up an intuitive message about a person you're with. Ask yourself, *Does this feeling seem to come from my Negative Ego? My subconscious? The superconscious?* Emotional messages can be driven by ego-related, fear-based feelings, concerns about whether you're better-than or worse-than others, what others think of you given that judgmental framework, and similar issues. Hindsight can help you learn to distinguish among feelings. For example, looking back some time later, what did your strong feelings about that person really mean?

Through Sensory-Visual Awareness

Intuitive messages may come by seeing pictures, colors, or symbols in your mind's eye. Focusing inside your head in the area just above your eye level may help. Visual messages are certainly noticeable, but you may not know how to interpret them. Dreams may be intuitive visual messages, so a good dream interpretation book may help you with any type of picture or symbol. (See Betty Bethards' *The Dream Book*.) Ultimately, it's your picture, and you must decide what it means.

You can enhance your intuition through imaging or visualizing. Record on paper the shapes and images that come to your mind during a period of deep relaxation and/or meditation or zoning. This might result in a mandala, symbolic geometry, or other meaningful diagram.

Through Kinesthetic Awareness

Intuitive messages may come as a muscle contraction or other internal body movement. It may come as inner sense of body movement, such as drifting, floating, soaring, or falling. Notice and ask yourself what this sense means. Your may also put yourself into *the zone* or a moving meditation by such movement-in-space as dance or sports.

Through Aural Awareness

Intuitive messages come to many people through words they hear in their head. You'll need awareness, practice, and evaluation of such inner hearing because it can be confused with Negative Ego chatter. Ask yourself, *Is this a better-than or worse-than type of message? Is it based on contracting emotions?* Sometimes the verbal messages are soft and brief; other times they're loud and repetitive. It may help to focus inside your head in the area just above your ear level. Ask for guidance from your Intuitive Self, your Higher Self, or other helpful source. Focus on the intention *for the highest good of all persons involved*, to weed out egomind messages.

You may encourage intuitive insights and receive intuitive messages through mentally toning or hearing inside your head, or through a variety of tones, chords, or songs. You can expand this by combining it with other sensory input. Let's take toning. The three chambers of your body are the head, chest, and pelvic chambers. Through your head you can *tone*, discovering sounds that vibrate certain parts of each of these three chambers. You can progress from toning to a broader range of sounds. After a while you can add movement by carefully listening to your natural sounds and following the impulses that arise from those resonances.

Through Olfactory Awareness

Certain odors, fragrances, and tastes may trigger strong associations for you, memories from the past, and other senses, emotions, and thoughts. Notice especially smells and tastes that have a vivid, sudden, or dramatic effect on you. Ask yourself what message may be implied here.

Through Associative Intelligence

Intuition often comes as a synchronistic experience—a coincidence or series of coincidences—when connections materialize and events fall into place. Notice these happenings and ask yourself what they mean and what hidden messages they hold. Do you detect some symbolism here? How can you interpret these symbols? Also notice situations where all options but one seem to disappear and times when an unwanted or unhappy experience turns out for the best.

Through Inner Knowing

An inner knowing message comes as a hunch, an awareness that events are flowing in a certain direction, a sudden relevant remembrance, an insight, or a sudden "a-ha." These are especially nice because they usually need little interpretation, but you must learn to notice them, pay attention to them, and act on them.

Sometimes intuitive insights come loud and clear—or in a subtle flash or a glimmer, a sense of knowing what's going on or what will happen. You feel it throughout your being, especially in your mind, but it's not purely verbal. It's the flashes and glimmers you must learn to notice, and you must learn to trust this type of knowing. Try asking yourself some questions that you can later check out, so that you can learn to recognize and trust this knowing. For example, when you've had a little flash about what's going on, ask yourself, *What did that flash really say? What does it mean? What does it tell me about what's going on and what is about to happen?* If you're not sure, ask for guidance from your Intuitive Self, Higher Self, or other guide.

Informing and Enriching Your Life

You can use your Intuitive Intelligence in every aspect of your business and personal life to bring the information you need and to enrich the quality of your life.

Answering Rational Questions

You can use Intuitive Intelligence to get answers to the rational who, what, where, when, why, and how questions. For example, you can ask the following types of questions and then listen quietly for answers that may come at off times in unexpected ways:

- What next? What should I create or do next in this project? In my life?
- Why is this coming up in my life?
- What decision should I make in this situation?
- Who can I connect with on this project?
- Where should I do this?
- When is the best time to move on this?
- How can I achieve this goal?

Enriching Your Life

Intuitive Intelligence can enrich your life in so many ways. Here are just a few examples:

- To get in touch with your life purpose.
- To create a future that's in line with your purpose.
- To find your unique niche in the world—and the activities that are part of your purpose.
- To guide your decisions and choices.
- To develop a greater vision and to exercise leadership based on that vision.
- To work with teams—and with people in general.
- To enhance your day-to-day work life—and all your relationships.
- To increase the depth of intimacy you're comfortable with—intimacy with yourself and others.
- To change your life in ways you want (for example, to stop smoking, break out of old habits and ruts, change careers, commit to new relationships, take risks).
- To assess, in any moment, the intuitive energy within your body and beyond your physical body.

You'll find many, many ways to develop your Intuitive Intelligence. You'll find enough ideas here to take you a long way, but because your intuition is without limit, you can grow and develop it throughout your life. The fun never has to end.

Innovation Showcase:
Marilyn Goldberg on Intuition

Marilyn Goldberg is CEO of Museum Masters International of New York. She's a business executive who relies on her intuition every day. Sometimes intuitive messages come through her senses. She says:

> I "smell" the person, the office, the home, the situation, the essence of who I'm dealing with. This is everything! I can tell about the true person after one visit to her home, or one dinner with her mother or child. Great businesspeople either have great family relationships, or none at all (but pretend to). Those with none have devoted their life to their work. I've devoted my life to my family and my work. I find this a much more balanced and loving lifestyle.

Marilyn also hears an inner voice that speaks when she has direct eye contact with people and when she notices the way they carry themselves. She hears messages when she gets a strong handshake, sees a head held high, or looks into deep sensitive eyes. She also hears the inner voice when she has bottom-line discussions with people and senses an inner security.

Because she trusts her intuition, Marilyn has been willing to take calculated risks. She says that without risk, she could have achieved none of life's major rewards: *Basically, I've risked everything for my dreams, for my independence, and for the opportunity to grow. I've succeeded by trusting my inner voice, all the time.*

How to Spark Your Intuitive Intelligence

Your intuition is just below the surface of consciousness. You just need some techniques to switch your awareness to that below-the-surface level so it can rise up into your conscious mind. To begin with, prepare yourself by adopting beliefs that open you up to your intuition. Then notice and work with your various mental states, ranging from the rational-active through various levels of meditation to the dream state. Meditate every day to tap into subconscious and superconscious levels. Spend as much time as you can in a state of beginner's mind and mindfulness that come from a focus on the Now and accepting What-Is in the Now. All these techniques help you to maintain a mind that's aware and open to new ideas. Practice using your intuition every day, beginning with small predictions and messages and graduating to more important visioning, problem-solving, and decision-making.

Sparkler #1: Adopt Beliefs That Nurture Intuitive Intelligence

The intuitive process is about receiving information in a way that's different from the way you get it when using Rational or Associative Intelligence. You get it at a speed that's faster, from a level that's deeper. The intuitive process involves the deeper accessing of your being. You receive waves picked up by your brain. The signals often come in quantum leaps rather than coming in recognizable continuous waves. You cannot direct the intuitive process, but you can prepare for it and you can develop it by adopting three beliefs:

1. *Belief in a larger reality*—that there is a larger reality than the one you perceive with your senses.

2.   *Belief in self-observation and change*—that you can mentally observe your thinking and your actions, learn from this self-observation, and make decisions to change your thinking and actions.

3.   *Belief in connection*—that you can connect or attune with the vibrations or resonances of others and with the Web of Life, and that attunement can bring you intuitive information.

Belief in a Larger Reality

You can think of this larger reality in many ways: as the universe, the cosmos, nature, All-That-Is, Source, God, Goddess. This all-encompassing reality must be one that you can believe in and can trust to be loving, kind, and safe, regardless of how your immediate environment may seem. To develop this belief, begin by focusing on a larger horizon and then allow yourself to move toward it. Your goal is to trust or think your way into, feel, or experience a largeness, an all-pervasiveness, a love so alive that it expands your limits until you lose your ability to describe it.

Expand your world. Make your belief system one that enables you to search ever-greater horizons. Relate your larger belief system in something all-encompassing to your everyday, limited existence. It should enhance your capacity for wonder and your trust that all things are possible.

Develop your capacity for wonder. Begin by admiring something, by being able to be surprised, and by experiencing a state of wonder. Experience gratitude for the wondrous.

Believe in the possible. Begin to trust your guesses and your hunches. Include them in your conversations. Allow yourself the freedom to guess—and then follow up to see if you guess was correct. When you open up to the belief that all things are possible, you open up to intuitive information that's otherwise unavailable to you.

Belief in Self-Observation and Change

Love all your glimpses of All-That-Is and continue your search into infinity. Ask, *Who am I?* Wait for the response. Be open to its coming in strange ways. Continue to ask that question again and again. Continually ask yourself and continually observe your responses. By deeply relaxing and focusing into that still place deep within, you enter rare vibrational levels.

You can also observe your thoughts, images, emotions, and actions in your everyday life. You do that by focusing on your inner life first, by observation and meditation. You can find guidance in those thinner inner ranges. Then, when your consciousness emerges to operate in the denser realities, you're better able to attune, harmonize, and heal your body-mind.

Observe your mind. Watch your mind when your thoughts are forming and let the thoughts come through even if they are not complete.

Belief in Connection

It is you who tunes in a *reality program* with your antenna-mind, whether you tune into the great or the trivial, the expansive inner-body or the contracting egomind, the fine or the gross. You can choose to tune yourself into any station on the entire range of energy vibrations in which you are embedded in this Web of Life. You create your reality partially by what you choose to select, to focus or concentrate on, to attune with. Attunement is becoming *one* with whatever station you are tuned into, and ultimately with the Web of Life itself. *At-one-ment* is a way of expressing the deep state of consciousness that can result from tuning in and receiving.

Attunement is also the practice of shifting into alternate states of consciousness, alternate mental states, or alternate intelligences. It is your job to tune in. You can choose the wavelength you wish to be on and receive whatever enters that range.

Sparkler #2: Tune into Varying Brainwave Frequencies

You've already learned something about brainwave cycles and how various states of mind can be defined by the measurement of your brain waves. Snapshot #1 illustrates how brain waves affect your level of intuition Through measurement and biofeedback processes, scientists have greatly advanced our knowledge of the roles that meditations and dreams play in the enhancement of Intuitive Intelligence.

Snapshot #1: Intuition and Brainwave Cycles

Intuitive Level	Brain State Experience	Per Second	Cycles
Intuition low	Rational, active	Beta	13 to 25
Intuition high	Drifting, light meditation or hypnogogic-before/after sleep	Alpha	8 to 12
Intuition very high	Deep meditation	Theta	5 to 7
Intuition very high	Dream state during sleep	Delta	1 to 4

When you are in the beta state, the rational, active level, your brainwave cycles have a dense, rapid frequency. The meditative states progress in depth of relaxation, from alpha to theta, and you retain mental clarity and waking consciousness in these states. Going deeper, your brainwave cycles become thinner and less frequent, until you reach delta, which goes through the dream state to the deepest level of sleep.

In certain key moments of your life, the thinnest wave vibrations become as practical as the densest ones. If you want to stop dividing and separating yourself from other people and from the Web of Life, open up to the entire vibrational range of energy in every person. Then you'll start connecting.

Sparkler #3: Meditate Every Day

Do you immediately resist the idea of doing something every day? Focus on this idea: You can commit only five minutes a day, that relaxed time just before you drop off to sleep at night, to do a brief meditation. Start with that tiny commitment and see what happens.

Meditation is the best path to building Intuitive Intelligence, according to most writers who have studied the subject and are highly intuitive themselves. You have nothing to lose in this process, because at the very least it boosts your health as a stress management technique. Relaxation—stress relief—can be your first meditative goal. The second goal is to allow and enjoy these periods of silence, when you let the joy of being alive wash over you. With that aliveness and in that silence comes the voice of intuition—whether it's spoken as an inner voice, inner vision, brief glimmer or flash of an idea, muscular tightening or softening, distinct emotion, or other form.

All you really need to excel in this process is the willingness to trust that you *are* intuitive and the willingness to practice meditation and other intuitive processes. Trust and practice are the keys. You can do it! Aren't you curious about your intuition? Encourage that curiosity. Practice trusting in your intuition, practice acting on it, and have fun with the whole process. Let your intuition invite you into your greatness—and don't be afraid to respond to it.

Sparkler #4: Move into Mindfulness

"In the beginner's mind, there are many possibilities. In the expert's mind, there are only a few," says Zen teacher Shunryu Suzuke as described by author John Kao. You boost your intuitiveness by getting back into your beginner's mind. You empty your mind in order to return to the first innocence of the child.

One way to do this is to let go of the need to solve a problem or generate new ideas and instead distract yourself. You redirect your concentration to subjects that don't carry the burden of anxiety, subjects with no connection to the task at hand. Mentally, take out a fresh piece of paper. Shift your mind from the task-fixated self that's harboring doubts and fears to a nonthreatening but vivid world of playing ball, dancing, singing, cooking, or anything you really want to do, can get caught up in, and enjoy doing. You achieve mindfulness by escaping the heavy, single-minded striving of most ordinary life.

Intuition comes in after you free yourself of old, limiting mindsets. That's when you allow new information, like a melody, to come into your awareness. Intuition flowers after you open yourself to new information and surprise, after you've played awhile with various mindsets, viewpoints, beliefs, and attitudes, after you've focused more on the *process* of creating something new than on the actual end results. This intuitive information may be full of surprises, and it may not *make sense*. If you resist and evaluate it on rational grounds, you may silence a vital message.

Purely rational understanding serves to confirm old mindsets and rigid categories. How do you stay open to experience? When your mind is set on one thing or on one way of doing things (often mindlessly determined in the past), you block intuition and miss much of the present world around you.

Sparkler #5: Practice Intuition Every Day in Every Way

Get in the habit of practicing intuition by using it to solve problems and make decisions—about everything from finding a parking place to knowing the best time to telephone a friend to playing the stock market (not using real money at first, of course).

Play Intuitive Games

Make up fun ways to test your intuition. For example, play an *artificial dreaming* game with a friend. Make up a story about your partner. Look into the future and see your partner's possibilities. Play with choices. Ask yourself, *What would happen if...?* Notice pictures that come, feelings that come. Watch especially for scenarios that evoke elation and enthusiasm. You can play with this for yourself, too. Then follow up to see how much of this actually happens and keep a record of your accuracy.

Here are some other simple intuitive games you can play each day:

- Before you leave home, note the exact time you will arrive somewhere.
- Before you shop, decide what the exact total will be on your grocery bill.
- Pick the date and time of the next rainfall.
- Before you go to sleep, decide what time you'll awaken in the morning. Don't set the alarm.
- Relax, go deep, and visualize a friend that you haven't contacted for a while. See what comes up. Repeat the process for two more friends. Write down the significant images, words, feelings, and other types of information that come up about each of the three friends. Contact your friends and ascertain the significance of this information.

Plan Your Future

Because your intuition can receive information from the Web of Life, all that is, has been, and will be, you can access it in order to tune into your future. For example, when you want clarity about what to create next in your life, go into a meditative state and ask your intuitive self, *What next?* If you have an idea about what's next but want to check it out, you can ask, *Will this be best for me and for the planet?* If you have any questions about what the future holds, ask your intuitive self and be willing for the answer to come to you in the manner your intuitive self selects.

Making business predictions in this high-tech age becomes more difficult every year. Who could have predicted the Internet back in the 1950s? It wasn't even conceivable at a time when IBM predicted that four mainframe computers would be enough to handle the needs of the entire world.

You can imagine something that resembles what is, but then it's not a true innovation. And you are limited in anticipating the New New Things down the road because the process of generalizing from what you can imagine is limited by your imagination. You can intuit a business future, but you may not be able to accurately predict it. Your predictions are only as accurate as your Intuitive Intelligence. By opening up to intuition and by practicing intuitive predictions, you can improve your predictive batting average.

What if you sense that you've received an intuitive message but you don't understand it? Try holding it gently in your mind, just letting it be. Relax and mentally say, *Tell me more.* Let the message turn over in your awareness. Let your mind drift away into stillness. By de-centering in this way, a gentle knowing may begin to emerge. If not, let it go and know that it may become clear at a later time. Tapping your intuition is all about relaxing and allowing. It doesn't seem to respond when you demand answers or struggle intensely to perceive answers.

Solve Problems

To spark intuitive problem-solving, pay attention to these suggestions for bridging the knowledge gap between the problem and a great solution:

- ❧ Acknowledge the power in your intuition.
- ❧ Articulate what you want to know.
- ❧ Formulate an intention.
- ❧ Get in touch with what you don't know.

You can think of the space between what you know and what you want to know as a knowledge gap that you want to fill with intuitive information. You can view the gap as an electromagnetic line that will magnetically attract intuitive information into it from all around. The goal is to mentally hold that space without filling it in with your biases, prejudices, or old ways of thinking. If you're open, intuitive information *will* be attracted into that magnetic space.

Snapshot #2: The Knowledge Gap

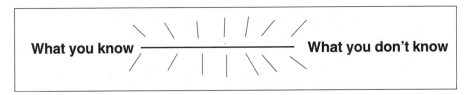

What you know ——————————— What you don't know

You may want to reframe the problem-opportunity as a basic question. Wait for answers to be attracted into the mind-space you've created, the electromagnetic gap. You may need to meditate once or many times, holding your question in mind. You may need to detach and play.

Make Decisions

Think of your intuitive ability as the inner knowledge of whether to say yes or no, to move toward an energy or away from it. Develop a sensitivity to both the yes and the no. Again this incorporates Basic Intelligence.

Survey all your options—the alternative decision paths you could take. Use your imagination to picture yourself actually going down a particular decision path, living out the decision. Allow your intuition to guide you in how this would play out as you imagine vividly how it feels, how it looks, how comfortable or *right* it seems. Do this for each major alternative you're considering.

Work with Symbols

You'll increase your Intuitive Intelligence by opening up to symbols. They can be very powerful because they can trigger a connection to your inner wisdom. If a symbol comes up in your mind, ask yourself, *What does this symbol mean?* If an answer comes easily, in a flash, it's probably intuition. You don't have to analyze it, figure it out, or work at it. If it doesn't come easily, you should wait and try another time when you may be more open, more relaxed.

Recognize the symbolism of synchronicity—meaningful and unexpected coincidences or unusual repetitive occurrences. For example, you've never witnessed an automobile rollover. Then within a month, you see three rollovers. Ask yourself, *What's the symbolism of these coincidences? Does it mean my world is turning upside down?* Synchronicities can be signs to take notice, even calls to action. If they were part of a dream, how would you interpret the symbolism? What is the emotional flavor?

Symbolism can also add power to your intuitive processes. Use favorite symbols that are powerful for you. For example, when you meditate, you can imagine a favorite geometric shape to focus on. Let it fill your mind as you say to yourself, *My intuitive mind will fill me with answers.*

Recognize Your Hits

Learn to recognize the intuitive hits that you get. For example, ask yourself, *What does an intuitive message feel like? Where is there energy that points to intuition? Where is there a certain vitality?* Notice patterns. Learn the language— the symbols slow down, be curious, play. Intuition works best when you place no pressure on yourself to be intuitive. So find ways to relax. Relaxed and open—that's the combination you want. Be aware of what's going on around you. Increase what you can notice, what you can find. Open up, be alert to all.

Practice is the most valuable way to boost your Intuitive Intelligence, but only if you review and assess your intuitive hits. Follow this process:

1. Write down your predictions.

2. Note whether your predictions turn out to be true or false. If a hunch turns out to be valid, you can chalk it up to intuition. If not, it was wishful thinking, a knee-jerk reaction, or some other subconscious process, usually triggered by egomind concerns. Intuition comes from the superconscious, a higher level of information.

3. Learn your patterns. After each successful outcome, review the mental, emotional, and physical clues you relied on in following an intuitive idea. This will help you learn about your intuitive patterns, for future reference.

4. Periodically look back to review and assess your accuracy and to learn how your intuition speaks to you. Review and assessment are the ways you learn to distinguish valid intuitive information from other types of information.

Sparkler #6: Adopt a Range of Workable Techniques

Senior executives apply intuition to identify problems, to streamline routine jobs, to pull isolated facts together, to balance purely logical analysis, to solve problems faster, and to judge character in job interviews, according to a Harvard Business School study reported by author Sandra Weintraub. But how do these executive build their intuition and tap into it? Here are some specific techniques for tapping your intuition—morning, noon, and night (see the Creative Processes at the end of this chapter for detailed suggestions):

- When you awake, review your dreams for messages.
- Prepare for the day; for example, ask, *What's important for me today?*
- Tune into your body, asking for information.
- Shift modes and activities when you need inspiration—to refresh and renew your mental state.
- Listen to music; experiment to see what's most conducive for you.
- Exercise vigorously to *cleanse* your mind and body and allow new awareness and sensitivity
- Take a 20-minute walk and then write three pages. (See the Walk and Write creative process on this page.)
- Notice flows of energy within you and around you.
- Tune into what's going on beneath the surface—with people and events.
- Trust your *little feelings* and hunches about people, places, things, and plans.
- Detach and play—play with words through metaphors, analogies, and other forms. Literally play at anything that may take you into the intuitive zone.
- Any time you get a chance, play games and have fun. Be playful and childlike. Collect toys, symbols, figurines, rocks, crystals, chimes, music tapes, pictures. Allow intuition to come in if it wants to.
- Draw sketches and build models of new products using various materials.
- Study pictures of all kinds to find new approaches to a problem.
- Practice using intuition to make plans, solve problems, and make decisions.
- Keep a running record of your intuitive hits.
- Meditate—with focus and purpose. Do it so often that your life is frequently a *walking meditation.*
- In the evening, review the day—to process the events, to learn lessons, and to think about what you want for tomorrow.
- At bedtime, program your dreams—to ask for dream-time answers, information, and experiences.

Creative Processes Using Intuitive Intelligence

Here are some creative processes that call upon your Intuitive Intelligence. Apply these processes to the problem-opportunity situations you encounter.

Walk and Write

Purpose: To bring up intuitive ideas and to channel egomind energy into creative channels.

This process is especially helpful when you're feeling frustration or anger.

Take a 20-minute walk: 10 minutes briskly walking away from your home or office and 10 minutes back. To boost the effect, make up a little mantra or sentence stating what you want to learn or establish during this walk. Repeat it over and over as you walk. Add a tune to it and sing it, coordinating it with the rhythm of your steps.

When you return, write three pages on any topic, even if you write over and over *I don't want to write*. You'll end up writing intuitive messages—solving a problem, coming up with what's next, or some type of intuitive idea.

Random Word Connections

Purpose: To build skill at using signs and symbols as springboards to intuitive knowing.

Hold a dictionary and form an energy bond with it as a potential source of intuitive messages for you. Formulate a question that has genuine meaning for you. Open the dictionary at random. Leave your mind blank as you let your finger spontaneously land on a word. If you get a highly technical word, move on to another.

Say the word. Read the definition out loud. Then keep on speaking, saying anything that pops into your mind, whatever is triggered by the random word. Let yourself go on to explore connections and images that range outside your personal experience.

If you get a strong intuitive hit about what the word means to you, shift your attention to this insight and explore its significance. If you want to ask for clarification, you can formulate another question. Then open the dictionary to another word and repeat the process.

Brainstorm: Team Intuition

Brainstorm with your team. First the team selects a facilitator and a recorder. The facilitator helps the team define the problem-opportunity, preferably before the brainstorming session, so each member will have time to mull over the situation. Express the problem-opportunity situation in a brief statement.

Team members volunteer ideas, insights, suggestions, solutions, and any other expressions they consider helpful to moving toward an eventual action plan, following these agreed-upon rules:

- ✎ No judgments are made about any suggestions during the brainstorming phase.
- ✎ All ideas, even far-fetched "wild" ones are welcomed and respected.
- ✎ The goal is to generate a large quantity of ideas; quantity is more important than quality during this phase.
- ✎ During the session ideas may be combined, piggybacked, or refined. Ideas may pop up and evolve, because one idea often triggers another.
- ✎ At the end of the session, the team takes a break and then returns (or returns at a later date) to further process and evaluate the ideas.

Brainwriting

Identify the problem-opportunity situation; express it in a brief statement. Team members sit in a circle and decide on a time period for individually writing down their ideas as they come up (at the top of a full sheet of paper or notebook).

At the end of the time period, each member passes his or her written ideas on to the next person and that person piggybacks on the original idea, writing on the same piece of paper, again within a specified time period.

At the end of the time period, members again pass on the paper for the next person to piggyback upon. The team may use three or more rounds of brainwriting.

When the rounds are completed, each member reads aloud the ideas on the paper she or he is currently holding. The team decides how to further organize and process this information, perhaps using a rational-creative technique.

Brainstorming with Visual Display

This technique is especially helpful in generating and deciding on alternatives when dealing with complex problem-opportunity situations. The team's ideas are displayed as they work on the project so members can begin to see interconnections, how one idea relates to another, and how all the pieces might fit together. It takes brainstorming several steps further in order to organize and deal with complex issues. Here's the process:

- ✎ The team brainstorms the problem-opportunity situation and expresses it in a brief statement. This becomes the *topic header* at the top of the display.

- ✎ The team next brainstorms the purpose of this project—why you are working on it, why it's important, and/or the end result or goal(s) you want to achieve—and expresses the major purpose in a brief statement that becomes the *purpose header*, with other purposes displayed under it as subheads.

- ✎ The team brainstorms all the major aspects, issues, opportunities, or solutions to the situation. Each one becomes a *header*. Related ideas will be displayed under that header.

- ✎ Finally, there should be a *miscellaneous header*, under which the team will post stray ideas that don't quite fit under any other category.

For complex projects, the team may want to do a brainstorming process and display for each phase of the project, such as 1) planning the entire project, 2) generating new product-service-process ideas, 3) organizing the resulting action plan, and 4) communicating the action plan.

The planning display will contain all the major ideas related to solving the problem or capitalizing on the opportunity. It forms the blueprint for the actions that follow. Each major idea becomes a *header*, and ideas generated under that heading become *subheads*.

The ideas display is an expansion of some of the ideas contained in the planning display. For example, a header from the planning display might become the topic header for the ideas display, and each of the subheads under that header in the planning display would become headers in the ideas display. Then ideas brainstormed in each category become subheads.

The organization display responds to such questions as: What are the tasks that we need to get done? When do they need to be done? and Who will do them? In this phase the team takes the goals and plan established earlier, and the ideas that have been generated, and breaks them down into team goals and tasks and individual goals and tasks. The team can actually add the answers to these questions to the appropriate locations on the planning display and the ideas display.

The communications display responds to such questions as: Who needs to know about this action plan? What do they need to know? When do they need to know it? and What media will we use to communicate the information?

Immerse Yourself in Ideas

Collect all the information, insights, suggestions, and ideas about your problem-opportunity situation, using every technique and method you know. In one sitting sift through all this information, including pictures and other visuals, experiences, and feelings.

Now put all this aside with the awareness that it will be incubating within you, cooking up new creative ideas. Shift your attention to completely different issues and activities. Let go of the need to solve this problem.

Allow your intuition to work with this information at its own pace and in its own way. Be open to various ways your intuition may reveal new ideas to you, including brief visual flashes, glimmers of ideas, murmurings of words of insight, as well as brilliant, clear pictures or words that relate a complete idea.

Shift from Rational to Intuitive Mind

Your intuitive mind alerts you by sending precognitive warnings in the form of images, dreams, gut feelings, and so forth. To recognize these signs, you must learn to shift out of your rational mind into your intuitive mind.

Step 1. Define your issue or problem-opportunity.

If you can clearly define the real issue or root problem-opportunity, you're more likely to get good results from the process. Form a question that focuses only on one problem or issue. For example, "What production method should we use?"

Intuition usually works best in response to a simple, focused question, so don't mix together several issues in the question. Be clear whether you prefer a variety of options or a simple yes-or-no answer and phrase your question accordingly. For example, *How should we roll out this product?* asks for a variety of options. *Should we roll out in May?* sets up a yes-or-no response.

Step 2. Relax and center your attention.

Start with deep breathing to slow down your bodily functions and move to a slower brain wave. Become still. Allow your Intuitive Intelligence to take over while your Rational Intelligence becomes inactive. Center by focusing all your attention on an imaginary point of light between your eyes. You can bring the light into the center of your head and down into the center of your heart. You can listen to peaceful music. You can focus on a geometrical shape or a mental picture. You can focus on quieting words such as *I am...serene, peace...be still,* or *ohm.*

Step 3. Let go of physical tension and open up.

Once your mind is quieted, relax your body through one or more of the SAOs in the Basic Intelligence chapter (Chapter 3).

Step 4. Elicit intuitive imagery.

Which intelligences do you bring in to play with your intuition? Your Sensory Intelligence—the five senses of seeing, hearing, smelling, tasting, touching? Your Emotional Intelligence—feelings of empathy, curiosity, wonder, etc.?

Step 5. Interpret the imagery.

If your senses or emotions bring to mind certain images, pictures, or fleeting glimpses of something, what does that imagery mean in your current situation? How does it help to answer your question? Try amplification and word association techniques.

Amplification: Start with a central image and continue to associate words and images with it until a significant meaning falls into place, or an *a-ha!* recognition pops up.

Word association: Start with an original word that came to you and that seems significant in some way. Think of other words that you associate with the original word and write them down, perhaps with connecting arrows.

Imagining a graph: Imagine a line graph, bar graph, pie chart, or similar visual that can indicate answers to your question.

Imagining a traffic light: Imagine a traffic light and see what signal it gives you: red for *no*, green for *yes*, or yellow for *wait*.

Step 6. Take time out.

If you don't come up with something that seems *right* or significant, take time out to let the question incubate in your subconscious mind. Become occupied with other activities, especially activities that you can become wrapped up in. Getting into flow is helpful.

Step 7. Return for insight and implementation.

Even if you got a significant answer to your question, often that answer will stimulate more questions. Notice if any come to mind and use the intuitive process on them. Then it's time for your rational mind to kick into action to resolve the issue or problem.

Consult Your Council of Advisors

Think of who you would choose as a council of advisors for dealing with this issue—people you admire, would trust, and who would be knowledgeable and wise in this area. Visualize these people sitting around you. Connect with them. What are they thinking and saying? Ask them specific questions and listen for answers.

Decision-Making: The Open Door

This process can help you intuit the best decision among two or more alternatives:

- Relax; then imagine the decision alternatives that are facing you.
- Imagine that each option is a different door. Visualize the options as unique doors. Make each a different color, design, and size—whatever mental images seem right to you.
- Scan the doors. Which door opens up? That's the alternative to take.

Tune into the Customer

This is a technique to focus on what your customers would welcome in the way of products, services, or processes for delivery of goods or services. The purpose is to connect intuitively with customers and to receive intuitive messages.

Formulate three or four key questions. The questions that follow will give you some ideas, but you'll probably have some questions unique to your situation.

- What do my top customers really want?
- What new product or service would delight them, even though they're not aware of a need yet?
- How much would they be willing to pay for this?
- How do they want to hear about it? How do they want it promoted?
- Where and how do they want to buy it? Through whom or what? Under what conditions?
- Which customers are really the target market for this new product or service?

Relax and allow yourself to enter a meditative state. Recall your key questions, one at a time. Imagine yourself attuning and connecting with your customers. Open up to intuitive messages. Afterward, write down any information that came up.

Intuit the Stock Market

You can practice applying your Intuitive Intelligence by investing in the stock market. First, do it without actually putting up your hard-earned dollars. Keep a record of your stock investments—how much money you make or lose over a specific time period.

Make Some Preliminary Picks

First, think of fields that interest you: the media, Internet, biotech, fashion, or other fields. Then think of specific corporations within a field that intrigue you, appeal to you, spark some interest within you. It's important to engage your Motivational Intelligence in this project. To spark your thinking, browse through an issue of *BusinessWeek* or another business periodical. Make a list of a dozen or so potential corporations or mutual funds. You can check the business section of your local newspaper or *The Wall Street Journal* to be sure that these corporations are sold on a public stock exchange.

Another approach is to go online to get information about hot stocks. *Marketplayer.com* has free charts showing which stocks are breaking out to 52-week highs on higher-than-normal trading volume. In addition, this Web site has powerful programs you can use to screen potential stocks using more than 100 variables. Another good place to find predesigned trend screens is *wallstreetcity.com*. *Quicken.com* screens for the fastest-growing companies in terms of sales and earnings.

After you choose a few stocks, focus on one at a time and imagine yourself invested in it. See how it feels. If a stock feels totally comfortable, think about finding something more exciting. Find a stock that feels comfortable but also a little daring and outrageous, a bit of a stretch in a direction that intrigues you. Pick three to five such stocks or mutual funds and write their names on index cards or sheets of paper.

Intuit the Trends

Intuitive coach Nancy Rosanoff recommends the following process: Put three to five stock cards face down and mix them up. Do a relaxation process. When you are fully relaxed, imagine that you are connecting with a universal source of information. See an image or symbol of this source and feel a flow of energy from this source into you. Snapshot #3 shows some symbols that might work for you.

Pick a card without knowing which stock it represents. With your eyes closed, imagine this stock represented by a blank line chart with specific days, weeks, or months across the bottom. Watch or sense the line graph as it moves across the days, weeks, or months. Allow it to move up or down, showing you what's going to happen. Alternatively, imagine an arrow that points up, down, or across, or imagine the words *up*, *down*, or *neutral*. Open your eyes. On the blank side of the card, draw the graph or arrow you saw or sensed, or jot down the word. Repeat this process for each stock.

Compare the results for the various stocks. How do you feel when you see the name of the stock and how well it did in your visualization? Do this exercise with three to five stocks each day for a while. You'll soon be able to sense the growth energy of stocks just by hearing their names. Let your Rational Intelligence feed into your Intuitive Intelligence by doing some selected reading that will help you understand trends in the fields you have selected. The key to this skill is to avoid running the show with your rational mind, and relaxing to allow your intuitive mind to do its thing.

Meanwhile, read the stock market reports to see whether your stocks actually go up, down, or stay about the same. Make notes, with dates, on each stock card. Track your progress to see how well your Intuitive Intelligence is building. If you want to improve, try variations on the visualization techniques.

Snapshot #3: Examples of Stock Market Symbols

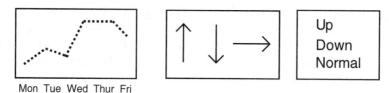

Mon Tue Wed Thur Fri

Pick Your Stocks

When you're ready, pick three to five stocks you want to actually invest in. Decide how much you would invest in each, and write that amount on the stock card. Play with timing, when to buy and when to sell. Just before the right time occurs, you may feel tremendous tension. Stay with it until the tension eases and the answer becomes clear. If in doubt, wait. Wait till the energy shifts and the path is obvious. As soon as you make a decision to buy or sell, write it on your card with the date.

Once you gain confidence in your ability to play the stock market, you're ready to put up some real money.

Finally, keep practicing the whole range of intuitive processes every day, and watch your power grow.

A Final Word

Now you're learning to pull all your intelligences together in ways that spark your Creative Intelligence. You're learning new ways to use your highest-level intelligence, the one that feeds you the innovative ideas you need—either through one of the other intelligences or directly as an inner knowing. How can you best bring this Creative Intelligence into your career and your workplace? Your company culture probably has its share of creative blocks, so your next step is to explore ways to ignite change in that culture so that you and your colleagues can thrive in the New Economy.

Part 3:

Using Innovative Skills
in Your Career and Workplace

Chapter 10

Thrive in the Innovation Age:
Open, Adaptive, Wholistic Thinking

The beauty of this industry (high tech) is the paradigm changes that sweep through it every five years, giving people a whole new reason to get excited.
Eric Schmidt, CEO, Novell

As a career woman in the midst of a New Economy, your innovative skills can launch you into a new arena. They can rev up the engine that makes your organization take off—whether you're the new hire, the CEO, or the owner of your own startup.

You'll naturally be looking at all aspects of creativity and innovation through two filters: your own personal career and the success of your organization. First you must become a more creative person, one who is creative in all aspects of life. You don't become creative because you walk in an office door. If creativity is part of who you are, than you *will* bring it to your career and your firm. That's how it works.

Now is the perfect time to be a creative person, because this is the age of complexity thinking, according to innovation experts Howard Sherman and Ron Schultz. That means that, first, you must become comfortable with a certain level of chaos. Key elements of the New Economy simply create more chaos—the continually evolving technological change, the lightning-fast global communication, a constantly shifting global marketplace, for example. Next, you need to detect patterns emerging from this chaos so that you can recognize new opportunities and the Next New Thing—as well as the problems such change can bring. You need to know when and where to bring order to the emerging patterns, and how to harness them for your own purposes. That means recognizing what paradigm you're in, when it is about to shift, and how this fits in with a typical high-tech life cycle.

Bottom line: You must open your senses and ideas to the new, adapt to the shifting changes, and take a wholistic view that allows you to frame a large picture—bigger than the activities that are swirling all around you.

Complexity Thinking

Complexity thinking allows you to deal with the ideas businesses are made of, and in turn lets you see the possible, the opportunities that open up. It's absolutely necessary for innovation in the New Economy. Here's a brief overview of complexity thinking—some clues that will help you see deeper into the patterns of what's happening all around you.

Levels of Complexity: Order – Complexity – Chaos

We might compare the levels of complexity with the various forms that water can take, from the very ordered, to the more complex, to the chaotic.

Order is contained, like an ice cube. Traditional business was relatively ordered.

Complexity is fluid and flowing, like water—less controlled than the ice cube but still following some sort of pattern. Complexity is like a deep sea of vast possibilities. Here people (and organizations) combine in unpredictable ways that affect the way other people (and firms) combine and change. People and organizations co-evolve, and something new emerges. People are living complex adaptive systems—as are the organizations that are made up of people. This is typical of business in the New Economy.

Chaos is like steam. It has no detectable pattern and its details cannot be understood. Without patterns, we can't imagine what will happen, nor analyze the circumstances under which things might happen, nor make any plans to deal with the unpredictable conditions. All we can do with chaos is to clear a small island of certainty and make small forward movements. People and businesses on the edges of major change, of paradigm shifts, experience chaotic conditions.

Business Components

We'll focus on complexity—an ever-changing environment, sometimes chaotic, but usually with clear, detectable patterns (if you know what to look for). Complexity thinking views a business as composed of:

- Interacting agents (executives, employees, customers, suppliers, competitors),
- That follow rules (values, ethics, laws, blueprints, procedures),
- And exchange influence (ideas, trust, goods, money),
- With the local and global environments,
- Altering the very environment they're responding to through their simple actions.

The four major elements of your career or business, from a complexity-thinking viewpoint, are:

4 Elements of Your Career	4 Elements of Your Business
Life purpose	Mission
Mental models (mindset, beliefs, strategies)	Mental models (ideas, theories, paradigms)
Methods, how-to's, guidelines	Procedures and rules
Actions (behaviors, activities)	Actions (behaviors, activities)

Life purpose, Mission. You must innovate if your career success is to survive. Today's businesses know they must innovate to survive. But innovations that are not in sync with your life purpose, or your company's mission, may produce confusion rather than growth.

Mental models. You have mental models of how you, and your organization, look in physical reality and of your human relationships and interactions. Are you open to changing your mental models as the environment around you changes?

Methods, procedures. Locking into methods and rules as a way to operate freezes the possible—keeps it from co-evolving and emerging—and eliminates real innovation.

Actions. Your ideas shape your actions. If your ideas are outdated, your actions will be irrelevant. Your actions are based in part on experience, but your mental models exist outside actions and experience. To create new mental models, you must be able to conceptualize the adjacent possibilities, which by their very nature have not yet been experienced.

Interaction of Elements: Innovation. When you examine the interactions between your mental models and the actions they bring about, you may recognize the need for new models. Therefore, innovation begins to take place.

Innovative ideas are the key to success. Your career can be only as successful as your ideas. Your business can be only as successful as the ideas of the people who operate it. In that sense your career *is* ideas, just as a business *is* ideas.

Einstein said, "Our thinking creates problems which the same level of thinking can't solve." To solve a problem or recognize a new opportunity, step back. Step outside your mental model. Remember: You are not your ideas. The true you is a self-aware center of consciousness. So you can look at any situation through a new mental model and adjust your actions accordingly. When you continually do this, innovative ideas emerge on a regular basis.

Traditional Vs. Complexity Thinking

You can understand complexity thinking by comparing it to traditional business thinking, which has been relatively mechanical, closed thinking. In contrast, complexity thinking must be adaptive, open, and wholistic.

Traditional: Mechanical, Closed Thinking

The Industrial Age was more ordered, slower paced, stable, and slowly changing, like an ice cube. People and firms could close themselves off from the rest of the world and still be successful. Closed systems could work.

Many people and businesses think as if, and act as if, they are in a closed system. When we try to close systems, we close off innovation and new opportunities. Though we avoid risk of change, we take the risk that our competitors will make us obsolete.

When you (or your firm) get stuck in old closed-system ways of thinking, you can't even recognize what is truly innovative.

Complexity: Adaptive, Open Thinking

The New Economy is ever-more complex and rapidly changing. It's less stable, but it's more fluid and flexible, like water. People and firms must be open, taking in what's happening in the world and sharing what's happening with them, how they're influencing and being influenced. Open systems survive and thrive, while closed systems decline and die.

Open systems are not mechanical, but emergent. They can arise only out of that which has directly preceded them.

Planning is essentially linear: looking at a flat plane of existence and trying to set a course for a person, or firm, that itself is necessarily nonlinear. You can move beyond merely focusing on the fixed targets that come from planning, and also focus on recognizing the Next New Thing.

Out of chaos and complexity comes self-organization. Among its many qualities, the open-adaptive business is able to self-organize its structures (relationships) and its rules for interaction at all levels of the business—and it's able to innovate. The business is nonlinear, which means that, at one extreme, small events may have no effect at all, and at the other extreme, they may bring about a paradigm shift of change.

Linear Vs. Nonlinear Thinking

This brings us to another way to recognize complexity thinking. It's nonlinear in nature, as compared with traditional linear thinking.

Linear Thinking

Linear thinking follows the belief that anything you can refer to has some independent, objectively verifiable status apart from the way it's formulated. It is an object that you, a subject, are observing. The observed thing is separate from you, the observer. Here are some traits of linear thinking:

- A focus on Rational Intelligence.
- A focus on past and future: Past $\longrightarrow$ Present $\longrightarrow$ Future
- A focus on activities as just a means to an end:
  Means $\longrightarrow$ End
- Space: points in space $(\cdots\cdots)$
- Observer vs. observed.
- Objects with their own objective nature are *out there.*
- The objective world is the same for all observers.
- Stability, status quo, little change, and slow change are typical.
- Mechanical system of many parts making up a whole.

- A focus on events that occur in a sequential manner.
- Mechanistic, sequential feedback.

Nonlinear Thinking

Nonlinear thinking follows the belief that information has more the character of a pattern, conveying a whole picture, rather than the parts of a pattern. Only from the pattern can you figure out the facts, the data, relating to a situation. You are part of that pattern, and you affect it. This process eliminates the distinction between the subject and the object. Here are some traits of nonlinear thinking:

- Focus on right-brain intelligences (Associative, Sensory, Intuitive).
- Spiraling, emerging, evolving.
- Liquid, flowing.
- Wholistic, all is Now.
- Organic systems that grow, learn, adapt, and co-evolve.
- Complex adaptive system of behaviors.
- A focus on events that occur in a parallel, interactive, and simultaneous way.
- Collaboration.
- Movement, flowing forward.
- Wholistic, intuitive feedback.

Left Brain Vs. Right Brain

Putting this all together, you can see that traditional thinking is a linear, closed-system, left-brain, rational-mind, mechanical type of thinking. In contrast, complexity thinking is a nonlinear, open-system, right-brain, adaptive type of thinking.

Closed-System Rational-Mind Mechanical Thinking

Here are some typical beliefs you hold when you engage in traditional thinking:

- Rational Intelligence is the only real intelligence.
- A statement is either true or false.
- We can objectively determine what is fact and not fact.
- All thinking and actions must conform to the facts.
- I can define what is.
- We can define the separate, static, external reality that exists out there.
- There are stationary forces *out there* that we can diagnose and analyze.
- Customers want either this or that.
- I am either the subject or the object, the knower or the known.

- ❧ Keep doing what worked in the past. Do more of the same.
- ❧ Closed systems with strong walls will prevent chaos from taking hold.
- ❧ Mechanical, linear thinking is what works.

Open-System Right-Brain Adaptive Thinking

You hold very different beliefs when you engage in complexity thinking. Here are some examples:

- ❧ Associative, Sensory, and Intuitive Intelligences must link up with Rational Intelligence.
- ❧ Reality consists of ongoing processes that are influenced by the ideas, languages, and actions of all the participants.
- ❧ What customers want is continually changing.
- ❧ I'm both the subject and the object, the knower and the known.
- ❧ There's not really an *out there* called the marketplace; there's only my (and my firm's) interactions with the other players.
- ❧ My clients and I are constantly modifying each other and co-evolving.
- ❧ Organic, nonlinear thinking is what works.

The Role of Boundaries

Because complexity thinking requires you to be open to your environment, what about boundaries? To begin with, you know that you (and your firm) must function as an adaptive system within your increasingly complex environment. Complex adaptive systems have arbitrary boundaries. Where you (or your firm) stop and something else begins is a matter of perception, so people will disagree about just where the boundary is.

Your boundaries (and your firm's) must be open enough for interactions to occur—for you to have new experiences, form ideas, and be influenced by aspects of other elements in the environment, such as lifestyles. You are shaped by ideas you have of yourself, as well as ideas you have of your environment. You must protect your boundaries, but they must be permeable, allowing ideas in and out, allowing the process of shaping ideas of others in your environment and being shaped by theirs. Idea boundaries are not physical, yet they are very real.

Emergence of the Next New Thing

The Principle of Emergence developed by Sherman and Schultz says: *What is possible at this moment is possible only because of the last level of possibilities that have emerged—the adjacent possible.*

How can you thrive in an age of complexity thinking? You focus on the possibilities that have just been realized—and see the adjacent possibilities that have just emerged because of it. In the Silicon Valley high-tech culture, all the focus is on the New Thing, then the New New Thing and the Next New Thing. Their way of talking about adjacent possibilities would be: You must focus on the New New Thing that has just come into play—and see the Next New Thing that's now possible because of it.

Emergent innovation is possible only when you (or your firm) are open to the adjacent possible. Then, what was once inconceivable becomes actualized.

Focus on the work unleashed by the previous emergence (the New New Thing). That work fertilizes the ground for the next emergence (the Next New Thing). Adjacent possibilities abound. Evolution is unstoppable. Emergence occurs. What might be inconceivable can be realized by taking very small and deliberate steps. To emerge is literally to *dive out*, to come out of the depths of complexity. Emergent innovation refers to that Next New Thing that arises out of the depths of complex interactions. It's an idea brought to life.

Until a previous possibility has come into existence, an adjacent possibility could not exist. Until personal computers appeared on the desks of many people, the Internet could not exist. Until the Internet existed, we could not have e-commerce.

You can develop adjacent possibilities in two ways:

1. Through co-evolving technologies: As technology develops, further technologies that were not previously even conceivable become possible.
2. Through mental models: As we develop new mental models, new possibilities for ways of formulating ideas that weren't possible before now become possible.

Finding the Next New Thing

Once an adjacent possibility becomes possible, it *will* occur. If you (or your firm) are not ready to innovate and act on the new idea, someone else will. Someone will discover it and create a startup based upon it. Will this new startup make your business irrelevant?

The people, and businesses, that succeed are those who are first within an industry to see an adjacent possibility and act upon it.

How quickly in this process of evolution can you recognize the adjacent possible? Can you focus on the here and now? Then can you free yourself from your current environment long enough to leap out for a moment and see the bigger picture around you—like the fish that jumps out of water? And form a new viewpoint? You may see the adjacent possible.

Need help seeing the adjacent possible? Work with team members. First, learn to ask good questions of each other with every problem that arises. A good question may start with a story. The story can relate ideas that link to something the listener already knows. From here you can move on to questions that naturally arise from your story. If a true meeting of the minds takes place, you and your team can co-evolve and open up to the adjacent possible—and innovation occurs.

Jean, a Silicon Valley trainer, told a story of trying to develop an Internet-based training course for employees. She told about working very hard to make the course effective, but employees avoided this course. They said they would rather attend a regular seminar with an instructor. She asked her team what they saw as the major barrier to making computer-based courses palatable to employees. This led to a series of questions and discussions about what makes an instructor-led seminar effective and how to incorporate those factors into a computer-based program.

Innovative Questions About the Next New Thing

Here are questions to ask yourself on a regular basis—and certainly any time you sense that some major shift is about to occur:

1. What is the New New Thing in my field? And what is the Next New Thing that this makes possible?
2. What are the adjacent possibilities (the Next New Thing) within my field that allow for the creation of something new?
3. How can I step outside myself (and my organization) and see how I'm managing my career, my organization? How can I imagine other possibilities?
4. How is my field changing as it co-evolves with all the people it touches?

Barriers to Finding the Next New Thing

Your old beliefs are your greatest barrier to seeing the Next New Thing. Beliefs based on what has succeeded in the past are especially blinding. What are the beliefs that led to ideas that guided the actions that made you successful, that made your company rich? You tend to cling to those beliefs, and they may be outdated and irrelevant in the current environment that is emerging. They can close down the open boundaries of unlimited possibilities. They may deny the complexity and change that are essential parts of all living systems. They make old ways of doing business *the way*. Rapid change is always occurring, so it's rare that the ideas that allowed your current success will work to bring about your next success.

How can you (and your firm) be more innovative? Begin by questioning all your old beliefs and ideas that keep you stuck. Innovation can take place only when we challenge our static ideas.

Innovative Questions for Learning from the New Economy

Ask yourself these kinds of questions any time you think that you (or your firm) need to learn from the New Economy:

1. How do I (and my firm) learn?
2. How can I tell when I (and my team) am learning—as compared to just reacting?
3. Do I (and my firm) reformulate the events in my world? How am I interpreting my experiences through a current mental model or story?
4. How does my life purpose (and my firm's mission) guide or limit my learning?
5. How do I (and my firm) use information in my learning process? Do I equate info with data and reports? How does this limit me? Is most of my information in the form of numbers?

   Where do I (and my firm) get most of my information?
6. What do I (and my firm) see as the relationship between learning, training, and information?

The Interaction of Thinking, Feeling, and Doing

Complexity thinking depends on an interaction of your thinking, feeling, and doing modes. It's only when your thinking anticipates your experience that true innovation can occur. Your feelings can spark the drive for innovation or squelch it. Still, it's important to remember that your true self is a center of self-aware consciousness; you are not your thoughts, feelings, and actions. You can observe them and recognize the many choices you have for how to think and act, which will in turn trigger the feelings you experience.

Thinking: Left-Brain Rational Intelligence

- Mental models.
- Theories.
- Concepts.
- Ideas.

Feeling: Midbrain Emotional and Motivational Intelligences

- Sensations.
- Feelings.
- Desire (will).
- Intention.

Doing: Brainstem Basic Intelligence

- Behaviors.
- Activities.

When you take an open-system, complexity approach, you're aware of how your experience interacts with your interpretation of that experience. You're aware of how you visualize and think about that experience. You're aware of the stories you tell about it and how those stories guide your actions in relation to the experience and how they define the outcome of that experience. When you look back on this process, you don't see a straight line. It's not linear.

For example, say you've heard about Anita Roddick, founder of The Body Shop International, and you dream of bringing her to your organization's annual conference as a speaker. Because her headquarters are in England and she's an extremely busy executive, you have little hope of making your dream a reality. Then you learn that one of your father's friends has twin daughters who, with their husbands, own four Body Shops. You contact one of the daughters, Pat. She agrees to meet you for lunch, and an amazing story unfolds. Pat's husband, Eric, formerly a travel agent, handles the details of Anita's travel and speaking engagements in the United States. She will be in your area for six weeks this fall, conducting a special graduate business seminar at a local university. She wants to do one speaking engagement each week and has expressed an interest in speaking with an organization like yours. Bottom line: She delivers a rousing speech to your organization, getting a standing ovation.

How would you interpret this experience? How would you visualize it and think about it? What stories would you tell yourself and others about it?

And how would these stories affect your current and future actions and experiences? Would you interpret these events...

- ❧ As synchronicity—indicators that you and Anita are on the same wavelength, tuned into the same forces and interest?
- ❧ As a sign that fate had predestined that you would come together in this way?
- ❧ As a set of lucky coincidences?
- ❧ As a matter of possibilities becoming probabilities?
- ❧ As random events having no particular meaning?

Each of these interpretations leads to a different story that you tell yourself and others about this experience. In fact, each will literally determine how you introduce Anita when she gives her presentation—a verbal story to the entire organization. Each interpretation is likely to affect the way you'll approach making a dream come true in the future. If you see the events as synchronistic, in the future you're likely to put your desire out there, keep your antenna up, follow leads, and trust the universe to help you bring it into reality.

Anticipate Paradigm Shifts

A key innovative skill you can easily develop is anticipating paradigm shifts that will affect your career and your firm. You need this information to predict the problem-opportunities you and your organization are likely to face and to develop some innovative ideas for preparing and responding to these events.

Know How to Identify a Paradigm

A paradigm is a mental model of how something works. To be considered a paradigm, according to business author Joel Barker, the model must include three factors:

1. A set of rules that
2. Establishes or defines the boundaries of the model and
3. Tells you how to behave inside the boundaries in order to succeed.

People who adopt a particular paradigm measure success by the ability to solve problems within the paradigm.

Think of a culture, society, worldview, organization, or business as a forest of paradigms. Each paradigm is a tree in the forest. For example, a business will have management paradigms, sales paradigms, human resource paradigms, and recruitment paradigms. We're defining a paradigm as a mental model, but it is also seen by various people as a set of beliefs or principles, a theory, a method, a protocol, standards, routines, assumptions, conventions, patterns, habits, common sense, consensus reality, conventional wisdom, a mindset, a frame of reference, traditions, customs, prejudices, ideology, and/or rituals. The forest of paradigms we find in a business, a culture, or a worldview are interdependent, so you never change just one paradigm. When you change one, it affects all the others, so they too must shift to some degree—from very slightly to dramatically.

Recognize Paradigm Cycles and Shifts

A paradigm shift is a change from the current model to a new model, with a new set of rules and boundaries. It's a new game that requires different behavior in order to succeed. For example, when women started moving into power positions 20 or 30 years ago, this was a major paradigm shift that has affected business, marriage, family, child-rearing, education, courtship, and perhaps most of the trees in our cultural forest. The mental model of what it means to be a good wife, mother, husband, and father all began to shift. People are still trying to figure out all the new rules and boundaries.

To identify where paradigm shifts are likely to occur, notice where people are trying to change the rules, because that's the earliest sign of significant change possibilities. When the rules change, the whole world can change.

Paradigm Phases

When do the rules change? When do new paradigms appear? Usually when someone figures out how to solve one or more major problems that cannot be solved using the rules and boundaries of the old paradigm. In effect, someone figures out how to do something better, something important that really needs to be done better, and enough people jump on the bandwagon to make a shift occur. Often it's when someone solves a problem in a new, strange way—not using the old rules. Such explorers often think this new way could be a new model for solving a wide range of similar problems. Let's look at typical phases of a paradigm shift, as shown in Snapshot #1, along with their relationship to the complexity-chaos process.

Snapshot #1: Paradigm Shifts: Technological Change

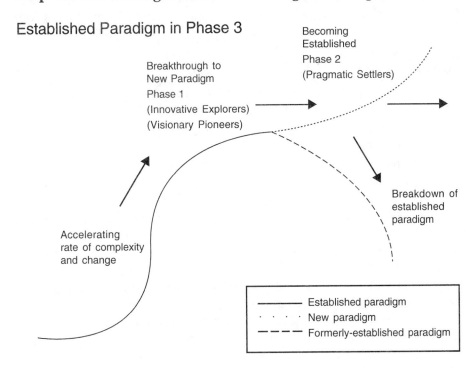

Established Paradigm in Phase 3

Breakthrough to
New Paradigm
Phase 1
(Innovative Explorers)
(Visionary Pioneers)

Becoming
Established
Phase 2
(Pragmatic Settlers)

Breakdown of
established
paradigm

Accelerating
rate of complexity
and change

———— Established paradigm
· · · · New paradigm
— — — Formerly-established paradigm

Well-Established Phase 3 of a Current Paradigm

- The well-established paradigm eventually begins to seem less effective.
- People in the field who are affected begin to lose trust in the old rules.
- Turbulence and a sense of crisis grow as trust is reduced.

Beginning Phase 1 of a New Paradigm

This is the breakthrough period when a new mental model is first proposed and tried out.

- Turbulence and crisis increase even more as paradigm conflict becomes obvious.
- People in the field become very upset and demand clear solutions.
- People begin to believe that one of the proposed new paradigms can solve a small set of significant problems that the old paradigm cannot.
- *Innovative Explorers* step forward to propose a solution—a new paradigm. It may be a radically new way of doing things, or it may be an old idea whose time has come.
- *Visionary Pioneers* take the lead to accept the new paradigm, based on their intuition that it will work.

During the Beginning Phase 1, the new paradigm is usually in competition with other paradigms that are also being developed to solve the problem. The paradigm that can survive to Phase 2 (Becoming Established) will almost always win—even if other paradigms would be better in the long run. For example, many people say Apple had a better computer operating system, but Microsoft found ways to make its operating system the one chosen by most computer users—so its system and related software became the New Paradigm.

Becoming Established: Phase 2 of a New Paradigm

This is the phase when Innovative Explorers, Visionary Pioneers, and Pragmatic Settlers who are entrepreneurial types can make great profits.

- As support and funding for this new paradigm grow, acceptance of it increases.
- Turbulence and crisis decrease as this new paradigm starts solving the problems and as people in the field realize that this is a new, more successful, way to deal with the world.

You and your organization will have a significant competitive advantage if you can anticipate paradigm shifts, obviously. Then you can become a *Visionary Pioneer* in adopting a new paradigm that allows you to lead people out of the old paradigm.

Meanwhile, what's happening with those competing paradigms that have been battling to get established as the new paradigm? Suppose these paradigm explorers face artificial barriers—such as government regulation, a distorted marketplace, or big companies that crush competition. Then their competing paradigms may not have much of a chance until the accepted New Paradigm has become established and has moved into Phase 3 (Well-Established). However, it's most likely that their competing paradigm—or a new competing paradigm—will appear and be accepted late in Phase 2. That's because there will be enough unsolved problems at this stage to trigger the search for new solutions. The need is felt.

Personal Impact of Paradigm Shifts

We can relate the paradigm shift process to complexity theory and chaos theory by focusing on the acceleration of change in today's workplace and society and how that acceleration builds to the point of breakdown of the old and breakout into the new.

Acceleration

Not only is technological change accelerating, so is every aspect of life. We all feel the acceleration of the pace of modern life. We have too much to do, there is more information coming at us, and it is more complicated and dense than ever. We don't have much time to spend on any one thing. We must move fast to keep up or we'll be left behind. We'll fail. Traditional boundaries are collapsing as we move into new situations at a faster and faster pace. Every area of human activity seems to be escalating at an exponential rate. Maybe you spend every free moment you can grab just cocooning to get ready for tomorrow's onslaught. The speed of the workplace, marketplace, and digital world has become the speed of your body-mind.

Breakdown

You reach a critical point where you can't go any faster. Your beliefs, attitudes, thinking, feeling, decisions, and choices will no longer handle the increasing tension. You may begin to question the beliefs and habits—those that you accepted without much thought. You may begin to challenge everything you see, to have doubts, and to be cynical. Even though you try harder to succeed, your efforts are no longer effective. You feel you must disconnect from the constant buzz in order to retain your sanity. You're right: In the breakdown phase, it pays to march to a different drummer.

You need fresh eyes and new thinking in order to decide where to go next. You must redefine who you are and what your skills, products, or services are. Things must dissolve, break down, destruct. Leadership becomes the ability to break down existing forms and to provoke others to do the same. Breakdown is a time of cleaning out, changing priorities, and giving up control.

Chaos

During the chaotic phase, no one knows for sure what they're doing or what's going on. Old forms have broken down, but new ones are not yet in place. It's a time with few, if any, rules, when identity begins to come apart. The old knowledge seems useless. Boundaries are moving, form is missing, and power relationships are shifting. You need to find the center within, to keep your head even when people around you are losing theirs. Get in touch with your purpose in life (tap your Motivational Intelligence) in this sea of chaos. The external boundaries and rules are gone, so each person's individual values and motivations are all that's left. In a world without form, images are the only way to think, for imagination is how the new forms will emerge.

Breakthrough

Breakdown and chaos release huge flows of energy from the previously stable system. This energy seeks out a new level of order and stability, and at this moment it becomes a *dissipative structure*, in the words of biologist Ilya Prygione. At this critical moment there is a qualitative break from the past and an entirely new world of possibilities opens up. The study of how new order arises from chaos is called complexity theory or chaos theory. You can gain the ability to entirely rewrite your perceptions of what lies ahead. Instead of dwelling on solutions, focus on discerning new paradigms, shifts in *how* you look at a problem.

How can you grow most effectively in these new, fast-moving, turbulent systems? What new patterns can you develop in response to new cultural and business demands? You need:

- New perceptual skills.
- New emotional paths.
- New relationship skills.

The most powerful element of building future scenarios is that it opens the door for you to begin tuning into your own personal sense of what lies ahead. You must be able to see unfolding patterns before they occur and as they occur. You must recognize what's happening in that subtle zone where what you already know is dissolving into something you haven't yet imagined. This is the threshold, the edge, the door to the future.

You must learn to think, sense, know, feel, and act in entirely new patterns. You must boost your intelligences—all of them. You don't have to do this overnight or in quantum leaps. Even tiny shifts in the right direction can change the path you take—and many tiny shifts eventually add up to a dramatically different way of functioning. The part of you that is getting smarter is the part that's beginning to focus in on what's really important: your personal strengths and your most passionate, heartfelt desires.

Paradigm shifts are regular events in the New Economy and especially in the world of high tech. Your knowledge of paradigms will help you recognize the patterns that reveal where you and your firm can profit from the high-tech life cycle.

Recognize the High-Tech Life Cycle

If you work in a high-tech field, you must understand typical high-tech paradigm shift patterns—which we'll call the High-Tech Life Cycle. Even if you work in a low-tech field, the high-tech world will impact you more and more, so you need to understand how it works. The High-Tech Life Cycle consists of four phases—Early Market, Niche Market, Whirlwind of Demand, and the Mall (Moore 1995). If you're part of this cycle, it's absolutely essential that your management team agree on which phase your product is in and what role your company is able to play.

Early Market—Phase I

Target Audience: Innovative Techies

Definition—Early Market Phase

Imagine that your company is an Innovative Explorer that develops a brand new category of product offering. This is a breakthrough technology that replaces a whole class of infrastructure. Innovative Techies must accept it because they influence the Visionary Pioneers who have the financial decision-making clout to adopt it.

Competition—Early Market Phase

Competition is among alternative breakthrough possibilities. Visionary Pioneers want a dramatic competitive advantage by adopting a new paradigm. The competition is other companies with their own new paradigms that are competing for the Pioneers' attention. How you win: Your idea has the ability to break through the problems that are blocking progress and your company is flexible enough to adapt your idea to the Pioneers' needs.

Role of Strategic Partners – Early Market Phase

A new paradigm of open architecture and inter-vendor cooperation emerged, introduced by Apple in the Apple II, and then broadly disseminated by the PC division of IBM and by Sun Microsystems. These companies recruited partners to fill the open slots inside their computer cases. This means whole products can get to market much faster because multiple companies compete to provide each part. Work on all the parts can go forward in parallel.

In open systems solutions, everything is assumed to plug and play. In reality, nothing really does in the beginning. The whole product is a barely complete core product that's surrounded by the custom services needed to make any particular application work. Visionary buyers take a product that may be about 80 percent complete and use it as the foundation for creating an application breakthrough. They must rely heavily on the service of systems integrators who pull the whole project together.

The initial question to ask about forming partnerships is: Are we partnering on a single revenue opportunity, for a potential revenue stream, or to capture market leadership? Market leadership is the only strategic reason to partner—because it focuses on the whole product that you must offer in order to win top position in a target market

Power Hierarchy—Early Market Phase

Power lies with the technology provider who attracts visionary buyers and the systems integrators needed to make the technology work.

Organizational Leadership—Early Market Phase

From the beginning, the company needs a cross-functional team to see it through the various phases. In the first phase the key leader needs product marketing expertise.

Niche Market—Across the Gap to Phase II

Target Audience: Visionary Pioneers

Visionary Pioneers are intuitive, independent risk-takers who are motivated to search out future opportunities and capitalize on them.

Definition—Niche Market Phase

Your company provides a usable product/service to a particular market niche—to the point that you have a satisfied customer. Your market is not yet defined by a particular product, but rather by your customers' application of your new technology. It's still the customers' market, not yours. They are your sponsors and your protectors, and you'll need that protective umbrella for a while. But this is your start in the mainstream market. Each niche requires its own whole product to be fully complete before it can adopt the new paradigm.

Short-Term Goal

To find the Visionary Pioneers with the most compelling needs to buy your new technology—then develop your technology into a whole product for this particular niche.

Long-Term Goal

To emerge as the Market Monster when you get to the Whirlwind of Demand phase. Look for that moment when it becomes more effective for the marketplace to organize itself away from niche markets and rally instead around the emerging product category of the Demand Phase. Now's when you must simplify, simplify, simplify your product to make it suitable for general-purpose use and easier and less costly to acquire and maintain. Remember: The Niche Market Phase is just a phase—necessary, but not one you want to get stuck in.

Key strategies—Niche Market Phase

- Meet customer needs. That's your top priority now.
- Focus on the economic buyer and end user in client organizations.
- Emphasize to buyers that return on investment is the reason to buy—money gained by solving a current problem or removing a current barrier.
- Differentiate your whole product for a single application.
- Partner with a company that can serve as a distribution channel that adds value to the whole product—to ensure that your customized solution is delivered to the end user in usable form.
- Base your prices on the value your product/service provides to clients.
- Avoid competition to gain niche market share.
- Position your products within vertical market segments (all the phases of delivering a product or service to an end user, within a particular niche market).

    ॐ   Give up an R&D-based product-centered approach and adopt a customer-based, application-centered approach. Vertical marketing requires becoming an adjunct to another industry's market—and giving up being the center of attention.

Competition—Niche Market Phase

How you win: Being the first to provide a differentiated whole product that solves a particular problem or allows a specific breakthrough. You must provide a whole product and you must be first to win in this phase.

Role of Strategic Partners – Niche Market Phase

To cross the gap and become accepted by Pragmatist Settlers, the company must develop a whole product, at first for a specific niche of customers. Now every part of the product must be part of the package, and no part needs to be created from scratch by a technician. To accomplish this as rapidly as possible, the lead company must recruit partners who will commit to completing one or more specified parts of the whole product. Here the network of informal partnerships is born.

The responsibility of the market leader is to make a market for the other partners. If the partnership really is strategic, giving the business away to the right strategic partner is the lowest-cost, highest-return investment in market development.

Power Hierarchy—Niche Market Phase

Power centralizes in the leader of the niche market attack, the company that has seen the market opportunity where nobody else did.

Organizational Leadership—Niche Market Phase

Marketing and finance people are key to making it across the high-tech adoption gap and gaining a toehold niche. In the Niche Market Phase, vertical market managers, partner managers, and market-focused sales teams take over. Now the company needs a hands-on leader who spends more time with the customers and the troops than reviewing reports or winning points with top management—with these traits and skills:

    ॐ   A team leader, very focused and disciplined in the approach to reaching goals.

    ॐ   Charismatic and personable with colleagues and customers.

    ॐ   Strongly committed to the end goal but with great flexibility about how to attain it.

Danger Signs—Niche Market Phase

Never go after a niche where the current expenditures on your category of product are larger than your current annual revenue. "Pick on somebody your own size" is the rule. To succeed in the Niche Market phase, you must win at least 40 percent of its new business over a 12- to 18-month period. Then word of mouth starts spreading the message that you're the Market Monster. That means your share of the next year's sales should go well beyond 50 percent. Pragmatic Settlers want to buy what other Settlers have bought.

How big a target niche can you handle? To answer that question, look at your goal for the coming year, how much you hope to ship. Say it's $10 million. At best you might get 60 percent of your revenue from your target niche, meaning $6 million from that niche. Remember: You must win at least 40 percent of this business, so 100 percent of that niche should be $15 million. That's the maximum amount this niche can spend next year if you are to end up being its dominant supplier. If you know it will be greater, you can't handle it. If you try, you'll create demand you can't fulfill, which in turn creates a market for some other competitor.

Leveraging Your Toehold—Niche Market Phase

Next you must leverage that toehold in order to sell to a related niche market, adapting your new technology to that particular arena. Moving from one niche to another, you work toward building a critical mass of niches. If you succeed, then your product becomes interesting to the Pragmatist Settlers in the larger marketplace.

Strategy: Sell to the end-user community, the economic buyer, the line manager in the end-user organization. Frame the buying issues in terms that economic buyers can understand and buy into. For example:

- Show how your product can solve some previously unsolvable problem that's costing them money.
- Show how this problem is part of the current IT infrastructure's paradigm for supporting their end users.
- Show that you can solve this problem because your new paradigm redesigns the end users' workflow to eliminate the root cause of the problem.
- Show that you've studied and understand their particular application requirements, so you not only have the necessary core product but the whole product they need.

Methodically work through all the elements of this whole product, showing your understanding of their business. This overcomes the resistance of Pragmatist Settlers in the organization and brings them over to your side. You become a true partner to your customer. You can charge any price that the Visionary Explorer sees is worth the investment.

Which niche do you target next? Generally, take a vertical approach. Say your technology is accepted for some specific tasks in the human resources function in a bank. If your technology can be applied to other departments within that same company, target those. If not, then target human resources departments in other banks. Then expand to human resources functions in another financial sector, such as investment companies. Expand from one related niche to another.

Taking a vertical approach during the Niche Market Phase will achieve your goal of building a critical mass of support for becoming the Market Monster.

Taking a horizontal approach will defeat it. Going horizontal into the mass market is tempting because that's where the big money is, but a premature entrance into the mainstream will permanently cripple your company and discredit the technology.

The Role of Niche Markets

Niche markets do the following:

1. They simplify the whole-product challenge in the early stages of the technology. You can earn Visionary Explorer customers immediately instead of having to wait for another round of development.

2. They are inherently profitable because you are replacing an inefficient problem situation.

3. They help you become self-funding, which gives you more control over the timing of your entry into the Whirlwind of Demand phase.

4. They represent territories of loyal customers that you can capture and who will sponsor your architecture in the *standards war* that will take place during the Whirlwind of Demand Phase.

5. They can be leveraged so that victory in one segment overflows into victories in adjacent segments. If the overflow is powerful enough, it can trigger the Whirlwind of Demand Phase.

Breaking Through Paradigm Barriers—Niche Market

Two types of paradigm shifts can shape the High-Tech Life Cycle: paradigm shock and application breakthrough. Each presents barriers that your company must overcome.

Paradigm shock may be experienced by end users or by the infrastructure that supports them—as a form of technological shock or as cultural/psychological shock.

For example, the electric car affects automobile owners as end users. The infrastructure that supports auto owners includes gas stations, mechanics, and corporations that employ owners. All must learn new ideas, make new investments, and adopt new behaviors. Their resistance can put a brake on adoption of new technology.

Your company must single out the issues of a specific niche segment and reduce paradigm shock by implementing a limited niche-specific solution that provides application breakthroughs. Later the company can support all the variations of a general solution set.

In the case of electric automobiles, the new hybrid electric-gas cars run 70 miles on a gallon of gasoline. This provides users an immediate operational savings and eases the transition from a gas to an electric infrastructure.

Application breakthroughs occur when the new technology allows end-user roles to dramatically change and improve, resulting in dramatic returns on investment or savings for the company that installs them. These breakthroughs accelerate the adoption of new technology.

For example, in phone services, paradigm shock for the Baby Bells included such new technologies as fax, conferencing, call forwarding, and caller

ID, but these did not provide significant application breakthroughs for end users. On the other hand, Voice Response Units did provide such a breakthrough by allowing companies to replace human telephone customer service personnel with automated telephone answering services. This provided large payroll cost savings.

Getting Ready for the Whirlwind of Demand Phase

Price point is a key indicator of readiness for the Whirlwind of Demand. For example, when your product price falls below $1,500, it gets you into the small office market, whereas falling below $1,000 enables a Whirlwind. Falling below $700 gets you into the home market, whereas falling below $300 enables a Whirlwind.

A Whirlwind needs the whole product as a plug-and-play commodity. As long as even one significant part requires scarce expertise in order to integrate it into the end user's situation, the market will have difficulty getting into the Whirlwind of Demand Phase.

One big signal for a Whirlwind is the emergence of a *killer application*. Killer apps supply universal infrastructure, are appealing to a mass market, and can become a commodity.

Whirlwind of Demand—Phase III

Target Audience: Pragmatist Settlers

Pragmatist Settlers tend to be analytical conformists who like to stick with their neighbors and are motivated to solve current problems. They consult with other Settlers to try to get a sense of when it's time to shift to a new technology. They want to see a clear market leader that's able to establish a vision and the architectures and standards that will make it work in the mainstream market.

Definition—Whirlwind of Demand Phase

During this phase the Pragmatist Settlers move together as a community. They apply these three principles:
1. When it's time to move, let's all move together.
2. When we pick the vendor to lead us to the new paradigm, let's all pick the same one.
3. Once the move starts, the sooner we get it over with, the better.

A new order, a hierarchy, is created in this phase. One company will emerge with at least 50 percent of the business: the Market Monster. This company will rake in about two-thirds of the profits during the life of this technology. Two or three companies will capture most of the remaining market and profits: the Big Munsters. Any number of smaller companies will emerge around the margins: the Little Munsters. It's only during this phase that all-out battles for market share make sense. All high-tech fortunes are based on winning this battle.

The Whirlwind occurs when the general marketplace for your type of product shifts its allegiance from the old architecture to the new. Now it's time to take your R&D investment and, with modest additional work, secure entirely new niches, which gives you a very profitable situation.

Mass-market adoption occurs. The demand for the new far outstrips the supply. The company that becomes the Market Monster is the one that can sell, sell, sell—capturing customers for the lifetime of the technology—and deliver, deliver, deliver a *whole product* that is feasible and usable. It is in this phase that huge revenues and profits are won and the company may become one of the Fortune 500.

If you become the Market Monster, you'll create a market for many Munsters. Every customer who buys your platform becomes a potential Mall Phase customer for the additional bells and whistles that Munster companies will create around your infrastructure. Munsters add value and enrich the whole product. Customers are able to do more with the technology, which drives more sales, which in turn attracts still more Munsters, who create more bells and whistles. The result is an ever-expanding whole-product family.

Becoming the Market Monster gives you many advantages: You can charge more money for your product, even if it has a bug or two in it. You ship the highest volumes, so you enjoy the lowest cost per unit. When you charge the highest price and achieve the lowest cost, your profit margins soar. You enjoy lower cost of sales because Settlers want to buy your products—so selling them is easy. In addition, Little Munsters will often pay you to let them create products that fit in with yours. Your product not only benefits generally from their supportive products, but your company immediately benefits, bottom line.

Key Strategies—Whirlwind of Demand Phase

1. Beat out the competition at all costs and establish a common standard for your infrastructure.
2. Focus on the infrastructure buyer within client organizations, ignoring economic buyers and end users.
3. Ignore return on investment as a reason buyers should buy.
4. Price competitively to maximize market share.
5. Focus on developing a reliable infrastructure and rapidly getting it installed.
6. Commoditize your whole product for general purpose use in horizontal, global markets.
7. Position your products horizontally as global infrastructure.
8. Distribute through low-cost, high-volume channels for maximum market exposure.
9. Attack competition to gain mass market share. In this phase, it's a zero-sum game, so every new customer you win is one that your competitors lose—for the life of the technology.
10. Just ship! Don't segment the market. Don't customize the product. Don't commit to any special projects. Just ship.
11. Do anything you can to streamline the creation, distribution, installation, and adoption of your whole product. Avoid friction and distraction.
12. Focus on supply chains and quality in order to avoid getting returned product.
13. Focus on your own organizational needs at this point rather than individual customer needs.

Competition—Whirlwind of Demand Phase

How you handle competition in this phase depends on your status in the marketplace:

As the Market Monster: Focus on the distribution channel. At the high end, it's a competition for good sales reps and at the low end for the most shelf space. When competing against Little Munsters, reset the standard, temporarily making their offerings obsolete, as Intel has done with its new chips. Big Munsters may come up with new innovations, and you must meet their challenge as soon as possible with your own versions.

As a Little Monster: Your reference competitor is the Monster's product, but your real competition comes from other Little Munsters. Your role is to fulfill overflow demand, to provide what's needed around the margins. Your strategy should therefore be: Take the money and run. Cash out the business every day. You have nothing to gain here except the sale itself. Invest in nothing; defend nothing. The only way you can ever become a Monster is through providing a differentiated whole product to a niche segment, thus becoming a Big Munster and then taking that product to a Whirlwind phase.

As a Big Monster: You have a major investment in your own technology. You are competing first and foremost for distribution of your product, simply to get access to the pent-up customer demand. You can focus and innovate within a local segment, staking out turf that's not yet committed to the Monster. You should adopt a Niche approach during the Whirlwind of Demand Phase. By carving out a niche or two, there may be a place for you when the Whirlwind is over.

In the meantime, remember that Pragmatist Settlers may want to support you as a safe alternative to the Monster, in case they need it. On the other hand, they don't want to upset the Monster's authority to set de facto standards. It's the market, not the Monster, that prevents you from overtaking the Monster and becoming the leader. This has to do with the current alignment of massive amounts of wealth and powerful interest groups that are already committed to the Monster's standards. You can be aggressive, but only go so far. You must keep your products current with the market's evolving standards. You can't fight the Monster on its own turf. Your question: What's the value of market share to me?

The Role of Strategic Partners—Whirlwind of Demand Phase

Once the product enters the Whirlwind of Demand Phase, the pressure is to drive costs down and reliability up, so the whole product must become increasingly plug-and-play. For example, the personal computer must come with all key software programs already installed, ready for users to plug it in and go to work. This means the Market Monster must eliminate the very partnerships that brought the product to Whirlwind readiness.

Power Hierarchy

Power is centralized here in the Market Monster company and its Big Munster partners. If it's a major technology, the market may select a Monster for each component. They are elected as the solution set within which every part is guaranteed to be compatible with every other part. The PC market is certainly major, allowing several Market Monsters. For PC operating systems market, it's Microsoft, and the Big Munsters are IBM and Apple. In PC microprocessors, the Market Monster is Intel, in hard drives it's Seagate, in DRAM memory it's Toshiba. For corporate client/servers, the Market Monster is Oracle and the Big Munsters are HP and SAP.

Organizational Leadership—Whirlwind of Demand Phase

During the Whirlwind, the line functions of manufacturing, purchasing, and quality control become crucial, as does human resources—all to provide the operational excellence that's needed to win. The original cross-functional team should become a product marketing council to ensure communication flow and problem resolution among the various line functions during the Whirlwind of Demand Phase

The company needs a leader who can function above the fray, see the forest without getting caught in the trees, and use fire prevention instead of fire fighting—a leader who is unflappable and disciplined, with a process-drive management style. The leader needs expertise in making systems work, both external and internal systems. External systems must help customers mesh the old and new paradigms to create a workable infrastructure that performs effectively. Many new hires are coming on board so key internal systems include human resources orientation, to get people off to a good start. On the financial side, cash-flow management is critical.

How to Become the Market Monster

Timing and luck are crucial, but there are some things you can do to improve your chances. For example, the two greatest whirlwinds of the 1980s each went through two rounds.

Midrange computers—computers at a power level between mainframes and personal computers—went through the Whirlwind first. Demand developed around DEC's minicomputer architecture, subsequently replaced by Hewlett Packard's Unix architecture, with Oracle's software providing the driving energy in both rounds.

Personal computers—smaller computers—went through an even greater Whirlwind. IBM provided the large-scale infrastructure and Lotus the software in the first round. Microsoft's Windows software and Intel's chips won the second round with no Monster hardware vendor. Big Munsters were Dell and Compaq.

Lessons that Oracle taught the industry about winning the Demand Phase include attack the competition ruthlessly, expand your distribution channel as fast as possible, and ignore the customer. Lessons that HP taught include just ship, drive to the next lower price point, and extend distribution channels. If you fail to supply any channel with your product, you leave that flank unprotected. Finding the next lower price point gives your company the first crack at a whole new customer base that wants to enter the market once prices get down to their level. Whirlwind markets will be served—it's not a question of if, but of who will do it. Lessons Microsoft and Intel taught include design partners in, institutionalize the whole product as the market leader, and then commoditize the whole product by designing out your partners. This is an essential part of the commoditization, fusing together as a whole what the market has endorsed as the standard set of component parts.

The market's goal: serve as many customers as possible by reducing cost and eliminating distribution friction. The fewer the component parts and suppliers, the lower the price can be. Market forces will make this process occur. The only question is how you align your strategy with it.

The market not only expects the Monster to dominate, it requires it. It's the Monster's job to beat out the competition so that one clear standard emerges.

Rules if You're Winning the Whirlwind

Don't try to control the Whirlwind; you can't. Serve the tornado by driving down prices and profit margins per unit.

Don't introduce breakthrough innovations during the Whirlwind. Stay the course with your old product architecture, coming out with upgrades instead of brand new technology. Continuous innovation favors market leaders, while discontinuous innovation favors market challengers.

Design service out, not in. Make the product as *plug-and-play* as possible, with minimal need for service from vendors, retailers, or service organizations.

Betting on Who'll Be Market Monster

How do savvy investors, Pragmatic Settlers, potential partners, and similar bystanders respond at the beginning of a Whirlwind battle for dominance? They place their bets on all likely winners. Then one by one they shift them away from each apparent loser toward the emerging winner. As soon as one competitor lags, they kill it immediately and reinvest that resource in the ones that are still gaining.

The Mall—Phase 4

Target Audience: Conservatives Resisters and Holdouts

Definition—Mall Phase

Growth comes primarily from serving your own installed customer base and not from attacking the base of other companies. For most customers, it's too disruptive to switch vendors. Now you must shift your strategy away from a focus on beating out the competition and go back to putting the customer first.

Key Strategies—Mall Phase

1. Sell to end users. Focus on their experience of the product and meet their individual needs.
2. Differentiate the commoditized whole product with add-on features targeted at specific niches.
3. Distribute through the same channels but focus on merchandising to advertise the add-on marketing messages.

4. Celebrate the add-on offers to gain margins above the low-cost clone.

5. Compete against your own low-cost offering to gain margin share.

6. Position yourself in niche markets that reflect individual preferences of end users.

Competition—Mall Phase

Strategies for dealing with the competition in the Mall Phase varies, depending on what role you're playing.

As the Market Monster: You can take a two-pronged attack. Attack the product-as-commodity market with a low-end offering. Attack the premium market with a series of add-on niche offerings. Continue to innovate enough to keep the Little Munsters scrambling. If you shift the standards a little, you give customers an easy-to-absorb add-on while making the Little Munsters reengineer their clone products in order to keep up.

As a Big Munster: Focus on marketing into add-on niches where you can retain the customer or on R&D investment hoping to create a new paradigm shift.

As a Little Munster: You provide the clone product. You can establish the rules by setting the lower price point in the market, which becomes the reference price for the Monster and Big Munsters. You compete by reducing overhead to an absolute minimum.

Role of Strategic Partners—Mall Phase

This process continues into the Mall Phase until add-on marketing is needed to differentiate the now-low-margin commodity. Now there are limited opportunities to again develop partner relationships.

Power Hierarchy

Power shifts to the distribution channel. In the PC industry, it shifts to such superstores as Comp USA.

Organizational Leadership—Mall Phase

Traditional management models become feasible, with key roles being product marketing, marketing communications, and product management. The company needs a leader who is people-oriented and focused on customer satisfaction and staff development.

A Final Word

In this chapter you gained some savvy about the type of thinking you must adopt in order to thrive in the Innovation Age. You understand how paradigm shifts can affect your career and your business. And you have some sense of how the high-tech life cycle works and why innovative thinking is the key to success in a high-tech world. Next you'll explore the Creative Intelligence Model in some detail.

The New Economy is a chaotic swirl of new ideas and global activity. It can be overwhelming, but now you've stepped back to view it from a bigger viewpoint. You know something about complexity thinking and its role in allowing the swirl to spin out innovations that you and your company can use to survive and thrive. This swirl involves paradigm shifts, which in turn contains a high-tech life cycle that helps you identify where your company fits into the shifting patterns that are constantly evolving. Apply these ideas to your own company in the Self-Awareness Opportunity that follows. Then you're ready to explore how Creative Intelligence provides the engine that drives this New Economy.

Self-Awareness Opportunity: Where's Your Company in the High-Tech Life Cycle?

If you're with a high-tech company, you can help your company know where it fits in this high-tech life cycle and what role it can play. This is a must for success—and all the key people must agree on this.

Step 1: Decide what *type* of product yours is. Only then can you identify which phase of the life cycle it's in. Deciding on a clear category is a must. If you identify your product as both A and B, you have nothing marketable. Stores have to know what department to sell it in, and everyone must know which products to compare it with so they can decide if the price is fair.

Step 2: Once you identify the type, you must determine whether this product category is in the Early Market, Niche Market, Whirlwind of Demand, or Mall Phase in order to know what strategies to adopt.

Step 3: Next, you must market-position the category of product as a whole—not your particular product. Only after you've completed these three steps can you move on to positioning your product or service.

Chapter 11

Ignite Change:
Creative Corporate Cultures

Futurist Mikela Tarlow says, "The spirit of our time is an emerging sense that all concepts are transient and all forms are changeable....It becomes not just a philosophy but a new emotional reality...demanding that we each become truly creative."

The future is in fact accessible to you now, if you know where to look. Tomorrow depends less on the direction of technology than on the direction of your own mind. To guide your team and your career through this future landscape, you must awaken your ability to see the unfolding patterns and paradigm shifts.

From the breakdown of old paradigms, and the chaos of swirling creative energies, emerges breakthrough to a new order. As the workplace and the marketplace become more volatile by the day, as old structures collapse, you can help to develop a culture that's more harmonious and innovative. You can attune to a greater energy Source and move forward, in step with an emerging global beat. Creative Intelligence can help you to move through this uncharted informational universe, unique in human history. It can help you to lead corporate culture change and to meet the challenges and opportunities of the New Economy.

Lead Corporate Culture Change

You can learn to make quantum leaps in your thinking—and lead others to do the same. The strong analytic skills that Rational Intelligence provides you, and that have been so effective in the past, are not enough for today's demands for innovation. The sequential, cause-and-effect type of change of the past called for having a vision, developing a plan, and reaping the harvest. But change now is better seen as energy and forces, which we understand through the instinct of our Basic Intelligence, the feelings of our Emotional Intelligence, and the insights of our higher-level Intuitive, Associative, and Sensory Intelligences. It's a world of subtle rhythms and mysterious forces rather than one of certainty, control, and clear rules. It can be mysterious and challenging, but the rewards for innovating can be huge.

To lead corporate culture change most effectively, adopt these strategies:

1. Identify corporate culture blocks to creativity.
2. Create an innovative environment.
3. Create change through new beliefs and mental models.
4. Create change through visions and symbols.
5. Use creative problem-solving.
6. Create change through new stories.
7. Use high-tech to free up creative energy.

Strategy #1: Identify Corporate Culture Blocks to Creativity

Corporate cultures often harbor creativity blocks. You may be able to influence your organization to remove such blocks. If not, you can at least reorganize them and move on to a more nurturing environment. Here are the usual suspects:

- Few goals or rewards for creativity.
- A rigid, mechanistic, authoritarian company structure.
- Autocratic managers who value only their own ideas.
- No training for creativity.
- Little or no support for creativity.
- Few, if any, creative successes to build upon.
- Punishing mistakes and failures and ignoring a willingness to risk and learn from mistakes.

Innovative Questions for Breaking Through Barriers

1. **Actions**. How are my firm's practices tied to situations that have changed? Are these practices taken for granted as habits?
2. **Change**. How would my firm know if the situation had gradually changed?
3. **Fads**. Are my firm's ideas based on business fads? And how do fad ideas differ from valid ideas?
4. **Openness**. Does my firm hold beliefs that aren't open to question? How has this come about? Does my firm try out an idea because it might work—or because of the person who has the idea?
5. **Key concepts**. Does my firm understand key concepts—such as *purpose, vision,* and *paradigm*—that help us tune into today's complex environment?

6. **Blame**. Does my firm look for someone to blame when things go wrong? How do we express this blame? How does this affect our willingness to innovate?

7. **Risk**. Does my firm need to be certain of the outcome before we make a change? How do we test for certainty?

Strategy #2: Create an Innovative Environment

Creativity is a natural function of the mind, just as breathing and digestion are natural functions of the body. But new ways of thinking may seem risky to you, and putting forth new ideas does risk rejection of those ideas. Such risk invariably arouses in most people some distrust, anxiety, or even downright fear. To manage the risk of being creative, you need faith in yourself and your work environment. You need a corporate culture that provides a challenging but trustworthy environment. Here are some basics:

- Safe, casual, liberating.
- Not so small as to be limiting.
- Not so big as to kill intimacy.
- Creature comfortable, but stimulating.
- Both open spaces and private spaces.
- Some areas free from distractions and intrusions.
- Time targets when needed, but flexibility when necessary.

Open Spaces

Consider two great advantages of open workspaces:

1. The great breakthroughs come when you cross the boundaries from your daily focus to what other people are focusing on.

2. Cross-pollination of ideas is critical to stimulating creativity. A new perspective can trigger a snowball of imagination and innovation.

Try these ideas:

- Provide team and project rooms rather than private offices.
- Use a conversation pit instead of a conference room.

Private Spaces

On the other hand, private spaces and nature are great creativity enhancers too. Here are some suggestions:

- Create hiding places—cozy nooks where people can go off and make fools of themselves in safety.
- Think in terms of a sanctuary for the shared values, perceptions, and goals of the people working on a particular project. Group microcultures breed in those spaces. Magic often occurs in these private out-of-the-limelight places.
- If team microcultures become more disruptive than creative, rotate them and integrate them with members from various departments.

- ❧ Consider renting a small farmhouse, beach house, or mountain lodge.
- ❧ Provide meditation rooms.
- ❧ Install shiatsu walking paths that allow people to walk and stimulate their accupressure points for great inspiration.

Play Spaces

Another key to enhancing creativity is to nurture the inner child's sense of play and humor that tend to open us up to new ideas. Here are some fun enhancers:

- ❧ Provide a *humor room* filled with games, toys, creativity books, and funny videos.
- ❧ Create an island of imagination amid the sea of routine demands. Create a playpen. Let the people who will inhabit these spaces help design them.
- ❧ Set aside a space that says clearly: Let those creative juices flow. That space should challenge assumptions and unleash imagination.
- ❧ Symbols and icons can define space. Use devices such as a blinking red light as a *do not disturb* sign.

High-Tech Spaces

High-tech spaces offer many advantages, including freeing up people from grunt work so they have time to nurture new ideas.

- ❧ Accumulate a CD-ROM and DVD library.
- ❧ Cyberspace is a welcoming place for artists and dreamers. Re-create the cyber cafes that are globally so popular—with computer monitors and network connections built into the tables. Techno-bohemians love to play in this relaxed setting.
- ❧ Technical tools, such as a high-end personal computer, speakerphone, state of the art videoconferencing system with groupware, and high-speed Internet connection can provide creative advantages. Some examples:
  - ◆ Drafting complex documents using templates of your own design to help you organize the process of doing deals.
  - ◆ Searching databases.
  - ◆ Sharing information.
  - ◆ Bringing collaborators in on deals.
  - ◆ Developing virtual teams.

Creative Example #1: Idealab's Spinoff Startups

Idealab is in the business of starting small businesses. The firm functions on the belief that individually empowered entrepreneurs generate way more value per unit of time—for their investors and for themselves—than people within a big corporation. Large companies need to learn how to break up their hierarchy in ways that tap into Idealab's innovative power.

Idealab plays the role of parent company. It generates and circulates important types of knowledge, such as its staff's expertise in building Web-based companies. But it's a two-way informational exchange, with the center dispensing it to the node startups, and the nodes feeding their learning back to the center. Picture a starburst built around a central core of intellectual competency. The informational leverage and the Creative Intelligence leverage are exponential.

Located in a renovated warehouse in Pasadena, California, Idealab's transparent bubble of an office is surrounded by loosely defined spaces. Each space is temporary home to an entrepreneur who is creating a startup company. In 1999 there were 21 of them, aided by a core staff of 20 employees. Idealab gives each startup the following resources:

- Some seed funding, usually less than $250,000.
- A package of shared services that includes recruiting, payroll, accounting, legal, graphic design, office space, and Web servers.
- Idealab's accrued wisdom about growing Internet companies.

In return Idealab gets a percentage of the spinoff's equity, from 20 to 50 percent.

The result is a network of separate but interdependent businesses, a cluster of nodes loosely tied to a central focus. Each business has an entrepreneur who takes direction from the marketplace, not a corporate center, to guide the company. These leaders focus on creating or finding a highly specialized niche.

Creative Example #2: IDEO's Open Spaces

IDEO of Palo Alto, California, provides another example of a creative culture. Here, people come to work in a big, open room. They interact with lightning-fast communications, and no secrets. The purpose is the leveraging of ideas. It works because everyone instantly grasps what's going on in everyone else's area. When customers call to report a problem, everyone can be involved within a few minutes.

The open room forces people to communicate and to develop skills that lead to better communication. The most important ingredient is openness, which echoes and facilitates dialogue. It also invites polite confrontation. When you see a problem in someone's area, you talk to him about it right now. It's easier in an open room.

Creative Example #3: Playpens at The Body Shop, Story Street, and Imagic

The Body Shop's headquarters office near London is filled with whimsical stuffed sculptures, Seurat prints, and a green pagoda. Anita Roddick actively embraces the *playground* image.

Story Street Studios in Harvard Square near Boston is blurring, even erasing, the distinction between work and play. This has energized its young designers, each self-employed, who lease space in the studios, for two good reasons:

1. Designers believe they do their best work when they can maximize free play.

2. The free-flowing physical space mirrors the truly creative person's pride and independence. The slightest suggestion of hierarchy implies bosses, and here everyone is a one-person company.

Executives at Imagic of Los Gatos, California, know that creative magic often occurs in collaborative team microcultures. They also found that inbred teams can take on the collaborative spirit of a semi-secret society. This air of *creative aristocracy* can be disruptive to cooperation throughout the rest of the company. Imagic responds by putting its game designers on integrated teams with members from other departments. It then makes heavy use of marketing input and concept testing before producing new games.

Strategy #3: Create Change Through New Beliefs and Mental Models

A business *is* its ideas, and these ideas eventually generate the structure and creative substance of the business. The mental models of the founders and leaders shape the ideas of the employees.

Mass Consciousness

You (and your firm) absorb the ideas that are accepted in the culture and field you live within—including the belief systems and histories that spawned the ideas. You get clues from this environment about which ideas are meaningful, useful, or relevant. We sometimes call this environment of belief and ideas *Consensus Reality* or *Mass Consciousness.*

The belief that slavery was normal and natural shaped societies before 1850. Extreme controls were considered necessary, so we had laws keeping slaves in their place, as well as physical restraints and such practices as banning literacy among slaves. This affected all of society, including the manager-employee relationship, which was more master-slave in orientation than it is today.

The belief in the world as a mechanical closed system shaped our ideas and relationships over the past 300 years, and still does to a great extent. The idea of open complex adaptive systems leads to very different ideas and actions. *How do we control behavior?* is a very important question in a mechanistic system and irrelevant in an open complex-adaptive system. What are the new beliefs and mental models that people need to adopt in order to build and thrive in a creative corporate culture within the New Economy?

Innovative Questions About New Beliefs

Ask these questions any time you want to lead corporate culture change in ways that spark creative thinking and innovative ideas:

1. How does my firm try to come up with new ideas?
2. How does my firm spread around new ideas?
3. How do people in my firm work with colleagues and team members to co-evolve new ideas?
4. Are people in my firm stuck in Rational Intelligence? Are we limited by the linear worldview of the rational mind?
5. What are the core beliefs, values, and mental models of my firm?

6. How are these related to our core mission and strategies?
7. How do my firm's beliefs limit what we accept as knowledge?
8. How does *what we already know* limit what we see as important?
9. How do my firm's rational-mind limitations and related beliefs affect the firm's bottom-line beliefs and priorities?
10. Are people in the firm applying new ideas to new actions in their work?
11. How do people resist changing their action patterns?
12. How do the firm and its people respond to change? How do we adapt or avoid adapting?

Mission and Mental Models

When you look at your firm's mission, look at the most abstract ideas you can imagine about what the firm is in business to do. The more abstract an idea is, the greater the number of other ideas it can include. Then you can select from those abundant ideas the ones that you can use most effectively to carry out the mission in the ever-changing and evolving reality around you. By expanding to an essence idea, you give shape to the other ideas that flow from it. This allows you to make distinctions between ideas that are important and those that are irrelevant. If you were a clothing design company, which mission statement would be the most powerful in the New Economy?

- To provide clothing to customers.
- To make the clothing Americans want.
- To provide stylish apparel for young people.
- To provide style and fashion.

The firm's mission and strategies (its core ideas) shape all its other ideas, and they shape the actions people take throughout the firm—in a continual interactive process of refining the ideas and shifting the actions. Actions are ways of exploring, expressing, and using the ideas. You find that some ideas lead to dead-ends, some need further development, and some are ready to use productively.

Strategy #4: Create Change Through Vision and Symbols

Creating a powerful vision with imaginative symbols can inspire people to high levels of creativity and achievement. Think of President Kennedy's challenge to the nation to put a man on the moon by the end of the 1960s.

Bausch & Lomb used the vision of a greenhouse to symbolize the process of product development—of ideas growing with careful nurturing in a controlled environment.

American Express used the vision of running the four-minute mile to represent company aspirations: to move to the front of the pack with record-breaking speed.

Jan Carlzon, CEO of SAS, commissioned a *little red book* of cartoons with text that visually communicates all aspects of the company's mission and strategies. For the first time everyone began working from the same playbook—in a fun-to-learn format. Carlzon brilliantly framed and crafted a company-wide challenge: *Put customers first.*

The seven aspects of a well-crafted challenge are language, context, mouth and money, preparation, discipline, complicity, and empathy.

1. *Language*. Use vivid language. Deliver your challenge in full costume, verbally and visually.

2. *Context*. Voice your challenge in the context of the times and events around you.

3. *Mouth and money*. There must be consistency between the status of the challenger and the seriousness of the challenge. Challengers must have the right status. They must be in a position to put their money where their mouths are.

4. *Preparation*. When you ask people to commit time, energy, emotion, and soul, think through what you're doing before you act. Creativity is born of experience. Don't jump in with both feet unless you know where you're headed.

5. *Discipline*. Commit to a deadline. All successful challenges are to some extent promises—of resources, of moral support, of personal participation, and of accountability. A promise to meet a deadline commits you to many other promises: You'll devote your mind, time, energy, anxiety, physical and human resources, money, influence, and more. As stagecraft, there's nothing like a deadline, a countdown, to capture your audience's attention.

6. *Complicity*. Your challenge must be a challenge to yourself as well as to the others.

7. *Empathy*. Simple acts of kindness make the difficulties of creative work easier to bear. Remember the crucial importance of making the creative person comfortable. Appreciate the difficult creative process. Stay loose, improvise, and look for empathic ways to present your positive challenges.

Strategy #5: Use Creative Problem-Solving

Look at these four business elements: mission, strategies, tactics, and procedures or rules. If you identify the root problem as simply a procedure or rule that's not working, you can just change it. That's relatively easy, because rules function at the surface. The deeper the root problem goes, the more difficult and comprehensive the change efforts need to be—with the company mission being the core level that directly affects corporate culture.

Innovative Questions About Problem Solving

Ask yourself these questions any time you want to lead your corporate culture in engaging in more creative types of problem-solving:

1. *Beliefs*. Regarding the problem I'm working on now, what are the basic beliefs that my firm has about it? How did we acquire these beliefs? How have they influenced our ability to be innovative?

2. *Intelligences.* Is the firm's thinking about this problem limited to rational, logical, step-by-step, observer-observed ways of thinking? What other intelligences can we use to solve this problem?

3. *Stories*. How does the firm limit or encourage people to share stories? How does this affect the firm's ability to solve problems or recognize opportunities?

4. *New level*. How can my firm break out into a higher, different level of thinking than the one that led to the problem?

Strategy #6: Create Change Through New Stories

How can you (and your firm) spread the word about a more open, innovative way of thinking and acting? Stories are a great way to point to new ideas, to distribute new knowledge in order to bring people up to speed.

To galvanize an organization's interest in a new idea, immerse people in it through listening to dramatic stories and watching or engaging in scenario simulations, such as role playing or acting out of dramatic experiences. Look for ways to make it real—in a multisensory, emotionally engaging way. People must become emotionally engaged before they will make a commitment to change.

People love stories, and various types of stories are the glue that hold together teams, companies, and cultures. Stories can take many forms, ranging from the smallest—little anecdotes, jokes, or slogans—to tales of how the company began, the Founding Legend. Other stories about the courage, daring, or perseverance of key people can also become company legends. Some stories fall into the archetype category and play the role of myths, which together make up the cultural beliefs and values that drive people's attitudes and actions.

The most powerful stories for creating an open adaptive firm are about the adventurers, renegades, tinkerers, and risk-takers out there on the fringe, the edge, the boundaries of the field. Tell stories about the breakthroughs they are making, the type of thinking that triggers the Next New Things, and successful ways of responding to them. Stories and metaphors about people, living things, and Nature are usually much more effective than those about things.

Innovative Questions to Identify Powerful Stories

Ask yourself these kinds of questions any time you want to help people to identify powerful stories that will help develop a more creative corporate culture:

- Which people are out there in the field, along the boundaries with the clients or customers?

- What new insights are happening out there on the periphery of the company?

- How can we get these people to tell their stories?

- How can we be sure they are brought into key company systems so they add to corporate learning and the word is spread to all?

- How can we continually reinforce the stories in ways that insure that people really hear and understand?

- How can we keep alive the key stories—the myths and legends that hold the culture together?

The teller-listener relationship creates interaction, and out of this something new, an innovation, an idea, emerges—when the story is new. How can we live in the new and the Now and still not get stuck in memory of the past or anticipation of the future?

Strategy #7: Use High-Tech Tools to Free Up Creativity

The computer and the Internet are just tools, but those tools increase the resources at our disposal so dramatically that change is more than quantitative. It's also qualitative. Let's look at some ways high-tech tools can increase our creativity.

Friction and Drag

Infotech decreases the forces of friction. We don't have to trudge to the library and muck around in the stacks, nor worry about lost information, nor retype the entire paper after we edit it, nor wait for a scheduled meeting to get reactions to our ideas. We don't have to wait for ideas to wend their way through the bureaucratic red tape, nor wait to find the right person. Drag and friction are minimal.

Computers serve us as almost limitless memory banks and tireless research assistants. This helps us keep our heads clear and ready for action. We don't have to remember unnecessary data for too long. The computer has it.

Distance and Speed

Infotech decreases distances—between customers and suppliers, between those who need services and those who supply them, and between employees and contractors. It allows outsourcing in more efficient and qualitatively different ways.

Infotech changes processes and speed. For example, marketing can be done at the same time as strategic planning or manufacturing. It decreases distance in terms of the location of physical work. Your Internet address is anywhere you want to be. It gives you great speed. For example, we're making dramatic improvements in product development time due to successful linking of designers, tool-makers, engineers, and vendors on computer networks.

Diversity

Infotech enables diversity, which in turn leads to a higher quality of creativity. Teams gain a wider range of skills and experience, as well as a more intimate level of cognitive style. It can help those who rely on intuition to keep track of the facts. Those who are data-oriented will find sources of inspiration. Technology can provide a common language across business cultures, a way of bridging the gaps. It can enhance collaboration. It can facilitate an unmatchable, powerful, and far-reaching connection. It's a way to create membership organizations. It's a way to manage the invisible collage of relationships among talent who may not work for the company. It's a way to protect subcultures within the organization.

Quantum computers

Computer science has melded with subatomic physics to create computers based on quantum particles—such as atomic nuclei, photons, and electrons—instead of silicon chips. Quantum computers use qubits of information, each equivalent to a traditional digital bit. Bits are either on or off, one or zero, but qubits can be both on and off at the same time.

Conventional computers step through calculations one at a time. But the effect between quantum particles, known as *spooky entanglement*, lets quantum computers perform all calculations simultaneously, as though in parallel. These two features allow quantum computers to perform massive computations in a fraction of a second. They're expected to be invaluable at creating uncrackable security codes and also at cracking others' security codes. They excel at storing and retrieving information in huge, unstructured databases. And they're great at simulating complex quantum phenomena.

A seven-qubit computer is in the experimental stage in 2001. Some experts predict that a 15-qubit computer—equivalent to the 2001 desktop PC—will be built by 2002 and that a 30-qubit machine more powerful than the most powerful supercomputer of 2001 will be built by 2004.

Meet New-Economy Challenges and Opportunities

Although the New Economy poses constant challenges to survival, it also offers incredible opportunities for business and career success. Take the lead in helping your company and its employees meet these challenges and opportunities by following these strategies:

1. Understand how size can block or enable innovation.
2. Adopt new principles for a New Economy.
3. Shift the focus from infrastructure to information.
4. Grow a new corporate structure to enhance creativity.
5. Enable virtual startups.

Strategy #1: Understand How Size Can Block or Enable Innovation

Increasing every day are the opportunities to start your own small firm, to work with a small firm, or to spin off a virtual startup from your large firm. The small firm is on the rise.

Before 1900 our economy was primarily agricultural, so we were a nation of small firms. Then, during the 20th century the industrial economy was dominant, and the number of huge firms grew dramatically. Now, in this high-tech information economy, small is in again. In 1970 about 20 percent of Americans worked for huge Fortune 500 firms, but by the early 1990s that number had dropped to only 10 percent. Meanwhile, the number of startup firms grew by leaps and bounds. We're now in a boom-time of self-employment and independent contracting, with more than 25 million people working as small business owners.

The trend toward small is offset by periodic waves of mergers that create huge multinational giants, but the overall trend is toward breaking up into small units, not conglomerating into larger ones. We're becoming a nation of business owners. The roots of this trend were put down in the 1970s with a series of shocks: 1) global competition, 2) new technologies, and 3) government deregulation. The overall effect has been threefold:

- ✎ More disruption and chaos in the marketplace.
- ✎ The return to power of independent-minded consumers.
- ✎ An exponential acceleration of change.

Giant companies now seem lumbering and incapable of competing. Owning the whole production chain has become a liability. Small companies, without the hierarchy or sunk costs of large corporations, can sense and respond to customer needs more quickly. They look outward, not inward. The market trends have turned the producer increasingly into the instrument of the consumer.

But large corporations do have a special advantage: They're repositories of certain kinds of knowledge that can't be readily circulated through arm's-length market-based buyer-seller transactions. Corporations will continue to play an important role as *communities of know-how*, especially those that value the learning corporation.

As a result of all this, huge companies are finding ways to break up into small entities. When an industry adopts information technology in a serious way, the companies within that industry tend to shrink in size within about two years. This is a world where buyers know buyers and sellers know sellers, a world of dense, information-enabled relationships, a network economy.

The Internet has enabled a world of tiny, autonomous businesses, each with one or a few people, who conduct transactions with one another in the market. Heartland Supply is a typical example: With a staff of five people, Heartland Supply sold $150 million worth of merchandise last year.

We've come full circle from huge to small companies, but at a higher level. The difference is the ability of small companies to self-organize. For example, SolarX is a virtual company of 12 or so engineers and manufacturers who came together over the Internet to design a new kind of solar home. They can work in concert, coordinating complex tasks without any overarching authority.

Strategy #2: Adopt New Principles for a New Economy

The New Economy is diffuse. It has centrifugal tendencies. It is uncontrollable. All this means that no person will be able to completely dominate the New Economy. Other comparisons of the old and new economies are shown in Snapshot #1.

Snapshot #1: Old vs. New Economy

Old Economy	New Economy
Established rules of hierarchy.	Culture of speed and the Holy Grail of partnerships.
A big sale could move your stock price by ½ point.	Stock prices move when you announce some new partnerships.
Market value accrues to those who do the right things.	Market value accrues to those who do the instantaneous things.
Growth of a new product reaches equilibrium and then shrinks.	New products create possibilities for more new products.
Economies of scale, adding many units, means big companies can sell for less.	New members can grow the network exponentially, exploding value.

What type of entrepreneur will represent the best of this new era? Every organization needs to consider these principles of the New Economy:

- For companies that create and sell information, nimbleness and speed matter most, not economies of scale.
- Responding to the fundamental, uncontrollable desires of the marketplace is what counts, not trying to control them.
- Creative people thrive in small organizations, not within big hierarchies. The smaller, the better.
- Corporate cultures need to provide an environment that maximizes the opportunities and occasions for creativity.

Innovation Breaks the Law of Diminishing Returns

The concept of diminishing returns has held sway throughout the industrial era. It says that a product or a company that gets ahead in a market will eventually run into limitations. The price of the product/service and its market share will reach equilibrium and growth will stop, resulting in diminishing returns for the company and investors. But innovation in the New Economy is breaking that law. These shifts make all the difference:

- From infrastructure to information.
- From bulk material manufacturing to design and use of technology.
- From processing resources to processing information—leading to innovations.
- From diminishing returns to increasing returns.

Diminishing-return companies still make up much of our economy because infrastructure still makes up most of what we think of as business. But a greater portion of even the old-style business is developing in the information arena. Most traditional corporations can no longer perform their operations without massive information systems.

Increasing returns within a company or a marketplace constitute a single continuous feedback mechanism. Here's how it works:

- Increasing returns within the company mean better ideas.
- These ideas improve the quality of the product or service.
- Better quality leads to better products and services, and even improvements in the infrastructure.
- These improvements lead to increasing returns in the marketplace, more revenue, more outlets, more customers, more brand-name recognition;
- These lead in turn to better ideas, processes, and systems.

Increasing returns within the system cannot be separated from those in the marketplace. The interaction back and forth between models and actions creates more and more innovation.

Innovative Questions About Feedback for Innovation

Ask yourself these kinds of questions any time you want to improve feedback for innovation in your firm:

1. How does my firm encourage or rebuff feedback?
2. Has my firm built into its processes and activities some way of getting and giving feedback?
3. What happens when we get negative feedback?
4. Which forms of feedback do we emphasize? Conversations, meetings, reports, performance data, customers, competitors, suppliers, external media, government, other?

Networking Increases Returns Exponentially

Economies of scale of the Industrial Age come from huge efforts by a single company to lead the competition by creating greater value for less money. The expertise developed by this company belongs to it alone. Industrial economies of scale increase value in a way that's primarily linear: by adding increments. Two plus two plus two symbolizes the linear growth.

In the New Economy the prime law of networking is known as the law of increasing returns. More brings more. Each additional member increases the network's value. This law is far more important now than the traditional concept of economies of scale because it increases value in an exponential way.

Exponential growth can be symbolized by two times two times two: the doubling principle. This produces an upward curve that keeps accelerating. Exponential growth is often viewed in terms of how fast its doubling times are. The doubling sequence of 2, 4, 8,16, 32, 64, 128, 256, 512, 1,024, 2,048, and so forth goes up to astounding numbers. A typical example is the lily plant growing in a pond. The plant doubles in size each day. In a large pond, there will be an impression of slow growth at the beginning. But in a matter of perhaps 20 days, the pond will be half covered. And on the very next day, the pond will be totally covered.

If you keep doubling the number 2, after 20 steps you reach two million. Keep doubling and shortly past 100 steps, you start to exceed the number of atoms in the universe.

The doubling principle usually applies to chain letters. In theory you could quickly reach every person on the planet. This can be beneficial if the message is constructive. Sometimes the message tells each person to send money to someone at the top of the list. Only the people at the beginning of the chain can profit because the expanding chain quickly reaches all the people on the planet who could possibly be interested in such a plan. Then it runs out of people who could possibly contribute money. That's why such schemes are illegal.

Networked increasing returns are created and shared by the entire network. One company or person may reap more of the gains of the increasing returns than another, but the value of the gains lies in the greater web of relationships. The increasing returns we see in Silicon Valley are not dependent on any one company's success. In fact Silicon Valley has in a way become one large, spread-out company. Workers and consumers tend to feel more loyalty to the network than to any one firm. The social web of Silicon Valley employees and entrepreneurs creates a true Network Economy. However, you can see that exponential growth clearly has its limits. The goal is to include everyone on the planet in the Network Economy. Some say we are only 1 percent into this process. The growth will seem slow for a while. Then we'll reach the point where half the people are included, and the next day all.

Strategy #3: Shift the Focus from Infrastructure to Information

The central event of the 20ᵗʰ century is the overthrow of matter.... Wealth in the form of physical resources is steadily declining in value and significance. The powers of mind are everywhere ascendant over the brute force of things.
John Casti, author

Infrastructure

Infrastructure usually refers to physical support systems and structures, but some people refer to old habits and limitations as infrastructure. That's because old ideas can be so strong and rigid. You can use them to build mental walls, to construct complex rules. Such rules are the counterpart of physical infrastructures. Rules can change only when you expand your mental model in a way that generates some new rules. Neither your current physical infrastructure nor your old rules can change themselves, and they can block innovation.

Information

Information is contained in the firm's mental models, patterns, and ways of informing and learning. The right information allows the infrastructure to work more efficiently at a lower output of resources.

You want a high ratio of information to infrastructure. If you get trapped by your infrastructure and pay more attention to it than to its flow of information, you lose the opportunity for real growth, and even survival. Your ability to create new mental models, again and again, is that point where the emergence of the new, innovation, happens.

Matter as a metaphor for things is giving way to a focus on process, pattern, abstraction, and ideas. Fewer resources are devoted to the infrastructure of things and more to information, the development and sharing of ideas. Businesses operate around core ideas, attaching all they do and say to those ideas—about the economy, the industry, management, marketing, the consumer, and so forth. In the New Economy new behaviors that emerge are informational rather than mechanistic and are based on these factors:

1. Technologies that are evolving rapidly and are so complex and far-reaching that they change how we do things and how we act, opening us up to new kinds of experiences.
2. The emerging possibilities that computers enable.
3. New ways of thinking—at a higher level than the one where our major problems arose.
4. Increasing globalization.
5. Co-evolution of the importance of wholistic right-brain thinking and the concept of people and businesses as Complex Adaptive Systems.
6. Changing views of history, social structures, and value systems.

For your company to see the emergence of the Next New Thing, to truly innovate, all these factors must co-evolve and keep up with each other.

Innovative Questions About Infrastructure-Information

You can't measure information, because it doesn't have location, weight, or width. It's not matter. All you can do is look at the process of setting goals and working toward them and ask questions that help you understand what's happening. Here are some questions to ask:

1. Where is my firm applying its financial resources?
2. What are we investing in?
3. Where are our key people focusing attention?
4. How are our key people spending the most time?
5. When we speak with people, what are we talking about?
6. What do our people communicate in e-mails and memos?
7. When we hold meetings, what are we communicating?

When you pull the answers together, assess whether your resources, time, energies, and communications are spent on infrastructure (things) or on information (ideas). Information is like your immune system: It's located throughout the organization.

Strategy #4: Grow a New Corporate Structure to Enhance Creativity

The marketplace and workplace are moving toward a world where responsibilities and decision-making are spread out all across the organization and the landscape. People interact with each other more as autonomous agents than as subordinates.

Such distributed open systems can respond and adapt more quickly to external changes than closed systems with decentralized decision-making. Such open systems offer more ways to innovate and more motivation to innovate. They allow solutions to problems to emerge from the interactions of the people throughout the firm.

In the New Economy, control lies with information. The firm has some measure of control, but only to the extent that its leaders provide ideas and formulations to themselves and to the people, ideas that can guide and shape their actions. The only control lies in the leaders' ability to shape people's actions. You can only do this through formulating ideas that work and, better yet, inspiring teams of people to formulate these ideas themselves.

New ideas lead to new shapes. Every aspect of an organization changes: what people do, how they go about doing it, how they should be compensated, how they work together, how they are evaluated, and what kinds of communications are needed. The shape that's emerging looks more like a fluid web than the old hierarchical pyramid, as shown in Snapshot #2. In the web-like flexible corporation, the executive team is central but doesn't dominate in the old hierarchical, isolated way as top management does in the traditional corporation. Cross-functional teams with team leaders sometimes include suppliers, customers, investors, and/or distributors in their deliberations.

Snapshot #2: Web Vs. Pyramid Structure

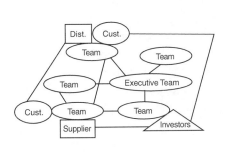

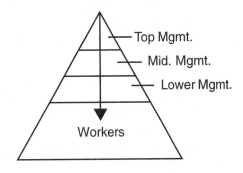

Flexible Corporation   ### Traditional Corporation

In a web-like corporation, what the company must do is supply information. Without this shift from central control to information-sharing, the company will spend its resources trying to maintain control mechanisms. By their closed nature, these control mechanisms make it impossible for the company to adapt quickly to local influences. Long-term success becomes impossible, too.

To avoid chaos in these free-form situations, company leaders must not close down and build walls. Instead they must provide more information—mental models, theories, ideas—to guide their actions and those of the employees. Traditional companies must realize that if they want to grow and develop, they must let go of centralized control and find a way to spread out authority and decision-making. Otherwise, people will give the feedback they think the boss wants to hear—not the feedback everyone needs to hear. Actually, within a web organization that has widely dispersed authority and decision-making, one where people interact within a free exchange of ideas, the word *boss* has no meaning.

In fact, it may be that the term *employee* is becoming obsolete and that *adaptive agent* is taking its place. Another way of saying this is that people associated with the firm function less as employees and more as change agents that enable the company to adapt to constant change.

How are other definitions changing? *Boss, job, workplace, customer, marketplace, profit, supplier, stockholder, board of directors*? Does a supplier become a board member or at times an employee? Do people no longer have jobs but skill portfolios and changing roles? Do fixed workplaces give way to mobile employees with mobile cabinets? Do you rotate the role of CEO so the firm isn't stuck reflecting one person's strengths and weaknesses?

Innovative Questions About Restructuring

1. What would happen if we spread out authority and decision-making throughout the firm?
2. Who would benefit and how in the short-term? In the long-term?
3. How can we remove unnecessary restraints on people?

4. What if each division or department of my company became a semi-autonomous operation?
5. How would relationships between departments and divisions change?
6. How would communication and feedback change?
7. When does my firm become overwhelmed? What factors lead to this? How is this connected with our current organization structure?
8. When overload occurs, what happens as a result?
9. How does the firm react to these system overloads?

Strategy #5: Enable Virtual Startups

In the near future, suppose someone calls you to develop a new enterprise. You may be able to do it entirely through the Internet, including these action steps:

- Make the necessary trademark search, background research, competitive analysis, and financial model through your computer linkages.
- Get the right legal advice through Lawyer-on-a-Chip, a service of leading law firms.
- Get legal documents your need almost instantly.
- Generate the documents you need digitally.
- Digitally scan your list of colleagues, friends, and associates for likely collaborators in a proposed new enterprise.
- Locate potential investors, scanning for investors who fit with your particular opportunity.
- Use a cybernetic agent to comb databases for market information.
- Prospect for experts, advisers, directors, and managers who might be interested and available in working on the new enterprise.
- Prepare a business plan and pro forma financial statements.

The bottom line: You could lay the foundation of a new enterprise in a day or so, instead of months or years.

What kinds of virtual startups are likely to be possible and successful in the near future? Here are a few ideas.

Cybernetic agents will help creative people to get their thoughts into digital form and represent their interests around the clock in a variety of virtual marketplaces.

Entertainment reviewers will save your time in selecting those programs that best meet your needs. For example, a respected movie reviewer could open a *movie tourist information stand* on the digital highway. Movie-goers dial up and ask for advice about certain films or for custom recommendations about movies playing that day. The charge for this service is perhaps 25 cents, but the review site fields a million calls a day.

Information gatekeepers are another type of entrepreneur that gathers branded information. They provide entry to desirable data or opinions. They create the means to greatly amplify the value of that information and the effectiveness of its distribution.

Security enforcers are essential in the Net Economy. A whole new class of information outlaws will arise. Therefore, entry to desirable areas of cyberspace in the future may require special skills, renown, money, prescience, or other distinction. Passwords may be a key aspect of the new software. People who can manage a new economic model, who can set financial standards, and who can develop their own versions of digital cash to reflect value—all these people will make much money.

Agent middlemen represent a whole new class of go-betweens. Technology will enable people on the creative side to enjoy a new level of privacy. Technology can create anonymity as well as access. Agents will need to provide access and to make sure that talent's price floats to a market level. Such agents guarantee fair exchange and ensure that transactions take place.

A Final Word

The challenges and opportunities of the New Economy are huge, global, and complex. Are you (and your firm) taking the lead as change agents? How is your corporate culture changing in response to these challenges and opportunities? Will you not only survive, but thrive?

You now have some tools for igniting corporate culture change. They'll come in handy as you apply your Creative Intelligence to a leadership role in your work team. It's true that two heads are better than one. And a team-full of heads is better yet. You're ready to explore the power of team synergy and how to spark innovation in that arena.

Chapter 12

Spark Innovation:
Leading Team Creativity

> When people feel that they are relevant, that their work matters,
> they will do amazing things.
> *Eric Schmidt, CEO, Novell*

W hat an exciting time to be a workplace leader—to spark innovation and lead team creativity. You can play many key roles, such as Power Coordinator, one who enables the power of team synergy, or Creative-Corporate-Culture Nurturer, where you apply what you know as a change agent to create the right team setting. Then there's your role as Founder of Self-Managing Teams, establishing teams that are highly innovative and entrepreneurial. You'll use strategies for striking that balance between challenge and support that is so essential for creativity to blossom. You can also play the role of Creative Collaboration Coordinator, where you prepare team members to collaborate and you support those collaborations that are likely to achieve innovative breakthroughs. Finally, you can be a Multicultural Team Creator, who brings together people from diverse backgrounds to generate even more new ideas.

Use the Power of Synergy

Synergy is one of the most powerful complexity processes for sparking innovation. It happens when teams toss ideas around in ways that co-evolve new ideas. It is the product of generative relationships where the ideas and actions of the team members combined generate more innovative ideas than they could produce separately. It's at play in improvisation, a process for moving to the Next New Thing.

Innovating from Co-Evolving Team Ideas

People can multiply the innovations they devise just by working together in a motivating team environment. Emergence of innovation is more likely to occur in a team setting than in an isolated setting. Emergence is an interactive, co-evolving process that depends on relationships and partnerships to shape the ideas from which innovation can arise.

Team Patterns

Self-organizing teams can be highly innovative, and they can follow a number of teamwork patterns that work. Maybe projects emerge from within, the brainchild of anyone, who then advertises internally for volunteers to become members of the project team. Perhaps in this and other ways, teams become self-organizing. In today's fast-paced workplaces, where we're always trying to do more than we can, it's important that people get along and enjoy working together. That's what creates the emergent phenomena—the breakthrough innovations to the Next New Thing. Any time two people interact, ideas get generated, and so do interpretations. Any other person who becomes part of that interaction will be influenced by it too.

Ideas Are the Key

If you want to understand why people act the way they do, see if you can find out what *ideas* led to those actions. People cannot act outside the paths structured by their ideas. If you want to change how people act, you must give them new ideas. You must experiment to find new ideas that work. Introduce a new idea. Pay attention to people's actions that seem connected to the new idea. The ideas that work to help you, or your firm, to carry out your mission— these are the *right ideas*. Better yet, inspire people and teams to dream up these right ideas and share them.

Who makes the decisions in a web organization? Decisions emerge out of a very complex system of interactions and agents setting up many local fields. Those ideas shape the actions of the CEO as much as other agents. The key question is: Does this happen in a way that makes the firm become more adaptive to its environment?

Innovating from Generative Team Relationships

Out of each team member's behavior emerges a team behavior that can't be understood or predicted by looking at the behavior of each team member in isolation. Out of the behavior of many teams comes still higher levels of organizational behavior, which again can't be explained just by analyzing each team in isolation from the whole.

The missing factor is sometimes called *synergy* or a *generative relationship*. A basic complexity principle is that the whole is greater than the sum of its parts. Synergy is one of complexity's most useful business tools. When two or more people or teams with diverse goals and independent, autonomous responsibilities work together on a common project, the performance of all the participants is improved. That's a generative relationship. It generates greater productivity and success than the people could achieve working alone.

For example, a technical representative finds a way to relate to customers that reveals specific product problems or the emerging needs of the customer. She shares that way of relating with the firm's other tech reps, and they start using it successfully. That's a generative relationship. When the tech reps start carrying this information back to production managers, who in turn use it to create better products, that's an even more generative relationship.

What's essential to a generative relationship is a measure of diversity among people and distance between them, as well as a shared direction that motivates them to bridge the distances that exist.

Innovating Through Improvisation

Closely related to emergence and synergy is improvisation. This occurs when team members feel free to play around with ideas, to piggyback on each other's ideas, to confidently step out with their own versions of what's next, and to listen appreciatively when others step out.

Have you ever been to a *jam session* of musicians? These are informal improvisation sessions, started by early-day jazz musicians, picked up by mid-century swing musicians, and carried on today by various types of musicians. They might loosen up late in the evening during a club date and stay on after hours. They might gather on a Sunday afternoon to jam. Jamming starts with a theme (a tune). The group members play around with it. They pass it around for first one and then another to take the lead. They fly with it, soar, as they create something new that's never been quite that way before. Yet it's a variation on a theme.

At the beginning of a jam session, the members agree on the tune and how it will generally be played. In a continual state of co-evolution, each musician (agent) is influenced by the interpretations and improvisations (innovations) of the other players—and a unique rendition of the music is the result—the innovative product. They're all contributing, but they're not necessarily playing the same notes at the same time. Each player knows that certain notes must be played (certain functions must be performed) and that individual players assume those responsibilities—stepping in when the time seems right for their talent to enter in. They listen to each other, each in turn emerging to play certain parts.

They all have a common goal: to individualize the theme to produce music that's somewhat different and sounds great. Each player has adequate knowledge of the discipline and the particular tune, as well as adequate performance skills, to be relaxed and flexible in playing her part and cooperating with the others.

From this scenario, innovation soars and cohesion produces something more and different than the players could create by playing alone and then putting it all together. They inspire each other. You hear something very different than you would if you listened to the pianist playing his part alone, the drummer doing his part, and so forth. Synergy occurs, a generating relationship emerges, and a whole new thing co-evolves.

Innovative Questions for Fostering Generative Team Relationships

Ask yourself these kinds of questions any time you want to boost creative team relationships:

1. Do I assume that my team's behaviors can be understood or predicted by looking at the actions of each member, one by one? If so, what do I miss?

2. How do I, and all team members, foster the co-evolution of ideas by the team?

3. Does my firm decide on the goals and then ask teams to develop only the way of getting there? Are the goals ever seen as open possibilities?

4. Does my firm, and team, look at markets and customers as being *out there* with a fixed identity?

5. Do I see myself (and do team members see themselves) interacting with people and groups of people, influencing and being influenced, co-evolving an ever-changing environment?

6. How do we deal with the unexpected? Which of the following reactions apply? Denial, rationalization, blame, incomplete data, sabotage? Welcoming the unexpected, incorporating it into the process?

Create a Self-Managing Team Culture

Generative team relationships thrive best in a self-managing team culture. Most well-educated people value being their own boss and contributing to a group effort, so they can adapt well to self-managing team situations. Some employees may need grooming for self-management, especially older employees who are conditioned to function in a hierarchical, top-down corporate culture. As a leader, you may need to set the stage for creating self-managing work teams in your organization. To create an environment where self-managing teams can flourish, use these strategies:

1. Encourage an attitude of enlightened self-interest that brings employees' personal goals into alignment with the team's and the organization's goals.

2. Encourage cooperation and friendly competition.

3. Promote team learning.

4. Nurture positive team feelings.

5. Allow team members' expression of feelings.

6. Lead in ways that enhance self-direction.

Strategy #1: Encourage Enlightened Self-Interest

Workers in traditional bureaucratic organizations typically adopt an attitude of narrow self-interest based on a sense of dependency on bosses. This attitude leads to negative politics and manipulation. To avoid that, rely on

Motivational Intelligence. Help team members link their personal goals to team and organization goals, to see how putting the team first can help them achieve more of their own career goals in the long run. Show members how the following activities will empower them:

Ask creative questions, such as "what if" questions—on a regular basis. Focus more and more on opportunities while also doing necessary problem-solving. Remember that even though creativity begins with the generation of ideas, it's also at work in the selection, development, and implementation of ideas.

Set personal work goals and activities that have meaning to you and are needed by the team. Focus on activities that have meaning, depth, and substance for the team.

Contribute to the team and its purpose, with an awareness of your unique contribution and the team's unique value. Be willing to give all you can give and to share as much valuable information as you can. See other teams in the organization as customers to be served. Focusing on contribution and service allows people to let go of struggles for control and territory.

Speak up and speak honestly. Put into words what you see happening. Tell people what's really going on within the team and what you see going on outside the team. Make only those promises you can keep. Admit your mistakes. Give feedback honestly and with respect, even if it's unpleasant. Critique people's performance to their faces, not behind their backs.

Support team members. What's good for the team is good for you and your career. Your success depends on the team's success. Support all team members in ways that build trust. Be willing to confront lack of support and actions that undermine trust—to process the feelings this arouses and to resolve the conflict it reflects. Be willing to reassign team members who refuse to *get it*.

Continually learn and gain mastery. Learn as much as you can about your job. Welcome new challenges and opportunities to learn new jobs and gain new skills. Perform well simply for its own sake, because it helps you to be your best.

The rewards for enlightened self-interest are autonomy and enthusiasm. As a team member, you pursue mastery, meaning, contribution, integrity, and service because your team is in charge of its own work. You do not perform just to please a boss. The team eventually operates as a group of entrepreneurs, scanning the environment, finding opportunities for new business ventures, creating visions of success, setting its own goals, and focusing on them as if the team were a small business.

Enlightened self-interest is a long-run strategy that requires team members to take a broader view and to envision future achievements. For it to succeed in the long run, organizational leaders must maintain integrity, deliver on promises, support the team, and earn their trust.

Strategy #2: Encourage Cooperation and Friendly Competition

To get the right balance of friendly competition and cooperation that sparks innovation, use Emotional Intelligence and Motivational Intelligence. Women tend to focus more on connecting and supporting, while men focus more on competing. To handle competition among employees or groups in a constructive way, first identify the kind of competition that's involved. Let's look at three major types: constructive group action, friendly competition, and destructive politics.

Constructive Group Action

Employees need to unite in constructive group action in order to continually reinvent the goods or services they offer in the marketplace. Otherwise they'll soon be looking for another company to work for. Women tend to be very comfortable with this type of cooperative effort within the organization.

Friendly Competition

Friendly competition occurs in many ways. An example is when a team member comes up with a great idea that needs a little more work, and each team member tries to be the one that finds the breakthrough solution that makes the idea workable.

Friendly competition also occurs when a team member wants a promotion and intensifies her performance efforts because she knows another member also wants the job. Each of them may develop personal, innovative approaches to their jobs as well as additional skills and traits needed for the promotion. They may set more challenging goals and higher standards for themselves. When a competitor gets the prize, the "loser" is generally able to take it in stride and work cooperatively with the winner. Most male leaders encourage friendly competition, believing that it creates challenge and interest. This style comes less naturally to most women, but when women see the overall benefits, they tend to be comfortable with friendly competition.

Destructive Politics

Total concentration on the process of winning and moving up the corporate ladder—rather than on the job at hand—is a warning sign of destructive politics. For example, an ambitious employee attempts to block a qualified peer's promotion, teams up with other peers to stop a front-runner, automatically sides with friends against enemies, and takes the attitude, *You scratch my back, I'll scratch yours, even if the company suffers in the process.*

Women are usually *not* comfortable with this type of competitive aggression, and for good reason: It leads directly to conflict. Such conflicts are especially difficult to resolve because of the deceit, manipulation, and hidden agendas involved. As a leader, let people know that you will not tolerate this kind of destructive politics. If you know someone is involved in that kind of behavior, nip it in the bud. You want word to get around: *That sort of thing just won't work. It's more likely to result in being demoted or fired than being promoted.*

Reward cooperation among competitors. Look for instances where members bring in competitors on projects and where they cooperate with competitors in meeting goals and in developing constructive, innovative approaches to implementing goals. Make sure these people are recognized and rewarded for working as a team.

Strategy #3: Promote Team Learning

Learning together is a major way to ignite team creativity. As team members work together over time, they begin to construct their own language, their own shortcuts for referring to the work. Their in-group language symbolizes their real sense of belonging. When it's working, members go far beyond learning *about* the business. They learn to *be* the business. They're not just observers; they're directly involved as full participants.

For example, when Xerox tech reps have a machine breakdown and it turns out to be a tough problem, do they go get their heavy procedures manual? No. They quickly find some symptoms and start to weave a story from these fragments of information. Because these machines can be very complex, some having 30 microprocessors, they might call in another tech rep. They tell their story and listen as their colleague recalls a similar tale from his own set of war stories. Noting similarities and differences among their stories, they begin to diagnose the current problem.

When they get back to the office, they begin to swap stories with other tech reps, who often have faced similar problems. They sit around telling their stories and listening to each other, embellishing and refining the stories that eventually travel around the grapevine to the entire corps of tech reps. Such storytelling is a natural, powerful way of learning to create new solutions to common problems as well as to uncover new opportunities to fill customer needs.

Strategy #4: Nurture Positive Team Feelings

Here's another strategy that will probably come more naturally to you than to your male colleagues, given your Emotional Intelligence advantage. Feelings underlie everything we do in business and are especially important in building positive team relationships and team spirit. The feelings most typical of top-performing teams are self-esteem, belonging, commitment, support, pride, trust, and mutual respect.

Self-esteem is the basis for all other positive feelings. Each member must be heard, acknowledged, and valued. Members must be able to be themselves and must feel that all members are treated fairly and equitably. Self-esteem grows when members see they have influence and can contribute to the team's successes.

Belongingness is a powerful asset to develop. Each member feels he or she belongs to a desirable group in which individuals are accepted for who they are, are respected for their uniqueness, and are rewarded for their performance.

Commitment to the team's goals and its successes grows out of the feelings of belonging and self-esteem and is based on being part of the decision-making process. Members see the decisions as their own and want to make them succeed.

Support for team members and for the team as a whole grows out of self-esteem, belongingness, and commitment. An important element of team spirit is the sense of "all for one and one for all" that impels members to root for each other and help out when they can.

Pride in the team's achievements, in its overcoming of obstacles and in its camaraderie, evolves as the other feelings develop and as the team works together in fruitful, positive ways.

Trust in one another and in the team develops from positive experiences. Members must discuss the types of behavior and attitudes that build or break trust. For example, when commitments are not met, confidentialities are betrayed, or dishonesty occurs, the team must discuss these actions and their impact on trust and team spirit. They must resolve any and all trust issues in order to achieve and maintain optimal team performance.

Mutual respect is essential. A team is a collection of diverse individuals, each with a unique character and potential for contributing to team success. The best team leaders capitalize on differences and do not try to force conformity to one ethnic, gender, or lifestyle standard, such as a straight-white-male standard.

Strategy #5: Allow Team Members' Expression of Feelings

Enabling the expression of feelings is another way to apply your Emotional and Motivational Intelligences. You know that feelings are part of every business transaction. All of us are thinking-feeling beings, and our feeling side is what provides the charge, the motivation, and the passion that makes things happen. Once people acknowledge this, they can begin to find ways to process the egomind emotions as they come up and to channel them into the expansive, enabling emotions that lie on the other side.

Recognize the Legitimacy of Feelings

Too often in business we treat almost any expression of feelings as inappropriate, embarrassing, and unprofessional. Actually, feelings are normal and human, and many effective leaders are coming to see that ignoring them creates more problems, long-term, than it solves. Everyone recognizes the need for certain boundaries in the expression of feelings. For example, physical violence in the expression of anger is not acceptable. But few corporate leaders have searched for constructive ways to help employees express their egomind feelings—such as hurt, disgust, sorrow, blame, anger, and rage—about workplace events.

Use Empathic Emotional Processing

You can use a variety of ways to deal with team members' emotions. Suppose an employee comes at you expressing strong, egomind emotions, such as blame and anger. Your natural reaction is probably to close off from these feelings. You either try to withdraw or stay in a neutral counseling mode, which keeps the contracting emotions in the employee's court.

Psychologist Dr. David Berenson, who has done extensive work in this area, suggests alternate ways of responding to others' emotions: If you use empathic emotional processing, you access your *own* feelings of blame and anger. You can do this by recalling a situation in which *you* felt blame and anger toward someone, perhaps a situation you haven't yet fully processed. You can then move through the emotional processing that ends with your releasing the egomind emotions. This process creates the psychological-physical space for you to move into the expansive emotions.

To process anger and other egomind emotions, use your Emotional Intelligence. Go fully into the emotions and let yourself move into any other emotions that come up. Fully experience all emotions that come up until you're ready to release them. When you're able to let them go, you'll feel yourself move up into more expansive emotions, such as relief and peace.

The key point is to let the egomind emotions flow, let them move, be willing to feel them fully, to release them, and to create space for the expanding emotions. By doing this, you can help the other person to fully experience his or her emotions and to flow with them, letting them move on to wherever they want to move. Through empathic resonance, you feel the emotions the other person is feeling, you take the lead in processing those emotions, and the team member in turn feels the movement of emotions that you're feeling. In this way, you help the team member to release the egomind emotions and to move into expansive emotions. You do this simply by *being with* the other person. Should you tell the team member what you're doing? Perhaps. Discussing the process is not necessary for it to occur, but it may be helpful.

Strategy #6: Lead in Ways that Enhance Self-Direction

A facilitative leadership style is essential for self-directed teams to survive and thrive. This style relies heavily on trusting, vibrant relationships. Here's where your Associative Intelligence can team up with other intelligences in building relationships with team members. As you role model ways of connecting that support and challenge members in expanding their innovative skills, team members will learn new relationship skills themselves.

You, as team leader, will be effective if you do the following:

- Be a team player while also being a leader.
- Focus on both team development (processes) and team performance.
- Use your coaching skills in the roles of mentor, tutor, and counselor.

Be a team player while also being a leader.

Balancing this dual role can help you build enough respect and influence to get cooperation from members. Then focus on team performance more than on individual performances and on getting results through each person's commitment to the team's performance rather than through control.

Focus on both team development (processes) and team performance.

Give special attention to structuring the team so everyone is clear about vision, goals, and values—even more than specific job responsibilities, which may shift and morph as the team progresses on a project. Help the team track and evaluate its own progress in achieving goals *and* in developing as a team. Lead the team in recognizing the processes it uses to get things done and in continually improving team processes.

Use your coaching skills.

Initiate the actions and processes needed to build a work unit into an excellent team. Involve the team members at the very beginning, then become a member of the team as the team starts developing itself. Model the behavior you want team members to develop by being a good team member—performing your own tasks and interacting with people in a team-oriented way. Coach members in the following ways:

Mentoring and helping team members understand what self-managing creative teams are all about, how company politics enters in, the values and biases of key managers, and career opportunities within the firm. The process may include helping a person gain political savvy, understand the way the organization works, learn how to build a support system or network, better manage his or her career, or develop greater commitment to team synergy and goals. Develop sensitivity to the values and biases of others.

Tutoring and helping team members learn new skills. This process can include helping team members to improve their innovative skills as well as their technical competence, to become an expert in an area, to learn more rapidly, to develop greater commitment to continuous learning, and to participate in ways that spark team synergy.

Counseling and assisting team members to expand their creativity, recognize opportunities, resolve problems, develop strategies, and boost team synergy. The process of counseling may include helping a person accurately describe a problem and its root cause, explore alternatives, gain technical or organizational insight, air strong feelings, understand some required change, or resolve some confusion or misunderstanding.

Help the Team Learn to Manage Itself

The more the team is able to direct itself, the more committed and powerful it will become. Teams can be empowered to perform virtually all management functions. For example, the team can learn to:

- Identify entrepreneurial opportunities and propose ways of responding to them.
- Set team goals and determine how they will be achieved.
- Solve those team problems that they have the resources to solve.
- Make decisions that they must carry out.
- Identify who will make what types of day-to-day decisions.
- Redesign jobs and procedures.
- Schedule the work (who will do what).
- Evaluate the work of the team and of team members.

To help your team work together to effectively take over key management functions, use these strategies:

1. Help the team create a shared vision and goals.
2. Promote self-management.
3. Help the team establish day-to-day processes.
4. Help the team learn how to grow into a Business Development Team.

Strategy #1: Create a Shared Vision and Goals.

When people are able to create visions of greatness and to make them a reality, they gain autonomy from bureaucratic dependency and the drag on productivity it causes. Everyone can and does have a vision. Often it's at the subconscious level because of their dependency on bosses or their pessimism about having any influence anyway. To make a vision reality, the team must continually develop clear, specific goals. Otherwise, members become apathetic or begin to focus on their own goals. The team must decide on strategies for continually creating shared visions and formulating the strategies and goals to bring them into reality.

Establish a Vision-Creating Process

To establish a vision-creating process for the team, ask members to share their concerns about work projects and then to imagine what and how the team might create in the future. Help them apply their Sensory Intelligence to the visioning adventure. Learn how to tell if the shared vision is viable.

Start with Concerns

One way to start the visioning process is to ask each member to pick an important project he or she cares about and is frustrated with. Then have them ask themselves why they care so much about it. They should keep asking why until they get to the root of the concern.

Imagine the Future

Next, ask them to imagine the team three years in the future—or some other relevant future time—in order to answer these questions:
- What does their ideal way of working with customers look like?
- What types of products or services are they providing and creating?
- What types of processes are they using?
- How do team members treat each other? How does the team interact with others in the firm?

Start a dialogue on these topics. Remind members that they're not likely to treat customers any better than they treat one another. If they're cautious, judgmental, and competitive with one another, they probably behave that way with customers. If they use fear and punishment to control a coworker, that coworker is likely to take out the resulting frustration on customers. The team's vision should reflect its members' deepest values about how people treat each other.

Identify the Signposts of a Shared Vision

Help the team develop the criteria for a good shared vision. What are the signposts that will let them know they're reaching a vision they can commit to? Here are some possible signposts:
- The vision has depth; it's personal and from the heart.
- It has clarity; it's specific, not vague.
- All team members feel a sense of responsibility for the vision and the team; they begin to talk of them as theirs, to transform in any way they want.

Let Each Member Contribute Talents

Lead the team in determining how it can use to best advantage each member's knowledge, skill, experience, and motivation. Do this by challenging, stretching, training, coaching, and supporting members—and encouraging them to do these functions for each other. The more skills a person has a chance to use, the more skills he or she tends to develop. Look for opportunities...

- To extend people's skills to other jobs within the team and within the larger organization.
- To expand the depth of a job area—from giving information about something, to developing new ideas about it, to solving problems and making decisions concerning it.

Team members need special skills in generating new ideas, in solving work problems and interpersonal problems, and in making team meetings work.

Strategy #2: Promote Self-Management.

You can be a role model in promoting self-management. First, master the strategy yourself. Then help team members master it.

Seek Team Members' Input

Ask for their ideas, opinions, and reactions. Don't judge them personally for the type of input they give (although you may not necessarily agree with the input itself). Never punish them, in any way, for what they say—either in the short run or in the long run. Listen actively, ask questions, paraphrase what was said, thank them, and resist having the last word.

Work Toward Consensus

The team should reach for general agreement on key issues because team power will be lost if people are divided. Encourage direct expression of thoughts, feelings, and concerns. Discourage and confront passive behavior, which is often an extreme form of withholding or an indirect strategy used to achieve a personal goal, such as getting others to feel guilty or sorry for them. Most passive-prone people have been getting their way since childhood by using passive strategies. They're usually not as vulnerable as they seem.

Promote Self-Evaluation

Give people the freedom to choose their own path to results. Encourage the team to structure work so that people do a whole job instead of a piece of it—or as close to a whole as possible. Alternatively, encourage cross-training and task rotation so members are more likely to stay challenged, interested, and enthusiastic. Provide regular feedback as quickly as possible. The most valuable feedback and evaluation are performed by the members themselves. Be sure everyone's performance is evaluated fairly. Give the team regular opportunities to evaluate team performance. Give guidance in how to measure performance—both how well the team is achieving its goals and how well it's doing as a team. Are relationships being built? How is team spirit? Are people cooperating? Are they working out differences? How are ground rules working?

Give Genuine Praise

The most powerful praise is specific and timely—normally just after performance. Give praise regularly, but keep it meaningful and sincere. Keep it separate from problems so it stands out as positive feedback.

Strategy #3: Establish Day-to-Day Processes.

Self-managing teams need to continually develop processes for helping their members respond well and adapt well—to change, to each other, to problems, to challenges, to the unexpected—often in new and different ways. They need processes to enhance their ability to identify opportunities that change may offer, processes for thriving on adversity and processes for dreaming up innovative ways around problems. These processes must ensure that members are able to influence and improve every aspect of the team's work, helping it to stay on a positive improvement slope. Routine processes include those that provide for:

- Team participation.
- Team decision-making.
- Communication.
- Conflict resolution.
- Customer contact.
- Challenge and support of the team and of members.

Team Participation Processes

All team members must actively contribute if the team is to achieve optimal synergy and team spirit. If even one member starts slacking off, hiding out, and otherwise not participating, his or her attitude will infect the others. To promote participation, the team might focus on such questions as:

- How do we want support to be expressed within the group?
- What balance between teamwork and individual work do we want?
- How do we want to handle internal competition? For example, what if we evaluated performance according to how much members contributed to other members' success?

The team can set clear, realistic standards and limits about such issues as being on time, getting tasks done on time, and scheduling breaks and days off.

Team Decision Processes

Decision power is a cornerstone of effective team development. When team members identify opportunities, generate ideas, solve problems, make decisions, and carry them out, the very process also reveals ways to get along together.

The team should focus on the things it has the power to influence. Once it decides on *content* matters—the tasks to be done—the team should have the power to implement those decisions. The group must also be able to decide *process* issues—how decisions will be made, whether majority vote or consensus will be the major mode, how minority rights will be protected, how the work will be structured and distributed, and the general ground rules of working together. Unresolved conflict about process can sabotage team productivity.

Communication Processes

Frequent communication is essential to team success. The best teams tend to contact each other and customers more, talk more, interact more, and meet more often—than less productive teams do.

Members must feel free to express themselves, especially to the leader. Informal channels must be open to pass on information, bring up new ideas, and make suggestions. The team must have the time and the means to communicate with each other, discuss issues, and share information. E-mail has made regular interaction much easier, and video conferencing is becoming common, so members can read voice tones and facial expressions as well as words. Still, face-to-face team meetings are extremely important. Consensus building works best when everyone can see everyone else—at least until virtual reality is able to provide this.

Processes for Conflict Resolution

Even the best teams will experience some conflict. Before it erupts, the team should decide how conflict and disagreements will be managed. Then, when a disagreement occurs, the team can focus on the *content* and not become bogged down in arguments over a process that may favor one side or another.

Processes for Customer Contact

Some leading-edge companies have found great success in assigning one team member to be the only company contact person for a particular customer. Instead of a valued customer being passed along from department to department, team to team, or employee to employee—that customer deals with one employee who has the authority and resources to meet all the customer's needs. That employee-customer relationship becomes solid, and the employee gains greater insight into what that customer needs and wants. True empowerment is being able to use the organization's tools and information to satisfy the customer.

Processes for Giving Challenge and Support

Individuals and teams function most creatively and passionately when they feel challenged to achieve and supported in pursuing that challenge.

Challenge

You—and all team members—can challenge yourselves and other team members to improve performance and to take on more challenging tasks by encouraging one another:

- To develop visions of greatness.
- To make a greater commitment to generating new ideas, finding the Next New Thing, and accepting more difficult and challenging tasks.

- To seek out and accept chances to learn something new, to stretch their capabilities, and to find ways to enable the learning process.
- To see the freedom they have to voice and try out their ideas.
- To enjoy friendly competition, primarily with previous self-achievement and also with team members and with other teams.
- To make a commitment to perform in new, more excellent ways, such as identifying performance problems and devising strategies to improve performance.

Support

When you support team members, you signal the importance of team autonomy and you promote trust. How can you show support? Here are some specific supportive actions:

- Find out what people need and want in order to do their jobs. Then offer assistance, run interference, and offer similar appropriate help. Provide the necessary tools to meet the challenges: the authority, information, supplies, staff support, and facilities to do the job.
- Provide training, coaching, and mentoring—showing a positive attitude and giving encouragement.
- Give rewards for achievement; if necessary, fight to get the rewards. Recognition is so rewarding and so inexpensive. Acknowledge team and individual ideas, innovations, projects, and achievements.
- Take a constructive, problem-solving approach to mistakes and view them as part of the learning process. When referring to a past mistake, for example, say, "This will give you a chance to follow through on the valuable know-how you picked up last month."
- Avoid dwelling on past histories, blaming, defending, and getting bogged down in details. Discourage blaming-victim behavior in others by staying in an idea-generating, problem-solving, problem-prevention mode.
- Back up the team and members in their well-meaning decisions and actions. For example, explain to higher management what the team is doing. Communicate support verbally and nonverbally.

The underlying message is this: *You can do the job. I'll be here for you. I'm rooting for you.*

Strategy #4: Grow into a Business Development Team.

Once your team becomes truly self-managing, it's time to take the next step. Business Development Teams (BDTs) act as entrepreneurs for the organization. They scan the environment and envision innovative new business ventures.

Know How BDTs Work

Here's where team and organizational flexibility are essential. For example, in many companies, project teams come together to work on a particular project and then may disband to join other teams and to work on other projects. When it comes to recognizing new business opportunities, the team may be quite solid and connected and may therefore agree on which opportunity to pursue and may stick together through one venture after another.

More often, someone in the company recognizes a business opportunity. Some people in their team get excited about it, but others don't. That won't necessarily block the development of the business venture. The people who go for the new idea may form their own new core team and recruit members from other teams to join them. Many high-energy organizations are flexible enough to allow and encourage such spontaneous, running-hot, rapidly evolving team activity.

Understand How BDTs Give a Competitive Edge

The demands of customers in an age of global competition are continually growing. To meet these demands, a new team intrapreneurship is emerging. Robert Reich, former Secretary of Labor, speaking on CSPAN-IV about the entrepreneurial spirit of many corporate employees, said, "We must begin to celebrate collective intrapreneurship, endeavors in which the whole of the effort is greater than the sum of individual contributions. The traditional we/ they approach to managing workers is giving a way to a synergy between leaders and teams of employees."

Alex Stewart defines such leading-edge companies as entrepreneurial firms that seize an opportunity to serve a tough market for a service or product on which their business must then depend. The firm is *pulled* by opportunities to create new wealth more than *pushed* by the resources it already has in place for doing business. The new type of entrepreneurial firm embraces its customers' needs and demands, sees the pressures created by such demands as business opportunities, and allows such demands to define the firm's mission. It sets about fulfilling this mission through focus on the actions that work teams must take to provide the products and services the customers demand or will welcome.

These demands may be recognized by people within your firm. Encourage them to develop a proposal to create a BDT, using people already working for the firm, outside contractors, consultants, and other persons with the needed skills. Once they come together as a BDT, members tend to act collectively as entrepreneurs. They often play above their apparent levels of competence— that is, above their heads. Often with little experience with conventional approaches, the members and teams work out procedures themselves. They manage by inventiveness and faith in the team process. With their new collective skills, and perhaps incrementally added inexpensive equipment, they find themselves creating careers and wealth.

BDTs and their members stretch past their previous abilities as they learn how to dream up products and services customers will love—as well as ways to solve customers' problems. They come up with procedures that manage to get the customer's total job done. Methods are learned incrementally and in practice. People on the floor are not second-guessed by intervening specialists, so business development is what counts—not the entrenched games people play. The challenging mission, which at first may be set from above, becomes redefined by the team members as their own. They assume a pride of ownership as they create a system that works, that grows, and that wins—and as they learn from their non-wins.

Create an Environment That Supports BDTs

BDTs arise from a combination of factors: tough competition, an entrepreneurial culture, customer focus, team-based corporate structure, and profit-sharing. Here are some guidelines for companies that want to support such teams:

- Keep each establishment small (no more than 100 people).
- Provide the resources the team needs to generate new business ventures.
- Recruit team members who have broadly, not specifically, suitable backgrounds and the ability to work well within groups. Promote them through career paths that start at the bottom and include lateral transfers, from job to job, so they get a wide-ranging view of company operations.
- Challenge members to understand matters they probably wouldn't learn if left to themselves. Share information.
- Ensure that everyone stays close to the customers in the short run but also scans the environment to see how customers can and will change in the long run.
- Encourage them to give some direction to the chaotic energy— such as holding a common vision, periodically setting new goals, and regularly prioritizing goals and activities.
- Let the team decide what procedures it needs to cope with pressures. Minimize staff (advisory) specialists, and seldom overrule your line (decision-making) members.
- Use measurements and appraisals that rely on customer delight and satisfaction as well as financial success.
- Give special rewards to people who create a new BDT and to all who excel at continuous learning and high performance. Give team members a sense of security; for example, honor promises of long-term reward. The high levels of global competition make team members feel vulnerable.
- Teach people to spark creative collaboration.

Spark Creative Collaboration

What next? That's what the world is always saying in a creativity-driven market. Businesses must adopt a cultural and organizational framework of *What next?* or, quite simply, they go out of business. Create or die—the choices are that extreme. To succeed in today's innovative, fast-moving business world, you need to understand and use creative collaboration. It's the stuff BDTs are made of. You need to know how to recognize a creative collaboration, a collaborative firm, and collaborative team processes. You need to know how to get a creative collaboration started and carried through to successful completion.

What Is Creative Collaboration?

Creative collaboration involves people from varying backgrounds and viewpoints coming together to find shared goals, developing creative responses to opportunities, and finding solutions to problems.

Shared, understood goals

Creative collaboration involves framing goals and problems in ways that inspire people to collaborate—as opposed to people doing their own thing and defending their own turf. It allows smart people with big egos to subordinate their egos while contributing to something significant and lasting. It creates a clearing that pulls people across different professional fields and allows them to create a common language.

New, shared understandings

Creative collaboration allows people to build shared understandings that lead to something new. The different perspectives and views in a collaboration are necessary to light the spark of creativity. Unity that contains diversity can be a magic pot of gold.

An act of shared creation

Most people usually think and work along the lines of a single frame of reference. Creativity occurs when people are able to connect different frames of reference in ways that result in creating or discovering something new.

Many types of people and projects

Creative collaborations involve the creation of new value by doing something radically new or different: scientific breakthroughs, landmark legislation, new products, and so on. Successful collaborative groups are often made up of motley crews, of new combinations of diverse people.

Future fact?

Whenever anything of significance is being accomplished in the world, it's being accomplished by people collaborating across professional and cultural frontiers. The future belongs not just to stars, champions, or technical wizards who think and work in isolation, but to collaborative people who think and work together.

The Collaborative Networked Firm

Companies immersed in the high-tech global economy are more concerned with nurturing creative people, with a view toward creating resources that never existed before, than they are with reducing personnel and costs. Their focus is on engaging customers in a dialogue about their goals and problems.

The main question is becoming: *What's missing in the way of innovative products and services?* Managers are asking, "What new patterns of relationships and interaction can we create to solve this complex customer problem?" They're following such role models as Bill Gates and Steven Jobs, who paid attention to what was missing, built it in collaboration with other firms, and delighted their customers. To boost the possibilities of creative collaboration, a firm needs computer technology that sparks creativity, as well as people who are turned on by exploring new ideas.

Computer Technology

Computer technology has enabled a new creative era. It expands the space for speculative thought through networks, groupware, and videoconferencing, which brings people an ever-widening array of ideas, opportunities, and challenges. It allows people to communicate instantly, and to freely feed the creative process. It brings together a wide diversity of people—and differing opinions are the raw material of the creative process. The power of creativity rises exponentially with the diversity and divergence of networked computer users.

Computers give you and your team members access to lots of information, which in turn allows you to engage in more creative conversations. You can't talk about what you don't know, but now you can find out by logging onto your computer. Your company can put online all kinds of information about business performance and project organization. Information technology, or infotech, is therefore one of the most important tools in the creativity toolkit.

Computer networks are nonlinear. They're wholistic, resembling the Web of Life, and through web connections they facilitate creativity. For example, they enable creative teams to have public conversations. They put people in touch with one another and create unexpected linkages across established organizational boundaries. They champion processes that, left to themselves, would go nowhere. They free us from concerns about how and where to get team members together. They provide speed, instantaneous transactions, and the ability to make transactions happen at all. A major type of computer linkage is groupware.

Groupware Environment: The Collaboratory

Groupware is software that connects team members' computers and allows them to brainstorm, argue, and collaborate online. People are easy to reach by groupware, which offers so much more than e-mail. Groupware takes teams a giant step closer to the brave new world of multimedia workgroup technology. It means they can set up their own private cyber-meeting, sometimes called a *collaboratory*.

Using their personal computers, team members can communicate their own ideas, instantly see each other's ideas, comment on them, edit them, take off on them, and vote on them—among other things. For example, a product development team can be from diverse backgrounds and areas of expertise. Members can be located all over the world, all over the building, or all over the room. When they connect via collaborative groupware, the level of joint creativity can be very high. Such cyberspace meetings often consist of talking or brainstorming around a theme, bringing in organizational information and experiences, sharing unique knowledge that each member possesses, and learning as a group.

Collaborative People

Collaborative people usually take some sort of leadership role, regardless of their actual position within the company. They have a vision of a possibility they want to realize. They know collaborations don't just happen by chance. They arise from the efforts of someone who is passionate about a possibility or opportunity. They're masters at building relationships and may have loud, exuberant conversations about what they want to create in the world, rather than staying silent or having muted, suppressed conversations. They're gifted at *being with* people in rapt concentration, listening with a high quality of attention. They're often masters at organizing, bringing people with diverse opinions and backgrounds together for the purpose of identifying opportunities, solving problems, or creating value. They recognize where their own views, experiences, or skills are limited and have a basic attitude of learning and a beginner's mind.

They're often masters of cyberspace relationships, the new marriage of computers and communications technology. Cyberspace allows conversations to happen any time, anywhere, free of the limits of time, space, and personal status. Because anyone can talk with anyone else at any time anywhere, cyberspace becomes a meritocracy of talent. Collaborative conversations will come to full fruition in the form of full-blown, multimedia video and data conferencing services. These are just around the corner.

As a collaborative person, you may be a chief negotiator, a strategic broker of joint ventures, or the head of a cross-functional team made up of people who can each make a distinctive contribution to the effort. You'll form networks of communication, commitment, and support that are much more effective than the usual corporate structures.

Collaborative Team Processes

Collaborative teams must have good communication processes—and to be creative they must ask and answer the right questions. The communications process is absolutely crucial for creative collaboration among team members. Here are some key components:

- ❧ Keep the process open.
- ❧ Focus on what you are *for*.
- ❧ Use beginner's mind.
- ❧ Get to know each team member.
- ❧ Make creative space.
- ❧ Ask key questions.

Keep the Process Open

Avoid reaching closure too soon. Creative work is exploratory, and in the early stages, everyone should check their disbelief and cynicism at the door. Become the innocent child. Reserve skepticism and doubt until assessment time. Keep communication open and nonjudgmental, even though you will of course need measurable results at some point.

Focus on What You Are for

Shift your way of thinking from *I'm against that* to *I'm for this*. Ask yourself, *If I'm against that, then what am I for?* For example, if you don't like the idea of packaging the product in plastic, are you *for* packaging it in recyclable cardboard? Instead of rejecting an idea you think is problematic, you can say *That's an interesting idea. I agree we need to change our package. Let's just explore one other option*. Think in terms of doubling and redoubling ideas. Avoid judging, evaluating, or criticizing at any point in the process. Instead speak of what you are *for*. Such positive-speak inspires confidence and nurtures the climate of openness to ideas.

Use Beginner's Mind

Pose questions that return the discussion to the state of the beginner's mind. You ask a question, get an answer, and then ask why. Do that five times and you will understand the essence of the situation. You'll break through a superficial understanding to reveal the more basic issues.

Get to Know Each Team Member

Use all of your intelligences to get to know a member. For example, ask exploratory questions to find out what's important in life to that person. Put yourself inside his or her head, encouraging feelings of empathy and compassion. This will give you a sense of the team member's personality and will help you to speak that person's language.

Make Creative Space

Creative, collaborative teams need the right environment to do their thing. The ideal play-space consists of several paradoxical elements:

1. It's both bounded (by one problem-opportunity or project) and open (to explore it freely).
2. It's both safe (for wild ideas) and charged with risk (the company must innovate or die).
3. Individualistic ideas are welcomed—and group guidance is sought (for example, a team leader reflects back the group voice at key times).
4. Little, individual ideas and stories are treasured—and so are big ideas, broad in scope and depth, that put all the little ideas into a framework or context.
5. Working alone is supported—and team and organizational resources support each member, allowing and helping each person to contribute.
6. Silence is okay—and speaking up is welcomed.

Ask Key Questions

The team must decide how to structure itself and how to function in order to generate a high level of creativity. Here are some penetrating questions the creativity team should ask:

Who is included? Should we include everybody, all employees?

Who will lead? Who will take responsibility for seeing that agendas are set and carried out? Who will define the task, establish milestones, call it quits? Will it be the team as a whole, a leader, or both? Sometimes one or the other?

Who is the store minder? The great continuing challenge of managing creativity is handling the tension between rational-mind discipline and the free play of sensory input, new associations, intuition, insight, and inspiration. The team must decide who will play the role of *store minder*, the one who grounds the chaotic energy in the reality of goals and profit margins. How will the tension between minding the store and free play lead to meaningful conversation?

What's the agenda? What's the venue? What kind of audience? What for? What's the purpose? The end result or goal? The product, purpose, service, or process that we're after? How will people define and evaluate the *product*? How will they draw protective lines around it? Determine its fate? Does the team decide or does the leader decide, or both?

Where does all of this take place? Under what conditions?

Rules for Success—Team Collaborations

Here are three rules for success in creative collaboration.

Rule 1: Create or find a project that makes a difference.

Ways to do this include:

- Find what you're passionate about and what you intuitively feel is an emerging opportunity.
- Talk with customers and colleagues and others about the bothersome issues they face.
- Ask people in your network about what's going on and what they're into.

Rule 2: Be a great collaborative team player and colleague.

Try these techniques:

- Think of yourself first as an effective team person.
- As a colleague, offer to help others who have their hands full.
- Bring together a diverse team and start a deep dialogue on a customer's needs, wants, and problems—to ground people from different disciplines in something real and to allow them to think and work together. Express your thinking as honestly as you can, being open to other takes on the topic. Think of this process as passing a ball of energy back and forth until a creative, shared interpretation emerges.

Rule 3: Be an expert in a distinct area that creates solid value.

Let people know who you are and what knowledge and skills you can contribute. Ask yourself, *What do I know how to do that's distinctly different?* or *What real distinctive value can I bring to the table in this project?* Create your own resume or marketing brochure based on your achievements and abilities, especially those that apply to groups and creative teams. Publicize what you can do to add value or team zest to your next project. Get on the talent list of five

CEOs, on other people's *Who's Who*, and on their preferred e-mail lists—to boost your chances of making a contribution.

Steps to Starting a Creative Collaboration

To get creative collaboration going, think in terms of having collaborative conversations. These may have five steps.

Step 1. Clarify the purpose of the collaborative conversation.

State clearly the specific purpose of the conversation. Speak to the *Why are we here?* question. Answers could include:

- ✎ To explore new possibilities or opportunities.
- ✎ To create a community of commitment that will go for a possibility.
- ✎ To create a strategic plan.
- ✎ To reach certain goals, solve problems, or resolve a dispute.

You can move an impossibility to a possibility by making a declaration—a shared commitment to a collaborative goal.

Ask yourself, *What role should I play in this phase? Who do I need to be?* For example, *I'll be a deeply purposeful, clear, and focused person.*

Think of purpose as a guiding light, a navigating beacon. Think of clarifying the purpose as focusing the conversation like a laser beam. Think of the purpose as a container that can hold whatever happens in the conversation. Decide how you'll *frame* the purpose.

Consider asking the group to reflect on these kinds of questions:

1. Is there a clear purpose for the conversation consistent with what matters to all of us?
2. Have we clarified a purpose for the conversation? One that's attainable?
3. Are the issues and problems we've defined solvable?
4. Will the way we've framed the goal or problem give us the results we want?
5. Will the conversation move the collaboration and learning along?

Step 2. Gather divergent views.

See divergent views more as a source of strength than a source of conflict.

Ask yourself who you need to be during this phase. You might decide, for example, that you'll be someone who is warm, outgoing, gracious, who sees other people's truths as something to learn from, who doesn't have to win, and who can listen.

Think in terms of empowering people to come to the table and to speak up honestly and respectfully. Treat everyone as colleagues regardless of official status differences. Acknowledge any unresolved issues that are relevant to the conversation. Recognize and validate the different opinions and viewpoints. Give up the need to be in agreement. It's more important at this point to get the differences on the table than to agree.

Create an environment where chaotic communication is okay, but slow down the conversation when people are being left out. People have different rates of thinking, talking, and integrating info. Take breaks when some people need time to digest the info. Remember, in any creative project, there's a period of chaos and confusion before the breakthrough to clarity when things fall into place and make sense.

Step 3. Build a shared understanding of divergent views.

The purpose is to allow people to expand their views to include others' views and to get on the same wavelength. Here are some suggestions:

- Weed out false assumptions about each other and about varying viewpoints.
- Inquire into each others' thinking, express emotions constructively, recognize other's defensive reactions, and work through those reactions.
- Have a spirit of curiosity about how other people see the world, themselves, the situation they're in, what they want to achieve, and how.
- Set aside your position for the moment and begin to ask questions and listen in a deep way to build shared understanding.
- Look for new ways of seeing yourself and the others, for new awareness that can create new openings for possibility and action.

Ask yourself who you need to be in this phase; for example, is it someone who is curious and asks questions with a real sense of curiosity, someone who enjoys listening? Think in terms of being real, honest, and a learner, of open-minded and open-hearted listening. Balance your desire to persuade asser-tively with the need to question with curiosity. Establish a trading zone where you can exchange something of value without having to agree on everything or even understand each others' basic assumptions.

Learn the stories of others in the group. Listen to what they say—for what they mean and how they think. Discuss all the issues that are important to this creative collaboration, even if you thought some were off-limits for discussion.

When hostile energy from a group member comes your way, try verbal Aikido, stepping aside mentally and letting it just go by without hooking you emotionally. Then suggest that the two of you find a way to move forward together, perhaps by asking some well-meaning, constructive questions.

Step 4. Create new options by connecting different views.

The purpose is to explore ways to creatively connect different views with an eye toward creating dramatically new, surprising, even delightful solutions. Creativity is more likely to occur when you have people from different frames of reference who think and work together on a shared goal. Here's a common pitfall: creating emotional tension when the views seem irreconcilable, leading to disillusionment with the whole process. The goal is creative tension that leads to a creative breakthrough and resolution. Key consideration: avoiding the pitfall of emotional tension and collaborative breakdown.

Think in terms of creation itself rather than artistic creativity. Invent new options by expanding your view to include others. There are always more possibilities and options than people are aware of. Open up to them, search for them. Expand your view to encompass opposing views that may look incompatible. Focus on what really matters, on areas of overlap. Forget for the moment areas that you can't resolve. Try thinking in terms of *both...and* instead of *either...or....*

Try putting the challenge or problem in one sentence, brainstorming multiple options, using metaphors to generate new ideas, using analogies to distinguish what's missing and to solve practical problems, immersing yourself in all the info, and then giving it time to incubate.

Step 5. Start a conversation for action.

Think of the creative process as a spiral, originating with new ideas that you can't quite express, that are then developed through metaphors and analogies, and that finally end in a sketch, a prototype, or a scale model. This becomes a shared workspace that allows you to see if you have a shared understanding of what to create and how, as well as to test your idea through a prototype to see if it really works.

Ask yourself who you need to be in this phase. For example, you may need to be a practical doer, someone whose obsessive-compulsive interest in the nuts and bolts of the project can mean the difference between successful action and just another idea. Or maybe you need to be a tinkerer with a desire to act by building something one chunk at a time.

Use language in a way that goes beyond predictions, descriptions, and explanations—to carve out a new possibility *between the lines*, to ignite passion in people's hearts and fascination in their minds, to cause people to jump into action.

At this stage, if the group is a work team, the chain of command is replaced by a network of commitments, communication, and support. It's like passing a ball of energy back and forth until the collaborative project is brought to completion.

Think in terms of getting prototypes completed quickly rather than in terms of elaborate planning. It's more like a creative frenzy than a leisurely pace. You can alter your strategies and plans as you take action. Too much planning, analysis, and time tend to douse the fires of creative passion, so keep it moving at a lively pace.

Making bold promises has a powerful impact on transforming your possibility into reality. Here's what you need in order to make a bold promise work:

- A committed speaker: someone who makes a bold promise and follows through.
- A committed listener: someone who holds you accountable and encourages you to make bold promises that stretch your mind and skills
- Conditions of satisfaction: what will be produced and delivered?
- A time frame.

Encourage Diversity in Multicultural Teams

The power of synergy in sparking innovation is most powerful when team members come from diverse backgrounds and life experiences. The U.S. workplace offers a gold mine of diversity. In fact, one of the most dramatic workplace changes in the United States is the movement of women and minorities into all types of positions, including executive, managerial, technical, and professional jobs. This makes it easier to put together a multicultural team. Try these strategies for managing diversity in a multicultural team so that everyone feels included and empowered:

1. Provide a team culture that reflects the team's diversity. Use your influence to create a corporate culture that reflects employee diversity.

2. Reap the benefits of diverse teams—such as less groupthink and more innovation—by providing a culture that meets their needs and wants.

3. Build your (and your team's) multicultural skills through a five-step process.

4. Understand each subculture's patterns, strengths, and issues in order to understand individual team members from that subculture.

5. Be a multicultural change agent.

Strategy #1: Provide a Culture that Reflects Employee Diversity.

About 57 percent of employees were women and minorities in 2000, and about 43 percent were European American (white) men. But these men held 95 percent of top management positions and 70 percent of middle management jobs. This imbalance is increasing, as 85 percent of new employees coming into the workplace are women and minorities, with European American men making up only 15 percent of newcomers, according to the Bureau of Labor Statistics. This means business relationships are more diverse than ever, and diverse groups have diverse issues that are important to them. Suppliers and customers are also increasingly diverse and international in scope. They, along with global competition, are changing the way we do business.

Understanding the issues of many women and minorities means understanding how companies have dealt with them—past, present, and future. We're moving from the old assimilation approach, through the legal approach, to valuing diversity and multicultural inclusion. All these approaches can still be found in various companies around the country.

The assimilation approach is based on the melting-pot myth. Most companies have traditionally assumed that all employees would assimilate into the corporate culture. However, people who don't look like the dominant workplace group (that is, European American men) have never *melted in*. To overcome the discrimination and workplace barriers minority employees have experienced, civil rights laws were enacted in the late 1960s.

The legal approach was originally based on Equal Employment Opportunity (EEO). These laws allow employees to directly complain about discrimination, but individuals find this a difficult path that usually entails one person proving an employer wrong. Most people who file legal action suffer informal blackballing in their industry and severe career setbacks.

Affirmative action (AA) works in the background for most employees but has proven much more powerful than EEO in opening career doors. It requires that all employers who obtain federal government contracts develop and implement AA plans for hiring and promoting minorities. Backlash and resistance to AA have been reflected in claims of reverse discrimination, lower job standards for minorities, and beliefs that minorities are hired or promoted into good jobs only to fill *quotas*, which are in fact illegal in nearly all cases.

Valuing diversity came to be seen as a way to prevent these backlash problems. This approach calls for an organization's leaders to make a commitment to learn about and promote diversity, to value diversity rather than seeing it primarily as a problem.

Multicultural inclusion goes beyond the melting-pot myth, the legal approach, and even the valuing diversity approach. It's a more action-oriented approach that's based on valuing diversity but goes further to find ways to shift the corporate culture itself, to make it more multicultural—in other words, to include all employees and to reflect their subcultures. The goal is to create a corporate culture that supports and nurtures all types of employees. To grasp this evolution of diversity approaches, examine Snapshot #1.

The key to the multicultural inclusion is that employees aren't expected to do all the adapting. The corporation meets diverse employees halfway by adapting the corporate culture to reflect employee diversity, creating a multicultural corporate culture.

Snapshot #1: Evolution of Approaches to Workplace Diversity

assimilation approach——>legal approach——> valuing diversity——> multicultural inclusion

Basis: melting-pot myth——>EEO/AA——>differences as assets——>multiculturalism

Strategy #2: Reap the Benefits of Diverse Teams.

Multicultural inclusion has many advantages, including:

- ∾ Attracting and retaining the best available human talent because of an open, inclusive corporate culture.
- ∾ Creating and innovating more powerfully by avoiding groupthink and pulling from diverse viewpoints and thinking patterns.
- ∾ Finding opportunities and solving problems more effectively due to increased creativity.
- ∾ Increasing productivity and reducing costs due to better problem-solving and innovation.
- ∾ Increasing customer satisfaction and loyalty due to better products and services, including better relationships with diverse customers.
- ∾ Gaining and keeping greater market share due to increased productivity, lower costs, and greater customer satisfaction.

- ✨ Improving the quality of management; making managers more open and flexible.
- ✨ Increasing organizational flexibility, opening up to new ideas and cultures, and providing for the diverse needs and wants of diverse employees.
- ✨ Contributing to social responsibility by giving everyone a chance to succeed in our society, which meets the need for diverse peoples to achieve harmony and unity while still valuing and respecting our diversity.

Attract and Retain the Best Team Members

If you want to attract and retain the best team members, you must meet their valid needs, show respect for them as individuals, and use multicultural skills in working with them. As qualified employees become more scarce, employers must become more flexible. They can no longer afford to convey the implicit message: *This is what we offer and how we do things. Fit in or leave.* Now they must adapt to potential employees who say, *These are my needs and goals; they must be met if I am to stay.* To retain good employees, your firm must be truly committed to treating all employees fairly and providing an inclusive, multicultural environment. Employers who appear to favor some personal orientations and stifle others risk paying the price of low productivity due to a restricted pool of applicants, employee dissatisfaction, lack of commitment, turnover, and even sabotage.

Meet Members' Expectations

Most of the women and minority employees coming into the workplace are from a new generation who expect something extra from their careers: meaningful work and a sense of making a contribution. Most, especially career women, expect to have a personal and family life and are less willing than older generations were to sacrifice all for career success. And most, especially ethnic minorities, are more resistant to fitting into a corporate culture that requires them to squelch important parts of their persona.

Communicate Respect

One of the basic principles of effective multicultural leadership is to signal respect for the unique characteristics of another's culture. Small gestures can communicate respect, such as greeting persons in their native language, taking time to chat and learn more about a person, and keeping their cultural and personal viewpoints and values in mind as you work together. Doing this effectively requires learning about diverse subgroups and building skills in relating to them.

Strategy #3: Build Multicultural Skills.

Culture is pervasive and complex—it includes virtually everything you experience in your reality. It's also pervasive, like the air you breathe. Therefore, you need a plan or process for learning more about your own culture and the cultures of other employees. An effective process for building multicultural skills—your own and those of your team—involves five major steps:

Step 1: Become aware of culture, its pervasive influence, and how cultures differ.

Step 2: Learn about your own culture to help you recognize those differences that are rooted in culture.

Step 3: Recognize your own ethnocentricity, the ways in which you stereotype, judge, and discriminate, and your emotional reactions to conflicting cultural values.

Step 4: Learn about other cultures you encounter in the workplace so you can recognize when cultural differences may be at the root of problems and so you can appreciate the contributions people from diverse cultures can make to the work situation. Focus especially on these aspects of each diverse group:

- Myths vs. reality—myths that reflect stereotypes and prejudices that people in the dominant culture hold toward members of this group.
- Background or evolution of the current unbalanced situation.
- Current profile—demographics that reflect current reality of people in this group.
- Cultural themes, patterns, and issues of this subculture or community.
- Leadership challenges and opportunities to provide support to members of this group and to help them contribute their talents.

This learning step is the heart and soul of the multicultural approach. We all have the human capacity to imagine ourselves experiencing what another human experiences. When you make the effort to learn about others' experiences, and when you open your mind to seeing the world as they see it, you grow personally by leaps and bounds. You become truly able to take the lead in managing diversity.

Step 5: Build interaction skills and practice new behaviors through case studies, role plays, and on-the-job experience.

Strategy #4: Understand Each Subculture's Issues.

Every cultural subgroup has its own unique set of values, habits, customs, life circumstances, and issues to resolve. Understanding the key cultural themes and issues of each group can give you great insight and power for building good work relationships and helping other team members do the same. If you can mentally slip inside a "different" person's skin for a time and see the world through that person's eyes, you'll gain great power in understanding the thinking and feeling and the issues most important to that person.

We know, of course, that each person is unique and therefore may not agree with their own group's consensus on an issue. On the other hand, when you know something about a person's cultural background, you gain clues to identifying questions that may help solve team problems. For example, May-Wan, an Asian American team member, is not participating in group discussions. You understand that Asian cultures tend to disapprove of women expressing assertive opinions. A key question would be, *May-Wan, how do you feel about speaking up in team meetings?*

Following is a brief example of an issue for each major group in the American workplace. For in-depth information on each group, see my book, *Diversity Success Strategies* (Butterworth-Hememan, 1999).

European American women

In fact, career women in all diverse groups often find themselves in catch-22 situations. For example, people expect women to be emotional, indecisive, and vulnerable. But business leaders are expected to be in control of their emotions, decisive, and able to roll with the punches. If women project the typical image, they're not seen as potential leaders. But if they project the *business leader* image, they're often seen as too hard and masculine, or even abnormal.

European American men

To some extent men from all diverse groups are expected to be aggressive, ambitious, and proud. But many corporate cultures are changing in ways that call for leaders who are cooperative and focus more on challenging and supporting others than on personal achievement. Many men are confused about what companies expect of them, just as they're confused about what the women in their lives expect. The dramatic changes in women's roles have had a major impact on men's lives.

African Americans

When African Americans have a problem with an associate, they typically take the bull by the horns and confront the issue directly. They go straight to the person, tell it like it is, and try to work it out immediately. To them this approach is real and honest. But to most other people in a workplace, it may be threatening and may imply anger that might erupt into violence. When European American, Asian American, and Latino American coworkers feel threatened by African Americans' "confrontation," "rage," or "violence," it's usually because they misinterpret their cultural behavior patterns.

Asian Americans

If you're an Asian American, you learn early on that one of the highest values is to control your reactions and to become mature enough to put relationships before personal concerns. As a result you may be very indirect about expressing criticism or disagreeing.

In fact, Asian Americans rarely show strong emotion, especially outside the family circle. When European American, Latino American, and African American co-workers conclude that Asian Americans are closed, secretive, inscrutable, and even cold, it's usually because they're unaware of Asian cultural values.

Latino Americans

Do you assume that many Latino Americans have a *mañana* (literally *tomorrow*) attitude, which implies they're not ambitious, productive go-getters, like European Americans? Actually, most Latino Americans are hard workers, but they may wait for orders from the boss. Their cultural beliefs include greater respect for authority than most European Americans hold—and greater acceptance of themselves as subordinates to a powerful boss. Also, Latino Americans tend to be more accepting of undesirable circumstances, often seeing such situations as God's will. When European Americans judge Latino Americans as lacking initiative, it's usually because they don't understand these aspects of their cultural background.

Gay Persons

Have you seen gay persons being avoided by coworkers who assume that gays don't have *normal* relationships? Coworkers have made such comments as, *I just don't feel comfortable socializing with Joe (a gay man), Maybe he'll come on to me sexually*, or *Maybe he'll get jealous of my friendship with a guy he's attracted to, when to me we're just hanging out*. Joe would probably say, *Hey, I'm me first and foremost, just a person. My sexual orientation is just one slice of the whole pie that's me. What's more, I'm very sensitive to the discomforts and fears of straight guys.*

Studies indicate that people in the gay community have a whole range of relationships, as people in any community do, and overall they're as likely to have "normal relationships" as people from any cultural group.

Persons with Disabilities

Do you think of persons with a disability as a quite small minority? Do you think of them as distinctly "different"? Actually, most people have some type of disability, usually fairly minor. Persons classified as *disabled* simply have a disability that affects their ability to perform one or more major life functions, such as walking, reading, or hearing.

They're not really *different* from the person who limps around occasionally with back trouble, the person who wears contacts, or the person who doesn't hear too well out of one ear. It's just a matter of degree. Even a person with a severe disability, such as paralysis from the neck down, may learn to live and work independently and may make significant contributions through his or her career.

Obese Persons

Many cruel myths and stereotypes surround obesity in our culture. The type of discrimination obese employees experience has an element of appearance bias and is related to skin-color discrimination, which is also a form of appearance bias. Obese persons also experience discrimination based on assumptions about what they cannot do, similar to that experienced by persons with disability. Actually, many obese persons are as healthy as most adults, depending upon the extent of their obesity and their age. Still, recent court rulings that support the employment rights of obese persons are based on their rights to "reasonable accommodation" under laws that protect the disabled.

Older Persons

How old is old? The answer to that question depends on which organization or law you refer to. Most stereotypes about older persons are some variation of *they're rigid, dogmatic, and forgetful*. Their younger co-workers may avoid them and may wonder why these "old folks" haven't retired or when they're going to retire.

Research indicates that aging itself does not cause any significant loss of intelligence, memory, or learning capacity. However, with age one's habits tend to come home to roost. People who abuse or neglect their bodies start paying the price in their later years, while people with good eating and exercise habits, and the right genes, tend to remain healthy and vibrant. People who habitually spend much of their time in negative thinking tend to become even more negative with age, while those who work on a positive outlook and self-growth become more delightful to be around.

Other Groups

Other groups that have distinct issues include American Indians, Arab Americans, Jewish Americans, and bi-ethnic persons (those whose parents are from two distinctly different cultural backgrounds). For example, the person whose mother is European American and whose father is African American tends to experience a unique type of cultural conflict while growing up.

Strategy #5: Be a Multicultural Change Agent.

By gaining multicultural skills, you can become an agent for change—to make the world a better place. If one leader can help one organization to thrive by creating an environment where diverse people can work effectively together, this can serve as a model for the entire world.

The Need for Role Models

After the Rodney King riots in Los Angeles, a local business executive said, "In this area the situation is so desperate and so in need of role models, that if we in corporations can't advance minorities so they can turn around and do what needs to be done in their communities, I don't see any of us surviving. The bigger picture we have to deal with is the minority situation in this country." We might add: The even bigger picture is the minority situation in Bosnia, Ireland, Israel, and the entire planet.

The Team as Change Vehicle

Research indicates that the most powerful way to overcome the walls of prejudice between groups is for members to need each other in order to achieve an important goal. This assumes that the persons relate to each other as equals and that communication is deeper than the superficial level.

For example, a multicultural condo community in South Central L.A. averted damage during the riots. Owners met the rioters at the gates and con-vinced them to leave. Their apartments had been converted from government-subsidized housing to condos the occupants could buy. They had formed a homeowners association with the common goal of creating a safe, attractive environment for their families. The walls of prejudice came down and lasting friendships were forged.

Self-managing teams of diverse employees provide exactly these ingredients of equality, meaningful communication, and interdependence in achieving important goals. As a team leader, you have an opportunity to take the lead in overcoming false myths, stereotypes, and prejudice in this country and in helping people to join together to create a better life for all.

A Final Word

Together, we've completed this leg of your journey into creativity, and I'm thinking of what I would wish for your future. As a woman, you have so many advantages in building innovative skills—from your Emotional Intelligence to your Intuitive Intelligence. Let yourself feel gratitude for these talents—gratitude is such a powerful emotion.

Now you have the Creative Intelligence model as a framework for understanding where and how to keep expanding your creative talents.

You've started to spark and grow each of your seven intelligences. Keep up the good work. Don't stop now.

You've used many creative processes that rely these seven intelligences. Apply them to the opportunities and challenges that surround you every day of your life. Watch your innovative skills blossom as old limits fall away.

Let your Creative Self soar.

Chapter 13

Find Your Niche:
New Startups, Shape-Shifting Giants, Profitable Gaps

A good place to work is where dreams get fulfilled and interesting things go on. 'Nice' can be a coverup for a lack of passion.
Eric Schmidt CEO, Novell

The New Economy offers you a wealth of opportunities for finding your niche: the perfect job and career where you can bloom and thrive. If you're a risk-taker, a dotcom startup of your own can be a real turn-on. It takes nerve, but the reward can be amazing. The founders of such dotcoms as *Yahoo.com* and *Amazon.com* are high-stakes risk-takers who understand that each major move can lead to dazzling wealth or to a wild wipeout. You may be a moderate risk-taker who would love to provide outsourcing services to a leading-edge high-stakes firm. Maybe you'd love to work for a high-tech startup with the possibility of moderate wealth through stock options. Or you may like the wide-ranging possibilities offered by a position in a large corporation.

Dotcom startups took the lead in forging the New Economy, but corporate giants are learning how to shape-shift into web-shaped organizations that can spin off their own dotcoms. The giants may have been slow to start, but they're rapidly shifting the shapes of their customer channels, their organizational charts, and their corporate cultures so that they can survive and thrive in the Net Economy. They're discovering ways to be almost as nimble as the fast-paced, innovative startups. Speed is essential for the constant reinvention, innovation, and alliance-forging that allow high-tech companies to survive and thrive.

Giants and startups alike are outsourcing many of their functions so they can focus their resource on their core business mission. When a team comes through with a breakthrough innovation, success depends on being the first to market. This is so crucial that it pays off to hire other firms to help get there first. Outsourcing opens up many opportunities for specialists, consultants, and other startups, creating new niches that alert entrepreneurs can fill. They're creating new firms everywhere, offering to do virtually any business function—from finding and furnishing offices to handling all a company's human resources tasks.

Developing your innovative skills gives you a great advantage in any of these New Economy niches, because virtually all executives say that finding talented team members is a constant quest. Having talent means your company will do more then ever to give you what you want on the job. That's because keeping good people is a top priority. It's an essential factor of the intense teamwork-based achievement that spells success in the New Economy.

Where is the best place for you, as a woman, with your particular talents, interests, and lifestyle needs? You set some career goals in the Motivational Intelligence chapter (Chapter 4). In this chapter you'll get a sense of the field of play that's emerging and how it might affect your niche and those career plans.

Thrive in the New Economy

To thrive in the emerging networked global economy, you need to understand the principles that make it work. You also must grasp how its assets differ from those most valued in the old economy.

10 Driving Principles of the New Economy

Editors of the Internet journal *Business 2.0* say these are the 10 principles that drive the new economy. (Many say that Rule 4 should come first.)

- *Rule 1: Matter.* It matters less. What matters are ideas and information, which in turn rely on people and the technology that people develop.
- *Rule 2: Space.* Distance has vanished. The world is your customer—and your competitor.
- *Rule 3: Time.* It's collapsing. Instant interactivity is critical and is creating accelerated change.
- *Rule 4: People.* They're the crown jewels, and they know it. Brainpower can't be measured, but it's the prime factor driving the New Economy. More than ever in history, huge value is being leveraged from smart ideas and the winning technology and business models they create. So the people who can deliver them are becoming invaluable, and methods of employing and managing them are being transformed.
- *Rule 5: Growth.* It's accelerated by the network.
- *Rule 6: Value.* It rises exponentially with market share.
- *Rule 7: Efficiency.* The middleman lives. *Infomediaries,* who gather information from various sources and provide it to users, replace intermediaries.

      ▹ **Rule 8: Markets.** Buyers are gaining dramatic new power, and new sellers are finding new opportunities.

      ▹ **Rule 9: Transactions.** It's a one-on-one game instead of faceless mass markets.

      ▹ **Rule 10: Impulse.** Every product is available everywhere. The gap between wanting something and buying it has closed.

Where Are the Real Assets? Capital Shifts

All this means that human capital (innovative skills) have become the most important asset that businesses must find and keep. No doubt about it, the Net Economy is based on brains, not brawn—and women have full equality in the brains department. In this realm, the only thing that counts is smarts. The only assets that really matter are intellectual assets—knowledge contained in the brains of knowledge workers and in networked digital documents and databases according to Don Tapscott. Creative people provide human capital, and they also generate new ideas that become knowledge capital, business plan capital, and organization structure capital—all to the benefit of the firm.

Net Generation Human Capital

Much of the brainpower that drives the startups comes from tech-savvy people in their teens and twenties. Infotech professionals, marketers, and business leaders know that nothing is more important than understanding the new Net Generation—its culture, psychology, and values, as well as how its members are changing the world.

To do effective knowledge work, people must be motivated, trust their fellow workers and the company, and have a real sense of commitment—not just compliance or going along with achieving team goals. This commitment can't be achieved with alienated, underpaid, and abused workers. In fact, most people of the Net Generation just won't accept unfair treatment. They have a new way to organize themselves: the Net. They know how to organize Net-based boycotts, how to penetrate secure company files, and how to take other actions their elders can hardly imagine. Companies that understand the Net Generation are likely to grow in value and earning power, while those that use the old industrial model of workers will shrivel and die.

Even customers are beginning to demand payment for the intellectual capital they provide companies. Here's their attitude: I provide information about myself that, with my permission, your company sells to others? I want a share of that transaction. I contribute to a product evaluation? I want compensation for it.

Inter-Networked Human Capital

Traditionally, human capital has been the sum of the employee's capabilities in the firm—her skills, knowledge, intellect, creativity, and know-how. Now this capital extends beyond the traditional firm, and companies can have it without owning it. For example, a Web-based firm can use the intelligence and know-how of thousands of employees belonging to its business-Web members.

Relationship Capital

Dynamic two-way relationships replace the old concept of the brand name as a one-way image that the vendor establishes through print and broadcast media. For example, *Amazon.com* has deep relationship capital with millions of customers who have invested their time and effort to personalize their relationship with Amazon, keeping a "wish list" of things they want to order, writing reviews for books they've ordered, and so on.

Knowledge Capital

To succeed in the New Economy, firms must manage knowledge, not just data or information. They must manage the creation, protection, development, and sharing of knowledge assets. Business leaders, in a 1997 survey, said that knowledge management has been more important to their success than business process re-engineering, the big management fad of the 1990s according to Don Tapscott.

Knowledge sharing is at the heart of this challenge, but people are uneasy with the idea. If you know your stuff, you can spread this knowledge and, like a multiplier effect, add knowledge to the knowledge base. Sharing by one person tends to trigger sharing by others, allowing them all to reach a whole new level of understanding. For example, when people in different schools in different countries collaborate over the Internet to work on projects, a whole new way of thinking is usually revealed, because of the diverse beliefs and ideas that are pooled.

Business-Model Capital

As business-model innovation determines competitiveness and wealth, industry by industry, business Webs are destroying the old model of the firm. In 2000 the Internet action shifted from a focus on B-to-C transactions (business to retail customer) to B-to-B transactions (business to business). New business models flared onto the scene daily—with some developing into a steady glow and others burning out.

There will be individual bubbles (in the stock market, industry worth, etc.) as many new business model companies will fail. But people are investing in new models of how wealth will be created—and we are only about one percent into the investment process according to author George Gilder. The risky thing to do is to invest in the old economy companies, profit or not, unless they are shape-shifting into New Economy success stories. The safe choice is to develop a new set of lenses for looking at firms.

Capital in New Organization Structures

CEOs of traditional giant corporations are asking in private, *Why is my structure killing me?* Old structures cause frictional losses because they consume energy rather than unleash energy. Obsolete concepts include the pyramid structure with its hierarchy and all that goes with it, such as line and staff, span of control, and job descriptions. These old structures and concepts eat up energy and make managers feel like they're running through mud, moving in slow motion.

A new model, new paradigm, is emerging that revs up human energy instead of draining it. The paradigm rule is that there are no rules except what works. So nimble, flexible firms are experimenting with strange new structures—with eliminating traditional structural boundaries, with web-like interconnecting structures, with structures that are more horizontal or flat, with fluid, mobile structures.

The new paradigm features a focus on roles, not jobs—because a job may not be the same from one month to the next. It includes internal venture capital models and internal partnerships—where a giant corporation shifts its shape by providing venture capital to an internal team of partners with a startup idea.

Welcome to the Innovation Age

A crucial result of these major changes, these paradigm shifts, is to bring about the Innovation Age. You don't have to wait for someone to appreciate your innovative skills. It's easy to find companies that will reward you handsomely for being creative. The Innovation Age is here, even if the traditional, dying companies don't realize it yet.

CEO and author John Kao believes this is the age of creativity because:

- That's where infotech wants us to go next.
- Creativity is where the Knowledge Age takes us.
- Many young people want and expect creative jobs.
- Customers respond to innovative products and services.
- Customization and design are more important than ever.
- Companies must constantly reinvent themselves in order to achieve growth.
- Global competition is about mobilizing ideas, talents, and creativity.
- The new management mindset is to foster creativity by setting direction, inspiring, listening, facilitating, and providing resources.

In this age of creativity, organizations must find creative people—as employees, managers, partners, consultants, coaches, and contractors. The competition for people with innovative skills has become a fundamental, unavoidable, do-or-die factor of business success.

Businesses must compete globally, and they must allow creative freedom to their people. These twin factors have loosened the ties that have traditionally bound together people, places, and organizations—over many years or a lifetime. What's emerging is a culture of the temporary, the ever-emerging.

These changes, along with the computer and the Internet, are triggering two additional cultural changes:

1. It's very easy for people to connect in cyberspace.
2. People feel a more powerful desire to connect with other people in person.

People enjoy the benefits of high-tech, and they also deeply want high-touch. If you gain skills in managing these cultural cross-currents, you'll be seen as a winner. You have a running start, because as a woman you probably value connection and relationships above all else. You have the people skills to develop powerful networks and maintain them. People in high-tech value the high-touch skills that you can bring to the workplace and marketplace, such as:

- Expressing concern, empathy, and compassion.
- Tuning in to people's feelings, concerns, needs, and wants.
- Bringing people into a team or other group and helping them to contribute and fit in.

Becoming More Innovative

You can make your niche in the Net Economy more innovative at the same time that the Net Economy makes you more innovative. You can tap into the wealth of information available through the Internet (infotech) to help you clear your mind, to find the space for more communication, and to hurdle barriers to dreaming up new ideas. Infotech is allowing even manufacturing firms to become idea factories.

Using Infotech

Infotech helps build three key conditions for creativity, according to John Kao:

1. Clearing the mind—returning to beginner's mind.
2. Clearing the space—opening the space for instant communication, a hidden space for team collaboration.
3. Clearing the beliefs that block your access to creative ideas.

Clearing the Mind

Infotech can enhance your awareness of emerging ideas and arouse your interest in those new ideas. It does this primarily by providing you, and your organization, with retrievable memory. Computers make it easy to record ideas, events, and experiences and to pull them up when you need them.

You gain awareness on a continuous-flow basis, rather than on an announcement or demand basis. You get information in two basic ways:

1. You instruct your software to give you what you need. Information providers then deliver the equivalent of a focused briefing.
2. You go Web surfing, a form of scanning or prospecting in cyberspace, much like thumbing through a book or browsing a library, but faster and easier.

Either way, the sheer quantity of ideas boosts your chances of achieving higher-quality results.

In the future your cybernetic agents will help you encounter dynamic and qualitatively interesting sources of expertise. They'll scan the world for you, looking for interesting events and reporting them on a network. You can carry out highly customized searches, surveying very specific customer groups, for example.

Clearing the Space

Infotech opens you up to wider, more diverse worlds. It lets you make new connections. It helps you develop prototypes of what you want to create, to dialogue with others about it, and to share knowledge with colleagues.

Groupware now enables you to have virtual meetings where any number of your colleagues can *talk* at once. The value of a network is exponentially proportionate to the number of its users.

Clearing Self-Limiting Beliefs

As more and more power is transferred from bureaucratic managers to nomadic entrepreneurs, the business world becomes dramatically different. New kinds of organizations emerge and people need new skills to assure trust and give-and-take in cyberspace. Everyone becomes a sort of *Me Company*, trading information with other Me Companies. Everyone becomes more of a decision maker and less of a subordinate. Your home desk may become as good a place to work as any other.

The Idea Factory

We've still got to have factories, but we must change their focus from mass production to continuous creativity. All companies must come to see themselves more or less as idea factories. We must apply the principle of interdependency:

Principle of Interdependency

Ideas are dependent on successful products.

Successful products are dependent on ideas.

Both ideas and products are dependent

on the effective management of creativity.

Our mindset is shifting from a mechanical, observer-observed separateness to a wholistic, interdependent connectedness. Competition is more about exploiting an aspect of interdependency, of being part of an ecological whole, than about beating out another company. Mastery is about moving from an abstract intellectual understanding of something to an understanding that's *cellular*, integrated into your worldview.

We have computer networks and related technology that let us play with ideas without the former limitations of time and space. We can preserve our creative energy while we vastly expand our creative choices.

Where Is Your Niche?

The Internet is creating new workplace roles according to Sean Donahue. All the job categories discussed here were bringing in well in excess of $60,000 in 1999. Do any of these jobs fit your profile—meaning the kinds of things that fascinate you, that you enjoy doing, that you do well? Do any of them represent a future career target that you're willing to aim for?

New Metric Analyst. A typical title is Director of Consumer Activity Analysis. In this job you dig beneath the surface of page views and traffic reports on Web sites to create a detailed picture of what's really happening. You spot patterns in user behavior data, such as visit frequency, visit length, who's shopping at certain times, and what they're buying. In Web companies you set advertising rates, identify cross-selling opportunities, reduce churn (rapid customer turnover), and develop new marketing strategies. You also help to make crucial decisions about strategic alliances and acquisitions by putting a dollar value on the traffic they might generate.

Virtual Organization Leader. A typical title is Account Manager. You assemble teams of experts from around the world to achieve specific goals on projects—meanwhile jumping from project to project. When a particular project is complete, you disband the team and move on to next project. The work is typically coordinated online.

Content Engineer. A typical title is VP of Engineering. You're responsible for the overall organization and presentation of a Web site's content. You work with almost every part of an Internet business, hashing out infrastructure requirements with the Information Technology (IT) department, assisting with marketing campaigns, strategizing with executives, and working directly with suppliers to gather product information.

Chief Community Strategist. A typical title is VP of Customer Support. You develop and manage all aspects of building a sense of community online. Your job consists of equal parts policy-maker, minister of culture, ombudsman, and operations manager. You serve as a direct link between the Web site's community members and the company's top executives. You develop reports for managers based on feedback from the Web site's message boards, its customer e-mail, and your own face-to-face meetings with community members.

Hacker Consultant. You simulate attacks from the Net or from an internal source in order to locate weak spots in a company's network. Then you work with clients to prioritize which are the most serious threats, and you suggest preventive measures and solutions to the company's vulnerability to potential hackers.

E-mail Channel Specialist. A typical title is VP of E-mail. You oversee outbound e-mail and you channel all e-mail operations, from product development and strategic planning to corporate policy issues. You define a policy for the use of outgoing e-mail to ensure that e-mail products provide value to customers and aren't just a cheap and easy solution for the company. You design subscription-based services that offer content that customers choose to receive—not spam. You oversee the testing of new products to learn what customers will find acceptable.

Consumer Experience Manager. A typical title is Chief E-commerce Officer. You monitor the total quality of a customer's experience, from shopping the company's site to the delivery of orders. You work with the content team and Web applications developers on new features and functions that will make the shopping experience better and easier. You oversee operations for the back end of the transaction process, such as order fulfillments, supply-chain management, delivery, and billing. You ensure that first consideration is given to how strategic decisions will affect customers.

Metamediary CEO. As the head of a Web site that sits between buyers and sellers, you're responsible for offering customers a centralized, unbiased source of information and resources related to a specific task, such as buying a home or car. You provide information for customers to educate themselves on the topic. You provide research options and prices. When a customer is ready to find vendors in the marketplace, you offer specific pricing information, comparisons, and reviews of a product or service. You come strictly from the consumer's point of view.

Chief Knowledge Officer. You're responsible for building and managing a company's internal knowledge management efforts. You create and manage a system that organizes vital information—including documents, databases, and people—in a reusable and searchable body of institutional knowledge.

Your first task is to extend the necessary technology infrastructure, including applications that capture, categorize, and retrieve information entered by employees or stored in company databases. You continually work on new applications to add functionality, scalability, and efficiency to that system.

You teach employees what resources are available and how to use the system. Your goal is to create an online collection of information—such as former project proposals, task methodologies, best practices, meeting transcripts, and documentation of employees' project experiences—that may be useful in additional projects or in ongoing employee training. You work with the CEO and the heads of the IT and human resources (HR) departments to align knowledge management with the company's overall strategy. You bring together the company's technological and people pieces.

Chief Internet Officer. A typical title is VP of Community and Marketspaces. You keep the company up to date in the Net Economy. You oversee online strategy and operations to bring success to the company's online efforts. You impart the firm's Web strategy and direction to employees. You create a revenue model and make crucial decisions, such as online marketing and distribution deals.

Consider People-Oriented Jobs

Women typically thrive on connection, tune into people, value building long-term relationships, and are skilled in maintaining relationships. People-oriented jobs are often a natural fit for women, but sometimes it's difficult to tell which jobs really use your people skills. You may think it's that HR job, only to discover you spend most of your time with a computer screen. So check out the actual job tasks in references such as John Wright's *The American Almanac of Jobs and Salaries* and talk to people who have actually worked in the jobs you're considering.

Explore New People-Oriented Fields

Many new people-oriented jobs are opening up in the New Economy. For example, ethnography is a people-oriented approach to designing new products based on how people think and act, according to reporter Peter Kupfer. It's used primarily by high-tech firms. Ethnographers seek answers to their questions in the disciplines of anthropology, ethnology, sociology, and psychology.

The traditional way of developing new products is for engineers to devise what they think people want. Or they devise something they like, or accidentally stumble upon, and then devise or discover a consumer use for it. This can work beautifully, as in the case of the Post-it note described in Chapter 6. But ethnographers believe that companies are more consistently successful when they first figure out the next new thing that their customers want and then design it for them. In the past, they've done that by taking surveys and meeting with focus groups. The new approach is to go out and be with people as they go about the activities that a new product or service might fit into.

People-in-Action Approach

Ethnography is a people-in-action approach that provides information you would be unlikely to discover without actually watching people using the product, service, or process that you're developing.

For example, before they installed expensive videoconferencing equipment in all their offices around the world, a major management consulting firm tested it in the offices of a few executives. Almost all of them turned the cameras off during conferences because they found them distracting.

In 1979 Xerox PARC (research branch) commissioned a study designed by anthropologist Lucy Suchman. She filmed office workers struggling to do copying jobs on a Xerox machine. She concluded that simplicity was more important than fancy features on a copier. As a result, Xerox now provides a large green button that can be pushed to make a single, hassle-free copy.

The Xerox study also revealed that the company's repair technicians often learned how to fix problem machines during informal chats with colleagues. So Xerox equipped their repair techs with mobile phones in order to facilitate exchanging this information.

Impact of Culture

The way people live is strongly influenced by their cultural environment. This in turn impacts the acceptance or rejection of a new product.

For example, one U.S. company developed a black cell phone to market in Latin American countries. The phone had many wonderful functions and was a real bargain. But it had little appeal in Latin American countries, where they prefer bright colors and simpler designs.

Chinese businessmen working in rural areas that had no telephone service developed an elaborate system of using pagers to send coded messages. When Motorola found out about it, a company team developed a two-way pager for that market.

One company did a study of how office workers in England function on the job. They learned that most phone conversations there involve some reference to documents. They developed DeskSlate, a device that connects to a phone and allows users to view a document and listen to a voice mail about that document at the same time.

Life in Europe revolves around the family—much more than it does in the United States. There, business conforms to life, as compared to United

States, where life usually conforms to business. How might this affect a product or service you plan to market there?

In the Middle East, savvy consumers learned to read the bar codes on cell phones to find out where they were made. They believed that cell phones made in the United States were more desirable. What can a savvy businessperson do with that kind of information?

Ethnographic Advantages

The ethnographic approach has at least two major advantages over traditional market research techniques such as surveys and focus groups:

1. It provides firsthand observations of what people do in their everyday lives (not just what they say they do).

2. It can be done relatively quickly. Most studies can be done in days or weeks, although others could take months or years.

Sapient, a firm of Internet consultants who pioneered ethnographic research, has a staff that includes historians, actors, theologians, literary critics, and a cookbook author. What's the common thread? They're all good at observing the relationship between people and culture and stuff. They believe that you can't design products for someone unless you can see the richness and uniqueness of the world. That's lost in the lab, so you must get out and observe people in action.

Apply Your People Skills

A paradigm shift that started in the late 1980s is still blossoming and growing more profusely than ever in the New Economy. Organizations, more than ever, have decentralized authority and decision-making and moved them down, even to the work-team level. These changes call for leaders with people skills, the kinds of skills women tend to excel in.

Corporate Culture Changes

These new needs have led to related shifts that are causing corporate cultures to change dramatically and rapidly in some of the following ways:

- Self-directed work teams increasingly make most of the decisions that affect their work. They increasingly network with other teams, persons, and outside resource people to accomplish their work.

- Creative and empowered employees are in. On the way out are employees with a few limited skills in doing the same old grind—and doing it as they're told.

- Successful leaders are finding ways to empower team members and are moving away from traditional control-oriented management styles.

- More women are available who have the education, experience, and career vision and are ready to accept the challenges and demands of the new responsibilities.

Leadership Changes

When we look at what companies need from their leaders these days, we can see that women's ways fit those needs quite well. Companies need leaders who:

- Use more flexible ways of viewing and identifying managerial talent.
- Achieve fast-paced informational exchange.
- Have a broad vision and a diverse portfolio of skills.
- Think creatively and contribute to needed innovation.
- Have an ecological mentality, stressing the interrelatedness of all things.
- Reconcile a concern for bottom-line results with a concern for people (in other words, leaders who focus on both the ends and the means).
- Are skilled at both planning and problem-solving.
- Have rich people skills, including communication, team facilitation, negotiation, and conflict resolution skills.

This profile fits the typical woman's leadership style and is opening more doors for women.

Apply Your Innovative Skills

The New Economy is an innovation-based economy. Leading-edge companies know that they must make their own products obsolete before someone else does. As soon as they develop a great product, the next goal is to develop a better one that will make the current one obsolete. Most large U.S. companies introduce more than one new product a day. Even back in 1995 Sony was introducing 5,000 new products in a single year.

Microsoft executive Kim Drew says, "No matter how good your product, you're only 18 months away from failure." Products come and go more rapidly all the time. The average time to create and manufacture a new product has dropped from 2,500-person days per product to three hours. About 90 percent of Miller's beer revenues comes from beers that didn't exist 24 months ago.

Companies must also obsolete their own businesses—creating a new type of business with new relationships before a competitor does. Toyota's motto is to reinvent your company proactively in order to ride the wave of change.

Do it now and then immediately work on doing it better. This is a key driver and variable in the economic activity and business success of today's companies. In the past, such inventions as cameras and photocopiers provided revenues for decades. Today consumer electronic products have a typical product life of two months. "Just in time" applies to everything from when goods are received from suppliers to when products are shipped to customers.

Human imagination is the main source of value in this high-tech world. The company's major challenge is to create a climate in which innovation is valued, encouraged, and rewarded. Most growth has been coming from small and medium-sized businesses, but even the giants are shape-shifting in order to catch up and move forward in the New Economy.

With the fast pace of change and complexity of markets, customers often don't know what's possible and what to ask for. Business leaders must innovate beyond what their customers can imagine. They must understand the needs of their customers. They must thoroughly understand what's possible with the emerging technologies—and then provide products and services that surprise and delight customers. To accomplish this, leaders must establish a climate in the organizations where risk-taking is rewarded, human imagination can fly free, and Creative Intelligence can blossom.

Consider Creating Your Own Startup

How about creating your own business startup? Women own 8.5 million of the businesses in the United States. They employ about 25 million employees, and their businesses generate more than $3 trillion in sales every year. This is a burgeoning trend; the growth of women-owned U.S. businesses is outpacing overall business growth by two to one.

If you think you might want to join these women entrepreneurs, here are the first, basic questions to ask yourself:

1. *Do I passionately want to create my own business?*

2. *What type of business do I want to create?*

3. *What ideas do I have for offering my clients something of value, something a little different, something more workable, more satisfying, or more delightful?*

4. *Do I have the experience and expertise to operate such a business?* Remember: You don't have to do it all. Most small business owners hire a CPA, consult with a lawyer on occasion, hire a cleaning service, and so on. No one person has the time, energy, and expertise to do it all. On the other hand, don't underestimate your experience and expertise. The leap into starting your own business should feel challenging to you, but not totally overwhelming.

5. *How much revenue do I need in order to pay all the monthly business costs and expenses—and pay myself enough to meet my minimal living expenses?*

First, you must scout around and figure out how much it will cost you to do business, including monthly payments on any loans that you get. Then you must figure out how much of your product or service you must sell each month in order to meet expenses. If you believe you can generate those sales, then you may have a viable business idea. From here, talk with people you know and trust to get all the information you can about making this type of business a success. Do your homework; search the Internet and the library. If you need to borrow money for your project, start developing a business plan that you can take to a banker, family member, or venture capital firm. You can buy software that will guide you through this process.

On the other hand, if you think you have a really innovative idea that's hot and timely, you may be able to get financing without a detailed business plan—on the merits of the idea itself. If you convince savvy angels or venture capitalists that your idea is great, they in turn may actually help you with the business aspects of the project.

The idea is the thing. Your mental model of how your business will provide the customer with value—with something a little different and delightful—is what determines your success. That and the continual renewal of your mental models as the environment changes. To quote Howard Sherman and Ron Schultz: "That 50 percent of all small businesses fail within the first year says more about the ideas, or lack of ideas, that foster those businesses than about competition, location, or their ability to move rapidly."

Building your innovative skills will mean you're the one who can come up with great new business ideas—the kind you need to start and maintain a successful business of your own. See the chapter on Motivational Intelligence (Chapter 4) for more suggestions on creating your own business.

Putting It All Together:
A Day in the Life of an Innovative Woman

Now you have explored the many facets of your creativity. You've become aware of your various intelligences, and you've begun boosting each of them. You've explored the ways you can use your creativity to spark change and innovation in your work team and throughout your corporate culture. You've learned many ways that you and your firm can thrive in the Innovation Age by becoming more open, adaptive, and wholistic—so that you can find new roles and profitable gaps where you can step into the marketplace niche that's just right for you.

Your next challenge is keep the ball rolling. How are you going to continue to tap into creative ideas for the ongoing changes you're bound to encounter in your life? One way of putting together all the information and skills you've gained from this book is to imagine a typical day in the life of an innovative woman—you.

Wake Time

Don't move—not yet! Indulge in a few precious moments to tap into your dream time. Allow memories to come up. Keep a pen and notepad handy to jot down highlights of your dreams. Ask your Intuitive Self, *How can I integrate these dream-time messages with my wake-time life?*

While you're still in a sleepy, relaxed state, close your eyes and imagine what you want to achieve and experience in the day ahead. Use your visualization skills to imagine the end results—the feelings, the people. Be there, charge it with emotion and passion, become one with the essence of that vision. Then use a letting-go technique.

Before Work

Listen to some inspirational music as you start your morning routine. Or listen to an audiotape or videotape with an inspiring message. Or do a bit of reading from an inspirational book or materials. Bottom line: Start the day on a high note—in touch with your Higher Self, Intuitive Self, Creative Self.

During Your Work Commute

Repeat one of the "before work" activities. Get in touch with your earlier vision of the day's experiences and achievements. Begin to plan the specifics of your day.

Throughout the Day

- Be aware of when you're using your various types of intelligence. Assess whether you're using each intelligence in a constructive way, allowing it to boost your creativity and your innovative skills.
- Think in terms of opportunities, of what you are *for*.
- Notice your behavior patterns and those of others.
- Notice when you're living in the Now and when you're in the past or future.
- Stay in touch with your feelings. Notice how they are connected to your thoughts. Are your thoughts focused on what you are *for*?
- Practice your empathy skills. Are you putting yourself in others' shoes?
- Keep top-priority goals in mind and whether your activities are "on purpose."
- Remember to put things together in new and different ways, trying out new associations and combinations.
- Open up to your inner vision, the imagination of your Sensory Intelligence—as well as your inner hearing and other senses. Allow intuitive messages to come in.
- Use the Relax-Visualize-Let Go process any time you need help or guidance. Remember to ask "What Next?" of your Intuitive Self. Use the RVL process also to reduce tension and to prevent stress buildup.
- Verbalize your thinking and feeling—talk it out and write it out—to bring up information through your Intuitive Self.

- ✎ Practice intuition skills by making little predictions throughout the day and noticing how they play out in physical reality. Learn from the associated feelings and other signals that you get during this practice.

- ✎ Work with your team (and others) on opportunities and challenges, on recognizing or creating the Next New Thing, and on staying open, adaptive, and wholistic in order to spark innovation.

Bedtime

Use the Relaxation-Visualization-Letting Go process. Ask your Intuitive Self how you can best use your dream-time tonight. Get in touch with any problems you're working on, anything new you want to create in your life, and/or any guidance you want. Program your dreams as you drift off to sleep.

Finally, as you build your innovative skills, notice how you are becoming, more and more, The Innovative Woman.

Bibliography

Austin, Nancy K. "First Aide," *Inc*., September 1999.

Barker, Joel A. *Paradigms: The Business of Discovering the Future*. New York: HarperCollins, 1993.

Berenson, David, interview, November 25, 1996

Bethards, Betty. *The Dream Book: Symbols for Self-Understanding*. Rockport, Mass.: Element, 1995.

Braden, Greg. *Awakening to Zero Point*. Questa, N.M.: Sacred Spaces/Ancient Wisdom, 1994.

Cairns, J., Overbaugh, J., and Hiller. 1998,"The Origin of Mutants," *Nature* 335, 142-145.

Capra, Fritjof. *The Web of Life*. New York: Anchor Books, 1996.

Carr-Ruffino, Norma. *The Promotable Woman*. Franklin Lakes, N.J.: Career Press, 1997.

Casti, John L. *Would-be Worlds*. New York: John Wiley, 1997.

CPS Publications, October 2000. Bureau of Labor Statistics and Bureau of the Census, *www.bls.census.gov*

Day, Laura. *Practical Intuition*. Derry, N.H.: Broadway Books, 1997

Dean, Douglas, and John Milhalasky. *Executive ESP*. Englewood Cliffs, N.J.: Prentice-Hall, 1974.

De Beauport, Elaine. *The Three Faces of Mind*. Wheaton, Ill.: Quest Books, 1996.

De Bono, Edward. *Serious Creativity: Using the Power of Lateral Thinking to Create New Ideas*. New York: HarperCollins, 1992.

Deutsch, David. *Fabric of Reality*. New York: Penguin, 1998.

Devlin, B., M. Daniels, and K. Roeder, "The Heritability of IQ," *Nature* 333, 1997, 468-471.

Donahue, Sean, "New Jobs for the New Economy," *Business 2.0*, July 1999, 102-109.

Dowling, John E. *Creating Mind: How the Brain Works.* New York: WW Norton & Company, 1998. (See the chapter on vision.)

Dunne, J.W. *An Experiment with Time* (on dreams). London: Faber and Faber, 1958.

Durden-Smith, Jo. *Sex and the Brain.* New York: Arbor House, 1986.

Economic Policy Institute, 1999; President's Council of Economic Advisors, 1990. Washington D.C.

Emery, Marcia, "The Intuitive Healer," *Intuition*, Jan/Feb 1999, 8-13.

Fleming, Tapas. *You Can Heal Now: The Tapas Acupressure Technique.* Redonda Beach, Calif.: TAT International, 1998.

Franquemont, Sharon. *You Already Know What to Do*. New York: Putnam, 1999.

Gilder, George. *Telecosm: How Infinite Bandwidth Will Revolutionize Our World*. New York: Free Press, 2000.

Goleman, Daniel. *Emotional Intelligence*. New York: Bantam, 1995.

Herman Group, The. Employee Survey for Shell Oil, 1995.

Higgins, James W. *101 Creative Problem Solving Techniques*. New York: New Management Publishing, 1994.

Horn, Robert E. *Visual Language: Global Communication in the 21st Century.* Bainbridge Island, Wash.: MacroVU Press, 1998.

Intuition, a bimonthly magazine published by Intuitive Media, Inc., San Francisco, Calif.

intuitmag@aol.com

Jensen, Rolf. *The Dream Society: How the Coming Shift from Information to Imagination Will Transform Your Business.* New York: McGraw-Hill, 1999.

Kao, John. *Jamming: The Art and Discipline of Business Creativity.* New York: HarperCollins, 1996.

Kupfer, Peter, "Designing Products Based on Real Life," *San Francisco Chronicle*, January 31, 2000, B1.

Lambrou, Peter and George Pratt. *Instant Emotional Healing: Acupressure for the Emotions.* New York: Broadway Books, 2000.

Langer, Ellen J. *Mindfulness*. Reading, Mass.: Addison-Wesley Pub Co. Inc., 1989.

Leonard, Linda Schierse. *The Call to Create*. New York: Harmony Books, 2000.

Maisel, Eric. *Fearless Creating*. New York: Putnam, 1995.

Moore, Geoffrey A. *Inside the Tornado: Marketing Strategies from Silicon Valley's Cutting Edge*. New York: HarperCollins, 1995.

Murphy, Dave "Not a Two-Bit Problem" *S.F. Examiner*, April 11, 1999.

Naparstek, Belleruth. *Your Sixth Sense*. San Francisco: HarperCollins, 1997.

Nierenberger, Gerard I. *The Art of Creative Thinking*. New York: Simon and Schuster, 1989.

Peirce, Penney. *The Intuitive Way*. Hillsboro, Oreg.: Beyond Words Publishing, Inc. 1997.

Pert, Candace. *Molecules of Emotion: Why You Feel the Way You Feel*. New York: Scribner, 1997.

Pollack, Willliam. *Real Boys*. New York: Random House Inc. 1998.

Reich, Robert, interview on C-SPAN, November 3, 1996

Rosanoff, Nancy. *Intuition Workout*. Santa Rosa, Calif.: Aslan Publishing, 1991.

Sheldrake, R., T. McKanna and R. Abraham *The Evolutionary Mind*. Santa Cruz, Calif.: Trialogue Press, 1998.

Sherman, Howard and Ron Schultz. *Open Boundaries: Creating Business Innovation Through Complexity*. Reading, Mass.: Perseus Books, 1998.

Skafte, Dianne. *Listening to the Oracle*. San Francisco: HarperSan Francisco, 1997.

Slywotzky et al. *Profit Patterns*. New York: Mercer Management Consulting, 1999.

Spangler, David. *The Call*. Riverhead Books, 1996.

Stewart, Alex. *Team Entrepreneurship*. Thousand Oaks, Calif.: Sage, 1995.

Tannen, Deborah. *The Argument Culture*. New York: Random House, 1998.

——. *You Just Don't Understand*. New York: William Morrow, Inc., 1990.

Tapscott, Don, "Mind Over Matter," *Business 2.0*, January 1999, 45-49.

Tarlow, Mikela. *Navigating the Future: A Personal Guide to Achieving Success in the New Millennium*. New York: McGraw-Hill 1999.

Tarlow, Mikela and Philip. *Navigating the Future : A Personal Guide to Achieving Success in the New Millennium*. New York: McGraw-Hill, 1998.

Tolle, Eckhart. *The Power of Now*. Novato, Calif. New World Library, 1999

U.S. Census Bureau Current Population Reports, Commerce Department, 1999.

U.S. Dept. of Labor, Bureau of Labor Statistics, March 30. 1999. *www. dol.gov/dol/wb/public/programs/1w&occ.htm*

U.S. Labor Department, Women's Bureau Fair Pay Clearinghouse, 1999.

Useem, Jerry, "Entrepreneur of the Century," *Inc*, 20th Annual Issue, 1999.

Weintraub, Sandra. *The Hidden Intelligence: Innovation Through Intuition*. Woburn, Mass.: Butterworth Heinemann 1998.

Wieder, Marcia. *Making Your Dreams Come True*. New York: Harmony Books, 1999.

Wolger, Roger J. "The Signs of the Times and the Time of the Heart," *Journal of Family Life*, Fall 1995, 26-36.

WSJ. Petzinger, Thomas. "The Front Lines," *Wall Street Journal*, March 12, 1999, B-1.

Index

About the Author

Norma Carr-Ruffino, Ph.D., Professor of Management at San Francisco State University, is the author of the bestselling book, *The Promotable Woman*. A well-known consultant and lecturer, she has made presentations throughout the United States, Europe, Asia, and Latin America. Her teaching and consulting expertise encompasses creative business problem-solving, leadership skills for women, and managing a diverse workforce.